Contents at a Glance

Table of Contents

About the Author

 **Alan Luber** is an author, journalist, computer expert, and consultant. Alan's first book, *Solving Business Problems with MRP II*, has been translated into Spanish and has sold well worldwide. He has also written dozens of articles that have appeared in both print and Web-based publications.

As a consultant, Alan helps companies implement Enterprise Resource Planning (ERP) and Supply Chain Management solutions. He also helps clients to reengineer business processes and manage large, complex information technology projects. Recent clients include Koch Industries, Inc.; Imperial Tobacco Ltd.; Frontstep, Inc.; and GSI Lumonics, Inc.

Alan has a B.S. in industrial engineering from Penn State. He worked for General Electric, Management Science America, and Digital Equipment Corporation before establishing ADL Consulting Inc., in 1994.

Alan spends his free time writing for fun, playing the piano, restoring photographs, losing at gin rummy to his youngest daughter (who clearly cheats), and collecting and selling baseball memorabilia. (Alan and his much older, less handsome brother Phil own the copyrights to the best-known interior color photos of Shibe Park [Connie Mack Stadium] in existence.)

Alan is married, has three daughters, and lives in Roswell, Georgia.

Alan would be pleased to hear from owners of small and home office businesses in the Atlanta area who require assistance in implementing personal computer disaster prevention and recovery plans.

Alan can be contacted through his Web site, http://www.alanluber.com.

Dedication

For Uncle Milt, who always listens.

For Eleanor, who always encourages and never second guesses.

Acknowledgments

Never have I seen a project of this magnitude move so rapidly from concept to contract to completion (only six months!). It couldn't have happened without the outstanding efforts of a great many people. I am truly in awe of their efforts and teamwork.

The Que Team

Working with Que has been one of the most pleasant experiences of my professional career.

I am grateful to team coordinator Sharry Gregory—the first person at Que to read my proposal—for recommending it to Que's management for consideration.

Huge thanks to Rick Kughen, my executive editor, for championing this project and driving it from submission to contract *within a week*! Rick, I still can't believe how fast you were able to make this happen. Thank you for all of your enthusiasm, encouragement, and efforts.

Thanks to associate publisher Greg Wiegand for approving the project and to my project editor, Tricia Liebig, for managing the entire production process.

The three cardinal sins an author can make in a book about solutions are overlooking a solution; considering a solution and rejecting it without informing the reader; and failing to explain a solution clearly to the audience. My development editor, Todd Brakke, added tremendous value in making *PC Fear Factor* "sin free."

It's difficult to write a book that addresses three different versions of Microsoft Windows. Thanks to David Eytchison, my technical editor, for ensuring that *PC Fear Factor* addresses the idiosyncrasies of all three operating systems.

Megan Wade, my production editor, played a dual role: copyediting and quality control. Megan's incredible attention to detail has made *PC Fear Factor* as close to error free as is humanly possible.

I want to also recognize the efforts of proofreader Suzanne Thomas, indexer Ken Johnson, interior designer Anne Jones, layout technicians Stacey DeRome and Cheryl Lynch, and graphic conversion technician Tammy Graham.

What a great team!

The Luber Team: It's a Family Affair

This book would not have been possible without the very tangible efforts of several members of my family.

I am most indebted to the other author in my family, my brother, Phil Luber, writer of the Harry Kline series of thrillers (`http://www.philipluber.com/novels.htm`). Phil's involvement and encouragement during every phase of this project was critical to its success.

Thanks to my oldest daughter, Michelle, for the generous use of her computer. It's impossible to write a book like this without access to a Windows 98, Millennium, and XP system, and I only had two out of three in my office.

Thanks to Mallie Bear Productions—my youngest daughter, Mallory—for developing
`http://www.alanluber.com`, the Web site that is integrated with *PC Fear Factor*.

Thanks to my middle child, Jessica, for assisting with promotional efforts.

Special appreciation to the artist in the family, my sister-in-law, Sherry Frank, for providing
the illustrations for *PC Fear Factor*. Somehow she managed to meet Que's deadlines while
dealing with a baby and a three-year-old. (Her secret: Do all your work after midnight.)
Sherry, I appreciate your efforts, but if you ever send me another fax at 2:00 in the morning I will have no choice but to hurt you.

The Software Vendors

A book that provides detailed instructions for disaster prevention and recovery has to be
100% accurate, lest the book be the source of, rather than the solution for, disasters.

Special thanks to Bill Tanner of NewTech Infosystems, developer of Backup NOW!, for his
input and review of Chapter 6; Jordy Berson of Zone Labs, developer of ZoneAlarm, for his
input and review of Chapter 5; David Rice of CyberScrub for his input and review of Chapter
5; Bill William of Symantec; and Al Price of AJSystems, developer of Express Assist.

Finally, I would like to single out the efforts of Daniel Stark of Symantec for daring to ven-
ture out of the traditional customer/Symantec communications protocol to review
Chapters 7 and 8.

To all of you: Your responsiveness in answering questions, addressing software issues,
and reviewing the manuscript for accuracy is most gratefully appreciated and has made
this a more comprehensive, accurate book.

The Infrastructure Provider

It is impossible to make a project like this happen without an extremely reliable broadband
Internet connection. I think it is worth noting that I have had less *cumulative* down time since
switching to BellSouth's Fast Access DSL 14 months ago than in a typical week with my previous broadband services provider. BellSouth is truly the Energizer bunny of broadband.

Last But Not Least

Thanks to Chip Dudley of Mirant and fellow Que author Harley Hahn for critiquing my Web
site and to Andy Wofford of `http://www.csriver.com` for providing Web hosting services.

We Want to Hear from You!

As the reader of this book, *you* are our most important critic and commentator. We value your opinion and want to know what we're doing right, what we could do better, what areas you'd like to see us publish in, and any other words of wisdom you're willing to pass our way.

As an associate publisher for Que, I welcome your comments. You can email or write me directly to let me know what you did or didn't like about this book—as well as what we can do to make our books better.

Please note that I cannot help you with technical problems related to the *topic* of this book. We do have a User Services group, however, where I will forward specific technical questions related to the book.

When you write, please be sure to include this book's title and author as well as your name, email address, and phone number. I will carefully review your comments and share them with the author and editors who worked on the book.

Email: feedback@quepublishing.com

Mail: Greg Wiegand
            Que
            201 West 103rd Street
            Indianapolis, IN 46290 USA

For more information about this book or another Que title, visit our Web site at www.quepublishing.com. Type the ISBN (excluding hyphens) or the title of a book in the Search field to find the page you're looking for.

Your personal computer: an unstable equilibrium.

When Disaster Strikes

My wife and I like to take walks at night. As we stroll through the neighborhood and glance into the lighted windows of houses, we see a community at work on their computers: mothers, fathers, sons, and daughters. In the old days they used to share the family personal computer. No more. These days, as we look into the houses, we can see each of them at work or play on their own computer. As I sit here writing these words, the average number of computers in homes having computers is 2.2, and by the time this book is published it will probably be closer to 3.

I know from experience that most people never even remotely consider the possibility of a computer disaster, let alone the impact that such a disaster will have on their lives. They take it for granted that their computer will always work, like the 10-year-old television in their family room. And when it doesn't—when the inevitable disaster strikes—I often receive a frantic telephone call from a friend or relative who knows that I am a computer expert:

> "Alan, my computer won't boot up anymore! Everything I've been work-ing on for the past two years is on it. How do I get it back?"

These kinds of disasters might not happen often, but like death and taxes, if you use a PC long enough, they're inevitable.

What Can Happen

You are probably familiar with the most catastrophic of all computer disasters—the hard disk failure, commonly referred to as a hard disk *crash*. But the mechanical fail-ure of this critical component is not the only reason I receive frantic phone calls. Here are some other causes of computer disasters:

- **Disasters caused by computer viruses**—"Alan, I can't find my MP3s anymore and all of my friends are telling me I emailed them a virus. Can you help me?"

- **Disasters caused by ill-behaved software applications**—"Alan, I installed a new software package and it trashed my computer. Can you help me?"
- **Disasters created by ill-behaved guests or family members**—"Alan, my computer stopped working. My son downloaded something and it doesn't work anymore. Can you help me?"
- **Disasters caused by good intentions**—"I decided to delete a lot of stuff off my computer that I didn't need anymore and now my computer speakers don't work. Can you fix them?"
- **Disasters caused by failure to perform routine maintenance**—"My computer has slowed to a crawl. Can you help me?"

Going beyond the types of crises that many users inadvertently inflict on themselves and others are those that come from above. Natural disasters caused by exogenous factors, such as fire, flood, theft, or lightning can be among the most frustrating forms of PC disasters because there is little, if any, warning and even less control.

Finally, there are disasters of a mysterious or unknown origin. All too often, due to the sheer complexity of computers, you can experience a computer disaster of mysterious or unknown origin. The fact is, personal computers are quintessential examples of unstable equilibriums. Like a person leaning backward in a chair, balancing himself on two legs, the slightest deviation from the point of equilibrium can precipitate a disaster. One day things are working fine when you turn off your computer, and the next day when you turn on your computer, they aren't. Something has caused some critical files on your hard disk to become corrupted, and unless you have the ability to recover from such a disaster, your computer has become the world's most expensive paperweight.

The Impact of Personal Computer Disasters

The impact of a personal computer disaster is far worse today than it was even a year ago and grows steadily worse each year as we find more and more ways to use our computers. With each passing year, our computers play a more central role in our lives. We store digital photographs, music, and videos on our computers, along with our important financial records and other critical documents. We depend on our computers to be available night and day so that we can keep up with email, e-commerce, e-banking, Web surfing, homework, investing, and a hundred other things—things that were once considered conveniences of life and are now considered essentials. Without a doubt, the computer has become the single most important appliance in the house. And perhaps, because it is perceived incorrectly as an electronic appliance, people incorrectly assume it will be as reliable as that 10-year-old television I mentioned earlier.

In effect, we've become a nation of super-users when it comes to computers. There probably isn't a person who is reading this who hasn't learned how to use several new computer applications in the past year. But most super-users still don't know the first thing about being a system administrator. So, each time we learn how to use a new application, we create more valuable data and expose ourselves to greater risk of losing that data because we don't know how to protect ourselves.

Most people are not so blissfully unaware that all their critical data can disappear in a nanosecond for any number of reasons, wreaking absolute havoc on their lives. Yes, those old family photographs you spent hours scanning into your computer can be gone in an instant. Oh, you can scan them again, but that only solves part of the problem: The hundreds of hours of labor you put into lovingly restoring your old photos using MGI PhotoSuite or some other photo application will have to be repeated after you rescan the photos onto your new hard disk.

In a world full of super-users, your PC's hard disk represents much more than raw data—it represents thousands of hours of labor that went into converting raw data into some finished product.

Ticktock, Ticktock

If you have never experienced a computer disaster, I assure you it is just a matter of time. The reasons can vary, but mostly it boils down to the following:

- We beat our hard disks to death.
- We have more computers than ever before.
- Our computing environment grows increasingly complex.

Most people never stop to think that their valuable, often irreplaceable data is stored on their computer's hard disk—a device that spins constantly at speeds of up to 7,200 revolutions per minute while data is read from or written to it at blinding speeds by a head that hovers millionths of an inch above the spinning disk. The personal computer hard disk, an amazing piece of technology capable of storing more than 120GB of data, is both the most important component of your computer and the most likely component to fail because it is, after all, a mechanical device. Years ago, we used our computers a few hours a day at most. Today, with the advent of broadband Internet connections and the popularity of telecommuting, we use our computers 10–14 hours a day. Given the service demands we place on our computers, it's amazing they perform as well as they do.

In addition to the excess stress we put on our hard disk drives, we also keep adding to the number of computers we use. The more computers you have, the more likely you are to have some type of computer disaster on at least one of them.

Finally, we keep adding to the complexity of our computing environments. In the old days, we had two or three applications installed on our computers and we generally used only one of them at a time, so there was little chance of them conflicting with each other in some mysterious way. In fact, until Windows 95 was released, you could use *only* one application at a time. All that has changed. At present, I have about 75 applications installed on my computer, including all the Microsoft Office applications; seven different programs for capturing, editing, and managing digital images; three programs that help me do business on eBay; a dozen performance and system management utilities; several programs for creating music and data CDs; a program to manage my finances; applications to manage peripheral devices; applications to browse the Internet; several programs for electronic communications…the list goes on.

At any given point in time, I have about a dozen of these applications running on my computer simultaneously. Some of these applications run constantly in the background, and some, like the application I am using right now to write this book, operate only when they receive my keystrokes and mouse clicks.

And therein lies a mega-opportunity for computer disasters engendered by software conflicts. Every time you install a new application on your computer, a real and significant risk is that it will cause some type of conflict with one or more other applications. Sometimes the problem is minor, and you can work around it. For example, I use a utility to stop pop-up ads from appearing on my computer when I am connected to the Internet. Unfortunately, this utility causes some conflicts with other applications that I use. But I am aware of the problems it causes, and I know how to work around them. More importantly, I choose to work around them because the benefits of having the pop-up stopper outweigh the problems it causes. I'm a lucky one, though. Many users are unaware of how a simple pop-up stopper might cause problems elsewhere in their computing lives.

Unfortunately, not all software conflicts are this innocuous. Many such problems are so serious that they can render your computer inoperable. Such conflicts don't always manifest themselves right away. The software program you just installed might cause a serious problem that goes unnoticed for days or even weeks, perhaps until you use it concurrently with some other program. This can make identifying the source of a conflict extremely difficult, let alone finding a solution or workaround for the problem.

Why So Many Applications?

It seems logical that we could reduce the potential for software conflicts if we could somehow reduce the number of software applications we install on our computers. Unfortunately, the trend is toward more rather than fewer applications. A number of reasons explain this:

- **New uses for personal computers**—We are constantly finding new ways to use our personal computers. In the past three months, I have installed several new applications on my computer to automate tasks I had been performing manually. For example, I recently downloaded and installed the United States Postal Service Shipping Assistant program, which I use to generate priority mail shipping labels.

- **Specialization**—I currently use seven applications to capture, edit, and manage digital images. By the time this book is published, I will probably be using more.

Why, you might ask, do I need not one or two, but seven programs to edit digital images? No, I'm not some expert in digital photography who needs a lot of complicated features. The answer is simple: Although all the programs contain overlapping functionality, each program does at least one very important thing much, much better than any of the other programs—so much better that it justifies using multiple applications.

- **Compatibility**—Sometimes, you need multiple, similar applications for reasons of compatibility. I use Microsoft's Internet Explorer as my primary Web browser, but I find that I can edit my eBay auctions much more successfully using Netscape Navigator. For some reason, eBay's software developers seem to favor developing software that is more compatible with Netscape Navigator than Internet Explorer. So, I find that I must have both Web browsers installed on my computer.

- **Ease of use**—Sometimes we install applications that make other applications easier to use. Entire software industries have sprung up around popular software applications. eBay is an excellent case in point. I use an application called *Auction Submit* to create and submit auctions to eBay, instead of using eBay's standard user interface. Auction Submit is easier and faster to use and has some additional capabilities, such as the capability to queue up a list of auctions and submit them all at once.

To summarize, don't hold your breath waiting for things to get less complex because our computing environment is becoming more complex with each passing day.

Help Is on the Way

Some computer disasters are preventable, and some are not. Most people don't know how to prevent the preventable disasters or how to recover from the unavoidable ones. I wrote *PC Fear Factor* for several reasons:

- **I hate it when bad things happen to good people**—I know that you have critical, irreplaceable information on your computer, and I don't want you to lose that information.

- **As much as I would like to help, I don't have time to help all of my friends and relatives with their computer disasters**—I have enough to do keeping my own three computers up and running—I just don't have the time to be a system administrator for every friend, neighbor, and relative who needs help in this area. (As I sit here writing this, I am on the phone with a friend who can't figure out how to get the case off his computer. Submitted for your consideration: If you can't figure out how to get the case off your computer, you probably have no business being inside your computer.)

- **It's darn near impossible to be a system administrator after the disaster has occurred**—Being a system administrator is all about taking the appropriate steps to prevent disasters wherever possible and to provide a means of recovering from those disasters that can't be anticipated or prevented, such as a hard disk crash. So nine times out of ten, there is nothing I can do for the person on the other end of the frantic phone call. It's certainly too late to prevent the disaster, and quite often there is no way to recover.

- **Nontechnical computer users need the kind of help provided by this book**—This book is not for computer nerds. This book is for the millions of people who use computers everyday to perform important tasks but don't have the slightest idea of how to protect themselves from any number of disasters that could render their computers nonfunctional, or, even worse, result in the loss or theft of their precious data.

Meet the System Administrator

I realize that I have been using the term *system administrator* without having defined it. I'll do so now.

The system administrator is basically a risk manager. His job is to keep things running smoothly by taking the necessary actions to minimize and manage risk. Specifically, the system administrator prevents computer disasters wherever possible and makes it possible to recover quickly and completely from unavoidable computer disasters. In a home computing environment, the system administrator installs and removes programs, takes data and hard disk backups, fixes problems, recovers from computer disasters, and implements safe computing practices.

Administrators in Action

At this point you might be wondering exactly what kind of actions a system administrator takes. As the title implies, some of the actions are purely *administrative*, for example, documenting and putting procedures in place to minimize risk.

Another role of the system administrator is to train and educate. You can have the best procedures in the world, but if even one member of your family fails to follow those procedures, all is lost. So, you must educate your family members on the importance of following procedure, as well as train them regarding the substance of the procedures.

A third role of the system administrator is to perform certain tasks on all computers on a scheduled basis to prevent disasters wherever possible and to make it possible to recover easily and completely from unavoidable disasters. This book discusses these tasks in detail and tells you how (and how often) to perform them.

The fourth role, the role you hope you never have to play, is disaster recovery. Interestingly enough, if you perform your other system administration duties with due diligence, disaster recovery can be a routine and worry-free task. The last time my hard disk failed, I yawned. Then I called Dell (my computer was still under warranty), and they came out to the house and installed a new hard disk. Within a few minutes I had initiated my disaster recovery. I was up and running again within a few hours after the new disk was installed. And I didn't lose a single byte of data.

Required Personality Traits

What personality traits should a system administrator have? A system administrator must have common sense and must be organized, disciplined, diligent, dedicated, and quite frankly, a bit paranoid. There's an old joke that goes something like this: "Just because you're paranoid, it doesn't mean they aren't really out to get you." That's actually a healthy attitude to have in a connected world because I assure you that somebody *is* out to get your computer, whether to harm it, steal information from it, or use it as a base from which to launch attacks on other computers.

The system administrator accepts responsibility. She doesn't bemoan the injustices of an unfair world. ("Woe is me, somebody infected my computer with a virus.") The system administrator unemotionally and maturely accepts that cyber terrorists exist and takes the necessary steps to avoid being a victim.

If you don't have these traits, don't worry: You will by the time you finish reading this book. I'll provide you with a structured framework for system administration, and I'll inject you with a healthy dose of paranoia with regard to what steps you should take to protect your data.

The Dog Ate My Computer

Part of my job as a writer is to anticipate and overcome the objections of my readers. To paraphrase Clint Eastwood as Dirty Harry, "I know what you're thinking." Specifically, some of you are no doubt thinking…

"Can't somebody do this for me? I'm not a computer expert, and I don't want to be a system administrator." Right. Nobody does. This is an all-too-familiar response. And it sounds reasonable on the surface. After all, we aren't a nation of auto mechanics. We take our cars someplace for routine maintenance and repairs. Why can't we do the same with our computers? But alas, computers are different. For one thing, you aren't going to lug a desktop computer somewhere to have someone perform maintenance activities. And while you could in theory pay someone to come to your house to be your system administrator, the cost would be prohibitive—if you could even find somebody willing and competent to do the job. Furthermore, computers require more frequent attention than cars. We take our cars in for service every few months. If you are truly committed to protecting yourself against all types of computer disasters, you need to perform some tasks on a daily basis and many others on a weekly basis.

So nobody is going to do the job for you. Oh, you might have a knowledgeable friend, neighbor, or relative who has the necessary skills to help you out, but as I mentioned earlier, these people already have a job administering their own computers—they don't have the time or inclination to be your system administrator, too. They just don't like you *that* much (grin). However, once you decide to accept the responsibility that is truly yours and yours alone—to administer your own computers—your expert friend, neighbor, or relative will probably be willing to lend a hand to help you become self-sufficient.

"I hear you, but is this really necessary?" Yes, it is. Let's continue with the car analogy for a bit. If your car doesn't start when you turn the key in the ignition, what's the real harm? Oh sure, you will be inconvenienced. You might have to get somebody to jump-start your car, or you might even have to have your car towed to the dealership. And you might need some neighborly assistance getting around for a day. But it's really nothing more than an annoying inconvenience.

But if you flip the switch on your computer and the hard disk spins and spins and spins and nothing else happens, it could be a disaster, unless you have followed the advice provided in *PC Fear Factor*.

"But I don't have the time." Would you rather spend a few hours a week performing the role of system administrator or risk having to spend thousands of hours recovering (or trying in vain to recover) lost data? Would you rather spend a few hours a week performing your system administration tasks or explain to an IRS auditor why you can't determine the cost basis of the Coca-Cola stock you purchased 20 years ago? I can assure you that "The dog ate my computer" is not an acceptable answer in an IRS audit.

"But I told you—I'm not a computer expert. I can't do this." And I'm assuring you that you don't need to be a computer expert to be a system administrator. All you need is *PC Fear Factor* to guide you down the path to serenity and security.

Do You Feel Lucky?

To those of you unwilling to take on the responsibilities of a system administrator, my message is that *you're an accident waiting to happen*. When disaster strikes, you can lash out and blame the world for your misfortune, as *Fortune Magazine* editor Stanley Bing did in his December 10, 2001, column, "Love Bug Bites." Stanley was upset to learn that evildoers infected his computer with a virus, causing him to lose all of his 3,500 MP3 music files. (He apparently had no backups, but that's another story.) I sent Stanley an email suggesting that he learn how to protect himself from future cyber attacks. I even pointed him to some articles I had written on the subject. I was genuinely trying to be helpful, but my letter was not well received. Stanley only wanted sympathy for his plight and went so far as to suggest in his response to me that I would be more successful as a writer if I were more sympathetic.

Stanley is right about one thing: I have little sympathy for people who refuse to take reasonable steps to manage risk. Don't get me wrong. I believe that people who unleash computer viruses should be severely punished, and I think laws around the world need to be updated to deal with these criminals more harshly. But to me, railing against this type of injustice is kind of like leaving your doors and windows wide open when you go to work and then bemoaning that scoundrels out there took advantage of the situation and robbed you. You can be a victim if you want and lash out at the evildoers, but *that still doesn't solve your problem*. In the final analysis, you have to take responsibility for your own safety.

But I hear you. You *still* don't want to be a system administrator. You're *still* not convinced of the necessity. Well, okay. You just might be one of the fortunate few who never have a problem with their computers and never even lose a single piece of important data. But before you decide to cast your fate to the wind, consider this: In the past four months I have had not one, but two hard disk failures. Had I not done all the things I will teach you in *PC Fear Factor*, my life would have completely unraveled. Every piece of financial data I have, every digital photograph I have, and every document I have ever generated would have been gone forever. Furthermore, I would not have had an easy way of getting my computer up and running again when I replaced my hard disk. In fact, had I not been a good system administrator, the easiest solution for me would have been to buy a new computer.

So, before you risk adopting a "hear no evil, see no evil" approach to system administration, you would do well to recognize that your position is eerily similar to that of the bank robber who found himself at the wrong end of Clint Eastwood's .44 Magnum in *Dirty Harry*. And as Dirty Harry asked when he pointed his gun at the bank robber, I ask you now, *"Do you feel lucky? Well? Do you?"* If the answer is no, you've come to the right place.

The Really Good News

I suspect that by now you have a new found awareness and fear of computer disasters. That's actually good news. The more concerned you are, the more likely you are to take the necessary steps to prevent most computer disasters.

But wait. There's more good news. This book is not going to require you to become a computer expert. I am not going to require you to learn how to do really drastic, difficult things like modify the Windows Registry. I have been using computers extensively for many years and I have never had to maintain the Windows Registry. I have always been able to find solutions for my problems that don't require such drastic action. I'm not trying to discourage you in your thirst for knowledge—If you have a burning desire to learn how to maintain the Windows Registry, by all means pick up a book such as Que Publishing's *Using the Windows 98 Registry* (ISBN 0-7897-1658-5). But you don't have to become a Registry expert to prevent or recover from computer disasters.

What Is the Windows Registry?

The short answer is it's a dark and foreboding place where mortals dare not enter.

The correct, technical answer is that the Windows Registry is a file (actually two files) within the Windows directory on your computer that contains critical information about all the hardware and software installed on your computer. If the Registry becomes corrupted, your computer might not work properly or at all.

The Windows Registry is a dynamic entity that gets updated automatically every time you install hardware or software in your system or remove hardware or software from it.

Every time you install a new program or new piece of hardware, the installation process creates entries in the Windows Registry that allow the application or hardware to be accessed and to function properly. Conversely, when you remove (uninstall) the program or hardware from your computer, all the entries in the Windows Registry that are associated with the program or hardware are (hopefully) removed.

Unfortunately, the uninstallation process does not always leave the Registry the way it found it. Over time, the Windows Registry can get cluttered with entries left over from programs and hardware that were installed and later removed from your system. In most cases, this debris is not harmful to your system.

But, to quote Paul McCartney, it's a good idea to "keep [your] fire engine clean." That is "a clean machine" is less likely than one cluttered with debris to result in a computer disaster somewhere down the line. This book will show you how to accomplish this task without having to learn about the inner workings of the computer Registry.

In fact, if you are ever tempted to modify the Registry, or if anyone ever suggests that you do so, I have but one word of advice: STOP! Unless you really understand what you are doing, you are more likely to do harm than good.

In addition to not having to be a Registry hacking expert, you don't have to know how to program. Nor must you know how to rebuild the contents of your entire hard drive from scratch to become a system administrator.

Finally, I am not going to recommend that you purchase a lot of expensive hardware to build redundancy into your computing environment. You will need to purchase some software packages to do the job, but I will show you how to purchase these packages as inexpensively as possible. Some of the products you need are free!

So the really good news is that you can learn how to protect your computer against disasters without having to acquire the technical skills of a computer expert and without having to spend a great deal of money on hardware and software to do the job.

Benefits

When you have completed reading *PC Fear Factor*, you will never have to worry about computer disasters again. You will be ready for whatever cyber-terrorists, mother nature, or anybody else throws at you. You will know how to stop all preventable computer disasters, and how to recover quickly and easily from unavoidable disasters. You will have learned how to perform some rather technical tasks without any technical knowledge. *You will be in control of your computing destiny, and that's a great feeling to have!*

How *PC Fear Factor* Is Organized

I have tried to organize the material in *PC Fear Factor* for the convenience of you, the reader and your reading habits.

As with most books educational books, learning will probably be easier if you read *PC Fear Factor* from beginning to end. However, I recognize that most people (myself included!) are spot readers by nature, and I have written this book with the spot reader in mind. So, if you dig into Chapter 6 and come across a term or concept you are not familiar with, you will probably find a reference to an earlier chapter to plug your knowledge gap. I have also repeated some concepts in several places to reduce the jumping around the spot reader will need to do.

PC Fear Factor introduces and uses a number of technical terms throughout. I realize it is unreasonable to expect a reader who is reading Chapter 7 to remember the definition of a term that defined in Chapter 2—even if you read the book in sequence. To make things easy for the reader, I have included a detailed glossary of terms.

A number of Internet links are referenced in *PC Fear Factor*—places you will need to go to get certain information. I don't want to force you to manually enter these long, complex links in their Web browsers. You will find all of these links, broken down by chapter and page and updated where necessary, at `http://www.alanluber.com/ pcfearfactor/links.htm`.

From the Base Up

The first two chapters of *PC Fear Factor* establish a knowledge base that will serve you well throughout the rest of the book.

Because some of you will probably time their purchase of *PC Fear Factor* with the purchase of a new computer, Chapters 3 and 4 show how to avoid a disaster before you purchase a computer and how to implement a disaster prevention plan for a new computer after you make your purchase.

In Chapter 5 you will learn how to prevent disasters related to cyber-terrorism.

The focus switches in Chapters 6 and 7 to preparing for the worst—the unavoidable computer disaster. Chapter 8 puts this preparation to good use and shows how to recover from computer disasters.

The last two chapters provide tips on how to keep your computer in top shape and how to avoid computer disasters.

Assumptions

The book assumes that you have some basic knowledge of Microsoft Windows and computer terminology. It assumes that you know how to perform such basic functions as creating folders and files, finding files on your computer, copying and moving files, renaming files, and deleting files. It assumes that you understand basic computer instructions, such as "Press Ctrl+Alt+Delete" or "Reboot." If you don't have these basic computer skills, I recommend one of the hundreds of good books on Microsoft Windows before you read this book. Depending on which operating system you have, consider purchasing the appropriate book from Que Publishing's *Easy* series for Windows:

- *Easy Windows 98* (ISBN 0-7897-1740-9)
- *Easy Microsoft Windows Millennium* (ISBN 0-7897-2405-7)
- *Easy Microsoft Windows 2000 Professional* (ISBN 0-7897-2187-2)
- *Easy Microsoft Windows XP Home* (ISBN 0-7897-2659-9)

I am deliberately steering you toward shorter books because you need not wade through an 800-page book to learn what you need to know about Windows to benefit from *PC Fear Factor*. These books are available in your local bookstore, from Amazon and other book e-tailers, or directly from Que Publishing at www.quepublishing.com.

This book assumes you are using one of the three supported consumer-oriented versions of Microsoft Windows: Windows 98, Millennium, or XP Home Edition. To the extent that instructions for certain tasks are different in these versions of Windows, multiple sets of instructions are provided.

If you are using Windows XP Professional Edition, be aware that there are a few minor differences between the XP Home and XP Professional user interface. For example, some features are buried a level deeper in XP Professional than in XP Home. Because Windows XP Professional is geared towards the corporate market, and because PC Fear Factor is geared towards home users, the minor differences between XP Home and XP Professional are not discussed in this book. Users of Windows XP Professional should be able to work through these minor differences without detailed instruction.

A Few Words About the Software Products Recommended in *PC Fear Factor*

I refer to a number of software products in this book. In fact, a whole chapter is devoted to tools you need to perform your duties as system administrator. These are products that I personally use and endorse. I receive no money if you purchase them, and you are certainly free to purchase other, competing products if you have a strong preference for another brand name. However, please recognize that I endorse the specific software products mentioned in this book for a reason: I know they work.

In some cases, I have tested several competing products that either don't work or are lacking with regard to functionality, ease of use, or reliability. I wish I could tell you that all of these software products performed flawlessly for me out-of-the-box. The truth is that I did discover a number of bugs that needed to be fixed. In fact, one of the additional, unexpected benefits you will receive is that I was able to convince software vendors to fix these bugs and issue patches to their software before recommending their products.

To ensure total accuracy, certain chapters of *PC Fear Factor* have been reviewed by the software vendors whose products are discussed therein. In reviewing these chapters, three of the vendors made comments to me to the effect that *PC Fear Factor* does a better, more accurate, more complete job of explaining their products than their own documentation! It gives me a good feeling that I am giving you more value in these unexpected ways.

If you enjoy reading *PC Fear Factor* only half as much as I enjoyed writing it, it will have been well worth the effort.

A Word About Instructions

It's difficult writing a book that has to serve the needs of users who might have any one of three operating systems: Windows 98, Millennium, or XP, because the instructions vary a bit by operating system. For example, instructions that read "Start/Programs" for Windows 98 or Millennium users would read "Start/All Programs" for Windows XP users. The differences are minor, and rather than burden the reader with a constant barrage of "If you are using Windows *<insert version>*…" type of instructions, I am trusting the reader to discern these very minor differences. I think it makes for a shorter and more readable book."

It only hurts when I boot up.

CHAPTER 1

The Root of All Computer Disasters

Revelations

In this chapter you will learn

- ❏ About the mysterious blue screen of death
- ❏ Why you are always just millionths of an inch and a cushion of air away from a computer disaster
- ❏ Why you should never have to partition or format your hard disk—even if you get a new hard disk
- ❏ How a lazy or incompetent technical support specialist might convince you to do something that results in a self-inflicted computer disaster
- ❏ Four categories of hard disk disasters
- ❏ Why your hard disk isn't perfect, even when it leaves the factory!
- ❏ When you should replace your hard disk

Overview

Computer problems are quite common, but not all computer problems qualify as disasters. This chapter provides a more formal definition of the term *computer disaster* and explains the root causes of such disasters.

You will learn about the basic physical components and the mechanical operation of the hard disk. You will also learn about the physical and logical structures contained on the most critical component of the hard disk—the platters that contain the data.

All of this will enable you to better understand the types of things that can cause computer disasters. You will also learn about the four major categories of computer disasters and the causes of each.

Finally, you will learn how you can sometimes determine when you are on the verge of a disaster and what you should do when you receive signs of impending danger.

Inconvenience or Disaster?

I talked a great deal about computer disasters in the Introduction without actually clarifying the difference between computer problems that are inconveniences and those that are true disasters. Let's make this clarification before we proceed further.

The following is a partial list of problems I have encountered at one time or another over the years with my computers:

- A dead monitor
- A broken floppy disk drive
- A broken CD-ROM drive
- A broken CD-RW drive
- A fried network card (that's right—fried by lightning)
- A broken Zip drive
- A broken power switch
- A bad cable (it took a long time to figure that one out; you just don't expect cables to go bad!)
- A broken keyboard
- A broken mouse
- The sudden inability to communicate with a peripheral device, such as a printer, scanner, or speakers

These are all significant problems that need to be fixed, some more quickly than others. They prevent you either from using your computer or from performing certain tasks on your computer. For example, a bad network card can prevent you from connecting to the Internet (if you have a broadband Internet connection or connect through a network).

But none of the previously mentioned problems qualify as disasters. Not even the dead monitor problem, which prevented me from using my computer at all for two days while I waited for a replacement from Dell, could be considered a disaster. Why? Because all these problems are easily remedied.

Most problems communicating with peripheral devices can be easily solved, often by doing something as simple as rebooting your computer or fixing a loose cable. (Some peripheral devices have communication idiosyncrasies. I have one old laser printer that will not work unless I wait until *after* my computer is finished booting up before turning it on.)

The broken components listed previously can all be replaced quickly, although you might have to refer to a repair book to learn how to replace an internal component such as a floppy disk drive. The only thing you will have lost in the process is the complete or partial use of your computer for a short period of time, and, if the computer is out of warranty, some money to replace the broken component.

Inconvenience? You bet. Disaster? Hardly.

What Qualifies As a Disaster?

What then, is a computer disaster? If I may paraphrase John Lennon, it's "a feeling deep inside." And it's not a good one. It's that feeling you get deep in the pit of your stomach when you are sitting in front of your computer and you just somehow *know* that something *really* bad has happened.

So, what could possibly leave you with the same deer-in-headlights expression the poor woman in Figure 1.1 has? How about something such as the following:

- The moment you realize somebody has accessed your computer over the Internet, stolen your passwords, and cashed out your brokerage accounts.

- When you click the My Pictures folder and discover that all your digital photographs have inexplicably disappeared.

- When you hear 30 people around the office shout in unison, "Why am I getting all of these emails from Robert?" two seconds after you, Robert, clicked the enticing email attachment named `Anna Kournikova.vbs`. (I talk more about the not-so-enchanting Miss Kournikova in Chapter 5, "Protecting Your Computer from Cyber-Terrorists.")

- When you turn on your computer and hear the hard disk spin, and spin, and spin—while your computer screen remains ominously dark.

- When you see the Microsoft Windows infamous "blue screen of death" 20 times a day, every day.

- When you try to open or save a file and receive an error message stating `Unable to access drive C:`.

- When you are unable to get any work done because your computer freezes up every time you try to use a certain critical application.

Are you beginning to get the picture? If you've used computers long enough, or know folks who have, at least one or two of these incidents probably rings all too familiar. So, let's formalize the definition of a computer disaster. A computer disaster is a computer problem that meets at least one of the following criteria:

- It results in the permanent loss of important, irreplaceable data.

- It results in the loss of work product that requires a massive expenditure of time and effort to recover. For example, you might be able to recover an earlier version of a document or digital image, but you might have to reapply a great deal of effort to bring that document or image back to its pre-disaster state.

- It results in the theft of important data, causing personal or financial ruin.

- It results in serious, perhaps irreparable, damage to your reputation as a responsible user in a connected world. For example, your reputation can suffer if you infect hundreds of colleagues with a computer virus. It's just possible that these people will no longer open your email messages.

- It transforms your computer into a paperweight for an extended period of time—several days or weeks—while you try to recover from the problem.

- It effectively prevents you from using your computer because you encounter constant problems that require you to reboot your computer.

The Blue Screen of Death: Everything You Ever Wanted to Know

The term *blue screen of death (BSOD)* refers to an ominous type of error message that all Microsoft Windows users receive from time to time. Even Bill Gates is not immune, having encountered a blue screen of death at the Comdex trade show in 1998 during a demonstration of Windows 98. (The video is still widely available on the Web for your entertainment.) To the best of my knowledge, nobody knows who first coined this now too familiar term.

The blue screen of death always occurs without warning and at the worst possible time (you should see the look on Bill Gates' face in the video). You're working on your computer, and suddenly, for no explicable reason, your entire screen turns a shade of shocking blue and an error message is displayed in white print on the blue background. The error message often starts with `A fatal exception 0E has occurred...` and ends with `Press any key to continue`, giving false hope that pressing any key will make the blue screen go away and take you back to a happier time. (I actually had a person ask me once where the "any key" was on his keyboard.)

More often than not, pressing any key just reveals another blue screen of death lurking beneath the first one. This process often continues ad infinitum. It seems as though your computer is mocking you. You almost expect to hear Clint Eastwood's Dirty Harry voice booming out of the speakers, daring you: *"Go ahead, press any key, make my day."*

FIGURE 1.1
*The blue screen of
death.*

What Causes the Blue Screen of Death?

The blue screen of death occurs when Windows encounters an unusual situation it
doesn't know how to handle, such as a hardware problem or software conflict. There
are as many specific causes as there are stars in the sky.

Sometimes, the BSOD error message is semi-helpful, indicating that a software
application (it won't tell you which one!) has caused a *general protection fault*, which
in plain English means that a software application has behaved badly by intruding on
memory (RAM) reserved for another application.

Some blue screens indicate that an *invalid page fault* has occurred, which in plain
English means that your software application was unable to find and retrieve information
your computer had stored temporarily in virtual memory on your hard disk. Information is
stored temporarily on the hard disk when your system runs out of real memory, also
known as random access memory (RAM). Adding real memory to your computer reduces
the need for your computer to store information in virtual memory on your hard disk and
can reduce the number of invalid page-fault-related blue screens of death.

The frustrating thing about blue screens of death is that the error messages don't tell
you specifically what caused the problem or how to prevent it from happening again.

From my experience, the vast majority (95% or more) of blue screens are software
related, caused by an ill-behaved application or a conflict between applications.

It follows that the more applications you have running concurrently on your computer, the more often you will see the blue screen of death. I get a blue screen of
death on my computer about once a week. I'm not happy about the situation, but
neither am I surprised or worried.

Since you can't plan for a blue screen of death, my advice is to save your work early
and often. Over the years, I have gotten into the habit of pressing Ctrl+S—the standard keystroke combination used to save your work in any Windows application—
every few minutes. I'm not even aware that I am doing it anymore—it's that
automatic. I can't remember the last time I lost more than a few keystrokes of work
due to a blue screen of death.

It is generally true that
each new version of
Microsoft Windows is
more stable than previ-
ous versions and that
the user experiences
fewer blue screens of
death. However, like
death and taxes, the
BSOD is here to stay.

What to Do When You Get a Blue Screen of Death

In most cases, when you get the BSOD, you have lost whatever you were working on (unless you were prescient enough to have saved your work seconds before you encountered the blue screen of death), and you will have to reboot your computer. If you *are* fortunate enough to get back to where you were without rebooting, your system is now unstable, and the smart thing to do at this point is save your work (if you can) and restart your computer to (hopefully) clear out whatever condition caused the blue screen of death. I recommend doing a *cold reboot*—shutting your computer down completely and then restarting it—to reset everything and get the cleanest reboot possible.

Sometimes, an application crashes (freezes) without causing the blue screen of death. If you are successful in exiting out of that application, you should assume that your system is now unstable. Rebooting might prevent you from getting a blue screen of death later.

Strange as it may seem, the occasional blue screen of death is usually nothing to worry about. Rebooting the system almost always solves whatever problem Windows had encountered, and the problem might not occur again for weeks, or the next blue screen of death you see might be caused by an entirely different, abnormal condition.

If, on the other hand, the blue screen of death occurs so often that it seems like your standard user interface, you have a very serious problem. You will need to determine whether a specific set of circumstances or a specific change to your system caused the repetitive problem. You learn how to diagnose system problems in Chapter 8, "Disaster Recovery."

The System Administrator As a Bodyguard

If you examine the criteria for a computer disaster, it should be clear that the root of all computer disasters is the computer's hard disk. Or, perhaps more accurately, the failure (or in some cases, inability) to guard against that which would destroy, corrupt, infect, or steal information on the hard disk.

The hard disk contains everything that is needed to operate the computer—the operating system, device drivers, software applications, and your data. Unlike the broken components discussed earlier, if your hard disk fails, you can't just install a new one and resume working. You will need to reinstall/restore the operating system, device drivers, software applications, and your data—a task that can take days or even weeks if you are unprepared for such a disaster.

The system administrator, as outlined in the Introduction to this book, is in a sense a bodyguard for the hard disk. The more you understand about what you are guarding, the better you can protect it. So without getting too technical, let's take a closer look at this electromechanical marvel to understand how it works, what can harm it, and most importantly, why it is prone to harm.

Understanding Your Hard Disk

In the next few sections of this chapter, you will learn about the basic physical components and mechanical operation of the hard disk. You will also learn about the physical and logical structures contained on the most critical component of the hard disk—the platters that contain the data.

This will enable you to better understand the types of things that can cause computer disasters. Immediately following this discussion, I will explain four categories of computer disasters that will draw upon what you have learned about the hard disk.

Basic Components

The computer's hard disk, as shown in Figure 1.2, is comprised of one or more *platters* that contain all the information on your computer—the operating system, drivers, applications, and data. (That's right—it's usually not a single disk. For example, a 120GB hard disk may be comprised of three platters, each of which is capable of storing 40GB.) This information is all magnetically encoded on the platters in billions of 0s and 1s. Information is stored on both sides of the platters.

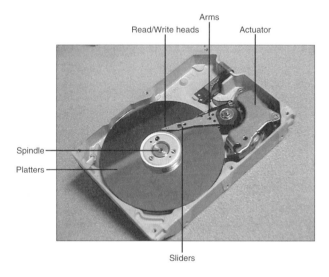

FIGURE 1.2
The hard disk revealed. (Note: The logic board is underneath and is not visible.)

The platters are mounted on a *spindle*, which is attached to a *spindle motor*. In most hard drives, the spindle motor spins the hard disk platters at speeds of up to 10,000rpm.

The hard disk has *arms* that are moved back and forth across the surface of the platters to precise locations by an *actuator*. A *slider* is attached to each arm, and an electromagnetic *read/write head* is attached to the slider. The read/write heads read data from and write data to the platters by either converting electrical energy to magnetic fields (to write data to the disk) or reversing the process (to read data from the disk).

The actuator moves all the arms across the surface of the platters in unison as a fixed assembly unit. Thus, all the arms are always located over the same respective position on each platter, forming an imaginary *cylinder*.

A *logic board* contains the electronics that control the other components of the hard disk. There are other components—cables, jumpers, connectors, and so on—that connect various components, provide power to the hard drive, and connect the hard drive to the motherboard.

A Cushion of Air

The actuator arm assembly travels at very high speed across the surface of the disk, but the read/write heads never actually touch the surface while your computer is on. Well, at least they're not supposed to. If the heads actually do touch the surface, you have what is known as a *hard disk crash*—the catastrophic failure of your hard disk. Under normal operation, the read/write heads hover a few millionths of an inch above the surface of the platter on a cushion of air created by the spinning platters. To put things into perspective, a speck of dust is about 200 times thicker than the space between the read/write heads and the platters!

A Closer Look at the Platters

(No, not the group that gave us such classics as "Smoke Gets in Your Eyes" and "Only You"—your hard disk's platters.) A hard disk's platters have physical and logical structures that allow data to be organized for easier access. The physical and logical structures allow the read/write heads to be directed to very specific locations on the disk to read and write data. Both structures are prone to harm, so let's take a few minutes to understand them better.

Earlier, I mentioned that all the arms move as a fixed assembly to the same respective location on all platters, forming an imaginary cylinder. The term *cylinder* is synonymous with *track*. It refers to the fact that the arms are located over the same track on all the platters.

The Physical Structure

The hard disk manufacturer places the physical structures on the platters through a process known as *low-level formatting*. This process physically divides each platter into tens of thousands of *tracks*, which are concentric rings around the disk. Each track is further divided into tens of thousands of smaller segments called *sectors*.

Tracks near the edge of the disk contain more sectors than tracks near the center of the disk because the track circumference at the edge is longer than the circumference near the middle. This structure allows the read/write heads to be directed to specific locations (addresses) on the disk to read and write data.

Logical Structures

The platters also have logical structures to facilitate easy access to data. These logical structures must be put on the hard disk before anything—even the operating system—can be loaded on the disk. The computer manufacturer puts these logical structures on the hard disk, which enables the manufacturer to load the operating system and applications so that the computer is ready for immediate use when it is purchased. These logical structures are applied through two processes, known as *partitioning* and *formatting*.

Partitioning

Hard disks are divided into one or more logical *partitions*. This is done with a special operating system command called FDISK. Multiple partitions make it appear as if you have multiple, independent hard disks on your computer. That is, each partition is treated by the operating system as if it were a separate hard disk. Thus, if you see two hard drives when you double-click My Computer, it most likely reflects that your hard disk has been partitioned into two partitions, or *logical drives* (or that you actually have two hard drives).

In the old days, Microsoft Windows could not manage partitions larger than 2GB. If you had a hard disk that was larger than 2GB, it *had* to be divided into multiple partitions. Happily, this limitation no longer exists, and computer vendors today commonly provide only one partition on the disk—even with disks that can store 120GB of data. I recently checked with Dell, Gateway, and Hewlett-Packard, and all three vendors provide a single partition on their Windows XP systems. However, Sony divides the hard disk into two partitions.

There are some advantages to having two partitions on your hard disk. For example, you can store your operating systems and applications on one partition and your data on another partition. This makes backing up your data separately from your operating system and applications easier.

However, the wise and safe thing for non-technical end users to do is live with whatever partitioning scheme the computer vendor has applied to the hard disk.

Formatting

The other logical structures are applied to the disk through a process known as *high-level formatting*, or more simply, *formatting*. This is done with a special operating system command called FORMAT. These logical structures permit data to be written to the platters and keep track of where data is stored. One of the important structures created by formatting is a *file allocation table*, an address table that keeps track of where everything is located on the hard disk and directs the read/write heads to specific locations on the disk. Formatting also organizes the disk sectors into larger groups called *clusters*. Individual sectors are so small that it makes sense to organize these physical entities into larger logical structures to more effectively manage data.

Thou Shalt Not FDISK or FORMAT

Before we go any further, I want you to promise me that you will not use the FDISK or FORMAT commands on your hard disk. (It is okay to format a floppy disk—just don't format your hard disk unless you *really know* what you're doing.) If you use

In one situation (described in Chapter 7, "Backing Up Your Hard Disk") it might be essential to have multiple partitions. Briefly, if Norton Ghost, the product recommended in *PC Fear Factor* for backing up your hard disk, is incompatible with your CD writer, you can work around this incompatibility by backing up one hard disk partition to another hard disk partition and then copying the backup to CDs. This is explained in more detail in Chapter 7.

As I mentioned earlier, in one unusual circumstance involving Norton Ghost you might want to create an extra partition on your hard disk. You would probably employ a user-friendly third-party tool (such as Partition Magic), rather than the FDISK command, to accomplish this.

Here's an easy way to understand the physical and logical structures on a hard disk.

Think of the hard disk as an office building. The physical structures on the platter (tracks and sectors) are analogous to the physical structures of the building (floors and offices). The logical structures on the platter—for example, the file allocation table—are analogous to the directory in the lobby of the office building. One provides a map of the disk; the other provides a map of the building.

The map of the hard disk tells the read/write head where to go. The directory in the lobby of the building tells you where to go.

The actuator and arms on the hard disk take the read/write head to a specific location on the disk; the elevators and your feet take you to a specific location in the building.

When you get to the correct location in the building, you knock on the door. Hopefully, the read/write head does not knock on the platter.

either of these commands without understanding the consequences, congratulations are in order—unless you're very lucky, you have just created your own computer disaster! You have made it impossible to access your data.

Why am I making such a big deal out of something that may seem so obvious? Because somewhere along the way, somebody—most likely a lazy or incompetent technical support specialist on the other end of the phone—is going to suggest that you reformat your hard disk to solve a problem. This is the standard response you can expect when somebody doesn't want to take the time to diagnose the root cause of a problem to find a less drastic solution. Reformatting your hard disk solves the technical support specialist's problem—it gets him off the phone. It doesn't solve your problem—it just creates a new set of problems. To paraphrase Nike, "Just don't do it!" I haven't had to use the FDISK or FORMAT commands in years, and you shouldn't *ever* have to use them, except perhaps to use the FORMAT command to format a floppy disk.

If you ever need to replace your hard disk due to a disk crash, your new hard disk will not be partitioned or formatted. The only time you get a disk that has been partitioned and formatted is when you buy a new computer with the operating system preinstalled. However, if you follow the instructions in this book, you will not have to partition and format your new hard disk because the recovery tool I recommend renders these steps unnecessary.

What Could Possibly Go Wrong?

Now that we understand the electromechanical operation of the hard disk and the physical and logical structures that are applied to the platters, let's take a few minutes to reflect on this amazing device.

What we have here is a set of actuator arms traveling back and forth from the edge to the center of the platters at speeds of 50mph, hovering a few millionths of an inch above platters traveling at 150mph, while read/write heads deposit and read data to and from microscopic tracks and sectors.

Gee, I guess nothing can go wrong here.

Actually, when you stop to think, it's truly amazing how reliable these electromechanical marvels are!

Now obviously, as reliable as these little devices usually are, a number of things can go wrong, and when they do you have the makings of a computer disaster. Let's take a look at the most common types of hard disk problems.

Hard disk disasters can be divided into four categories:

- Damage to physical structures on the platters
- Damage to logical structures on the platters
- Damage to data due to human error
- Damage to other components of the hard disk that render the disk unusable

Damage to Physical Structures

In the next two sections I take a closer look at each category of hard disk disaster. These disasters can range from a hard disk crash to general wear and tear as you use your PC.

The Hard Disk Crash

A hard disk crash occurs when the read/write heads come into contact with the spinning platters, instead of hovering a few millionths of an inch above the surface. This can be caused by a number of things. One possible culprit is dust. The hard disk components are encased in a dust-free (but not airtight) environment to prevent damage from contamination. Special air filters are designed to keep the hard disk dust free, but occasionally a speck of dust can get through these filters. Or perhaps the clean-room manufacturing process wasn't as clean as it should have been. Recall that a speck of dust is about 200 times thicker than the gap between the read/write heads and the platters. If the dust speck gets between the heads and the platters, you have a hard disk crash.

Hard disk crashes can also be caused by a sudden power surge, jarring or mishandling of the computer while in use, or the failure of one of the hard disk components such as the actuator or spindle motor.

Wear, Tear, and Age

The more you use your computer and the older your hard disk gets, the more likely it is to develop problems related to wear, tear, and age.

The platters on the hard disk are coated with a special magnetic media. The read/write heads write to the disk by creating magnetic fields that polarize the magnetic media. Over time, the media can develop physical imperfections, which show up as bad sectors when you use a utility to check your hard disk for errors. Once your hard disk starts to develop bad sectors, you are at risk of losing data.

Your Hard Disk Isn't Perfect

We'd all like to think that our children and hard disks are perfect. While I can't speak for your children, I can assure you that your hard is not perfect—not even on the day it leaves the factory. Hard disks contain millions of sectors, and it would be cost prohibitive if not impossible to manufacture a hard disk with zero defects. Hard disk manufacturers test each hard disk thoroughly, sector by sector, and use a process that marks the bad sectors as being unavailable for use and hides them from software utilities that check hard disks for bad sectors.

So, while a new hard disk is never perfect, it will always *appear* to be perfect. If additional bad sectors develop after the disk is put into use, these bad sectors *will* show up when you use a program such as Microsoft Windows' ScanDisk to check your disk for bad sectors.

A number of data recovery/hard disk management utilities are designed specifically to identify defective sectors, mark them as bad, and move the data that was in those sectors to good sectors. These tools are often able to recover and restore damaged data by rereading the damaged sector many times (positioning the read/write head in a slightly different position each time) and piecing the results together to reconstruct the data.

I strongly advise you *not* to use these utilities in an attempt to extend the life of your hard disk. Hard disks, unlike people, never get better once they get sick. Once your hard disk starts to develop bad sectors, the process is likely to accelerate. If you continue to use your hard disk after it begins to develop problems, you are at risk of losing data, even if you are using a data recovery utility. I replace my hard disk as soon as it develops bad sectors, and I strongly advise that you do the same. I inoculate myself against the costs of doing so by purchasing a three-year parts and labor warranty on my computers. I am writing this book on a computer that is now on its third hard disk and second floppy disk. The repairs have not cost me a cent, and I have a year left on my warranty.

Damage to Logical Structures

If the logical structures on your disk are damaged, the computer will be unable to find the data on the disk, even if the data has not been damaged. Let's go back to the office building analogy I used earlier. If somebody removes the directory (the file allocation table) from the lobby, the offices are still there, but you will have a very difficult time finding the right office.

Computer viruses can harm the logical structures on your hard disk. Some computer viruses are designed specifically to overwrite the file allocation table and the backup copy that is kept on your hard disk.

The file allocation table can also suffer damage if you shut down or reboot your computer without going through the normal shutdown or reboot process. You might be forced to do this if your computer freezes up or if you get the blue screen of death.

Damage Caused by Human Error

"We have met the enemy and he is us!"

—Walt Kelly, *Pogo* comic strip, Earth Day 1971

Walt Kelly may just as well have been talking about personal computers when he coined this now famous phrase. When it comes to personal computers, truer words have never been spoken. Well-intentioned but uninformed users are the cause of most hard disk disasters.

Such users open attachments that contain viruses, delete critical data or system files from their computers, and follow bad advice from other well-intentioned but uninformed users.

They install improper applications, and they uninstall applications improperly.

They say yes when they should say no, and no when they should say yes in response to dialog boxes that pop up on their computers.

They install antivirus software but never configure it correctly or keep it up-to-date.

Ah, well, to err is human, to recover is divine.

Learn Before You Leap

Human error comes in many guises. When I first became interested in digital photography, I scanned some old family photographs into my computer and spent a great deal of time digitally restoring them to remove blemishes, stains, and scratches; adjusting the sharpness and brightness; and so on.

The scanning process was incredibly easy. The scanning software seemed to have some intelligence built into it, so I just accepted whatever default settings the scanner selected for file type and scanning resolution.

Big mistake.

Over time, I began to notice that my digital images were degrading. After much investigation, I learned that I had been using a low-quality file format for digital images.

The moral of the story is as follows:

Don't embark on a major, labor-intensive, computer-related project until you have taken the time to become a subject matter expert. Learn before you leap.

Damage to Other Hard Disk Components

For the most part, we have been focusing on one component of the hard disk: the platters. It makes sense to put so much emphasis on the platters because most computer disasters revolve (pun intended) around some type of damage to the platters.

However, your hard disk can also fail for a number of other reasons, including a bad logic board, bad spindle motor, or bad actuator. Such instances are rare but not unheard of.

In the next few sections, you learn how to recognize when problems like these occur and what to do when they appear.

How Do You Know When Things Are Going Wrong?

Many computer disasters occur without warning. A speck of dust gets wedged between the read/write heads and the platters, precipitating a hard disk crash. A lightning storm causes a power surge. A new insidious computer virus spreads so rapidly that your hard disk gets infected before any of the antivirus software vendors can update their software to protect you. There is no way to predict such disasters.

In some cases, there are warning signs that you should heed. If you start to experience problems retrieving data on your hard drive or saving data to the hard drive, you are on the verge of a computer disaster. You will likely receive an error message stating `Unable to Access Drive C:` when this happens.

If applications that have been working without any problems suddenly start behaving improperly and your computer locks up frequently, you might be on the verge of a computer disaster.

Microsoft Windows comes with a utility called ScanDisk that can help you determine whether your hard disk is going bad. ScanDisk will run automatically when you restart your computer after an abnormal shutdown—for example, a shutdown caused by a blue screen of death. (You can also run ScanDisk manually from within Windows. This is discussed in Chapter 4, "A Disaster Prevention Plan for Your New Computer: Part 2, Before You Try.")

I suggest that, if ScanDisk runs automatically when you boot up your computer, you allow ScanDisk to finish its task, rather than accepting the option to quit. Although the time to complete varies with the size of the hard disk, this should take only a few minutes.

When ScanDisk runs automatically, it looks somewhat like a blue screen of death. The first thing ScanDisk does is check the hard disk for errors in data files or the file allocation table that might have been caused by the abnormal shutdown. If it finds any such errors, it attempts to fix them.

The only time you really need to be concerned is if ScanDisk is unable to finish its standard check. In such cases, ScanDisk recommends that you perform a thorough surface scan of the hard disk to check it for physical errors. This process can take a very long time, depending on the size of your hard disk. The last time I ran a thorough scan, it took about 16 hours to check a 40GB disk.

If the thorough surface scan finds any bad sectors, your disk is going bad and you should replace it as soon as possible. I also recommend that you stop using your computer until you replace your hard disk. If you continue to use your computer at this point, you are at serious risk of losing data.

What Should You Do When Disaster Strikes?

Even if you do follow all the recommendations provided throughout this book to prevent computer disasters, some disasters are unavoidable. You can't prevent a hard disk crash, and you might not even be able to prevent your computer from becoming infected by a new, rapidly spreading virus. You also can't protect your computer from a family member who fails to follow safe computing practices, and you certainly can't predict or prevent computer disasters of mysterious, unknown origins.

When the inevitable disaster strikes, your computer's hard disk will suffer serious physical and logical damage. So, you must have a way to recover from such damage without losing valuable data or time. Chapter 2, "The Threats and the Tools," tells you which tools you will need to prepare for a hard disk disaster, and Chapters 3–5 focus on disaster prevention. Chapter 6, "Backing Up Your Data," and Chapter 7 show you how to prepare for the worst, and Chapter 8 shows you how to recover from any kind of hard disk disaster imaginable.

The Threats and the Tools

Revelations

In this chapter you will learn

❏ How disaster prevention and recovery software vendors confuse consumers by encroaching on each other's turf

❏ How to avoid common mistakes that render your surge protector useless

❏ Why you shouldn't back up your data to your hard disk

❏ How to avoid a disaster when buying a CD writer

❏ Why the free firewall provided in Windows XP is not as good as another free firewall you should download and install

❏ How rogue applications invade your computer (the culprit will surprise you!)

❏ How you can replace the 80-step email backup and restore process provided by Microsoft with a simple 2-step process

❏ Why deleting your data and reformatting your hard disk still doesn't prevent other people from recovering your deleted files

❏ Why Windows Registry cleaners often do more harm than good

Overview

Assuming you've read this book's Introduction and Chapter 1, "The Root of All Computer Disasters," you are probably experiencing some anxiety at this point. You realize that at any second, you could be the victim of an extremely disruptive, destructive computer disaster, and you're probably wondering what to do.

Well, cheer up. The rest of this book is dedicated to mitigating your fears by giving you the knowledge, tools, and instruction you need to take control of your computing environment.

This chapter has two purposes. It will educate you about things that threaten your computer (lightning, hackers, viruses, and so on), and it will tell you what tools you will need to protect yourself from these threats and to recover from unavoidable computer disasters. Later chapters explain how to configure and use these tools.

Be advised that you are going to have to spend money to acquire some of these tools. If you have more than one computer, you will have to spend more money. Hopefully, this does not come as a surprise to you. You spend money for other types of protection—a burglar alarm for your house or car, various types of insurance, a safe deposit box to protect your valuables, and an annual physical to protect your health. This is just one more instance of spending money to protect something of great value. If the cost of these tools concerns you, compare it to the cost of losing your data or the use of your computer for several weeks. Or compare it to the cost of paying a professional data recovery service $1,000 or more to try to recover data from your hard disk. (Breathe easy—you won't have to spend anywhere near that amount of money to purchase the recommended tools!)

In addition to the tools recommended in this chapter, you will use some standard utilities that come with Microsoft Windows, such as the disk defragmentation tool and the ScanDisk utility.

However, I am conscious that most people need to live within a budget. For that reason, I have divided the list of tools into three main categories:

- **Required tools**—You must have every tool listed in this section to adequately protect yourself against computer disasters. No excuses, no exceptions.

- **Recommended tools**—The tools in this section are recommended but not absolutely essential if you are on a tight budget.

- **Optional tools**—These are other useful tools, but you should consider purchasing them only if you have money left in your budget *after* you purchase the required and recommended tools, and only if you feel at risk from the threats these optional tools address.

The Tool Selection Process

One of the most challenging tasks I had in writing this book was to select a suite of tools to recommend to my readers.

In the Introduction, I explained that one of the reasons we use so many different software applications is that we live in the age of specialization. As an example, I indicated that I use several programs to edit and manage digital images because each program does at least one very important thing much better than the other programs.

I have taken the same approach in selecting the tools I am recommending to you in this chapter. I believe you will benefit more using five specialized tools, each of which performs one critical task extremely well, than using one tool that performs all five functions in substandard fashion. This approach is more expensive, but your data is very valuable, and you would not want to cut corners to reduce the cost of protecting something that is priceless.

Turf Wars

Part of the issue here is that with the passage of time, each software vendor encroaches more and more on other software vendors' turf, without providing the same level of functionality. For example, Zone Labs—the developer of ZoneAlarm, the software firewall recommended in *PC Fear Factor*—has added functionality to its product to scan email for viruses. However, even Zone Labs' most robust version of its firewall, ZoneAlarm Pro, is not a full-fledged antivirus software product and should *not* be used as a substitute for Norton AntiVirus, another product recommended in this book.

Similarly, Norton AntiVirus has a feature called Wipe Info that allows you to permanently erase files from your computer as you delete them. But it lacks many critical disk wiping features found in CyberScrub, another product recommended in *PC Fear Factor*.

Microsoft jumps into the turf war more and more with each new release of Windows. For example, with Windows XP, Microsoft provides a software firewall called ICF (Internet Connection Firewall). However, as you will see later in this chapter, ICF is not nearly as robust a firewall as ZoneAlarm. Figure 2.1 illustrates how these various tools invade each other's turf.

Needless to say, this overlap creates a lot of confusion in the marketplace because products give the appearance of being something they are not.

FIGURE 2.1
Turf wars!

I will be discussing many different categories of tools. In any given category, there are many different products from which to choose. For example, there are more than a dozen products designed to perform data backups, several well-known antivirus software programs, and dozens of software firewalls.

I evaluated several products in each category, but I do not profess to have evaluated *every* available product.

Where there are choices, there are tradeoffs, and there is seldom one "right" choice. In selecting products to recommend in *PC Fear Factor*, I used criteria I thought would benefit you.

Functionality

The product had to perform the functions necessary to protect your computer from the specific threat/disaster.

Reputation

The product had to be well-known and widely used in the marketplace. I did not want to recommend beta-ware or a product that is not proven in the marketplace. Less-proven products would be more likely to create problems and conflicts on your computer.

Reliability

The product had to be bug-free. As I noted in the Introduction, some of the recommended products did not perform flawlessly out of the box, but the software vendors have fixed these problems at my insistence. Having conducted thorough testing, I have every reason to expect that you will have a pleasurable, bug-free experience with the products recommended in *PC Fear Factor*.

Of course, vendors could introduce new bugs into new versions of their products that are released after *PC Fear Factor* is published. I have no control over that. However, I will reevaluate new releases of the products recommended in *PC Fear Factor* and post any bug related issues at http://www.alanluber.com/pcfearfactor/softwareupdates.

Ease of Use

PC Fear Factor was written for end users, although computer experts should also derive substantial benefits from the book. But because most of you are end users, ease of use was an important consideration in recommending any product.

It is important to distinguish between the terms *easy to use* and *easy to understand*. A product that is easy to understand has such an intuitive user interface that you might not even have to refer to the documentation to figure out how it works. Only the best software developers can develop products that are easy to understand.

Some products are difficult to understand because the user interface is not intuitive and the documentation is not geared toward end users. Yet, once the operation is clearly explained, the product is easy to use.

I have tried to select products that are both easy to use and easy to understand. I was not 100% successful in this objective. Although all the products in this book are easy to use once you get the hang of them, one or two are somewhat difficult to understand, owing to poor documentation and a nonintuitive user interface. This book bridges the gap in such cases, making the product both easy to use and easy to understand.

Why Ease of Use Is More Important Today Than Ever

Ease of use is especially important today because of two very alarming cost-saving trends in the software industry: (1) the trend toward incomplete and poorly written documentation, and (2) the trend away from free telephone-based technical support.

More and more companies are adopting what I call a "customer no-service" business model, keeping their customers at arm's length. The first attempt to implement customer no-service was voice mail, or as a friend of mine refers to it, *voice jail*. I sometimes think that the idea behind voice jail was to force customers through such a complex and tortured maze of menu choices that they would get frustrated and hang up.

The second phase of customer no-service was to eliminate phone support entirely. Every day, I come across another company that doesn't even provide a phone number on its Web site. Many of these companies provide support *only* via email. Some augment email support with a knowledge base or a list of frequently asked questions on their Web sites.

The third and current phase of customer no-service has been to make it increasingly difficult to get email support. Some companies go to great trouble to avoid email contact with their customers. They do this by forcing customers through a convoluted path on the Web site before arriving at a place from which they can launch an email to technical support. I suppose the fourth phase will be to make customers pay for email support.

The net result of the customer no-service business model is that anytime you have a question, you might have to wait a day or two to get an answer (if you have the patience to figure out how to even submit your question, that is). And even then, the answer might be wrong or incomplete. (One company uses software to scan email questions for key phrases and automatically compose a response. The response is usually way off target.)

But customer no-service, engendered by the Web, is here to stay. So, unless a product is easy to use and easy to understand, you can "easily" spend days or weeks going back and forth through the tech support email transom to get your questions answered.

Windows 95 is not addressed in *PC Fear Factor* because Microsoft no longer supports it. Windows 2000 and Windows NT are not addressed in *PC Fear Factor* because these operating systems are not geared toward home users. However, all the principles and some of the products discussed in *PC Fear Factor* should apply equally well to Windows 2000 and NT users.

Compatibility with Different Versions of Windows

The product had to support the various home-user-oriented versions of Windows: Windows 98, Millennium, and XP.

Compatibility with Each Other

The suite of products had to play well together; that is, they couldn't conflict with each other and cause blue screens of death or other problems.

For example, I eliminated one product from consideration—a file backup tool—because it did not play well with Roxio's Easy CD Creator, another product recommended in *PC*

Fear Factor. The software vendor in question recommended uninstalling and reinstalling Easy CD Creator before and after using its program—hardly a viable solution. (Talk about a customer no-service solution!)

Compatibility with Other Popular Application Software Programs

The recommended tools had to be compatible with other widely used software applications, such as Microsoft Office.

Obviously, I can't provide an ironclad guarantee that a particular product won't conflict with some other application you have installed on your computer. Every computer is its own unique form of unstable equilibrium. So, while it would be unusual for any of these products to cause compatibility problems with other applications you have installed on your computer, it is certainly not out of the question. If a particular product I recommend doesn't play well in your computing environment, consider one of the alternatives.

Compatibility with Device Drivers

I eliminated one file backup software product from consideration because it was incompatible with a couple of very popular brands of video cards. For reasons that escape me, the software vendor could not make its product function with the video drivers for these cards. (I give the vendor credit at least for noting this in the product documentation and integrating a compatibility test into its trial product download.)

Price

I'm not going to recommend a $200 software product if a $50 product can do the job nearly as well.

Positive, Hands-On Experience

I personally use every product recommended in this book. I am not recommending anything based on how the documentation says it is supposed to work, but instead am making my recommendations based on how it *really* works. And you can be certain that if a product is recommended in *PC Fear Factor*, it really *does* work.

How to Make Your Purchases

You have already been kind enough to spend money on *PC Fear Factor* (for which I am most appreciative), and here I am asking you to spend more money on disaster prevention and recovery tools. The least I can do is show you how to minimize the expense of acquiring the recommended tools.

Alternative Software

The suite of tools I recommend in this chapter provide a proven path for protecting against and recovering from computer disasters, but are not the only options at your disposal. Other tools are available, and you might want to use some of them, especially if a different tool came preinstalled on your computer. For example, although I recommend and discuss Norton AntiVirus in this book, your computer might have come with McAfee's VirusScan or Trend Micro's PC-cillin already installed, and you might not want to incur the cost of changing tools. This is perfectly understandable.

If you do decide to replace a preinstalled tool with one that I recommend in this book, you should uninstall the old tool before installing the new tool to avoid software conflicts. This is especially important with antivirus software.

Appendix B, "How to Install and Remove Programs from Your Computer," provides instructions on how to install and uninstall programs properly in Microsoft Windows. It is extremely important that you follow these instructions; otherwise, you will most certainly suffer a self-inflicted computer disaster.

Finding the Best Price

I buy just about everything over the Internet, including all the products I refer to in this chapter. If the item can be purchased from multiple sources, I use the price comparison feature on CNET.com to comparison shop for the best price. Here are general instructions on how to use Cnet's price comparison tool:

1. Go to http://www.cnet.com/.

2. Click the Price Comparisons link in the upper-left corner of the screen.

3. In the Find Pricing and Availability field in the upper-right corner of the screen, enter the manufacturer's part number or product description of the item you want to check. For example, to check on pricing for the Tripp Lite Model TLP 810 NET surge protector, enter **TLP810NET**.

4. Cnet will display a list of suppliers for the requested item in a matrix showing the supplier, supplier rating, price, shipping charge, and stock availability.

5. Click the column marked Price to sort the results in price sequence.

6. Select a supplier and click the appropriate link to place your order. It's that easy.

Of course, price is not the only purchase criteria—you need to consider shipping costs, return policies, and whether the vendor is reliable. I will cover these in due course.

The eBay Alternative

I also recommend that you consider purchasing these products on eBay. You can often find brand-new, factory-sealed products at great bargains on eBay. You might also want to consider purchasing used merchandise on eBay to save additional money. However, do not purchase a used surge protector, as it might no longer offer full protection.

You also need to consider how good a job the vendor does in protecting your credit card information. One of the vendors I had used was recently hacked, and all its customers' credit card information was stolen. I and thousands of other customers had to cancel our cards and get new cards. Unfortunately, it is difficult to evaluate how good a job e-tailers do with regard to making their systems hackproof. You usually don't find out about their security problems until after the fact, as I did.

If you buy a software product on eBay, be sure you are purchasing the latest version of the product. Do not bid on the auction unless the version is clearly specified.

Also, understand whether you are purchasing the original equipment manufacturer (OEM) version or the retail version of the product. The OEM version might leave out certain features found in the retail version. If you purchase the OEM version, be sure you understand what features (if any) are missing and whether they are important to you. In the sidebar "The Mystery of the Windows XP Backup Utility," later in this chapter, I discuss a specific, important example of how the OEM and retail versions of Windows XP vary and how this impacts users of the OEM version of Windows XP.

Finally, make sure you are not buying counterfeit software. Many eBay sellers are legitimate wholesalers or retailers using eBay as an alternate distribution channel, but the old adage *caveat emptor* (let the buyer beware) applies.

To eBay or Not to eBay (or Hamlet in Pig Latin)

I advise you *not* to purchase anything on eBay unless you are already an experienced eBay user or have the assistance of an experienced eBay user. Experienced users know how to determine if the merchandise being offered is genuine, if it is in working condition, and if the seller has a good reputation for delivering merchandise that works as advertised. In other words, an experienced eBay user can help an inexperienced user manage and mitigate his eBay risk.

Tips for Comparing Prices and Ordering Over the Web

If you do not have a great deal of experience purchasing over the Web then you should know that there's more to keep in mind than just the price.

Most importantly, when comparing prices among e-tailers, be sure to include the shipping charge in your comparison. Some vendors offer unbelievably low prices coupled with outrageously high shipping costs. They are trying to lure you in, hoping you will not notice the shipping charge. Cnet shows both the product price and shipping charge in most cases. But sometimes the shipping charge is unclear. For example, a range of charges will be shown.

If the shipping charge is unclear, you can begin the online ordering process and take it far enough to determine the actual shipping charge without completing the order. You can then go back and compare the total cost to that of other suppliers. If you are bidding for an item on eBay, be aware of the shipping charge associated with the auction. eBay charges sellers a commission based on the selling price, so some sellers keep the selling price low and the shipping charge high to reduce eBay commission charges. (I'm sure it's just a matter of time before eBay figures out how to combat this practice. It's not unusual to see an item offered on eBay for $1 with a $20 shipping charge.)

Besides shipping charges, you should keep the following in mind:

- **When comparing e-tailer prices to retailer prices, remember that local retailers charge state tax**—Compare the retailer's price plus state tax to the e-tailer's price plus shipping to get a true comparison.

- **Most of the suppliers allow you to check their inventory online**—I prefer to order only from vendors who have the item in stock.

Low-Priced Pitfalls

Beware of vendors who offer incredibly low prices on items that are not in stock. When I was a brash, arrogant young lad working in my father's drug store, a customer came in and asked for a pack of Polaroid Land Camera color film.

"That will be $5.60," I said.

"$5.60!! That's highway robbery. I can buy it for $3.18 at Korvettes!"

"Well, why don't you buy it there?" I asked.

"They're out of stock."

"Well," I replied, "When *we're* out of stock we sell it for $1.99."

He paid without another word.

Moral: If it sounds too good to be true, it probably is.

- **Order from reputable suppliers**—Cnet provides a supplier rating for each supplier listed. I have personally used and had very positive experiences with the following suppliers: Buy.com, Gateway, CDW, Page Computer, and PC Connection.

- **Try to consolidate your shopping**—You can reduce shipping costs by purchasing several items at the same time from the same supplier.

Once you've dealt with all the cost issues, there's still one more important item to check. Before clicking that Buy button, make sure you understand the supplier's return policies. Some suppliers charge a restocking fee, particularly for electronic equipment, and some will not accept returns on opened software. This can negate the cost savings.

Required Tools—Hardware

You are not going to have to spend a great deal of money on hardware. You only need two devices: a surge protector and a CD writer. You may already have both, but even if you have both pieces of equipment, I strongly recommend that you read this section as it contains important information about the proper use of surge protectors and CD-RW hardware/software compatibility issues.

A Surge Protector

A surge protector (also referred to as a surge suppressor) is a critical piece of equipment that protects your computer and its peripheral devices (scanner, printers, cable modem, router, and so on) from voltage spikes. There are many possible sources of voltage spikes, the most common one being a nearby lightning strike. (That's right—you don't have to suffer a direct hit to be affected.) Left unprotected, your computer can suffer serious physical damage—including a hard disk crash—from such voltage spikes.

The surge protector sits between your equipment and the electrical outlet. That is, your computer and all its peripheral devices should be plugged into the surge protector, and the surge protector should be the *only* thing that is plugged into the wall outlet.

Recommended Features

Not all surge protectors are created equal. In fact, many products labeled as surge protectors are really little more than power strips that provide scant protection for your computer.

When shopping for a surge protector, you should ensure that it meets at least most, if not all, of the following standards:

- **It is UL listed**—An organization called Underwriter's Lab sets the standards for surge protectors. Any surge protector you purchase should have a UL-certified logo.

- **It provides a high level of protection**—A good surge protector has an energy rating of at least 800 joules, peak surge protection of at least 60,000 amperes and a let through voltage of no more than 330 volts.

- **It includes surge protection for all wires that are subject to voltage spikes**—A good protector includes built-in jacks for your telephone line, coaxial cable, and Ethernet cable. This means that you can run your telephone line through the surge protector if you are using DSL or a fax/modem to connect to the Internet, or your cable line through the surge protector if you are using cable modem for a broadband connection. The Ethernet cable connection allows you to protect the network card in your computer. You probably have a network card if you have a broadband Internet connection. Few surge protectors boast all these features. The majority of surge protectors on the market today only protect against surges through electrical wires.

- **It has at least eight outlets**—If you think this is a lot of outlets, think again. I am currently using six of the eight outlets on my surge protector to protect my computer and a variety of peripheral devices. Don't buy a surge protector that has less than eight outlets.

- **At least three of the outlets are "fat outlets"**—That is, three of the outlets have a large amount of space between them. This allows you to plug up to three transformers into the surge protector without blocking other outlets. Many peripheral devices have large transformer plugs, so this is very important. (It doesn't help much to have 8 outlets if three transformers effectively use 6 of them!)

- **It has a long power cord (10') with a 90° angle space-saving plug**—I don't have a lot of space between my desk and the wall, and neither do most users. A space-saving plug fits very nicely within most space limitations.

- **It has diagnostic LED indicators and an alarm**— A good surge suppressor has one indicator that verifies that the surge protector is working properly and another indicator that verifies it is grounded properly. More importantly, for those of you who don't like to crawl under your desk to confirm that your surge protector is still providing protection, it has an audible alarm that sounds if the surge protector is no longer working properly.

- **The surge protector comes complete with other cables**—Some protectors include an extra telephone cord, network cable, and coaxial cable with the unit. This enables you to connect your phone line, cable modem, and router (if you have one) through the surge protector without the need to buy additional cables.

Recommended Products

I recommend the TLP810NET surge protector from Tripp Lite (see Figure 2.2). It meets all these criteria for a relatively low price of $36 (including shipping when purchased over the Web). The TLP810NET surge protector is rated for 2,518 joules, a peak surge current protection of more than 90,000 amperes, and a let through voltage of 330 volts.

Another thing I like about the Tripp Lite is that the fat outlets have support around them. That is, the body of the surge protector supports enough of the transformer so that the weight of the transformer doesn't cause it to pull itself out of the outlet. (Otherwise, you have to stick a book underneath the transformer for added support.)

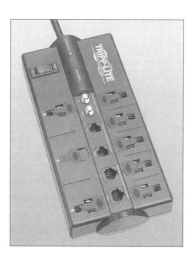

FIGURE 2.2

The Tripp Lite TLP810NET. (Photo courtesy of Tripp Lite.)

For the complete specs on the TLP810NET, visit `http://www.tripplite.com/products/suppressors/specs/index.cfm?model=TLP810NET`.

For a complete and up-to-date list of links listed in *PC Fear Factor*, go to `http://www.alanluber.com/pcfearfactor/links.htm`. This will eliminate the need for you to manually key these links into your Web browser.

Used = Bad!

I've not seen the TLP810NET for sale on eBay, but other Tripp Lite products are for sale, so it is likely that the TLP810NET will show up on eBay from time to time. However, remember that you should never purchase a used surge protector. As mentioned earlier, there's a very good chance it's no longer fully functional.

If you don't need Ethernet cable protection and don't have many fat transformer plugs, you can save about $13 and purchase a surge protector such as the Stratitec S5280. The Stratitec S5280 has 12 outlets (no fat outlets) and provides excellent surge protection.

The Stratitec S5280 sells at Sam's Club for about $20 plus tax. It comes with two telephone cables and a coaxial cable. For the complete specs on the Stratitec S5280, go to `http://www.stratitec.com/S5280MS.html`.

Surge Protectors Tips

The first rule of surge protectors is to replace them periodically.

Most people are unaware that the components within a surge protector that protect your computer wear with use. You should replace your surge protector every three years. Also, replace your surge protector immediately if the protection indicator light on your surge protector stops working or the alarm sounds. This means that your surge protector is no longer functioning properly. It's a good idea to check the light on your surge protector periodically and after a thunderstorm.

Secondly, use your surge protector properly.

The surge protector is an oft misunderstood and misused piece of equipment. Some people use the power switch on their surge protectors as their on/off switch for their computers and other electronic equipment. Bad idea! Do *not* turn off your computer by turning off the power switch on your surge protector. By doing so, you totally disable the surge protector—it is no longer protecting your computer!

The surge protector must be plugged into a grounded three-prong outlet. Plugging your surge protector into an adapter that converts the three-prong plug into a two-prong plug will prevent your surge protector from doing its job. The whole idea of the surge protector is to absorb the surge and send it to the ground. If it can't send the surge to the ground, the next least path of resistance is your computer.

Finally, don't use your surge protector as a substitute for common sense.

Don't get bold just because you have a good surge protector. If you are in the house when there is a thunderstorm, stop using your computer(s) and unplug your surge protector. Lightning can't harm your surge protector or computer if it can't get to it. However, it is *extremely important* that you also unplug your telephone line and coaxial cable from the surge protector. Surges don't just come through power lines; they come through telephone lines and cable lines as well. In fact, you should unplug these other lines from the surge protector *before* you unplug the surge protector from the wall outlet.

A CD Writer

The system administrator has many important tasks to perform, but perhaps the two most important tasks are to periodically back up data and back up the entire hard disk.

To perform these backups, you need some type of backup device to capture the information. I recommend that you use a CD writer for the following reasons:

- CD writers are getting faster each year. I have a very old model, and it takes me about 4 hours to back up 10GB of information. The newer 36X models can cut that time down to less than an hour.
- If you do not have large amounts of data, backing up your data can be as simple as dragging and dropping files to a CD-R or CD-RW disc.
- More and more vendors of backup software are supporting the ability to back up to CD writers.
- CDs are reliable and hold large amounts of data (700MB). While tape drives can hold more data on a single tape, it is still reasonable to back up large amounts of data onto CDs.

What About Tape?

Prior to the widespread use of CD writers, the most popular backup device was the tape drive. I have a rather strongly held opinion about tape drives, based on personal experience, and here it is:

Do not, *under any circumstances*, consider using a tape drive as your backup device. Tape drives are extremely slow, and the media is very unreliable. I have had brand-new tapes fail right out of the box on several occasions.

Prior to using my CD writer as my backup device, I used a parallel port tape drive—that is, a tape drive that attached externally to a port on the back of my computer.

It took more than 24 hours for me to back up 8GB of data and just as much time to restore my data the one time I had to use my tape backup to perform a disaster recovery.

And I hasten to add that my recovery was not painless. When I tried to restore from my most recent tape backup, I received the following error message about 22 hours into a 24-hour restore: `Unable to read media`.

The good news is I was able to restore from an earlier backup. The bad news is that my earlier tape backup was so old that it took me 4 full days to bring my hard disk back up to its pre-disaster state.

Tape drives are so slow that it is impractical to make backups as often as you should, and they're so unreliable that they are the backup equivalent of Russian roulette.

Another problem with tape backups is that they don't allow direct access to files. If you want to restore a particular file, you have to wait while the tape drive spools to the location of that file on the tape.

There is one rare but notable exception to this rule. Later in this chapter, I recommend Norton Ghost as a hard disk backup tool. I also discuss the fact that there are compatibility issues between CD-RW hardware and CD-RW software. If Norton Ghost is unable to write directly to your CD writer due to compatibility issues, you can back up one partition of your hard disk to another partition and *then* copy the backup to CDs using another software package that is compatible with your CD writer. This two-step backup process is discussed in detail in Chapter 7, "Backing Up Your Hard Disk." Note that even in this exception, backing up to a hard disk partition is just an interim step toward the ultimate goal of transferring your backup to external media.

Avoiding Hard Disk Backups to Another Hard Disk

A friend of mine was recently telling me all about his backup strategy. He was backing up his data from his C: drive to his D: drive. What he didn't realize—and what I hope you *do* realize after having read Chapter 1—is that his hard disk had two logical partitions.

Backing up from one partition to another partition on the same hard disk affords almost zero protection against computer disasters. (About the only thing it protects you from is yourself, should you accidentally delete one copy of the file.) It's tantamount to keeping duplicate copies of your precious photos or documents in two different drawers in the same desk as "extra protection" against theft or fire.

Even if you have two different hard disks in the same computer, I advise against backing up from one hard disk to another. A direct lighting strike could take out both disks. The only safe way to back up to a hard disk is to link two computers together and back up to a hard disk on another computer.

You must back up to media that can be stored external to your computer to have any real level of protection.

So don't back up to another partition or to another hard disk on the same computer. To paraphrase John Travolta in *Broken Arrow*, "It's **not**...a good...idea."

How to Buy a CD Writer

If your personal computer doesn't have a CD writer, you have two choices:

- Purchase and install a CD writer.
- Buy a new computer.

The second option is not meant to be facetious. If your computer is so old that it doesn't have a CD writer, you might be due for a new one for any number of reasons.

Avoid External Drives

If you decide to purchase a CD writer for your computer, please be advised that you should not purchase an external USB, FireWire, or parallel port device. As you will see in Chapter 7 and Chapter 8, "Disaster Recovery," disaster prevention and recovery software products often must work from out-side the Windows operating system using DOS to communicate with your CD writer. Unfortunately, DOS can't communicate with USB, FireWire, or parallel port devices. For more information, see `http://service2.symantec.com/SUPPORT/ghost.nsf/docid/2001102516563825`.

However, I realize that not everybody can go out and buy a new computer just because it would be nice to have a CD writer, new operating system, and some other new capabili-ties. With that in mind, I offer the following tips for purchasing a CD writer. (Please note that there are hundreds of models of CD writers on the market, and the models are con-stantly changing, so it would not make sense for me to offer a specific recommendation.)

Consider the Age of Your Computer Before You Buy

This is important for two reasons. First, if your computer is very old, you might have to replace it in the near future for other reasons. A good, fast CD writer costs about $150. While that might not be a fortune, it doesn't make sense to invest that much money in a computer that is on its last legs, any more than it makes sense to put new tires on a car you will probably sell in a few months.

The age of your computer is also important because it can seriously hamper your ability to find a compatible CD writer. Two years ago, I tried unsuccessfully to install a CD writer on a Windows 95 computer. I spent the better part of three days on the phone with tech-nical support from both vendors—the computer vendor and the CD writer vendor—trying to work around the conflicts the installation process created. In my case, the CD writer conflicted with, of all things, the monitor's video driver. (I know—it doesn't sound logical, but computer problems seldom are.) I never did get the problem resolved. I eventually sold the drive and purchased a new computer. To this day, my efforts to install that CD writer rank as the single most frustrating and unsuccessful task I have ever undertaken.

I hasten to add that a friend of mine installed the exact same make and model of CD writer on his newer, Windows 98 computer without any problems. He was up and running in minutes. (It probably also helped that the same company manufactured both his computer and CD writer.)

This discussion brings us back to a point I made earlier, one that will be a recurring theme: *Computers are unstable equilibriums.* Installing a new device on a computer can and often does create problems. The greater the difference in age between your computer and the device you are trying to install, the more likely you are to have compatibility problems. The point is, you will never know until you try.

Stick with a Name Brand

Buy from companies such as Hewlett-Packard, Plextor, or Sony. In the event that you do have problems installing the CD writer, you have a better chance of getting quality technical support from the top-tier companies than the no-name companies. Check out the company's Web site before you make your purchase to find out what type of support it provides.

Minimize Compatibility and Support Issues

If you have a Hewlett-Packard computer, get a Hewlett-Packard CD writer. If you have a Sony computer, get a Sony CD writer. By staying with one vendor, you are less likely to run into compatibility issues. And if you do run into problems, you have to deal with only one company to get technical support. Any time you have to work with two companies to resolve a compatibility issue, things can quickly degrade into a finger-pointing exercise. I have had personal experiences in this regard that even Ripley would have trouble believing. On more than one occasion, I have gotten two different vendors on the phone at the same time using two different lines. I then reversed the phones and held them together so that the two vendors could talk to each other and work together to resolve my compatibility issue!

Make Sure Your PC Meets the Minimum Requirements of the CD Writer

Make certain the CD writer is compatible with your operating system. Be certain that your computer meets the minimum requirements for processor speed, memory, and hard disk capacity.

Make Sure Your CD Writer Is Compatible with the Software Recommended in PC Fear Factor

Three of the products I recommend in this book—Symantec's Norton Ghost 2002, NewTech Infosystem's NTI Backup NOW! Deluxe, and Roxio's Easy CD Creator—need to work with your CD writer. Each software vendor provides a list of supported CD-RW drives. Be sure the drive you purchase is on all three lists.

The NTI Backup NOW! Compatibility list can be found at `http://www.ntius.com/support/supdrives.cfm/`.

The Norton Ghost 2002 CD-RW drive compatibility list can be found at `http://service2.symantec.com/SUPPORT/ghost.nsf/docid/2001102516563825`.

The Roxio Easy CD Creator CD-RW drive compatibility list can be found at `http://www.roxio.com/en/jhtml/cdrdatabase/static/supportedrecorder3.html?_requestid=898547`.

The CD Writer/Software Compatibility Issue Explained

You may be wondering exactly what is the issue here? Why do software packages have to be designed to be compatible with different makes and models of CD writers? After all, any software application can write files to any floppy disk drive, Zip disk drive, or hard disk drive. *Why is it so darn difficult to write to CD drives?*

The answer is quite simply a lack of standards in the world of CD writers. No, that's wrong! It's the exact opposite: too many standards and no one standard to which everybody adheres.

I contacted Plextor about this issue, and here is their response:

"Each drive requires special drivers to support the CD Writing functions. Standards will eventually come into play, but for now we all have to live with the fact that drive support patches must be written for each drive. All CD-RW hardware manufacturers provide drives to the various CD-RW software companies, and those companies then write the drive support patches for the CD-RW software they're working on. We make the hardware; they figure out how to use that hardware with their software. The reality is that CD-RW software companies provide CD-RW drive support patches for all CD-RW drives, regardless of who makes the drives."

More on the CD Writer Compatibility Issue   Although Symantec, NewTech Infosystems, and Roxio all publish lists of supported CD writers on their Web sites, I should point out that the list is not always correct for three reasons:

- **Software vendors don't always test their products as thoroughly as they should**—Vendors have been known to assume (often incorrectly) that if their product works on one CD writer within a product family, it will work on other CD writers within the same family.

- **Because each computer is its own unique unstable equilibrium, a CD writer that tested well in the software vendor's lab may not work on your computer**— Symantec goes so far as to state this explicitly on its Web page that lists supported CD writers for Norton Ghost: *"Because computers differ considerably from each other, Symantec cannot guarantee that Ghost 2002 will work with these drives on all computers."*

  I didn't experience any problems with Norton Ghost in this respect, but I did have difficulty using NewTech Infosystem's Backup NOW! on one CD writer that was on NewTech's officially supported drive list. Fortunately, Backup NOW! allows you to download a trial version of the software, so you can find out if it is compatible before you purchase the product. Norton Ghost does not provide a trial version, but I have tried it with four makes and models of CD writers with no problems.

  For the record, the compatibility issue I experienced with Backup NOW! occurred when the software had to span the backup set to the second CD, so if you test the software make sure you take a large enough backup to span multiple CDs. I should also note that Backup NOW! worked fine on other CD writers I used for testing.

- **A CD writer that is *not* on the official supported list might work just fine with these software applications**—For example, I recently used Norton Ghost to take a hard disk backup of my daughter's computer. Her computer has a new 24X Sony CD writer that is not on Symantec's supported drive list, but Norton Ghost worked like a champ. I had no problems at all backing up her hard disk to CDs.

You should also note that only certain versions of some software products support certain makes and models of CD writers. For example, the Roxio CD writer compatibility list has a column titled Supported from Easy CD Creator, which means your version of Easy CD Creator must be equal to or later than the specified software version to ensure compatibility with that CD writer.

Of the three products recommended in *PC Fear Factor* that use CD writers, you are least likely to experience CD-RW hardware/software compatibility issues with Roxio's Easy CD Creator, which has been tested for compatibility on hundreds of drives.

As you can see, the CD writer compatibility issue is a real conundrum. The issue will get less problematic over time, as a common standard emerges for CD writers.

What About DVD Writers?

DVD writers are starting to show up as standard equipment on personal computers, and over the next two years, DVD writers will likely replace CD writers as the backup device of choice. A DVD writer can store more than seven times as much information on a single disc than a CD writer, which means you don't have to swap discs as often if you have to back up large amounts of data. To put things in perspective, you would need 19 CDs to back up 12GB of data and only 3 DVDs to do the same job.

The problem with using DVD writers as backup devices today is that most vendors of backup software currently support only CD writers. I contacted Symantec and asked when it plans to provide a version of Norton Ghost that is compatible with DVD writers, and the only response I received is that it would give this serious consideration in the future. NewTech Infosystems, developers of Backup NOW! Deluxe, were more definitive in this regard. The next release of its Backup NOW! product, version 3.0, which should be available by the time this book is published, will allow users to back up data to DVDs. Also the current version of Roxio Easy CD Creator already does support recording to DVD.

However, I caution readers that we will have to suffer through DVD recording hardware/software compatibility issues just as we are now suffering through CD-RW hardware/software compatibility issues. Additionally, there are multiple competing standards for recordable DVD formats: DVD-RAM, DVD-R, DVD-RW, DVD+R, and DVD+RW.

The DVD Evolving Technology Quagmire

I caution anybody about jumping on the DVD writer technology bandwagon too soon. The technology is still evolving, with multiple incompatible formats and there are a number of problems, not the least of which is false promises.

Despite initial claims to the contrary, the first generation of DVD+RW writers could only write to DVD+RW (rewritable) discs, not DVD+R (write once) discs. Unfortunately, the DVD+RW discs are more expensive than DVD+R discs and are not always compatible with other devices that play DVDs. Thus, if you made a DVD+RW of your home movies, it might not play on your DVD player. (In some tests, DVD-RWs failed to play on 7 out of 10 DVD players.)

The second generation of DVD+RW drives began arriving in the market during the summer of 2002, featuring support for DVD+RW and DVD+R.

I suspect that there will be other evolving technology issues, and I caution readers about buying a DVD writer until at least the third generation of devices is on the market, which will be sometime in 2003. Personally, I plan to wait until 2004 before making the transition. By then, the technology issues should have been ironed out, the devices will be much faster, and the recording media will be much cheaper!

Required Tools—Software

In this section, we discuss those software tools that are absolutely essential to protect your computer against preventable disasters and to recover from unavoidable disasters. This includes the following types of tools:

- Firewall software to protect your computer against hackers.

- Antivirus software.

- Disk imaging software to back up your entire hard disk. (The term *disk imaging* is explained later.)

- A special tool to back up your email information and browser bookmarks.

- File backup software to back up your data.

- A disk scrubbing tool to permanently erase deleted files from your hard disk. (If this sounds a bit confusing, an explanation is forthcoming.)

A Personal Firewall

The term *firewall* probably conjures up a vision of a cinderblock wall between units in an apartment complex. Just as a cinderblock firewall prevents fire from penetrating into an apartment on the other side of the wall, a computer firewall prevents hackers from penetrating your computer's hard disk.

What Is a Computer Hacker?

The negative connotation associated with the term *computer hacker* is a relatively recent phenomenon. Prior to the existence of the Internet, the term *hacker* simply referred to a person who was obsessed with computers and programming.

Today, the term *hacker* is synonymous with cyber-criminal. A computer hacker is someone who tries to gain unauthorized access to computers to perform criminal activities. Such activities include

- Stealing important information, such as passwords, account numbers, documents, and email.

- Deleting files and programs from your computer.

- Using your computer as a base from which to launch attacks on other computers. By doing this, hackers hope to hide their tracks and avoid detection.

A firewall is absolutely essential if you spend a significant amount of time connected to the Internet. The more time you spend on the Internet, the more your computer is exposed to hackers. If you have a broadband Internet connection, your machine is exposed to the Internet whenever it is turned on, whether or not you are trying to access the Internet. Thus, firewalls and broadband Internet connections go hand in hand.

A *router* is a piece of equipment that allows computers to be connected to each other and to the Internet in a local area network. Routers are designed to support either wired or wireless networks. A router is a specific example of a general class of devices referred to as *residential gateways* in home computing environments.

Firewalls can be software or hardware based. While it is beneficial to have both types of firewalls installed to maximize your protection, I recognize that most of my readers are not going to spend $100 to purchase a router to provide a hardware-based firewall—especially when they can obtain a good software firewall for free! (That's right—this is one tool you won't have to pay for if you accept my recommendation.)

How a Firewall Works

Firewalls have the intelligence to allow invited guests into your computer—for example, Web sites you visit—while blocking uninvited guests. Think of a firewall as a bouncer with a guest list.

Firewalls employ a variety of technologies to accomplish this task. One widely used technology is *packet filtering*. Without getting too technical, a firewall can filter the packets of data that are arriving at your computer to determine whether the arriving data is part of an ongoing conversation/connection that *you* initiated or whether an unauthorized user is trying to initiate a new connection/conversation with your computer. Firewalls make this determination by checking for an acknowledgement bit on information flowing back and forth between two computers. The presence of an acknowledgement bit tells the firewall that the communication is part of an ongoing conversation. If the information coming to your computer does *not* have this acknowledgement bit, the firewall knows that somebody is attempting unauthorized access and blocks the communication (see Figure 2.3).

FIGURE 2.3
How firewalls work.

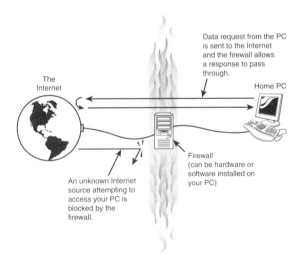

Firewalls Are Not Foolproof

If somebody wants to break into your house badly enough, and if he has the right skills, he can find a way around your burglar alarm system and locked doors.

The same thing is true for your computer. If somebody wants to hack into your computer badly enough, and if he has the right skills, he can find a way around your firewall and locked ports. (In this context, a port is a virtual [logical] doorway to your computer.)

Nevertheless, firewalls are very effective deterrents for the same reason that burglar alarm systems are.

Your local police will tell you that the best way to avoid being burglarized is to make your house less attractive than other houses in your neighborhood. You do this with deterrents—installing a burglar alarm system, keeping your doors and windows locked, leaving lights on when you go out, getting a dog, leaving a Cher CD playing, and so on. Burglars have plenty of choices. If your house is armed with deterrents, the burglar will likely go next door.

Most hackers are like burglars, except that the "neighborhood" is the Internet. Hackers write programs that roam the Internet, probing for vulnerable computers. If the hacker comes across a computer that has a firewall, he generally looks for a more vulnerable target.

So, the good news is that most hackers are not specifically trying to hack into *your* computer—like burglars, they are just looking for easy access. Just as an alarm system makes your house less attractive to burglars, a firewall makes your system less attractive to hackers.

Corporations and Web sites are another issue altogether. Corporations and Web sites are often specific targets of hackers for any number of reasons. Hackers might be trying to steal secrets, commit fraud, or get revenge on a former employer. Corporations and Web sites use an entirely different class of firewalls. Just as museums need a better burglar alarm system than houses, corporations need better firewalls than home computers.

Recommended Features

Not all firewalls are created equal. In fact, some firewalls only monitor incoming traffic. In this section, you learn why it is also important for firewalls to monitor and control outbound communications from your computer. You will also learn about other essential software firewall features.

A good firewall should have all of the following features:

- **The ability to monitor and block unauthorized incoming traffic**—That is, the ability to block unsolicited, unauthorized attempts by others to initiate conversations with your computer.

- **The ability to monitor and control outbound communications from your computer**—If somebody has installed a rogue application (see the following sidebar) on your machine, that application may try to steal information from your computer and send it back to the application developer via the Internet. A firewall that monitors outbound communications alerts you when an application on your computer initiates contact with the Internet.

Earlier, I told you to think of a firewall as a bouncer with a guest list. If your firewall monitors outbound traffic, think of your firewall as a teacher who doesn't allow a student to leave the room without a hall pass.

With regard to server rights, think of a firewall as a company that *always* and *only* allows certain people—for example, those in the public relations office—to listen to and respond to requests for information about the company.

- **The ability to manage and control server rights**—There may be certain situations where you want to allow people to initiate contact with your computer in some controlled fashion. In such instances, your computer acts as a *server*. That is, it "listens" to requests for information from the Internet and responds to those requests. A good firewall allows you to specify which applications have server rights—that is, the right to act as a server and respond to incoming requests. Certain programs, such as the popular file sharing application KaZaA, require server rights in order to function. Granting server rights doesn't grant people access to everything on your computer. In the case of KaZaA, for example, it grants people access to a special folder called My Shared Folder within the KaZaA program files folder. Having said that, it could be rightfully argued that if you allow someone to stick a toe in your computer, he might find a way to get his whole foot in! Nevertheless, a good firewall allows you to limit the extent to which you grant server rights to applications that reside on your computer.

- **The ability to designate certain computers as trusted computers**—This feature allows you to use file and printer sharing on a local area (home) network, as well as share files directly with other computers on the Internet (for example, computers belonging to relatives) as if they were on your local area network.

How Do Rogue Applications Get Installed on My Computer?

As the name implies, a *rogue application* is an application installed on your computer without your permission or knowledge for the purpose of performing dastardly deeds. The two most common types of rogue applications are spyware and Trojan horses. Both of these applications are discussed in detail later in this chapter.

Rogue applications can get installed in a number of ways, but the primary culprit is often that exceptionally good-looking person who stares back at you when you look in the mirror. If you download freeware (free programs) from the Internet, these free programs might contain hidden rogue applications (spyware) that roam your machine, steal data, and send it back to the freeware developer.

If you do not protect your system adequately against computer viruses, your computer can get infected with a Trojan horse that does the same thing.

Other, less critical but desirable firewall features include

- **The ability to put a temporary lock on all Internet communications**—If you are leaving your desk, you might want to prevent all communications with the Internet while you are gone. The Internet lock is as effective as turning off your computer. Some firewalls provide an Internet lock with a bypass option to allow certain applications to bypass the lock when it is engaged.

- **The ability to trace people who attempt to hack into your computer over the Internet**—Think of this feature as similar to that of tracing a telephone call. Instead of tracing a phone number, the software traces the hacker's Internet protocol address (the address that uniquely identifies each computer on the Internet). For most home users, this feature is not essential. It is more useful in corporate environments where the corporation is more likely to be a specific target of a hacker, rather than a random victim.

Recommended Products

Many well-regarded personal firewalls are available on the market, including Symantec's Norton Personal Firewall, McAfee.com's Personal Firewall, Internet Security System's BlackICE PC Protection (formerly BlackICE Defender), and Zone Labs' ZoneAlarm.

These are all good products. I have used BlackICE PC Protection and ZoneAlarm and have been pleased with both products.

I recommend ZoneAlarm for three reasons:

- It has all the essential features described in the previous section.
- It is very widely used and well regarded.
- The price is right. ZoneAlarm is free to home users. Of course, you will receive occasional reminders to upgrade either to ZoneAlarm Plus for $39.95 or ZoneAlarm Pro for $49.95, but you are not required to upgrade. For a comparison of all three products in the ZoneAlarm firewall product family, go to `http://www.zonelabs.com/store/content/company/products/znalm/comparison.jsp`. Briefly, the other two versions of ZoneAlarm provide hacker tracking functionality, which is missing in the free version.

You can download ZoneAlarm from `http://www.zonelabs.com/store/content/company/products/znalm/freeDownload.jsp`.

In Chapter 5, "Protecting Your Computer from Cyber-Terrorists," I provide detailed instructions for configuring and using both ZoneAlarm versions.

If you have reason to believe your computer might be a specific target of hackers, rather than the object of a random port probe, you should consider ZoneAlarm Plus, ZoneAlarm Pro, or BlackICE PC Protection. These programs can trace the source of the hacking activity. Once you have tracked the source, you can report the offender to your Internet service provider or other authorities.

What About Windows XP's Internet Connection Firewall?

Windows XP comes equipped with its own firewall, Internet Connection Firewall (ICF). However, I recommend that Windows XP users use ZoneAlarm instead of ICF for the following reasons:

- ICF does not monitor and block unauthorized outbound traffic, so it affords no protection from rogue applications that have been installed on your computer.
- ICF interferes with file and printer sharing if you have a local area network (home network).

Even Microsoft seems to go along with this. On its Windows XP support Web site (`http://www.microsoft.com/windowsxp/pro/techinfo/planning/firewall/icffaq.asp`) Microsoft compares ICF to third-party firewall products and states:

"In many cases ICF does not have the rich feature set provided by these products. This is because ICF is intended only as a basic intrusion prevention feature. ICF prevents people from gathering data about the PC and blocks unsolicited connection attempts. ICF is intended for users who connect to the Internet but would not normally purchase a firewall from the store."

As you already know, you don't have to purchase ZoneAlarm—the basic version is free. Truthfully, I am bewildered as to why Microsoft would go to the trouble of providing a tool that is not as robust as other, proven, free tools.

Antivirus Software

Antivirus software is a critical weapon in the fight against computer disasters. Antivirus software helps to protect your computer from viruses, worms, and Trojan horses, terms that are explained in the following sections.

Know the Enemy

Although viruses, worms, and Trojan horses are really three different things, they tend to be lumped together generically, which makes things a bit confusing.

A computer *virus*, using the term *virus* in its generic sense, is a program that is usually designed to do damage to your computer and spread to other computers. A virus inflicts its damage by delivering its *payload*. The damage can be as minor as changing your Internet home page, or it might be so major as to destroy critical files on your computer or even reformat your hard disk! Some viruses deliver their payloads immediately, and some are designed to activate on a certain date or event. Some viruses affect the performance of your machine without damaging anything, and some merely unleash torrents of email, bringing the Internet to its knees. Denial-of-service viruses direct massive amounts of traffic at a specific Web site, which prevents legitimate users from accessing the site.

Viruses can be designed to attack specific files or types of files on your computer. For example, a virus can be designed to erase all files with a certain extension, such as all executable program files.

Some viruses are designed to attack specific applications or operating systems. If you are not running that application or operating system, you are not at risk.

Some viruses have a relatively benign payload or no payload at all.

The first computer virus was found in 1986. Today, more than 61,000 known computer viruses exist, and more are being developed every day. Viruses are a much bigger problem today than in the early days of personal computers because the Internet enables viruses to spread all over the world in a matter of hours.

Know the Perpetrators

At this point, given the destructive nature of viruses, you might be wondering, "Why do people create viruses?" The answer is simple: because they can. There is no logical answer. You might as well ask why people commit any type of random, motiveless crime. I think my daughter summed up things perfectly, when at the tender age of three she observed astutely, "It's a yucky world!" (On that occasion, I was informing her that she had to share her toys with her baby sister.)

Having said that, we should all be aware that terrorism in the future will not be limited to the physical destruction of property and loss of life. We already know that terrorists are extremely computer literate, and it's a sure bet that future terrorist attacks will include computer viruses that are intended to wreak worldwide economic havoc.

The perpetrators of viruses are now starting to mimic legitimate application software vendors. They come out with "new, improved" releases of specific viruses that have more virulent payloads or are intended to prevent detection by antivirus programs. Viruses designed to escape detection are known as *stealth* viruses. Thankfully, virus writers mimic application software vendors in another way—they release "products" that haven't been debugged. Some viruses have bugs that prevent the payload from ever being delivered!

Viruses, Worms, and Horses, Oh My!

Three categories of pests can invade your computer:

- Viruses
- Worms
- Trojan horses

(Actually, the third category, Trojan horses, are just viruses or worms that are cleverly packaged.)

Let's examine these three terms and provide more specific definitions and examples.

Viruses

A *virus* is a malicious program that attaches itself to an application (known as the *host*) and causes damage whenever that application is run.

A recent example is the W97M.SMDM.A virus. This virus attaches itself to the Microsoft Word Normal.dot template—the default template used for all Microsoft Word documents. The virus is activated on the 5th of March, June, September, and December (don't look for a logical reason for this). Once activated, it causes all the files on the C: drive to be deleted the next time the computer is rebooted. As The Church Lady from *Saturday Night Live* would say, "Isn't that special?"

On April 27, 2002, AOL's Instant Messenger software was hacked by a 17-year-old who said, "I'm doing it because I can, and I will." He added the following with respect to AOL's security holes: "I'm only hoping that they are upset, and realize that they can't just program everything like 7th graders. If you are using a program that's got as many loopholes and gaps as Swiss cheese, then prepare for the consequences."

Worms and Trojan Horses

A *worm* is a malicious program designed to automatically spread itself across the Internet, often by mass mailing itself to the contacts in user's address books.

A *Trojan horse*, as the name implies, is something that is not what it appears to be. Specifically, a Trojan horse is a virus or worm disguised as something that is harmless, funny, sexy, or perhaps even helpful. Most worms are packaged as Trojan horses.

For example, the `W32.Mylife.J@mm` worm is disguised as a screensaver. Like many worms, it arrives as an attachment to an email message. The message itself has a subject of `Sexy Screen Saver` and the following text: `Hi, look to the screen saver. It's very funny. Bye.` If you are foolish enough to "look to the screen saver," the worm deletes all the files on your hard disk and mass mails itself to everyone in your address book.

Most Trojan horses try to entice you with things that are funny or sexy, or both. The most famous Trojan horse of all time is the Anna Kournikova worm, in which the payload was disguised as an email attachment that appeared to be a salacious picture of the comely tennis star. (Another Trojan horse, "Naked Wife," did not spread as quickly for some reason. I guess it's all in the packaging.)

Don't Nobody Speak English No More?

Because most email-distributed Trojan horses can only deliver their payloads if you click the email attachment, the message text is intended to entice you into doing so. One of the observations I have made over the years is that these email messages tend to be written in very poor, terse, or awkward English, such as the message that accompanied the `W32.Sircam.Worm@mm` worm: `Hi. How are you? I send you this file in order to have your advice.`

I suspect that many viruses are written by people in other countries—people who don't speak English very well. An awkwardly worded email message that has an attachment should always set off bells and alarms in your mind.

As I sit here writing this, I have just received six email messages containing the malicious W32.Klez worm/Trojan horse (see Figure 2.5). This Trojan horse is particularly devious in that each message has a different subject, message, and file attachment name. The most devious of all these messages is displayed in the message preview pane of Figure 2.4. In this message, the virus is cleverly masquerading as, of all things, a virus removal tool! I especially like this part of the message:

> NOTE: Because this tool acts as a fake Klez to fool the real worm, some AV (antivirus) monitor maybe cry when you run it. If so, ignore the warning and select 'continue'.

Note once again the bad English in the message text.

FIGURE 2.4

The Klez Trojan horse even masquerades as a virus removal tool!

How Your Computer Gets Infected

Your computer can get infected with a virus or worm in several ways:

- By clicking an email attachment that contains a virus.

- From infected media you insert in your machine, such as an infected floppy disk, Zip disk, or CD. There have even been cases where commercially sold software contained infected media.

- From Internet Web sites that download viruses to your computer without your knowledge.

- From an infected file you download from the Internet.

- From an infected file somebody sends to you. For example, if somebody sends you a Microsoft Word document that is infected with a virus, your computer will become infected when you open the document. (I once received a virus this way from the CEO of a major corporation, who used a Word document to send out the company's preliminary quarterly results. He was mortified, to say the least.)

A new breed of virus has recently been unleashed on the world. In the past, you actually had to click an email attachment to execute the virus. Recently developed viruses can be activated merely by opening an email message, or worse, simply by previewing it without opening the message.

Even more recently, somebody has cooked up a "proof of concept" virus named Perrun that can deliver its payload through a JPG graphics file. Such a virus could be used as a blueprint for spreading viruses via commonly shared JPG and MP3 files in the future. What I would like to know is, whose sick idea was it to call this a "proof of concept," as if this is something that will benefit mankind?

How Do I Know If I Have a Virus?

If you have a worm, it is likely that you will find out very quickly—not from your doctor, but from angry friends who are in your Outlook Express address book. If you have a particularly destructive virus, say, one that reformats your hard drive, it will be pretty evident that you have a virus. If your computer begins to behave oddly, you might have a virus. Examples of odd behavior include

- A significant change in performance—the virus slows your computer to a crawl
- Strange error messages or screen displays

Of course, the only way to determine for certain that you have a virus is to use your antivirus software to scan your system for viruses, something you should do once a week. Remember—some viruses lay in wait for an activation date, and there would be no obvious evidence of a virus on your computer prior to that date.

How Does Antivirus Software Work?

Each virus has a unique, recognizable pattern known as a *signature*. Antivirus software programs scan everything that arrives at your computer—downloaded files, email messages, and so on—for all known virus signatures. When a virus is detected, the software springs into action and eradicates it before you can do harm to yourself.

Unfortunately, whenever a new virus is unleashed on the world, it takes time—hours or sometimes days—for antivirus software companies to analyze the virus, determine its signature, and provide customers with a means of inoculating themselves against the virus. Because of the lag time, some antivirus software programs contain heuristic scanners that monitor your computer for suspicious activity. Such scanners are of limited value and can yield false positives.

Recommended Features

Beware of software applications that provide some antivirus capabilities, such as email scanning, but that are not full-fledged antivirus products. A good antivirus program must have all of the following features:

- The ability to detect, block, and quarantine all known viruses.
- The ability to scan your computer's hard disk and other media (floppies, CDs, Zip disks) for computer viruses.
- Redundant layers of virus protection—for example, a separate perimeter defense that scans arriving email.
- The ability to block vicious programs called scripts from automatically running on your computer.
- The ability to scan outgoing email for viruses to prevent you from infecting others.
- The ability to automatically update your antivirus software. This is absolutely critical. If you have to manually update your software to inoculate your computer against the latest viruses, your computer can get infected if you forget to update your software just one time!

Additionally, the software vendor's reputation and support are as important as the product features. Your antivirus software vendor should provide instructions and tools for virus removal and should have a reputation for product quality. There have been instances in the past where updates from certain antivirus software vendors have trashed customers' computers.

Recommended Product

When choosing an antivirus product, stick with one of the big three: Symantec's Norton AntiVirus, McAfee's VirusScan, and Trend Micro's PC-cillin.

I personally use and recommend Norton AntiVirus. It has a clean, easy-to-understand user interface, and Norton does a very good job of keeping the product up-to-date with the latest virus signatures. Although Symantec does not provide free phone support, I have used email support for numerous Symantec products on many occasions. I have always received responses within 24 hours, and the responses were almost always clear and helpful. In the event that further clarification of an answer is required, the response to my follow-up query always came very quickly.

The list price for Norton AntiVirus is $49.95. If you perform a price comparison on Cnet, you can purchase it for about $28 including shipping. However, your best bet is to purchase it on eBay. I purchased my copy of Norton AntiVirus 2002 Professional Edition on eBay for $12 including shipping.

You can learn more about Norton AntiVirus at Symantec's Web site (`http://www.symantec.com/nav/nav_9xnt/`).

I provide detailed instructions on how to configure and use Norton AntiVirus in Chapter 5.

If you purchase a new version of Norton AntiVirus to replace an older version, you must uninstall the older version before installing the new version. You should also be certain that all other programs are shut down before you install the product.

When the Cure Is Worse Than the Disease

It pains me to inform you that antivirus software programs occasionally cause serious problems.

McAfee has issued virus signature updates in the past that have caused problems. One problem forced users of Windows NT 4.0 to reinstall their operating systems. Another problem caused computers to freeze up. (I personally know people who were affected by the latter problem.)

Details regarding these problems can be found at the CNN Web site at the following links:

`http://www.cnn.com/2000/TECH/computing/12/21/mcafee.damages.nt.idg/`

`http://www.cnn.com/2000/TECH/computing/11/07/mcafee.windows.freeze.idg/index.html`

One Norton AntiVirus update also created problems, causing Windows 2000
systems to become unresponsive and require a reboot. You can find the
details at this link:

`http://news.com.com/2100-1001-242914.html?legacy=cnet`

I don't know about you, but I find it especially frustrating when a program that
is supposed to prevent serious problems ends up creating them!

System Backup Tool

Thus far, I have been discussing tools that help protect against computer disasters.
When the unavoidable happens—you suffer a hard disk crash, your hard disk gets a
virulent new virus, and so on—you will need the ability to recover from the ensuing
disaster.

A system backup tool—one that can back up your entire hard disk—is an essential
disaster recovery tool. There are two types of system backup tools: file-based
backup tools and disc imaging tools.

File-based tools copy files from one location to another, and disk imaging tools
make an exact copy—a clone—of your hard disk. A disk imaging tool is the better
choice for a complete system backup for the following reasons:

- **They tend to do a more complete job**—File-based backup tools might not back
  up hidden files if they are not configured properly. This is not a concern with
  disk imaging tools.

- **They are more reliable**—Disk imaging tools work from outside the Microsoft
  Windows environment; file backup tools work from within Windows. Because
  disk imaging tools work from outside the operating system, they do a more
  reliable job of backing up the operating system.

- **It is easier to do a system restore from a disk image**—A disk image includes
  all of the hard disk's logical structures. This means that when you restore
  from a disk image, you do not have to partition and format your hard disk first.

Recommended Features

A disk imaging tool is the most important tool of any recommended in *PC Fear
Factor* because it gives you a critical safety net—the ability to recover from an
unavoidable computer disaster. It is essential that your disk imaging tool have the
following features:

- The ability to back up your hard disk directly to CDs.

- The ability to automatically span media when the backup is too large to fit on
  one CD.

- The ability to restore your hard disk directly from your backup without having
  to prepare the hard disk in any way.

- The ability to automatically size partitions on your hard disk during the restore process. This enables you to back up a 20GB hard disk and restore to your newer, larger 80GB hard disk without any problems.

- Built-in error checking to ensure that the disk image is an exact duplicate of your hard disk.

- The ability to password-protect your hard disk images.

As always, good technical support is another essential requirement for any software application.

Recommended Product

I use and recommend Symantec's Norton Ghost, a rather contrived acronym for general hardware-oriented system transfer.

Norton Ghost has all the required features and is the market leader in disk imaging software. Norton Ghost's corporate edition has been used for years by major corporations and is used by more than half of the Fortune 500 companies.

In addition, Norton Ghost has a feature called Ghost Explorer that is very useful in testing backups.

Unfortunately, Norton Ghost falls into the "easy to use but difficult to understand category" of tools I mentioned earlier in this chapter. Symantec is aware of this, and the Norton Ghost user manual goes so far as to say that the product is "designed for technically proficient users." Also, Symantec's press releases have described Norton Ghost as "the most powerful disk cloning and imaging solution for the power user." *Technically proficient users? Power user?* This language would throw a scare into a lot of people.

The real problem with Norton Ghost, in my opinion, is not that the product is difficult to use, but that the documentation is difficult to understand. It is the documentation that is geared for technically proficient users, not the product. I will bridge this gap when I explain how to use Norton Ghost in Chapters 7 and 8.

Norton Ghost automatically spans across multiple CDs when making a hard disk backup, and it is even nice enough to automatically eject each CD when it is done, cueing you to install the next CD.

The Evolution of Disk Imaging Software

Disk imaging products were not originally intended to perform system backups and restores. The original and still primary use of these tools is to allow corporations and computer manufacturers to quickly load identically configured computers with identical software configurations.

Notice the emphasis on "identical." You can't create a disk image from one computer and successfully restore it to another computer unless the two computers have identical internal hardware configurations (same video card, sound card, DVD-ROM, CD writer, and so on). Remember, the Windows Registry contains information about your computer's hardware configuration. If you restore a disk image (which obviously includes the Windows Registry) to a computer having a different hardware configuration, I would be surprised if the computer would even boot up. It would be like using your house key to open somebody else's door. This is one reason you only transfer data from one computer to another when you purchase a new computer, and not the entire disk image. (Another reason is that the new computer is likely to have a newer operating system and newer versions of the applications you currently have. It just doesn't make sense to buy a new computer if you are going to limit your benefits by installing an old operating system and old applications.)

The list price for Norton Ghost is $69.95. If you perform a price comparison on Cnet by searching for "Norton Ghost," you can purchase it for about $55 including shipping. However, your best bet is to purchase it on eBay. I purchased my brand-new, factory sealed copy on eBay for $15 including shipping.

You can learn more about Norton Ghost at Symantec's Web site (`http://www.symantec.com/sabu/ghost/ghost_personal/`).

I provide detailed instructions for using Norton Ghost in Chapters 7 and 8.

Norton Ghost and Windows XP

You might hear rumblings to the effect that Norton Ghost is not compatible with Windows XP.

The bad news is that there *is* a compatibility issue. The good news is that the incompatibility has absolutely no impact on you if you use Norton Ghost to back up directly to CDs. In fact, if Norton Ghost is compatible with your CD writer, kindly skip the rest of this section!

The Norton Ghost/Windows XP compatibility issue is related to the Windows file system. A *file system* is a method used to store and organize files on your hard disk. The two file systems currently in use in various versions of the Microsoft Windows are file allocation table (FAT) and new technology file system (NTFS). The newest version of Windows, Windows XP, supports both file systems. Older consumer versions of Windows (Windows 95, 98, and Millennium) work exclusively with the older FAT file system.

Suffice it to say that NTFS has many performance and security advantages over the older FAT file system. For this reason, most computer OEMs use the NTFS file system with Windows XP.

The Norton Ghost/Windows XP compatibility issue is related specifically to NTFS. When you use Norton Ghost, you have the option of cloning an image to a hard disk partition. As I mentioned in Chapter 1, if Norton Ghost is not compatible with your CD writer and you have two partitions on your computer, you can clone an image of one hard disk partition to another partition and then copy the cloned image to CDs using software that is compatible with your CD writer. This is where the Norton Ghost/Windows XP compatibility issue might come into play. With the current version of the product—Norton Ghost 2002—you can't clone an image to an NTFS partition. Thus, the workaround you might want to use if Norton Ghost is incompatible with your CD writer will *not* work if your only alternative is to clone an image to an NTFS partition.

The reason for this incompatibility is that Norton Ghost 2002 works outside Windows in a DOS environment and DOS can't access NTFS partitions.

Please note that you can back up or restore an NTFS partition, so Windows XP users will not have a problem if they have to perform a disaster recovery using their Norton Ghost hard disk backup. The only thing you can't do is clone an image to an NTFS hard disk partition.

Finally, although *PC Fear Factor* does not focus on the Windows 2000 or NT operating system because they are not geared for home users, it is worth mentioning that the same issue exists if you choose to use Norton Ghost with either of these two operating systems.

Email and Bookmark Backup Tool

Amazingly, most people fail to back up their email and browser bookmarks when they back up their data. I think some people falsely assume that their email messages are stored on their Internet service provider's (ISP's) server. Unfortunately, once you receive your email, it no longer resides on the server—it only resides on your local machine.

I also believe that it just never occurs to most people to back up this extremely important data. People naturally tend to think in terms of backing up Microsoft Word documents and Excel spreadsheets, but the idea of backing up email and Internet Explorer favorites just never occurs to them!

The Microsoft Solution

Microsoft provides very detailed instructions for backing up your email and address book on its Web site. To see these instructions, go to this link on the Microsoft Web site:

```
http://support.microsoft.com/default.aspx?scid=kb;EN-US;q270670
```

I think you will agree that Microsoft's process is extremely complex. It requires the user to perform 31 separate steps to backup her email folders, address book, email account information, and newsgroup account information. Restoring this information is a 24-step process.

Microsoft's backup process is also incomplete. It fails to back up message rules (the rules you can set up to route messages to certain folders) and blocked senders (a list of people from whom you do not accept email). To accomplish this task, you have to perform another process, which you can find at this link on the Microsoft Web site:

```
http://support.microsoft.com/default.aspx?scid=kb;en-us;Q276511
```

You can, of course, configure your email account properties to leave a copy of your email message on your ISP's server. However, your ISP has a limit on how many MB of data you can store on the server—usually 5MB or 10MB—and you will broach that limit very quickly, particularly if you often receive attachments with email messages. Once you have consumed your available space, you will be unable to send or receive any new mail until you purge messages to free up space.

Practically speaking, it makes sense to store your messages on your local machine. You also have more control over your backups. I, for one, am not willing to trust my ISP to back up my email messages. Nor do I like confidential messages residing on somebody's server any longer than necessary.

This process requires 13 steps to back up message rules and blocked senders and is so complex that you need to export individual entries from the Windows Registry. Restoring this information is a 12-step process.

So in total, if you use Microsoft's instructions for backing up all your Outlook Express data, you must perform 44 steps to back up the data and 36 steps to restore the data. And neither of these two processes backs up your Internet Explorer browser bookmarks!

Unless you are a masochist, you will want a tool to automate this process.

Recommended Features

A tool that backs up your email and browser bookmarks should have the following features:

- The ability to back up all your email information, including messages, the Windows address book, email preferences, the blocked senders list, email rules, and electronic signatures.
- The ability to back up your browser bookmarks.
- The ability to selectively restore this information or restore all of it.
- The ability to restore to any system—not just the system on which the backup was performed. This enables you to migrate your email and browser information from one machine to another.
- The ability to do all of the above in just a few quick keystrokes.

Recommended Product

For the past several years, I have been using a wonderful product called Express Assist, a product of AJSystems.com. (As usual, all good things come from Canada, including my spouse.)

Express Assist backs up all your Outlook Express email folders, address book, message rules, and blocked senders in one easy step (see Figure 2.5). As a bonus, it also backs up your Internet Explorer favorites.

FIGURE 2.5

Express Assist replaces 44 steps with 1 easy step.

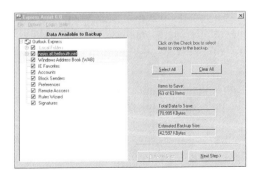

If you are using Microsoft Outlook (instead of Outlook Express), AJSystems has a complementary product called Outback Plus.

Express Assist is only available directly from the developer. It costs a very reasonable $29.95, as does Outback Plus. You can download Express Assist from this link:

`http://www.ajsystems.com/ea2kdnload.html`

You can download Outback Plus from this link:

`http://www.ajsystems.com/obpdnload.html`

I provide detailed instructions for using Express Assist in Chapter 6, "Backing Up Your Data," and Chapter 8.

AJSystems is currently developing a new, omnibus product called eaZy Backup that will work with all popular email clients and Web browsers. As of the summer of 2002, the product was in beta test.

CD Burning Software

If you don't have a significant amount of data to back up, you can use the drag-and-drop approach to backing up your data. (The term *drag-and-drop* refers to the process of copying files from your hard disk to a CD, the same way you would copy them to a floppy disk or Zip disk.) Simply drag and drop your data files to a CD-R or CD-RW. To use this approach, you need CD burning software.

Even if you do not use the drag-and-drop approach to backing up all your data, dragging files to a CD is a convenient way to back up individual files that you work on frequently between complete data backups. As I sit here writing this chapter, I save the file to my hard disk every few minutes and drag a copy to a CD-RW in case I have a hard disk crash or power outage.

Recommended Features

The drag-and-drop approach to backing up your data essentially requires you to be able to use a CD-RW disc the same way you would use a floppy disk or Zip disk. The CD burning software must have the following features:

- It must be ISO 9660 compliant. ISO 9660 is a standard that allows different computers with different operating systems to access files on CDs.

- It must support drag-and-drop functionality. That is, it must allow users to treat CDs as a giant floppy disk.

- It must provide the ability to format and erase CD-RW disks.

Recommended Product

Roxio's Easy CD Creator is the most widely used CD burning software on the market. Easy CD Creator is actually a suite of products that allows you to create audio, video, and data CDs. The product of primary interest to us is DirectCD, which provides the ability to drag and drop your files to a CD-R or CD-RW just as if it were a floppy disk, Zip disk, or hard disk.

There are many other CD burning software products on the market you might consider, but be aware that Easy CD Creator has the largest list of compatible CD-RW drives of any CD-RW software I have come across.

Windows XP comes with a very limited feature subset of Roxio's CD burning software. After using it, my feeling is that most users should upgrade to the actual Roxio product.

The list price for Easy CD Creator Platinum is $99.95. If you perform a price comparison on Cnet, you can purchase it for about $77 including shipping. The full retail version of the product is generally available on eBay for about $50, and you can find the OEM version selling on eBay for about $10.

Note that only the latest version of Easy CD Creator (versions 5.1 as of this writing) is compatible with Windows XP.

You can learn more about Easy CD Creator at Roxio's Web site:

`http://www.roxio.com/en/products/ecdc/index.jhtml`

I provide detailed instructions for using Easy CD Creator's DirectCD in Chapter 6.

Recommended Tools—Software

The following tools are strongly recommended but are not as critical as the tools described in the previous section. Of course, that's a relative statement. I have placed a disk scrubbing tool in the recommended tool category, but if you are constantly working with confidential information, you should consider it a required tool.

File Backup Software

File backup software formalizes and simplifies the file backup process by providing a framework of functionality around the process. It facilitates the backup process by making it possible to take a baseline backup of all your data and then supplement it with daily backups of changes and additions to your data.

The following section will help you determine whether you need a formal file backup tool or whether the drag-and-drop approach will satisfy your needs.

Drag and Drop Versus File Backup Software

As was discussed in the previous section, the drag-and-drop approach to backing up your data is fast, easy, and convenient, particularly if all your data fits onto one CD. This solution is still viable when you have more data than can fit on one CD if you can easily break up your data into CD-size chunks. For example, you might back up all your MP3 files to one CD, your digital photographs to another CD, and the rest of your data to a third CD.

The drag-and-drop approach starts to become less practical if, like me, you are backing up 8GB of data. Now you need a calculator to divide all your data into CD-size chunks so you can drag and drop your files onto 12 CDs. You also need a good memory (or a pencil and paper) to keep track of which files you have already backed up. It can be done, no doubt. But there are better solutions, and the more data you have to back up, the more likely you will want to consider a file backup tool.

A good file backup tool performs automatic media *spanning*. In plain English, this means you don't have to manually divide the data into CD-size chunks. All you have to do is select the files you wish to back up and start the backup job—the software will tell you when to insert the next CD.

What About Disc Imaging?

Earlier in this chapter, I recommended Norton Ghost as a hard disk backup (disk imaging) tool. You may be wondering, *Why can't I use Norton Ghost to back up my data? After all, you told me it made a complete copy of my hard disk. And it does automatic media spanning. Why are you asking me to spend more money?"*

In truth, Norton Ghost *does* back up all your data, along with your operating system and applications. And Norton Ghost even has a feature called Ghost Explorer that allows you to restore individual files from your hard disk backup.

However, there are some disadvantages to using Norton Ghost as a data backup tool. For one, Norton Ghost is not a selective tool. You can't back up *only* your data, unless you have multiple partitions on your hard disk and have all your data stored on a separate partition. In such a case, you could use Norton Ghost to clone (create an image of) the partition that contains just your data.

Alternatively, you could back up all your data to a compressed file on your hard disk, use a file splitting tool to break the file into CD-size splits, and copy the files to CDs. I have considered and rejected this as an alternative worthy of discussion in *PC Fear Factor*. It's cumbersome and complicated. If you really have that much data to back up, I recommend a file backup tool.

The Data Partition Fallacy

Storing all your data on a separate data partition on your hard disk is not as easy as it sounds, and it might not even be possible for many people. You might not realize it, but you probably have applications on your computer that play hide-and-seek with your data. These applications don't allow you to determine where to save your data—they automatically store your data in a predetermined location, and that location is always on the same hard disk partition where the application resides. The subject of hide-and-seek data is covered in more detail in Chapter 6.

Another disadvantage of using Norton Ghost to back up your data is that it lacks important features that make it easy to keep your backups up-to-date, such as the ability to perform daily incremental or differential backups (see the following sidebar).

What Are Incremental and Differential Backups?

File backup tools allow you to take a *baseline backup* of all your data and supplement it with either daily incremental or differential backups.

With an *incremental* backup, the software only backs up files that have been added or modified since the last backup. With a *differential* backup, the software only backs up files that have been added or changed since the last *baseline* backup. Basically, incremental backups are additive of changes, whereas differential backups are cumulative of changes.

> Differential and incremental backup strategies are mutually exclusive: You take a baseline backup, choose a daily backup strategy, and stick to it until you take your next baseline backup.
>
> If this brief explanation is not crystal clear to you, please don't be concerned. I discuss and explain baseline, incremental, and differential backup concepts in more detail in Chapter 6. My only purpose in bringing up the subject here is to make you aware of the differences between disk imaging and file backup software.

If you are able to create a hard disk image in less than an hour, either because you have a very fast CD writer or very little information in total (operating system, applications, and data) to back up, you might be more inclined to consider using Norton Ghost as your sole backup tool. In such a scenario, it would be practical to back up your entire hard disk every few days.

To summarize, the drag-and-drop solution is the simplest, easiest way to back up your data. If the drag-and-drop solution is impractical because you have a large amount of data, I prefer a file backup tool to a disk imaging tool because you can selectively determine which files to back up and file backup tools provide other features not found in disk imaging tools.

Recommended Features

A file backup software product must have all of the following features to justify the additional expense of purchasing the software instead of using either a disk imaging solution or the drag-and-drop backup solution:

- The ability to back up directly to CDs
- The ability to automatically span media when the backup is too large to fit on one CD
- The ability to create and save backup jobs—a set of instructions for performing a backup that can be stored and executed
- The ability to perform differential backups
- The ability to perform incremental backups
- The ability to easily search for and restore individual files from a backup, either to their original locations or an alternative location
- The ability to password-protect backups
- The ability to automatically include a date and time stamp in the name of the backup file for easy reference later
- The ability to compare backup files with the original files to verify that the backup was done correctly

Recommended Product

My quest for a reliable, easy-to-use file backup tool was a long one. Many backup tools try to be so flexible that they end up confusing the user with choices, terminology, and the product's user interface. And quite frankly, some of tools I tried just flat out did not work for a variety of reasons.

I use and recommend NewTech Infosystems NTI Backup NOW! Deluxe. It's easy to use, easy to understand, reliable, and has all of the recommended features in a backup tool (I just wish they would change the product name to something shorter.)

The list price for Backup NOW! Deluxe is $79.99. I was unable to do a Cnet price comparison, but you can save more than $20 off the list price by purchasing this product at buy.com using the following link:

```
http://www.us.buy.com/retail/product.asp?sku=20345828&loc=105
```

You should be able to purchase the product on eBay for about $30, which is an outstanding savings of $50 off the list price.

You can learn more about Backup NOW! Deluxe at the NewTech Infosystem's Web site:

```
http://www.ntibackupnow.com/
```

A new version of Backup NOW!, version 3.0, should be available by the time *PC Fear Factor* is published. This new version has several important features:

- **The ability to back up to DVD writers.**

- **Improved speed**—The new version is said to be 30% faster than the current version as of this writing, version 2.5.14.

- **Intra-backup recovery capability**—Nothing is more annoying than having some type of computer problem when you are 8 CDs into a 10-CD backup. Most backup software packages require you to start over again when this happens. Version 3.0 of Backup NOW! allows you to pick up where you left off, saving you time and media.

Backup NOW! Deluxe also comes with a disk imaging tool. I've not tested it and prefer to stay with the hands-down industry leader in disk imaging software, Norton Ghost.

I provide detailed instructions for using NTI Backup NOW! Deluxe in Chapters 6 and 8.

The Mystery of the Windows XP Backup Utility

The good news is that Windows XP comes with its own file backup utility. The bad news is that it is very difficult to obtain. The backup utility is not included in the default installation of Windows XP Home Edition. You must manually install it from the \VALUEADD\MSFT\NTBACKUP directory on your Windows XP CD-ROM.

Would that it were that simple.

OEMs do not install the Windows XP backup utility on new computers because it is not part of the Windows XP Home Edition OEM installation kit provided by Microsoft. Nor do OEMs include the Windows XP Home Edition CD-ROM with the computer. Instead, they include a system recovery disc. The system recovery disc does not include the VALUEADD folder (the folder that contains the Windows XP backup utility) because it is not part of the Windows XP Home Edition OEM preinstall kit Microsoft provides.

Nor can you download the backup utility from the Microsoft Web site or anywhere else that I am aware. So, if you purchase a new computer with Windows XP Home Edition preinstalled, you do not have access to the backup utility. In fact, unless you purchase the retail version of Windows XP Home Edition (or the upgrade disk) or know somebody who has the disk, you do not have access to this utility.

For more information on why you can't get this utility, visit http://support.microsoft.com/default.aspx?scid=kb;EN-US;q311246.

The Windows XP backup utility does come preinstalled in the Windows XP professional edition.

I am hearing mixed messages with regard to the Windows XP backup utility. Some people say it can't back up directly to CDs. Others say it can back up to CDs but can't span CDs. As I have been unable to get access to this utility, I can't definitively state what it can and can't do. But I am concerned enough about what I am hearing to wonder if this utility, like Microsoft's Internet Connection Firewall, fails to make the grade as a useful tool.

Backup Utilities in Other Versions of Microsoft Windows

Windows Millennium comes with a backup utility that is also MIA (missing in action), the apparent victim of a leave-out in the OEM version of Millennium.

Windows 98 comes with a backup utility that was actually included in the OEM version, and it actually works. However, it can't back up to CDs, nor can it break the backup file it creates into CD-size chunks (file segments) that can be copied to CDs. You would need to use a third-party disk spanning utility to transfer the backup to CDs. Personally, I think it is simpler and more reliable to purchase and use a utility that does everything you need out of the box.

A Disk Scrubber

The term *disk scrubber* probably conjures up visions of the ball scrubber on the fourth tee of your favorite golf course. No, we aren't going to give your hard disk a bath, but we are going to "scrub" your disk clean to prevent people from stealing your data. For those of you who think such a tool is unnecessary, I have a couple of unpleasant surprises:

Surprise #1: Most people think that the simple act of deleting a file deletes the data off your hard disk, making it impossible for somebody to steal the data. Do you think that nobody can recover your tax return after you delete it from your computer? Not true. Deleting a file doesn't delete the data at all—it merely deletes the file from your hard disk's index, the file allocation table. (Well actually, that's not exactly correct. Deleting the file doesn't even delete the filename in the directory—it just changes the first character of the filename to tell your computer that the file can be overwritten.) So, the deleted file is actually still on your hard disk. Eventually—days, weeks, or perhaps months later—it will be overwritten when your hard disk needs the room to store another file. But for an indeterminate period of time, the data is recoverable (or partially recoverable) with a specialized tool that can find and "undelete" deleted files.

Surprise #2: Reformatting your hard disk does not delete the data either—it merely wipes the entire index clean. So, once again, a person with a specialized data recovery tool can recover data off your disk.

In either case—deleting a file or reformatting your hard disk—a person with the right tool might be able to recover your data. That's good news if you need to recover the data, and it's bad news if you are trying to prevent someone from stealing your data.

Simply stated, a disk scrubber is the electronic equivalent of the paper shredder. Disk scrubbers (also known as disk wipers, file wipers, or file shredders) delete files in such a manner that they can't be "undeleted." You will recall from Chapter 1 that the data on your hard is encoded in magnetic media as billions of 0s and 1s. A hard disk scrubber overwrites files as you delete them with a random pattern of 0s and 1s so that the files can't be recovered.

Argggh!

Today's Argggh! award goes to the popular television show *Law and Order*. To their credit, the producers of *Law and Order* try to weave a thread of technology into their stories. To my disappointment, though, they frequently get things wrong. In one episode, the cops were unable to recover data off the suspect's hard drive because "the suspect defragged their hard drive." Come on folks—get your facts straight. Defragging your hard drive does not delete data—it reorganizes your data for more efficient access. The proper terminology would have been "the suspect scrubbed their hard drive."

When Do I Need a Disk Scrubber?

At a minimum, you need a disk scrubber when you sell your PC or give it away. You would certainly want to remove all sensitive data from your PC before disposing of it. If you work with critical information everyday, you might want to use a disk scrubber on a more regular basis to protect yourself from hackers.

Maybe I'm Amazed

Maybe I'm Amazed is a great Paul McCartney song from 1970. It probably also describes how Sir Paul felt when he learned that his asset management firm Morgan Grenfell sold an obsolete PC without first wiping the disk. The PC contained 108 files pertaining to Paul's personal finances, as well as financial data for other institutions. For more information, go to http://www.theregister.co.uk/content/archive/9137.html.

The point is, even corporations forget to wipe their disks!

In the Introduction, I noted that one of the reasons hard disks fail is that "we beat our hard disks to death." Hard disk scrubbers generate wear and tear on the hard disk's magnetic media by overwriting files as they are deleted. Depending on which file scrubbing algorithm is used, the area can be overwritten several times for extra security. So, in terms of preserving the life of your hard disk, it might not make sense to scrub every file.

Recommended Features

Some hard disk scrubbers have only the most rudimentary file wiping capabilities. They can wipe files only as they are being deleted (not after the fact), and the file wiping algorithm is inadequate to prevent data recovery.

It is essential that a disk scrubber include the following features:

- **The ability to erase files either as you delete them or after you delete them**— Chances are, you deleted thousands of files before you purchased a disk scrubber. Many of these files are still recoverable. They exist, in whole or in part, in two areas of your hard disk: free space and slack space. *Free space* is clusters on a hard disk where Microsoft Windows is allowed to write file information. These clusters might be empty or might contain data from files that have been previously deleted but not yet overwritten with new files. *Slack space* is space at the end of a partially used cluster that may contain data from files that were previously deleted. Many disk scrubbers can only protect you from a point in time going forward—they can't erase the sins of the past. Even if you install a disk scrubber the day you purchase your computer and use it religiously, you would probably still want to wipe the free space and slack space on your hard disk as a precautionary measure before selling your computer.

- **It has multiple scrubbing methods (algorithms)**—A good disk scrubber should have different scrubbing algorithms, ranging from low security to high security. The highest level of security should meet or exceed the United States Department of Defense standards for the permanent erasure of digital information (U.S. DOD 5220.22).

- **The ability to scrub traces of online activity**—A disk scrubber should be able to erase all traces of online activity, including temporary Internet files and deleted email messages.

- **It should integrate seamlessly with Windows**—When you right-click a file or the recycle bin, you should have the option to erase the file or the contents of the recycle bin beyond recovery.

Recommended Product

I recommend and use CyberScrub as a disk scrubbing tool. It has all the required features and a clean, intuitive user interface. CyberScrub provides five file scrubbing methods, and the highest level of security exceeds Department of Defense specifications.

CyberScrub is available in two versions, a standard version for $39.95 (Internet download) or $49.95 (purchase CD), and a professional version for $49.95 (Internet download) or $59.95 (purchase CD). The primary difference between the two versions is that the professional version offers the higher-security Department of Defense disk scrubbing algorithm, which prevents the recovery of data using specialized hardware tools. The standard version should be sufficient for most home users.

For more information about CyberScrub, go to `http://www.cyberscrub.com/page500.html`.

I provide detailed instructions for using CyberScrub in Chapter 4, "A Disaster Prevention Plan for Your New Computer: Before You Try," and Chapter 7.

An Update Sniffer

The term *update sniffer* is one that I have coined to refer to an application that has the ability to scan your computer, determine what application software and system software—drivers, operating systems, and so on—is out of date, and provide links to the available updates. (To be honest, my brother Phil came up with the term, but I liked it so much, I stole it.)

As your computer gets older, the likelihood of a computer disaster increases if you haven't kept your computer up to date. For example, a newly installed software application or hardware component might be incompatible with an old device driver, precipitating a computer disaster that could prevent you from booting up your computer.

You might have purchased your computer from Dell, Hewlett-Packard, or Gateway, but the fact remains that your computer is a multi-vendor affair. The sound card, video card, network interface card, DVD-ROM, CD writer, monitor, hard disk, and so on are all manufactured by different companies, and they all require software drivers to function.

On top of the multi-vendor system software environment, you probably have dozens of applications installed.

If you had to manually check every system software component and application software component for available updates, updating your computer would be a difficult, error-prone task. You would likely miss some important updates, and you might install the wrong device driver, precipitating a self-inflicted computer disaster.

An update sniffer solves this problem. An update sniffer scans your computer and compiles a list of all installed applications and system software. It then finds available updates and gives you the option of installing them.

CNET provides an excellent, free update sniffer called CatchUp, which can be downloaded from `http://catchup.cnet.com/catchup/cu/setup/setup.html`.

Chapter 9 provides detailed instructions on how to use CatchUp, and helpful advice on how to determine whether you should install a particular update.

I don't mean to imply that you should apply *every* available update to your computer. There are advantages and disadvantages to keeping your computer up to date. Computers are unstable equilibriums, and certain types of updates have a well-deserved reputation for precipitating computer disasters. Generally speaking, you should only apply an update to your computer if the update provides benefits that justify the risk. This subject is discussed in more detail in Chapter 9, "Keeping Your Computer in Top Shape."

A Download Manager

Many of the tools I recommend in this chapter can be downloaded via the Internet, and some of the tools are even cheaper when you purchase them in this manner.

Even if you have a broadband connection, it can take quite a while to download large program files over the Internet.

A download manager can significantly reduce the time required to download such files.

Software vendors frequently provide users with the ability to download a file from different servers at different locations. A download manager identifies all the locations from which a file can be downloaded and determines which location will provide the fastest download time.

Additionally, a download manager can optimize the use of your bandwidth. The download manager breaks the file into several pieces, downloads the pieces concurrently from multiple locations, and then reassembles them.

Recommended Product

I use and recommend Speedbit's Download Accelerator Plus (DAP). Once installed, Download Accelerator Plus automatically kicks in whenever you download a file from the Internet (see Figure 2.6). All you have to do is click the Start Download button.

DAP comes in two versions. The basic version is free. The premium version, which removes the banner advertising that comes with the basic version to improve bandwidth utilization, is $29.95. I have been very content with the free version.

For more information about DAP, go to `http://www.speedbit.com/#`.

FIGURE 2.6

Download Accelerator Plus breaks the file into segments and downloads the pieces concurrently from multiple locations.

Recommended Hardware: A Residential Gateway

The term *residential gateway* is a generic way of referring to a device that sits between your computer(s) and the Internet. Such devices serve as gateways to the Internet, allowing multiple computers to share one broadband Internet connection.

Residential gateways also enable your computers to share information directly with each other. This is known as a *local area network (LAN)*.

A residential gateway is optional if you have one computer connected to a broadband Internet connection. Although it is not absolutely required for multiple computers to share one broadband connection (Microsoft provides a little used feature called Internet Connection Sharing that allows one computer to serve as a host computer to other computers that need to connect to the Internet), a residential gateway is the recommended and most commonly used approach for sharing a broadband Internet connection.

The most popular residential gateway device is a router.

Residential gateways provide two very important functions that are pertinent to this book:

- They serve as a natural firewall between your home computer(s) and the Internet.
- They allow you to network your computers together, which can help you save money on software tools and provide you with some supplementary backup strategies. These supplementary strategies are discussed in Chapter 6.

The Residential Gateway As a Firewall

Residential gateways use a method of communication called network address translation (NAT). NAT enables multiple computers to share an Internet connection. Think of NAT as a traffic cop that directs (routes, from the term *router*) information from the Internet to the computer in your house that requested the information. But this traffic cop also offers you some protection from intruders!

One of the benefits of NAT is that it serves as a natural firewall between your home computer(s) and the Internet. NAT blocks unsolicited attempts by computers on one side of the gateway (the Internet) to communicate with the computers on the other side of the gateway (your computers).

Prior to installing my router last year, my software firewall registered and blocked dozens of probes each week. Since I installed my router, very little unsolicited traffic makes it through the router to my software firewall.

For the best firewall protection, I recommend that you use both a software- and hardware-based firewall. Thus, even if you have only one computer, you might want to consider using a router as an extra barrier against hackers.

The Economics of Residential Gateways

Residential gateways vary widely in price, depending on the features you require. A basic four-port router costs less than $75 and allows four computers to share an Internet connection and communicate with each other. Routers are readily available on eBay.

More expensive devices designed to work with a variety of home networking technologies such as Ethernet, wireless communications, USB port, or phone wiring can run as high as $400. The advantage of purchasing one of these more expensive devices is that you don't have to run Ethernet cable through your home. The objective of such a device is to deliver a home network in a box.

The cost of a residential gateway is offset partially by some savings associated with having your computers linked together on a home network. For example, if you are using a file backup software program, you can purchase one software license, install it on one computer, and backup data from other computers on the network.

Because home networking is beyond the scope of this book, I will not get into a detailed discussion of how to select and install a residential gateway. The devices generally come with very detailed installation instructions, and help is always available from the manufacturer's Web site.

My personal preference is to use a simple router with a wired Ethernet network. You will have to spend some money to wire your house with Ethernet cable, but this will be offset by the lower cost of the residential gateway device. Wired Ethernet networks are faster and more secure than wireless Ethernet networks. (Chapter 5 discusses the security problems associated with wireless networks.)

Your Shared Internet Connection and Your ISP

If you decide to purchase and install a router to share a broadband Internet connection, your ISP is not going to assist you with the installation or if you have problems with your connection, as you have implemented an unsupported solution.

Think about it. There are hundreds of residential gateway devices on the market. Some use wired Ethernet, and some use wireless Ethernet. Some allow you to connect your computers using phone lines or USB ports. *It would be unreasonable to expect your ISP to have the expertise to support whatever solution each customer decided to implement.*

Some ISPs offer a supported, multiuser residential solution. If you want a supported, multiuser connection, you will most likely need to buy the residential gateway from your ISP. This allows ISPs to standardize on one piece of equipment, which in turn makes it easier for them to support the solution.

Some ISPs will even come to your residence to install multiuser connections for you. However, ISPs are searching for user-friendly self-install solutions.

In cases where your ISP refuses to support a router of any kind, check to see if your router supports a feature called MAC Cloning. Once configured, this feature causes your router to appear to be your PC's network card to your ISP's computers.

Optional Tools—Software

This section provides information on three optional software tools: spyware detectors, adware detectors, and Registry cleaners.

Spyware Detectors

Earlier in this chapter, I discussed how a good firewall could block outbound communications for rogue applications that had been installed on your computer, such as spyware.

Unfortunately, your firewall might not identify the application by name and do nothing to help you delete the application from your computer.

You might want to consider purchasing Spycop, a software program that as of this writing can detect 286 different known malicious spyware programs. Spycop is like antivirus software in the sense that it scans your computer for known spyware programs and is updated frequently to recognize new spyware programs. Similar to antivirus software, you need to keep your software updated to have maximum protection.

Spycop can be downloaded from `http://www.spycop.com/`. It costs $49.95, but unlike antivirus software, there is no annual subscription fee for keeping it up-to-date.

Unfortunately, Spycop can't rid your computer of spyware—it can only identify whether one of these known malicious programs is present on your computer. You will have to search the Internet to find instructions for eliminating specific spyware programs found by the scan.

The threat from spyware today is not nearly as great as the threat from computer viruses. That may change over time. It is possible that within the next few years, anti-spyware software will be as critical to the health as your computer as antivirus software.

Spyware is discussed in more detail in Chapter 5.

Adware Detectors

Adware is similar to spyware in that both "applications" gather information about you and send it back to the developer. However, there are two important distinctions between spyware and adware:

- **Adware gathers the information with your implicit permission**—This is because the developers of adware disclose that the software is being installed on your computer. Adware is typically bundled with some other application (usually a free application) that you want to install, such as KaZaA. The developers of the application make their money by partnering with adware companies.

- **Adware programs are by definition less nefarious than spyware programs**—Spyware programs are out to steal your financial information, passwords, and so on and use that information to do you harm. Adware programs observe your Web surfing habits and use that information to target you with spam advertising.

Sometimes, adware is tightly bundled with an application. If you remove the adware, you can no longer run the application. Sometimes, however, the adware is loosely bundled and can be removed without affecting your ability to use the application. You must conduct research on the Internet on the particular application that installed the adware to determine which is the case.

I use and recommend a free adware detection and removal program called Ad-Aware. Ad-Aware can be downloaded from `http://www.lavasoft.nu`.

Adware is discussed in more detail in Chapter 5.

Registry Cleaners

Any Windows-based application you purchase includes an install program and an uninstall program.

The install program installs the application and adds entries to the Windows Registry to allow the program to function on your computer.

The uninstall program uninstalls the application and should also remove the Registry entries that were added previously by the install program.

If the uninstall program does an incomplete job of removing all the program's Registry entries, your Registry can become cluttered with debris over a period of time, and this can affect the performance of your computer. It can also cause other problems. For example, if the uninstall program does not remove all the program's Register entries, you might be unable to reinstall it at a later date.

A number of software tools are available that are designed to help you clean the Windows Registry of such debris. Called Registry cleaners, some of these programs even take over the application uninstall process to ensure the complete removal of the application from your system.

I have investigated several of these programs and have come to the following conclusions:

- **They frequently cause more harm than good**—I have read dozens of reviews from users who have tried these programs, and in my opinion, the risk is not worth the reward. A significant percentage of users report that these programs are buggy, and several indicated that just installing a Registry cleaner caused serious problems with their computers. Some reviewers reported that the cleaners recommended the removal of important Registry entries that rendered their computers inoperable.

- **You can keep your Registry relatively clean by following some simple procedures**—Most importantly, you should never install a software application on your machine without first checking out the reputation of the application and the application developer. I discuss this in more detail in Appendix B, "How to Install and Remove Programs from Your Computer."

- **Registry cleaners are not as important as they used to be**—Registry cleaners came about in the first place because many application software developers did a terrible job of writing uninstall programs. Happily, this is much less of a problem today than it was several years ago. Uninstall programs are more well-behaved today. In fact, the latest version of Norton's popular CleanSweep program does not include a Registry cleaner, although earlier versions of the program did.

I do not have a Registry cleaner installed on any of my computers, and I have never had any Registry-related problems. So, rather than burden my readers with a tool that can cause more problems than it solves, I will focus on how to keep the Registry clean through administrative procedures.

Optional Hardware: Uninterruptible Power Supply

Earlier in this chapter I discussed surge protectors, which protect your computer from voltage spikes. However, surge protectors do not protect your computer from loss of data or hard disk damage caused by the sudden loss of power. An uninterruptible power supply (UPS) provides a backup battery source of power to your computer that protects it from brownouts, blackouts, and other types of electrical interference. The backup battery is constantly being charged by your AC power source.

Inexpensive UPS units keep your computer running for a few minutes, which gives you time to save your work and shut down your computer normally. Larger, more expensive units provide more outlets, more power, and more features. For most home users, the objective is to keep your computer running for a few minutes so that you can save your data and shut down your system normally.

There are several types of UPS units. The most inexpensive is a *standby* UPS, in which power transfers from AC to the UPS backup battery in the event of an outage. The transfer occurs very quickly—in a few milliseconds—but there is some small risk that you might lose data while the battery kicks in, depending on the characteristics of your computer's power supply.

The most expensive type of UPS is an *online* unit. With an online unit, the UPS battery, which is always being charged, is always providing the source of power to your computer. Therefore, there is no transfer time when the power fails.

For most home users, an inexpensive standby UPS coupled with a surge protector is an adequate solution. An inexpensive UPS might or might not include surge protection. Regardless, I would be inclined to use a surge protector in conjunction with the UPS because most UPS units do not provide surge protection for Ethernet, phone, and coaxial cables. So, I would plug the surge protector into the UPS, and the UPS into the wall.

Do You Need a UPS?

I think the answer to this question depends on two things:

- How often you lose power
- How often you save your data; that is, how much data you are likely to lose in the event of an outage

I do not have a UPS myself—we rarely experience blackouts or brownouts—and I am fanatical about saving my data every few minutes. When we lost our power for about 2 hours the other night, I only lost about 5 minutes worth of work on my Excel spreadsheet. But I will probably purchase a standby UPS for one of my computers in the near future because they are relatively inexpensive (about $75).

Selection Criteria

The basic parameters for determining how powerful a UPS you need are as follows:

- **Load**—How many pieces of equipment will the UPS power?
- **Runtime**—How much runtime do you require from a UPS at maximum load?

Unfortunately, product specifications for uninterruptible power supplies are very confusing. It is not my purpose here to turn you into an electrical engineer. I understand that you could care less about the difference between volt-amperes and watts. You just want a unit that will run for a specific amount of time with the equipment you have plugged in and powered up.

Fortunately, American Power Conversion (APC), a manufacturer of various types of power availability equipment, has a wonderful UPS selector tool on their Web site at `http://www.apcc.com/template/size/apc/index.cfm`.

This tool allows you to fill out an electronic form that describes the characteristics of your computing environment—the type of computer, processor type, monitor size, number of drives, computer peripherals, and so on. On the next page, you specify your preferences, such as the amount of runtime you require in the event of a power failure, the percentage of extra power you require for future expansion, and so on. Finally, you click the Show Solution button and a specific APC UPS model is recommended. You can purchase this model, or you can print out the spec sheet and go comparison shopping on the Internet or in your local stores.

A Disaster Prevention Plan for Your New Computer: Part 1, Before You Buy

Revelations

In this chapter you will learn

☐ The biggest single mistake most people make when they purchase a new computer

☐ The myth of local support

☐ The danger you face when you take or ship your computer offsite for repair

☐ The incredible benefits of having identically configured computers

Overview

This chapter and Chapter 4, "A Disaster Prevention Plan for Your New Computer: Part 2, Before You Try," are intended for readers who plan to purchase a new computer in the near future. From the moment you say, "Dear, let's buy a new computer," to the moment you put that new computer into service, the decisions you make and actions you take have a profound impact on how disaster-free life will be with your new computer. These two chapters teach you how to minimize your risk.

People buy new computers for many reasons. Perhaps your old computer died or has an underpowered processor by today's standards. Perhaps you want the latest hardware and software technology—a DVD writer, Windows XP, a larger hard disk, or more memory. These are all very nice things.

Don't be in a hurry to sell your old PC! In Chapter 10, "Tips for Avoiding PC Disasters," I discuss how you can use your old PC as a buffer against computer disasters on your new PC.

But in my opinion, the nicest thing about getting a new computer is that you get a clean slate, or as Billy Crystal put it in *City Slickers*, a "do over." You get the rare opportunity to reap the benefits of being a good, competent system administrator from day one. If you take advantage of that opportunity, your new computer—*your new unstable equilibrium*—will be less unstable and less prone to computer disasters throughout its useful life. And if disaster strikes, you will be prepared.

Whenever you buy a new computer, you perform the following three tasks:

1. You decide what type of computer (brand, model, and features) to purchase.

2. You purchase the computer and put it into service.

3. You dispose of your old computer (unless of course your old computer becomes a family member's new computer).

This chapter and Chapter 4 are based on the assumption that your old computer is a Windows 95, 98, or Millennium system and that your new computer is a Windows XP system. The instructions and screen shots in these chapters reflect that distinction.

Most people don't give these tasks a great deal of thought. They go down to their local store, buy a computer that is on sale, bring it home, set it up, and start using it. If they have no use for their old computer, they sell it to a friend or donate it to a local school.

It is precisely because most people *don't* put much thought into these three tasks that they are likely to experience computer disasters. In this chapter and Chapter 4, I provide you with a disaster prevention plan for your new computer by defining a structure and process around the tasks of buying a new computer, putting it into service, and disposing of your old computer.

In this chapter, I focus on how to avoid a disaster before you buy. I explain why so many people make fundamental mistakes in the way they go about purchasing a new computer and how these mistakes lead to computer disasters.

This chapter explains why technical support and service/warranty should be the two most important purchase criteria for people who are not computer experts. It reyeals, to the surprise of many I am sure, where you are most likely to get the best support for your new computer.

You will learn how to prevent your data and identity from being stolen if you need to take or ship your computer offsite for repair, and you will learn how to configure your new computer to accomplish these five objectives:

- To buy the best value—the lowest total cost in use
- To minimize the chances of a computer disaster during the life of your computer
- To ensure compatibility with disaster recovery tools
- To facilitate the process of transferring data from your old computer to your new computer
- To economize without sacrificing performance so that more of your budget can be allocated for disaster prevention

Finally, I discuss the merits of having identically configured computers if you plan to purchase more than one computer.

The Importance of Buying Value

My observation is that many people use the wrong purchase criteria when they buy a new computer because they don't understand the difference between a commodity purchase and a specialty purchase.

By definition, a *commodity* is a mass-produced, unspecialized, consistent, reliable product. A battery. A pack of floppy disks. A light bulb. A gallon of gas.

When we purchase a commodity item, we only care about one thing: price. When we go to the store to buy a pack of AA batteries, we don't worry about special features, reliability, service, or technical support. We know the features; reliability is safely assumed; performance is predictable; and we know we will never need service or technical support. The commodity purchase transaction is simple: *Give it to me, and give it to me cheaply.*

Now let's talk about *specialty items*. When we purchase a specialty item, we base our purchase decision on a number of factors:

- Price
- Features
- Reliability
- Service/warranty
- Technical support

In other words, when we buy specialty items, we buy *value*—the lowest total cost in use—not price. If you save $300 by purchasing a cheap computer and, over the life of the computer, you have to spend an additional $800 in upgrade, repair, and support costs, have you really gotten a bargain?

Many people incorrectly believe that computers are commodities, and they base their purchase decisions almost entirely on price. *It's the biggest mistake they can make, and they pay dearly for it later.*

Yes, computers can be mass-produced. But that's about the only thing they have in common with commodities. If you have been reading this book in order, you understand that computers are extremely specialized, complex products.

More importantly, you understand that personal computers are unstable equilibriums. To those who argue that personal computers are becoming a commodity, I reply that a product that is by nature an unstable equilibrium will *never* be a commodity.

And consider this. When we buy a computer, we don't just use it, or use it up, the way we do a commodity. We change it constantly by adding and removing applications, and often internal and external hardware. And anytime we do so, we run the risk of needing service and technical support because any change can tip us from the point of unstable equilibrium toward disaster.

Why People Mistake Personal Computers for Commodities

It's not surprising that people mistake personal computers for commodities. For one thing, computers are far less expensive today than they were 10 years ago, even though they are far more powerful. There is a presumption that anything that can be mass-produced at a low price is a commodity.

Adding to the confusion is the fact that computers are sold as commodities. When you buy a specialized product, you expect to get assistance with your purchase decision from somebody who has specialized knowledge. Unfortunately, whenever I walk into my local electronics, office supply, or even computer store, the only assistance I typically receive is from a low-paid high school kid who knows as much about computers as he does about life. (The last time I walked into my local store, I couldn't even test drive any of the computers. The computers were set on the Windows password screen, and none of the employees knew the password!) So, the assumption is that you know what you want when you walk into the store, just like you do when you go to buy that pack of AA batteries. All of this reinforces the false notion that a personal computer is a commodity purchase.

Weighting the Purchase Criteria

I recently received a call from a relative who needed help with his computer. A local mom-and-pop shop had built the computer for him at a "really great price." The only problem was that it had stopped working a few months after he purchased it, and mom and pop didn't provide technical support.

This isn't the first time I have received such a call. It never ceases to amaze me that the people who are most likely to need technical support (those who are the least skilled in fixing computer problems) are the ones most likely to base their purchase decisions entirely on price! If you fall into this category, understand that you should be willing to pay *more* money to buy a computer that is also backed by great service and support.

I would suggest to you that if you are not a computer expert, you should weight your purchase criteria according to Table 3.1.

Table 3.1   Personal Computer Purchase Criteria

Criterion	Weight
Price	10%
Features/Performance	10%
Reliability	20%
Service/warranty	25%
Technical support	35%

That's right—I am recommending that 60% of your purchase decision be based on service and support. If you weight your purchase criteria this way and proceed accordingly, you will be much less likely to experience a computer disaster down the line.

The Myth of Local Support

A good technical support organization is an important buffer against computer disasters. A skilled technical support specialist can help you recover from many types of computer problems without having to resort to a worst-case disaster recovery scenario that requires you to restore your entire hard disk. I find that non-technical people are often concerned about buying computers from direct sellers such as Dell or Gateway because of the support issue. They assume that they will get better technical support from a local retailer. They understandably but erroneously equate proximity with support. The fact is that the high school student who probably couldn't answer any of your questions when you were in the store didn't get any smarter *after* you purchased your computer.

Now, I'm not saying you shouldn't buy your computer at a local retailer. I'm just saying that the best technical support is much more likely to come directly from the manufacturer, regardless of where you purchase your computer. When your computer doesn't boot up, you stand a much better chance of getting expert help calling Hewlett-Packard's customer support number than you do calling Office Depot. If you accept the premise that your best support is likely to come from the manufacturer, you should consider direct sellers such as Dell Computer and Gateway Computer as well as retailers when you purchase your next computer.

It's difficult for many people to understand that phone support from the manufacturer is better than local support from the retailer, but that's generally the way it is. The people who build the product know and support the product. The retailer who sells the product knows how to ring you up at the cash register.

Please! No letters from owners of mom-and-pop shops. I am sure there are some local PC shops that provide excellent support. But the risk of inadequate service and support from a local shop is, in my opinion, simply too big a risk to take for anyone who is not a computer expert.

I am also aware that there are some smaller, regional PC manufacturers. Again, to minimize risk, I feel obligated to steer my readers toward the top-tier computer companies.

I have to mention Sony here, as Sony has a growing presence in warehouse, electronics, and computer stores. I think Sony produces an excellent product. I have a Sony laptop and have been thrilled with it. My daughter has also been very pleased with her Sony desktop. In fact, I think Sony is a great choice for computer experts who need reliability, but not service and support, because Sony's support and warranty (one year) are much weaker than the big four.

Your New PC: Selecting a Hardware Vendor

This section explains how to minimize risk when buying a new computer. The four biggest players in the U.S. home market are compared from the perspectives of technical support, service, reliability, and warranty.

Minimizing Risk

Unless you are a computer expert, I advise you to purchase a computer produced by a company that has a superior reputation for technical support, service, and reliability. Yes, you might save a few hundred dollars buying an off-brand machine or a locally built, no-name computer. You might even get a well-built machine with quality components. But you probably won't get the kind of technical support you can get from a top-tier manufacturer, and in the end the money you save might prove to be a false economy.

The Big Four

In the U.S. market, the four biggest PC companies account for more than 54% of all personal computer sales: Dell (25%), Compaq (12%), Hewlett-Packard (9%), and Gateway (8%).

Dell and Gateway are direct sellers. Gateway has a number of "country stores" around the country to support the direct selling process, whereas Dell sells only via the Web and over the phone.

Hewlett-Packard and Compaq sell through retailers and direct to you over the Web. Although Hewlett-Packard and Compaq are now one company, they are still functioning as two separate companies as of this writing, and they have different reputations (as well as different policies) for technical support, service, and reliability. So, for the purpose of this discussion, I will treat Hewlett-Packard and Compaq as separate companies.

IBM is not included in the big four because it has essentially given up on the home market.

Beyond the big four, there are dozens of smaller players, but in the interest of minimizing risk, I focus on the top four players in the U.S. home market.

Technical Support, Service, and Reliability

Let's see how these four companies compare in terms of technical support, service, and reliability. I should point out that computer vendors change their support/warranty plans often. Please check the vendors' Web pages for the latest information about support/warranty plans. Because prices for various support/warrant options change frequently, I have opted not to include pricing in *PC Fear Factor*.

Dell Computer

In *PC Magazine's* 2002 best and worst survey of personal computer vendors, for the second year running, Dell was the only major vendor to receive an A rating in the Home Use category for desktop computers. Dell was ranked number one in the following important home use subcategories:

- Highest percentage of problems solved over the phone
- Lowest percentage of PCs sent out for repair (only 5%)
- Highest percentage in prompt resolution of problem
- Highest rating in tech support knowledge

Speaking from personal experience, I agree with the survey. I have found that Dell's technical support people are very knowledgeable and well trained. More importantly, they are very skilled at guiding non-technical people step-by-step through even the most complex problem-solving process.

Dell offers a variety of phone support options when you make your computer purchase, including one-year, two-year, three-year, and four-year phone support. Dell's 24/7 phone support is always toll-free, regardless of which plan you choose.

Gateway Computer

Gateway received an overall grade of B+ in *PC Magazine's* 2002 best and worst survey, up from its 2001 B rating.

As of this writing, Gateway is the only vendor among the big four to offer a lifetime phone support option.

I've not had much experience with Gateway computers so I can't offer any anecdotal evidence that either supports or refutes the *PC Magazine* survey. Gateway has been consistently losing money over the last two years and it would be reasonable to be concerned about whether it will survive. Nevertheless, Gateway continues to go after the home market aggressively and offers some real bargains to consumers.

Compaq Computer

Compaq has the unenviable distinction of being the only major vendor to receive an E rating in both the 2002 and 2001 best and worst survey. In fact, Compaq was the only vendor to rate significantly worse than average in every subcategory (overall satisfaction, satisfaction with reliability, units needing repair in the last 12 months, satisfaction with repair, and satisfaction with technical support).

Compaq offers options for one-year, two-year, or three-year toll-free phone support.

I've not had any personal experience with Compaq computers so I can't offer any anecdotal evidence that either supports or refutes the *PC Magazine* best and worst survey.

Hewlett-Packard

In *PC Magazine's* 2002 best and worst survey, Hewlett-Packard received an overall grade of D- in the home-use category; a significant drop from its 2001 rating of B. One would hope that the Hewlett-Packard/Compaq merger would have resulted in Hewlett-Packard pulling Compaq up to its standards. Early results seem to indicate that, if anything, Compaq is dragging HP down.

Speaking personally, I have had positive experiences with Hewlett-Packard. I have several Hewlett-Packard peripheral devices (although I have never owned a Hewlett-Packard PC), and I have been generally pleased with Hewlett-Packard's technical support. The people are knowledgeable, and I can usually get my problem resolved in one phone call.

Hewlett-Packard offers two phone support options. The standard support agreement is for one year and provides toll-based phone support. Thus, if you are put on hold for 20 minutes when you call for technical support, it's your dime.

Hewlett-Packard offers an extended three-year support upgrade that provides three years of toll-free phone support. (This option is not available to residents of Florida or Washington State.)

Web-Based Technical Support

Technical support isn't limited to phone support. All the major computer vendors provide valuable support on their Web sites, including access to driver updates, BIOS updates, and other software patches to keep your PC up-to-date. They also provide a knowledge base of previously asked and answered questions. In many cases, you can find the solution to your problem or answer to your question in the knowledge base without having to call tech support.

It's worth nothing that when it comes to Web support, Gateway really raises the bar. Gateway is the only vendor to offer remote assistance. Its remote assistance capability allows a Gateway technical support specialist to chat with you online and take control over your desktop remotely (with your permission) to fix your problem. So, instead of having a technical support specialist talk you through a series of complicated steps to fix the problem, the specialist can take control of your desktop (while you watch) and fix the problem for you. This service adds value for you and actually saves Gateway time and money, as a technical support specialist can often fix a problem faster than she can talk you through the solution. As Gateway says, "It's like having a personal technician standing next to you."

What Is a Driver?

A *driver* is a small computer program that enables your computer's operating system to communicate with an internal or external component. A printer driver enables your computer to communicate with your printer. Other drivers enable your computer to communicate with your video card (which controls your monitor), sound card (which controls your speakers), network card, modem, hard disk, CD writer, keyboard, mouse, and so on.

The manufacturer of the specific device—for example, the sound card—provides the driver for that device, *not* the computer manufacturer. Device manufacturers periodically release updated drivers. A new driver might be released to correct problems, add features, improve performance, or support new technology. I explain how to keep your computer's drivers up-to-date in Chapter 9, "Keeping Your Computer in Top Shape."

What Is BIOS?

BIOS (basic input output system) is a program that your computer's microprocessor uses to get the computer started when you turn it on. When you press the power button on your computer, the BIOS checks all the major components of your computer to make sure they are working properly. The BIOS also manages the flow of data between the computer and all its attached devices. For example, the BIOS directs your computer to check your floppy disk drive first and then boot from the hard disk if nothing is found in the floppy disk drive.

The BIOS program is created and maintained by the manufacturer of your computer's motherboard, which, as the name implies, is the main circuit board in your computer, which everything else plugs into. Motherboard manufacturers periodically release updated versions of the BIOS to fix problems in earlier versions.

Service/Warranty

Do you feel comfortable about opening your PC to replace a hard drive, floppy drive, DVD-ROM, or CD writer? Do you know how to do so without risking harm to yourself or your computer?

If the answer to these questions is no, you should purchase a computer from a company that offers onsite support as a service/warranty option. Let's compare the big four companies with regard to warranty support.

Dell Computer

Dell offers the option of a one-year, two-year, three-year, or four-year at-home service warranty. If you have a hardware problem, Dell sends somebody to your house the next business day to replace the bad component. Dell also offers a CompleteCare accidental damage protection warranty that covers damage caused by surges, drops, and spills. It's a pricey extra, and I advise against it for a desktop computer, unless you have a habit of spilling your coffee on your keyboard or just dropping your computer. The CompleteCare package might make more sense for a laptop computer, especially considering how laptops get handled by airport security.

I have had extensive experience using Dell's at-home service warranty. Dell subcontracts this work to BancTec Computer and Network Services (http://cns.banctec.com/), and BancTec does an excellent job. When you have a problem, Dell ships the replacement part to BancTec and BancTec comes to your house to install the part.

Over the years, I have had Dell/BancTec come to my house to replace such components as network interface cards, hard disks, floppy disk drives, and Zip disk drives.

Dell does not take its *at-home* literally. If you have a laptop computer and are on the road, Dell sends the service technician to wherever you are. I live in Atlanta, but I have had Dell send service technicians to Wichita to replace parts on my laptop computer. I have always been back up and running within 48 hours, and in most cases, within 24 hours.

Hewlett-Packard

Hewlett-Packard offers the option of a one-year warranty or three-year warranty, but you have to ship the computer back to HP or take it into an authorized service center if you are unable to install the part yourself (assuming you can determine what is wrong with the computer).

Compaq Computer

Compaq offers the option of a one-year, two-year, or three-year warranty and will service your computer in your home provided you live within 60 miles of a Compaq service center and that the part is "difficult to replace." For example, Compaq requires the customer to replace cards that plug into the motherboard, but it will replace things like hard disks and DVD-ROMs.

Gateway Computer

Gateway offers the option of a one-year, two-year, or three-year warranty, but it is entirely up to Gateway's discretion as to whether it sends a technician to your house to replace a part, requires you to bring the computer into a Gateway store, or requires you to ship the computer back to a Gateway facility. Gateway pays for shipping.

Warranty: Summary

If you need your computer every day, Dell is clearly the way to go. With the other major vendors, you might have to take your system in to a repair center or ship it back to the vendor's manufacturing facility, and you will definitely be without your computer for a longer period of time. Even if you purchase a computer from a local retailer who offers support, you will have to bring your computer back to the store and will probably be without your computer for several days, or perhaps weeks. In my view, computers are just too essential in today's connected world to take the risk of being without one for days or weeks.

Avoid Despair—Prepare for Repair

This is perhaps the most important warning you will receive in *PC Fear Factor*.

Do I have your attention? Good.

If you do *not* have an at-home service warranty and you have to take or ship your computer offsite for repair, you must first prepare your computer as if you were getting ready to sell it. For example, you must back up all your data and use a disk scrubber to erase it beyond recovery from your hard disk. The last thing you ever want to do is have your precious data sitting on your hard disk when your computer is not in your possession!

Chapter 4 discusses all the things you would normally do to prepare a computer for sale (see the section "Preparing Your Old Computer for Disposal or Redeployment"). You need to perform virtually all these steps when you bring or send your computer in for repair. (The only exception is that you don't need to delete your applications.)

It is extremely important that you follow these instructions to the letter. For example, if you delete your data but do not erase it beyond recovery, the data can be recovered while your computer is in the shop. If you delete your data files but forget to delete your email and email account information, the person at the repair shop can read (**and receive!**) all your email. Even worse, she can *send* mail under your name. Think of the possible ways somebody with a sick sense of humor or malicious intent can do damage!

Preparing your computer for offsite repair is such a giant pain in the derriere that, for me, it is yet another reason to buy from Dell. In all the years I have owned Dell computers, I have never had a computer leave my house for any reason until I sold it.

If your computer is "dead" and you do not have an at-home warranty—for example, if your power supply has gone to meet its maker—you have a problem because you will be unable to prepare for offsite repair. This further illustrates the importance of an at-home warranty.

Buying the Right Features

This section covers five topics related to configuring your computer with the right features:

- Buying the features you need up front
- Feature-related problems with bargain basement PCs
- How to purchase a compatible CD writer
- Buying the right features to facilitate the transfer of data from your old PC to your new PC
- Features you can economize on to make a larger percentage of your budget available for disaster prevention

Getting the Right Features Up Front

Many people skimp on features when they purchase a computer to keep the price down. They figure they can always add some other optional piece of hardware at a later date. I think that's a false economy.

My strong recommendation is that you include everything you need or might need during the useful life of your computer in your initial purchase. There are three reasons for doing this:

- **Anytime you add hardware to your computer, you run the risk of incurring a computer disaster**—In theory, you can install a new piece of hardware, boot up your computer, and everything will work properly. Microsoft calls this Plug and Play. In practice, I have always found changing the hardware configuration of a computer to be a risky proposition. The reality I have experienced is often referred to as "plug and pray."

- **All your components will be covered by technical support**—If you add a component later and it causes some type of problem or disaster, technical support is not going to assist you.

- **The components will be less expensive if you purchase them bundled with your PC**—Although it might sound silly, a bundled PC is worth less than the sum of its individual parts. If you've ever purchased after-market options for automobiles, you probably know what I mean.

In short, if you buy it all at once as an integrated system, you know all the pieces will play well together and be supported by the computer vendor, and you will get the best price. If you add components later, you are more likely to experience a computer disaster.

Beware of Bargain PCs That Skimp on Features

You see it everyday in the newspaper—ads for computers at incredibly low prices. Unfortunately, many of these computers are underpowered recipes for disaster. To keep the price low, the manufacturer skimps on RAM (random access memory). Most bargain computers come with 128MB of RAM. The problem with this is that it forces your computer to store more information in virtual memory on your hard disk. And the more swapping your computer does between RAM and virtual memory, the more likely you are to encounter the dreaded blue screen of death (BSOD) "invalid page fault" message. Make sure your computer has at least 256MB of memory, although I personally recommend 512MB. Not only will you be less likely to see the blue screen of death as your normal user interface, but your computer will perform better as well.

Vendors skimp in other areas on bargain computers, such as monitor size and hard disk size. A bargain isn't a bargain if the monitor is too small to allow you to do your work or if you run out of space on your hard disk 6 months after you purchase your computer.

Getting a Compatible CD Writer

These days, CD writers are standard equipment on personal computers. It is critical that you verify that the CD writer included with your new PC is compatible with the disaster recovery tools recommended in *PC Fear Factor*. Three of the products

I recommend in this book—Symantec's Norton Ghost 2002, NewTech Infosystem's NTI Backup NOW! Deluxe, and Roxio's Easy CD Creator—all need to be able to write data to CDs. Each software vendor provides a list of supported CD-RW drives. Make sure the drive included with your purchase is on all three lists.

The NTI Backup NOW! Compatibility list can be found at `http://www.ntius.com/support/supdrives.cfm/`.

The Norton Ghost 2002 CD-RW drive compatibility list can be found at `http://service2.symantec.com/SUPPORT/ghost.nsf/docid/2001102516563825`.

The Roxio Easy CD Creator drive compatibility list can be found at `http://www.roxio.com/en/jhtml/cdrdatabase/static/supportedrecorder3.html?_requestid=898547`.

If You Are Buying from a Retailer

There are two ways to check the make and model of a computer's CD writer if you are purchasing your computer in a retail store. You can ask a store employee, "What's the make and model of the CD writer on this computer?" and watch as his eyes glaze over. It's fun, but it doesn't get your question answered. Fortunately, you can also check for yourself, provided that somebody in the store knows the Windows password so you can access store's display model. Here is how you can check the CD make/model:

1. On the store display model, click Start, My Computer to bring up the My Computer window.

2. Click View System Information to bring up the System Properties window.

3. Click the Hardware tab.

4. Click the Device Manager button to bring up a list of all the devices installed in your computer.

5. Click the little plus sign (+) next to DVD/CD-ROM Drives. The plus sign will turn into a minus (-), and you will see the make and model of any optical drives (CD-ROM, DVD-ROM, CD-RW, and so on) connected to your system. The CD writer is the device labeled CD-RW (see Figure 3.1).

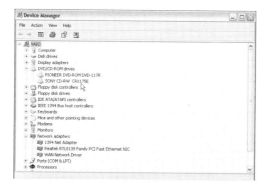

FIGURE 3.1
Write down the make and model of your CD writer.

6. Write down the make and model number and compare it to the list of drives supported by Norton Ghost, NTI Backup NOW! Deluxe, and Roxio's Easy CD Creator.

You will need to recheck the make and model number of the CD writer when you set up your new computer. Computer manufacturers use multiple sources for components, and it is entirely possible that the computer you brought home has a different CD writer than the store display model. This is even more likely if the retailer has restocked inventory since setting up the display model. If the CD writer is not the same one you saw on the store model, you will have to verify that the CD writer is compatible with your software applications. If it is not, you will need to return the computer.

Windows XP: One Step Forward, Two Steps Back

If you are currently using an earlier version of Windows and are already familiar with the Device Manager, you might be thinking, "Gee, it sounds like several more steps are required to get to the device manager in Windows XP than in Windows 98."

And you would be correct. The cynic in me requires me to think that Microsoft likes to play hide-and-seek with existing features with each new release of Windows. And several features in Windows XP are buried several layers (mouse clicks) deeper than in previous versions of Windows. What value this adds to the customer escapes me. In Chapter 4, you will see how Microsoft has taken this practice to a new extreme in Windows XP by not only hiding a utility that has been part of Windows forever, but also stripping it of its name, making it all but impossible to find.

If You Are Buying from a Direct Seller

If you are buying a computer from a direct seller, call the sales department and ask them to provide the make and model number of the CD writer they will be using to build your computer. If the company uses several makes/models of CD writers and can't guarantee which one will be in your computer, get the complete list and verify every make/model against the supported lists. It may be a pain, but it can save you a lot of headaches later.

If one or more of the CD writers used by the direct seller is not on the list, you have three options:

- You can explain the situation to the salesperson and see if he will work with you to make certain that one of the supported drives is used on your computer.
- You can take your chances and place the order. These companies have a 30-day no-questions-asked return policy, and you do not have to pay for the return shipping. So, if the CD writer is not compatible, you can return the computer. (You can even order a second computer and repeat the cycle. What fun!)
- You can buy a different brand of computer at your retail store.

If You Can't Find a Compatible CD Writer

In spite of all your efforts to ensure compatibility, you might have difficulty finding a CD writer that appears on all three software vendors' lists of supported CD writers. But don't give up hope. As I mentioned in Chapter 2, the CD-RW hardware/software compatibility lists are not always accurate, and sometimes this can work to your advantage. You might be able to determine if a particular make and model of CD writer is compatible with a software application by calling the vendor or posting a query in the software vendor's knowledge base. A positive response from the vendor or another user might enable you to proceed with confidence that the CD writer will work even though it is not on the officially supported list.

Buying the Features You Need to Support Data Migration

"What we've got here is...failure to communicate."

—Strother Martin, in *Cool Hand Luke*

The term *data migration strategy* refers to the approach you use to transfer all your data from your old computer to your new computer.

Data migration is a relatively new concern for home PC users. As recently as 3 years ago, I could fit all of my data easily on a 100MB Zip disk. Today, thanks largely to digital audio, digital photography, and digital video, I have 8GB of data to migrate—the equivalent of 80 100MB Zip disks. Furthermore, as hard disks get larger, we'll find more ways to fill the available space. A few years ago, I would have thought hard and long about the merits of storing a 30MB music video on my hard disk. But now that I have an 80GB hard disk (which is small by today's standards), I don't even hesitate to store files that large. I even have some 100MB files on my hard disk.

You should determine your data migration strategy *before* you purchase a new computer because it might have a bearing on how you configure your new computer, as illustrated below: A friend of mine recently purchased a new computer. He set it up next to his old computer and readied himself to begin the task of migrating several gigabytes of data from his old computer to his new one.

He stared at the computers for several minutes. His gut told him something was amiss, but he couldn't figure out what it was. Suddenly, it dawned on him. His old computer had a Zip drive but no CD writer. His new computer had a CD writer but no Zip drive. (Neither computer had a network card, which would have enabled him to set up and transfer data across a home network.)

What he had there was a failure to communicate. He could back up his data to Zip disks on his old computer, but he couldn't insert them in his new computer.

Had my friend thought of this, he would have configured his new computer with *both* a Zip drive and a CD writer. He probably would have used the Zip drive on his new computer only one time—to migrate data from his old computer—but it would have solved his problem because it would have allowed him to easily transfer data in large, 250MB batches from one computer to the other.

Let's look at some possible data migration strategies:

- **The home network strategy**—If you have your own local area network, data migration is a no-brainer. You merely move your data across the network from your old computer to your new computer. It's as simple as dragging and dropping files from one location to another, once you have configured your network for file sharing. If you have a home network, you will need to be certain your new computer is configured properly to connect to your network. For most people, this means having a network interface card.

- **Use a direct cable connection between computers**—Another approach to migrating data from one computer to another is to connect the two computers with a null modem serial cable, also known as a LapLink serial cable or serial file transfer cable. You can purchase this cable at your local computer store. This cable connects to the serial port on the backs of both computers. If you use this approach, Windows XP has a file transfer wizard that will help you transfer files from your old computer to your new computer.

  The big disadvantage of this approach is that it is painfully slow—20 times slower than transferring data over a wired Ethernet home network. I have about 6GB of data on my computer, and it takes about 90 minutes to move that much data from one computer to another across my wired Ethernet home network. With a LapLink serial cable, it would take about 36 hours to move the same amount of data. In my opinion, this approach requires too much effort to transfer a small amount of data and is too slow to transfer a large amount of data.

- **CD writer to CD writer**—If your old and new machines both have CD writers, data migration is no problem. You back up your data to CDs on your old computer and restore your data on your new computer. The same approach works if you have a Zip drive on both computers.

- **The "you've got a friend" Strategy**—If you can back up your data to Zip disks, a friend might be able to move the data to a CD for you.

The home network strategy is the fastest, easiest way to transfer data but is clearly the most complex solution to set up. I recognize that many readers will choose other, simpler strategies using Zip disks or CDs to transfer data between machines.

There is no "right way" to migrate your data. The right way, by definition, is the way that works and is easiest for you!

Select a data migration strategy you are comfortable with, and configure your new computer with the features needed to execute that strategy.

Where You Can Economize on Features

I realize that it may seem like I'm pretty busy spending your money. I've advised you to buy from a top-tier vendor, buy the best service and support policy available, and include all the features you might ever need at the time of your initial purpose.

So you are probably wondering, "How can I follow your advice and still stay within my budget?"

Here are a few areas where you can economize to free up funds for disaster prevention:

- **Buy the slowest available processor**—I am currently working on a 733MHz Pentium III computer that I have had for two years. It still seems lighting fast to me, and it was the slowest available processor on the market when I purchased my computer. If I were to buy a new computer right now, the slowest available processor on the market is still more than twice as fast and a generation removed from my current processor. And the difference in price between the slowest and fastest available processors is $450.

- **Reuse your monitor**—If you intend to sell or donate your old computer, consider keeping the monitor and buying a new computer sans monitor. This will save you $200 or more. (Of course, if your old monitor is only a 15'' monitor, it is probably time to upgrade to a larger size.)

- **Reuse your speakers**—If you already have computer speakers, keep them—don't sell them with your old computer. If you have to buy speakers, don't spend a lot of money unless you plan to use your computer as your surround sound home theater system.

- **Unbundle your software**—You can buy your Norton AntiVirus bundled on your Dell computer for $59, or you can buy it on eBay as I did for $12.

Additionally, time your purchase. Look for special rebate offers around the holidays and when school starts. Rebates can save you an additional $100–$200. Direct sellers often offer free shipping as an incentive, which will save you about $100.

The Sales Tax/Shipping Charge Trade-Off

If you buy your computer at a local retail store, you will pay sales tax. If you purchase your computer from a direct seller, you will not pay sales tax but you will pay for shipping.

If you purchase a $2,000 computer, shipping will be less than the sales tax, and if you purchase a $1,000 computer, shipping will probably be more. Figuring an average sales tax of 6%, the breakeven point is about $1,600. (Your break-even point may vary, depending on the sales tax in your state.) But when a direct seller offers free shipping, you avoid *both* sales tax and shipping charges, and that's a real bargain!

The Benefits of a Single Computing Environment

If you are buying two or more computers at the same time for your home or home office, I strongly recommend that you have each computer configured identically.

I'll even go one step further: If you are planning to purchase one computer now and another within the next few months, you will be far better off if you can somehow manage financially to buy both computers at the same time and have them configured identically. (You might even be able to negotiate a better price if you purchase your computers at a retail store.)

I purchased three identical computers two years ago, and I couldn't possibly overstate the resulting benefits.

Having identically configured computers provides two advantages:

- It makes diagnosing and solving computer problems/disasters easier.
- It reduces your workload as a system administrator.

Let's examine each of these benefits in more detail.

Solving Computer Problems

Your new computer is really much more than a computer. It is a computing *environment* made up of the following components:

- The computer itself, including all of its internal hardware devices
- The device drivers
- The Windows operating system
- The preinstalled applications

When I use the term *identically configured computer*, I am referring to having the same preconfigured computing environment on each machine.

Each of the components of a computing environment can be viewed as a variable that could be the possible cause of a computer problem or disaster. A bad hardware component. An ill-behaved device driver. A corrupted file in your operating system. A buggy software application. Any of these could prevent your computer from functioning properly. If you have two identically configured computers, it is much easier to isolate and eliminate variables to determine the root cause of a problem.

For example, one day I found myself suddenly unable to connect to the Internet from one of my three machines. Did I have some type of software problem? A problem with my router? A bad Ethernet cable? A bad network card? A problem with my Internet service provider?

Because the problem occurred the day after a thunderstorm, I wondered if lightning had fried one of my network cards. Because both computers were configured identically, I was able to swap network cards with confidence that I was not introducing any new variables. When I swapped the cards, the machine that was working stopped working, and the machine that wasn't working suddenly had no problem connecting to the Internet. At this point, I knew I had a bad network card and called Dell. They sent me a new card and my problem was solved.

Reducing the System Administrator's Workload

Each computer is its own unique unstable equilibrium, which is just a way of saying that every computing environment is different and therefore fragile in its own unique way(s). When you purchase identically configured computers, you have to manage only one unstable equilibrium—in other words, one computing environment.

This makes the system administrator's job easier in many ways. For example, if I install an application on one computer and it works without causing any problems, I know that it will most likely work on my other identically configured computers.

When I find a way to change my computer to make it more stable, improve its performance, or solve a software problem, I can make the same change on all three computers with confidence that it will have the desired effect.

When I purchased my three identical computers from Dell, for example, I had a problem with the preinstalled CD burning software, and I was unable to create audio CDs on any of the machines. After spending a considerable amount of time on the phone with the software vendor, we determined that the software was conflicting with some other preinstalled files that my computer didn't even need. We solved the problem simply by renaming those files to effectively hide them from the computer. And since I had only one computing environment to deal with, I was able to solve the problem on all three machines by making the exact same change.

Making Sure Your Identical Computers Really Are Identical

When you order a computer from vendors like Dell or Gateway, you can specify the exact make and model of sound card and video card to be included in your computer. You can't, however, specify the exact make and model of hard disk, DVD-ROM, or CD writer.

Since Dell uses multiple sources for these components, your identical computers might not be identical after all. You may get one brand of CD writer in one computer and another brand in the other computer—even though both computers were ordered at the same time!

For this reason, I suggest that you order over the phone rather than over the Web if you are buying from a direct seller. When you place your order, tell the salesperson that the computers must be configured identically, including the make and model of the hard disk, DVD-ROM, and CD writer. The salesperson will want to sell you more than one computer and should be eager to accommodate you, even if it means following up on your order personally.

CHAPTER **4**

A Disaster Prevention Plan for Your New Computer: Part 2, Before You Try

Revelations

In this chapter you will learn

- ☐ The biggest single mistake most people make *after* they purchase a new computer

- ☐ Why your new computer is especially vulnerable to computer disasters

- ☐ A great feature in Windows Millennium and Windows XP that helps you recover from certain types of computer disasters

- ☐ The important utility Windows XP tries to hide

- ☐ Why you might want to delete some of the applications that were pre-installed on your new computer

- ☐ Secret, private information about you that is automatically created and stored on your computer without your knowledge

Overview

Congratulations! If you are reading this chapter, you have just purchased (or are about to purchase) a new computer.

Stop! Don't use that new computer just yet. I know you're itching to enjoy the blazing speed, Windows XP, and all the other great features on your new machine, but please hold off until you read this chapter. Otherwise, you will rob yourself of the opportunity to give yourself a "do over" if things go wrong.

The biggest mistake most people make when they buy a new computer is to begin using it immediately, without implementing a disaster prevention and recovery plan.

In this chapter you will receive detailed, step-by-step instructions on how to put your new computer into service and how to prepare your old computer for disposition if you are selling it or giving it away.

Here are a few notes before you begin:

- There are a few places in this chapter where I refer you to later chapters for instructions on how to perform specific tasks required to put your new computer into service. If you have not already done so, I suggest that you take time now to read and familiarize yourself with Chapter 5, "Protecting Your Computer from Cyber-Terrorists"; Chapter 6, "Backing Up Your Data"; Chapter 7, "Backing Up Your Hard Disk"; Chapter 8, "Disaster Recovery"; Appendix A, "The System Restore Feature"; and Appendix B, "How to Install and Remove Programs from Your Computer." Or, if you prefer, you can wait until I refer you to specific information in those chapters.

- This chapter is based on the assumption that your old computer is a Windows 95, 98, or Millennium system and that your new computer is a Windows XP system.

- Finally, I suggest that you read this chapter in its entirety *before* you actually begin the process of putting a new computer into service. I think the journey is always easier if you know in advance where you are going and how you are going to get there. You may even come up with some additional steps that are specific to your situation!

Before You Use Your New Computer

Although your computer is *always* vulnerable to disasters caused by viruses, hackers, hard disk crashes, and human error, it is most vulnerable to disasters during the first month of ownership. Here is why.

You will probably make more changes to your computing environment during the first month of ownership than you will over the rest of your computer's useful life. During the first month, you will add dozens of software applications, add peripheral devices, set up your email accounts and Internet connection, delete preinstalled applications you don't need, and so on. Any single change that you make can cause dozens of changes to be made automatically behind the scenes. The risks inherent in making hundreds of changes to your computing environment are amplified due to the fact that you are in a great hurry to get things done. You want to minimize your down time while transitioning from your old computer to your new one, and your haste to complete the transition process can precipitate a disaster.

Consider some of the things that could go wrong during the transition process:

- **Software applications and peripheral devices that worked in your old computing environment might not work or work together in your new computing environment**—Your new computer probably has a different operating system than your old computer and a different set of preinstalled applications. On top of this base computing environment, you will be installing applications and peripheral hardware devices that you have been using for years. There is no guarantee that your new computing environment will work well with all of the applications and peripheral devices you had on your old machine. For example, older versions of such applications as America Online, MusicMatch Jukebox, Nero, Easy CD Creator, Norton AntiVirus, McAfee VirusScan, and Logitech mouse drivers are known to be incompatible with Windows XP.

- **Problems can occur during the installation process**—Whenever you install an application or a peripheral, there is a possibility that something can go wrong. Sometimes you can fix the problem easily by uninstalling and then reinstalling the application or peripheral. But sometimes the simple act of installing an application or peripheral can, for lack of a better term, *trash* your computer.

- **You might delete something you shouldn't**—New computers come with a suite of installed applications, some of which you might not want to use. It's pretty easy to delete something of importance by accident while you are purging these unwanted applications off your new computer.

- **You might forget to remove something from your old computer**—There's nothing like finding out that in your haste to get up and running on a new computer that you forgot to delete your financial records and tax returns from your old computer. Naturally, you'll realize this just after you've sold it to a neighbor who just happens to be an IRS auditor!

- **You might experience problems with some of the applications preinstalled by the computer manufacturer**—For example, the last computer I purchased included a preinstalled application that consistently crashed my computer with a blue screen of death.

- **Your new computer might become unstable for some unknown reason**—Somewhere along the way, while you are making hundreds of changes to your new computer to prepare it for use, your computer could simply stop functioning for some mysterious reason.

Well, have no fear. In short order I will teach you how to prevent many of these problems and how to recover should the transition process go badly.

Preparing Your New Computer for Use: A Step-By-Step Guide

This section contains a step-by-step guide for preparing your computer for use. The process is broken into three major subsections:

- "Pre-Transition Steps"
- "Setting Up, Powering Up, Checking Up, Backing Up!"
- "Creating Your New Computing Environment"

For a complete and up-to-date list of links listed in *PC Fear Factor*, go to http://www.alanluber.com/pcfearfactor/links.htm. This will eliminate the need for you to manually key these links into your Web browser.

If you have the recommended file backup software product, NTI Backup NOW!, installed on your old computer, the Upgrade Advisor will tell you that the software is not compatible with Windows XP.

This is not true. The reason you get this message is because two different versions of NTI Backup NOW! are included on the install CD (or, as we say in the software biz, two different executables): a Windows 98/Millennium version and a Windows NT/2000/XP version.

To keep my instructions as simple as possible, I have made a few assumptions:

- **You have a CD writer on both your old and new machines**—If this is not true, you might have to tweak some of these instructions to reflect your computing environment.

- **You have an Internet connection**—I should mention that your job as a system administrator will be a great deal easier if you have a broadband Internet connection (cable modem, DSL, and so on), as it gives you the ability to quickly download software updates.

- **You are using the tools I recommended in Chapter 2, "The Threats and the Tools"**—If you want to use different tools, that is fine, but *PC Fear Factor* refers to the tools I recommended.

Pre-Transition Steps

The following steps can be performed *before* you get your new computer. This speeds up the actual transition process.

Step 1: Identify Windows XP Compatibility Issues

As indicated earlier, some of your existing application software and peripheral devices might not be compatible with Windows XP. In some cases, you will need to buy completely new versions of an application software package. In other cases, you might be able to fix the software compatibility issue by downloading a patch to your existing version. Hardware compatibility issues can usually be resolved by installing the latest software for the peripheral device.

There is no complete list of software applications and hardware devices that are incompatible with Windows XP. However, Microsoft does provide an Upgrade Advisor tool you can download and run on your old PC. This tool examines the hardware and software components on your old PC and identifies compatibility issues.

Please note that I am *not* suggesting you use the Upgrade Advisor for its intended purpose—to help upgrade your old PC to Windows XP. In fact, in Chapter 10, "Tips for Avoiding PC Disasters," I advise you to *never* upgrade your computer's operating system.

However, running this tool on your old computer can help determine whether the applications and peripheral devices installed on or attached to the computer will cause any problems on your new Windows XP system.

You can download the Upgrade Advisor from `http://www.microsoft.com/windowsxp/pro/howtobuy/upgrading/advisor.asp`.

The Upgrade Advisor is a large file—35MB—so a broadband Internet connection is essential to download this tool. If you don't have a broadband connection, perhaps you can get a friend who does to download it for you and copy it to a CD.

When you run the Upgrade Advisor, it examines your computer and provides a report of incompatible hardware and software components (see Figure 4.1). You can ignore the incompatibility issues pertaining to internal hardware components since they won't apply to your new computer. Pay attention to the list of incompatible software applications and any peripheral devices (printers, scanners, and so on) that may require new software to function with Windows XP.

FIGURE 4.1
You can download and run the Windows XP Upgrade Advisor on your old computer. This helps you determine which software applications and peripheral hardware devices might be incompatible with your new Windows XP computer.

Step 2: Obtain the Latest Software for Your Peripherals

If your peripheral hardware is more than a year old, the chances are good that the manufacturer has released new application software and new drivers.

In fact, if your new computer has a different version of Windows than your old computer, you might *have* to obtain new software for your peripheral device—software that is compatible with your new operating system. (The Upgrade Advisor may have already alerted you to this issue.)

Using your old computer, go to the printer manufacturer's Web site and check for the latest software for your specific printer model. Compare the revision number on the software/driver to the revision number on the CD that came with your printer. If a newer version is available, download the software and copy it to a CD. Mark the CD so that you can find it later when you need to install it on your new computer.

For example, let's assume you have a Hewlett-Packard P1100 Photosmart printer. Here is how you would find the latest software for your printer:

If you are downloading several different updates, you might want to store them all in one folder on your hard disk (storing each update in a separate, clearly named sub-folder) and then copy the folder over to a CD when you are done.

1. Go to the HP Web site, `http://www.hp.com/`.

2. Navigate the Web site to get to HP drivers. (You can find the driver section on most sites under links with labels like Drivers, Support, Downloads, and so on.)

3. Enter the model number **P1100** and click the arrow.

4. Select the operating system for your new computer.

5. Look at the revision level date for the HP photo printing software and printer driver. Compare this revision number to the revision number on the CD that came with your printer. If the revision number on the Web site is higher, download the software and copy it to a CD.

Getting the Installation Instructions

You will need instructions to install your peripheral device on your new computer. You will find these instructions in your user guide. If you can't find your user guide, or if the user guide does not provide Windows XP installation instructions (which might be different from earlier versions of Windows), you should be able to find installation instructions on the vendor's Web site. Print out a hard copy of the installation instructions because you will need them later when you install the device on your new computer.

Repeat the process for your scanner and any other peripheral devices you have connected to your PC.

Step 3: Make a List of Every Application You Want to Install

Make a list of every application you want to install on your new computer, including the tools recommended in Chapter 2.

Some vendors, like Hewlett-Packard, give you the option of ordering the software on a CD. They generally only charge you for shipping and handling. This is a good option if you do not have a broadband connection, as the programs can be quite large and take hours to download over a 56K modem connection.

I recommend that you do *not* install any new applications—applications you are not currently using on your old computer—during this transition process. New applications introduce new variables into your computing environment, and it is best not to introduce additional variables while preparing your new computer for use.

Instead, I suggest that you wait until your computer has been in service for a few weeks before you install any new applications. By doing so, you will be able to more easily isolate any problems caused by a new application.

Step 4: Buy New Releases of Old Software Packages

If you are using versions of software packages that are several years old, I suggest that you buy the latest versions for installation on your new computer.

The latest release of any software package is more likely to be compatible with your new computing environment than an older version. For example, only the latest version of Roxio's Easy CD Creator (5.1 as of this writing) is compatible with Windows XP. Similarly, Norton AntiVirus wasn't compatible with Windows XP until its 2002 version.

Additionally, if your software is several years old, the latest release probably has some new features you would enjoy using.

Microsoft's Upgrade Advisor will help you determine which of your existing packages are not compatible with Windows XP. The next thing you must do is verify that the newest versions are compatible with Windows XP. You can find out whether a specific version of a software package is compatible with Windows XP by visiting the software vendor's Web site. Alternatively, Microsoft's Web site provides a catalog of applications that are certified to be compatible with Windows XP. The Windows Catalog is probably available directly from your Start button on your new computer. If it is not, you can find this information at `http://www.microsoft.com/windows/catalog/catalogshell/shell.asp?page=2&subid=22`.

As usual, you will find the lowest prices on eBay for most software packages.

Some of the tools recommended in Chapter 2 are acquired by downloading the installation programs over the Web—for example, ZoneAlarm. I suggest that you download these installation programs on your old PC and copy them to a CD so you can install these programs quickly on your new computer.

Step 5: Determine Whether Your Applications Are Compliant with Windows XP's System Restore Feature

Windows XP has an excellent feature called System Restore that is quite useful in helping users recover from certain types of computer disasters. (This feature is also found in Windows Millennium but is not present in Windows 95, 98, or 2000.)

System Restore is essentially a limited "do over" tool. It works automatically in the background, taking and storing snapshots of critical system files on your computer whenever you make a significant change to your computing environment. Each snapshot is called a *restore point* and has a unique date and time stamp. If a change to your computing environment renders your computer unstable, you can use the System Restore feature to restore your computer to its previous stable state without losing any of your data.

The System Restore feature has significant positive implications for users of Windows Millennium and XP. If you are using Windows 95 or 98, you are more likely to have to resort to extreme disaster recovery measures—restoring your entire hard disk from a backup—than if you have Windows Millennium or XP. The System Restore feature provides a less extreme way of recovering from certain types of computer disasters.

Observations Regarding System Restore

I feel that Microsoft's inclusion of the System Restore feature in Windows Millennium and XP validates my oft-made assertion that computers are unstable equilibriums. Basically, Microsoft is admitting that even the most seemingly innocuous change to your computing environment can precipitate a computer disaster and is providing a tool to help you return your computer to its most recent point of unstable equilibrium.

While I am grateful for having such a useful disaster recovery tool, I can't help but note that the need for such a tool is a sad commentary on the complexity and instability of personal computers.

You should also be aware that the System Restore feature has limitations. Restoring to an old system restore point can create more problems than it solves. For example, if you are somehow able to trace a computer problem to a change you made 30 days ago, you can't restore your system to that point without also undoing all the changes you made since then. The System Restore feature is most helpful if you *immediately* notice a problem after making a change to your computing environment. This way, you can restore your system without unintentionally backing out other changes.

System Restore Compliance: What It Is and Why It's Important

Certain events automatically trigger the creation of a restore point. One such event is the installation of a new application. Thus, if you install an application that trashes your computer, you can restore your computer's critical files to the point just prior to the application install because the installation process automatically triggered the creation of a restore point before the program was installed.

But there's a catch: The application's install program must be, to use Microsoft's exact words, "System Restore RestorePT.API compliant." In plain English this means the application's install program triggers the automatic creation of a restore point only if it is written specifically to integrate with the System Restore feature in Windows.

You can safely assume that the most recent releases of Microsoft applications are System Restore compliant. You can also reasonably assume that software products logo-certified for Windows XP are System Restore compliant. Beyond that, you should attempt to confirm whether a specific application you intend to install is System Restore compliant before you install that application. Unfortunately, my experience has been that application software vendors do not post such information prominently on their Web pages. You will need to search the knowledge base on the software vendor's Web site or contact technical support to ask the following specific question:

> *"Is your application's install program System Restore RestorePT.API compliant? That is, will the application trigger that automatic creation of a restore point when it is installed on a Windows XP system?"*

If you get an affirmative response from a knowledgeable authority, you can reasonably assume that the installation process will trigger the automatic creation of a system restore point.

If the application is not System Restore compliant, or if you are unable to definitively make that determination, all is not lost. The System Restore feature allows you to manually create a system restore point, which I advise you to do prior to installing an application you suspect or know is not System Restore compliant.

The System Restore feature is enabled by default within Windows, so you won't have to worry about activating this feature when you get your new computer.

Appendix A contains a more detailed discussion of the System Restore feature, including instructions on how to manually create system restore points and execute the restore process.

Step 6: Download the Latest Application Software Patches

Even if you have the current version of a software package, there might be software patches that are available on the vendors' Web sites. These patches are designed to fix problems with earlier releases, make the software compatible with new equipment or Windows XP, or provide additional features.

You might already have installed these patches on your old computer, but you will have to reinstall them on your new computer after you reload the base version of the software you own.

You will generally find software patches in the Download or Software Updates section of the vendor's Web site. The patch will generally include release notes that describe the fixes provided by the patch and instructions for installing the patch. I suggest that you read the release notes and determine whether it makes sense to install the patch. For example, if the only purpose of the patch is to support equipment you don't have or to support a foreign language, you really have nothing to gain by installing the patch. In fact, you have more to lose because, although patches are designed to fix problems, they sometimes cause problems.

Some software vendors issue incremental patches, and some issue differential patches. With incremental patches, you must apply all patches to a particular software release in sequence to get the latest patch—even if some of the patches add no particular value for you.

With differential patches, you need only apply the latest patch to a release to get up-to-date. Read the installation instructions carefully to determine whether the patches are incremental or differential.

Copy these patches to a CD so that they are ready to install on your new computer. Each patch you download will have a filename, and sometimes the filenames are unclear. If this is the case, rename the file and include the product name and patch number in the filename. This will be helpful when you apply the patches later.

Step 7: Capture Your Network Settings

This step is required if you have a broadband Internet connection or if a home network. If you meet either of these criteria, you need to capture the network settings from your old computer so you can replicate them on your new computer. Otherwise, you can skip this step.

You are not required to understand what all these network settings mean. I am not trying to make networking experts out of you. The objective here is to simply make sure that you configure your new computer with the same network settings as your old computer to ensure your ability to connect to the Internet and with the other computers in your house.

The easiest way to capture this information is to take a snapshot (screen shot) of this information. Here are two easy ways to do this:

1. You can use a screen capture tool like Snag It (`http://www.snagit.com/`) to take screen shots.

2. You can use the Print Screen button on your keyboard to take a screen shot. To capture a screen shot, press the Print Screen button on your keyboard (you won't see anything happen when you do this). Then, open Microsoft Word or Paint, and press Ctrl+V to paste the screen image into the application. Then, save the file.

Perform the following steps to find and capture your network settings on your old computer:

1. Right-click the Network Neighborhood icon on your desktop and select Properties.

2. A Network window opens (see Figure 4.2). Take a screen shot of each of the three tabs (Configuration, Identification, and Access Control) on this window.

FIGURE 4.2

The Network properties window.

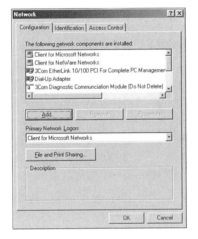

If you have two monitors, you may choose to have your old and new computers on side by side when it is time to transfer this information. If you use this approach, you do not have to take and print screen shots.

3. On the Configuration tab, find an entry in the network components window that refers to your TCP/IP settings for your network interface card (NIC), select that entry, and click Properties.

4. A new screen with seven tabs appears (see Figure 4.3). The tabs are as follows: IP Address, WINS Configuration, Gateway, DNS Configuration, NetBIOS, Advanced, and Bindings. Click each of these tabs and take screen shots.

5. Print out all the screen shots and place them in a file folder. You will need them later in this chapter when you are ready to connect your new computer to the Internet and your home network.

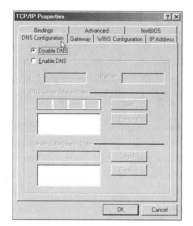

FIGURE 4.3

Take screen shots of the information associated with all seven tabs.

Step 8: Capture Your Application Options, Settings, and File Associations

Most applications allow you to set options or settings that control the way the applications work in your computing environment. Usually, these settings are found under Tools/Options, Edit/Preferences, or Options/Settings on the application's menu bar. For example, if you open Microsoft Word and select Tools, Options, you will see 10 tabs where you can change the settings that determine how the application functions. The same thing is true if you select Tools, Options in Outlook Express.

If you have been using your old computer for several years, you have probably changed the default settings on many of your applications. You might not even remember doing so!

In fact, you won't realize how many changes you have made until you install the applications on your new computer and suddenly discover that everything is working differently than it did before. This can precipitate a data loss disaster, as illustrated by the following example:

> You are using a photo editing application to edit your digital images. The installed default Save File settings save your digital files as a grayscale, medium-quality JPG type file.
>
> But you work with color images, and you always want to save your files in the high-quality, uncompressed TIFF format instead of the compressed JPG format. So, you change the default Save File settings to always save your files as 16 million color TIFF files instead of grayscale, medium-quality JPG files.
>
> *The years pass.*
>
> You get a new computer and reinstall all your applications. But you forget to change the installed default Save File settings on your photo editing application.

By default, Windows hides the file extensions from you, but they are there even if you don't see them when you look at a filename. It is easy to modify Windows to show the file extensions, but most people—myself included—feel that they only add clutter to the user interface.

If you are unsure of a file's extension, right-click the file and select Properties. Information about the file, including its extension, will be displayed.

You begin editing an existing image, working painstakingly for an hour to remove scratches and blemishes. You save the image, and voilà!—your beautiful color TIFF file has been converted to a lower-quality, black-and-white JPG file. There is no way to undo the change! Not only have you lost all the work you just performed, but you have also lost your color TIFF image forever if you do not have a backup!

This type of scenario happens more often than you might think. So take a few minutes now to open each of your applications and take screen shots of each application's options and settings. Print them out and put them in a folder. You will use this information later in this chapter when you install your applications on your new computer.

File Associations

Every file in Windows has a *file type*, which is determined by the *file extension*—the letters that follow the dot at the end of the filename. For example, in the filename `chapter3.doc`, the file extension is doc.

The association of a particular file type with a specific application is known as a *file association*. Almost every type of user-editable file in Windows has a file association. When you double-click a user-editable file to open it, it opens with the associated application. Thus, when you double-click a file that has a doc file extension, it opens in Microsoft Word.

Some file associations are unique. For example, doc is uniquely associated with Microsoft Word, xls with Microsoft Excel, and ppt with Microsoft PowerPoint.

Many file associations are not unique, but they still have a *default file association*—an application that opens when you double-click the file. For example, I can open a JPG graphics file from within seven different applications on my computer, but if I just double-click the file to view it, it always opens with my Irfanview graphics viewer because I have Irfanview set up as my default graphics viewer for JPG files.

If you want your new computer to have the same default file associations as your old one, you will need to take a few minutes to investigate your current computer's default file associations. Simply double-click different file types and observe which application opens.

Table 4.1 provides a list of commonly used audio, video, and graphics file types that are not uniquely associated with one application.

Table 4.1   Common File Types

File Extension	Type of File
.mp3	Audio
.wav	Audio
.avi	Video
.mpeg	Video
.jpg	Graphics

File Extension	Type of File
.tiff	Graphics
.bmp	Graphics
.gif	Graphics
.pcx	Graphics

Once you have determined your file associations, open the applications to determine where the associations are specified. You will usually find the file associations under Options or Preferences.

For example, one of the applications I use is the Irfanview graphic viewer. Under Irfanview's Options/Properties menu, I can select which file extensions I want to have associated with Irfanview.

Take screen shots of all your file association settings from within the applications you use. Print them out and put them in a folder. You will use this information later to set the same file associations on your new computer.

Make sure you identify all your file associations. If you do not, when you double-click a file on your new computer, the file might open with a different application, or it might not open at all. If this happens, you can then associate a file type with an application to fix the problem.

File Fight!

Ever notice your file associations changing automatically? No, it's not a poltergeist at work. Your applications are waging a war for control. The battle for control typically begins when you install a new application that has the ability to play the same types of media files as other applications that are already installed on your machine. Often, applications ask you before changing file type associations, but some may automatically seize control over your media files. To fix this problem, some applications have a setting called Reclaim File Associations. If you enable this option, the application automatically reclaims file associations that another application has stolen. Of course, if you allow two competing applications to reclaim file associations, the applications will continue to fight with each other. Every time you open an application, the file association changes.

Step 9: Assemble Materials

You will need to assemble the following materials before you begin the actual transition process:

- **Pen and paper**—You will need this to write down phone numbers and any error messages you receive and to keep a log of everything you have done.

- **One hundred blank, new, unformatted CD-R or CD-RW discs**—Make sure you purchase discs that are compatible with the highest speed of your new CD writer. This will make your job go faster. The CDs you purchase in a store will be unformatted. Do not format the CDs, as you will be using these CDs to take backups, and Norton Ghost does not work with formatted CDs. (You might not need all 100 CDs, but better to be safe than sorry. And if you purchase 100 CD-Rs on a spindle, you can get them for about $20 on sale.)

- **Two dozen new, formatted floppy disks.**

Old Media = Bad Media

Use new media—CDs and floppy disks—to reduce the chance of infecting your machine with a virus. This is especially important because you will be performing some of the preparation steps with your antivirus software disabled.

- **All the software you need to install on your new computer.**
- **A phone**—While it might seem like an odd item to have in a list such as this, at some point during the process you might need to contact the computer vendor or a software vendor to resolve some type of problem. I find it helpful to have a hands-free telephone—either a speakerphone or a headphone—so that I can talk and type in comfort at the same time (a speaker phone or headphone also makes it easier to put up with any long hold times). If you do not have a phone in the same room as your computer, use a cordless phone, and make sure you have a charged backup battery. If you have a dial-up Internet connection, try to use a different phone line if you have to call technical support so that you can be online and on the phone at the same time.
- **The technical support phone numbers for your hardware vendor and software vendors.**

Customer No-Service, Part 2

When talking with technical support, try to avoid getting disconnected at all costs. If you are using a cordless phone, don't let that battery die on you in the middle of a call! If the battery starts to beep, pick up another extension to keep the connection open while you change your battery. Most tech support people do *not* have direct extensions, and you will be unable to reach the same person again if you get disconnected. This can be very frustrating, especially if you have been working with one person for a long time on a particular problem. If you get disconnected and have to call back, you will end up talking to somebody else and you will waste a lot of time getting that person up to speed on the problem.

The unwillingness of most companies to provide their tech support people with dialable phone extensions to facilitate continuity-of-contact until a problem is solved is yet another example of the customer no-service business model discussed in Chapter 2.

I also suggest that you get the tech support specialist's name and give the specialist your phone number and ask that he call you back if you get disconnected. Some will and some won't, but it's worth a shot.

Step 10: Organize Your Workspace

You will need to have access to your old and new computer during the transition process, so make sure your work area can accommodate both computers. If your table or desk is not big enough for both computers, set the old one on the floor near your new computer. You will need an Internet connection in the room where you are doing your work.

Make sure your work area can remain undisturbed for the duration of the transition process.

Step 11: Schedule Time

The transition process could take one or two full days, depending on how many applications you have to load, how much data you have to migrate, and how many problems you encounter. Some steps will require your full undivided attention, some can be performed unattended, and some will require your attention every so often to change CDs or click a button on Windows dialog boxes.

Setting Up, Powering Up, Checking Up, Backing Up!

The big day has arrived. Your new computer has been delivered (or you have just picked it up at the store), and you have completed all your pre-transition steps. You're ready to go.

Step 1: Unpack Your New Computer and Set It Up

Unpack your new computer. You will find that the computer comes with a number of CDs. These CDs should have the software that was preinstalled on your computer, including Windows. You will not need to do anything with these during the transition process. However, it is extremely important that you keep all these CDs and their associated documentation in a safe place. If you ever have a problem with your computer, you may need to reinstall some of this software.

Set up your new computer. Most vendors provide a quick setup diagram, and most connections are color-coded, so it shouldn't take you more than a few minutes to make the required connections, which are as follows:

- Connect the monitor to the computer.
- Connect the mouse and keyboard to the computer.
- Connect the speakers to the computer.
- Plug the monitor, computer, and, if necessary, your speakers into your surge suppressor.

Connections You Shouldn't Make

Do not hook up any other peripheral devices to your new computer yet (like a printer or scanner). Doing so will prompt your computer to search for drivers, and you do not want to alter the virgin state of your computer the first time you boot it up.

Also, do *not* hook your new computer up to the Internet. The last thing you want is to have your hard disk wiped out by a virus or a computer hacker before you have even installed antivirus software and a firewall.

Step 2: Power Up!

Turn on your new computer. The first time your computer boots up, it might take longer than usual as your computer goes through some routines to finish installing Windows. You might be required to register Windows XP before you can use your machine. Normally, you can do this over the Web, but you should do this by phone because your new computer is not connected to the Web yet.

Step 3: Check CD Writer Compatibility

Using the instructions provided in Chapter 3, "A Disaster Prevention Plan for Your New Computer: Part 1, Before You Buy," check the make and model of your CD writer in the device manager and reconfirm that it is compatible with your CD writing software. In the case of my recommendations, this would be Norton Ghost, NTI Backup NOW! Deluxe, and Roxio Easy CD Creator. If the CD writer is not compatible with these applications, take or ship the computer back.

Step 4: Check for Identical Computing Environments

If you've purchased more than one computer with the specific objective of having them configured identically then set up both computers, navigate to the Device Manager using the instructions provided in Chapter 3, and confirm that each computer has the same make and model of

- DVD-ROM
- CD writer
- Hard disk
- Hard disk controller
- Display adapter
- Sound card
- Network adapter

If the configurations are not identical, contact your direct seller or retailer to resolve the issue before you proceed further. You might elect to return one of the computers, and it might not make sense to proceed until you are confident that you have identical computing environments.

Step 5: Disable Your Antivirus Software

Antivirus software may have been preinstalled on your new computer, and the software may have started automatically when you booted up your machine. You need to disable your antivirus software until later in the preparation process. If your antivirus software is enabled, it can interfere with certain steps in this process and create problems. For example, it is not a good idea to have your antivirus software enabled when you are checking your hard disk for bad sectors or when you are installing new programs.

Since you will be rebooting your system many times during the preparation process, you need to configure your antivirus software so that it does *not* automatically protect you when you boot up.

Open your antivirus software's user interface from the Start, Programs menu. For Norton AntiVirus, click Options and then uncheck both Enable Auto-Protect and Start Auto-Protect When Windows Starts Up. Later, when the preparation process is complete, you can reenable the software.

You are at no risk of getting viruses so long as you do not connect to the Internet or insert any infected media into your floppy disk drive or CD drive. I'll instruct you when it's time to reenable your antivirus software.

Step 6: Check Your Hard Disk for Bad Sectors

Chapter 1, "The Root of All Computer Disasters," discussed the fact that no hard disk is perfect when it leaves the factory but that the hard disk manufacturer hides the bad sectors so that the new hard disk *appears* to be perfect. That is, if you run a utility to check your hard disk, it should not find a single bad sector. If you do find a bad sector, the hard disk has suffered damage since it left the factory.

So, the first thing you should do is make sure that your hard disk is perfect, or more accurately, *appears* to be perfect. You accomplish this by running a standard Windows XP hard disk error checking utility to perform a thorough surface scan of your hard disk. A thorough surface scan attempts to read and write to every sector on the hard drive to identify any bad sectors. (The thorough surface scan will not harm the data currently on your hard disk.)

In previous consumer versions of Microsoft Windows, this utility was called ScanDisk. In the spirit of The Artist Formerly Known as Prince, Microsoft has changed the name of ScanDisk in Windows XP to The Utility Formerly Known as ScanDisk, which is to say it no longer has a name. I can tell you where to find it and how to run it, but I can't tell you what to call it. I could keep referring to it as "the Windows XP hard disk error checking utility," but from this point forward I will simply use the term *TUFKAS*, an acronym for The Utility Formerly Known as ScanDisk, to refer to this Windows XP utility.

Before you run TUFKAS, make sure that your computer was not configured at the factory with a screensaver. You do not want a screensaver running in the background while you are running TUFKAS, as it will slow down the utility and can even prevent it from finishing. To check for a screensaver, do the following:

If you have an earlier version of Windows, ScanDisk is found in the Programs, Accessories, System Tools folder. Because TUFKAS has no name within Windows XP, it is obviously no longer in the System Tools folder and can't be found the way normal programs are found.

To be perfectly accurate, I cannot absolutely guarantee that TUFKAS has the same exact functionality as ScanDisk. It would probably be more correct to refer to the Windows XP utility as "the utility that replaces ScanDisk."

1. Right-click your desktop and click Properties.

2. Click the Screensaver tab, set the screensaver to None, and click OK.

TUFKAS is very sensitive to other applications and processes that might be running on your computer. You might not even be aware of these processes because they may be started automatically when you boot up your computer. If TUFKAS is having trouble running to completion, you might eventually see an error message indicating that TUFKAS has been restarted more than 10 times. This means that other processes running in the background are preventing TUFKAS from running to completion.

The best way to ensure that TUFKAS runs to completion is to boot up your computer in safe mode. This is a special way of booting your computer without loading the applications, background processes, and drivers that would normally load. The only drivers that are loaded in safe mode are the drivers for your keyboard and mouse and a generic video driver that enables you to view your monitor only at low resolution. Normally, safe mode is used to troubleshoot Windows problems. In this case, you are using it to ensure that TUFKAS will have exclusive access to your hard disk.

To boot up your computer in safe mode, restart your computer and repeatedly press the F8 function key until the Startup menu displays (see Figure 4.4).

FIGURE 4.4

The Windows XP Startup menu allows you to control how Windows XP boots.

```
Windows Advanced Options Menu
Please select an option:

   Safe Mode
   Safe Mode with Networking
   Safe Mode with Command Prompt

   Enable Boot Logging
   Enable VGA Mode
   Last Known Good Configuration (your most recent settings that worked)
   Directory Services Restore Mode (Windows domain controllers only)
   Delogging Mode

   Start Windows Normally
   Reboot
   Return to OS Choices Menu

   Use the up and down arrow keys to move the highlight to your choice.
```

Use the arrow keys on your keyboard to choose option 3 for safe mode.

When your computer finishes booting in safe mode, the video display will look "funny." This is perfectly normal—safe mode just loads a basic, low-end video driver that is incapable of high-end graphics. The next time you boot up your computer normally, the video display will be back to normal. However, you might need to rearrange some of the icons on your desktop. Again, this is perfectly normal. After your computer has booted up in safe mode, perform the following steps to run TUFKAS:

1. Click Start, My Computer.

2. Right-click the drive to be checked for errors (usually Local Disk C:), and select Properties (see Figure 4.5).

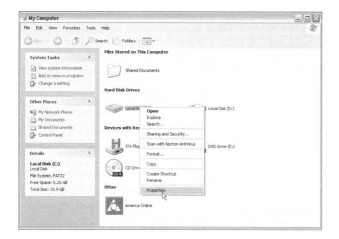

FIGURE 4.5
Navigating to TUFKAS.

3. Click the Tools tab.

4. In the Error-checking section, click Check Now.

5. Check the Scan for and Attempt Recovery of Bad Sectors box and click Start (see Figure 4.6).

FIGURE 4.6
Starting TUFKAS.

6. Let the error checking utility run to completion. Do not do anything else with your computer while the program is running.

A thorough surface scan could take many hours, so be patient. The larger your hard disk, the longer it will take. Because this process is rather like watching paint dry, you can leave your computer unattended while TUFKAS is running—even overnight if you wish.

TUFKAS will display a report on the screen when it has finished running. No factory-new PC should have a hard disk with errors on it, so if the report indicates any bad sectors, you should return your computer. (If the computer vendor tries to convince you that it is normal to have some bad sectors on your hard disk, don't believe it. It's not normal, and it's not acceptable. It's a precursor of bad things to come.)

In earlier versions of Windows, you could select multiple partitions simultaneously and run ScanDisk against all the partitions. With Windows XP, you can scan only one partition at a time. (Don't look for a logical reason.)

Also, in earlier versions of Windows, you could select an option that displayed a message as soon as ScanDisk found a bad sector. Sadly, this option no longer exists with TUFKAS, so you will have to allow the program to run to completion before you get the results.

While time-consuming, I recommend taking *two* complete disk images, labeling them "Virgin 1 backup" and "Virgin 2 backup." This provides additional protection against bad backup media. The newest CD writers are so fast that you can probably do a virgin backup in less than an hour.

Even if you have two or more identically configured computers, I recommend that you take a disk image of each computer. In theory, this is not necessary, but in practice it's a good idea, especially because Windows XP has a product activation feature that eventually causes problems if you use a backup from one machine to restore another machine.

If your hard disk has more than one logical partition, you will need to run TUFKAS separately for each partition. If either partition has bad sectors, you should return your computer. (Refer to Chapter 1 for a discussion of hard disk partitions.)

When TUFKAS has run to completion on all partitions, reboot your computer normally.

How Often Should You Perform a Thorough Surface Scan?

Because it takes many hours to perform a thorough surface scan on a large hard disk, this is not something that I do or recommend as part of normal maintenance. If you develop hard disk problems sometime after you put your computer in service, you will probably become aware of them without having to run a surface scan. For example, you will be unable to read from or write to your hard disk. Once I have put my computer into service, the only time I ever perform a thorough surface scan is to confirm what I already know in my gut— that my disk has developed bad sectors.

Step 7: Create a Restore Point

If you've gotten this far, TUFKAS ran to completion and did not detect any bad sectors on your hard disk. Congratulations. You have a good hard disk.

Before you do anything to change your virgin computing environment, follow the instructions in Appendix A to use the System Restore feature to manually create a restore point for your computer. This provides you with the option of restoring your system to this point in time should something go wrong while you are preparing your new computer for use.

Step 8: Take a Full System Backup

Before you do anything to change the initial state of your computer, you need to take a full system backup. Paradoxically, you need to make one change to the initial state to take the full backup—you need to install disk imaging software. As you'll recall, in Chapter 2, I recommended Norton Ghost for this purpose.

Install Norton Ghost following the general instructions for adding and removing programs in Appendix B.

After you have installed Norton Ghost, take a complete backup (image) of your hard disk. The instructions for using Norton Ghost to take a disk image are found in Chapter 7.

This backup will serve as your ultimate "do over." Should something terrible happen during the rest of the transition process, or even months later, you will be able to perform a disaster recovery to restore your new computer to its near-initial state. (I say "near-initial state" because if you use this backup to perform a disaster recovery, Norton Ghost will appear on the recovered disk.)

This initial backup will probably require fewer than 10 CDs, depending on how many applications were preinstalled on your computer. Label the backup "Virgin Backup." Be sure to put the name of the computer (if you have more than one computer) and the date on each CD, and be sure to number the CDs in sequence as the backup proceeds.

Creating Your New Computing Environment

In this section, you will perform the remaining steps required to create your new computing environment. If something goes drastically wrong during this process, have no fear—you can always restore your hard disk from your virgin backup and start again.

Step 1: Change Your Monitor's Resolution (Optional)

This step is optional. Your video card was preset at the factory at a default resolution. However, depending on the size of your monitor and the quality of your graphics card, you might want to change the resolution to something that is more to your liking. A higher resolution will display more information onscreen. To change your resolution, perform the following steps:

1. Right-click the desktop, select Properties, and select the Settings tab.
2. Under Screen Resolution, move the slider bar in the direction of More or Less to go to a higher or lower resolution, and then click OK (see Figure 4.7).

You don't need to be concerned about doing any harm to your system by changing the monitor resolution—Windows will not allow you to make choices, either in resolution or color depth, that your video card can't support.

FIGURE 4.7
Changing your monitor resolution.

Step 2: Select Programs to Uninstall

Most computers come with several preinstalled programs. You may want to uninstall any programs you know you will never use. For example, if you have an Internet service provider, you will not use AOL or CompuServe, and you can safely remove these programs if they have been installed.

It is generally a good idea to remove the old version of a program first before installing a new version. This results in a cleaner install and can get rid of files that are no longer needed. One exception to this is if the new version of the software is sold as an upgrade (at a reduced price). Some of these applications allow you to insert the original CD during the install process for verification, but others require that a previous version be present on your hard disk for the upgrade to successfully install. In either case, this is how publishers attempt to ensure that you paid the full price at some time in the past.

There is no hard and fast rule that says you have to remove programs you don't need. I do it because I don't like to clutter up my hard disk with what I consider to be garbage. The more garbage I have on my hard disk, the less room I have for really important stuff (like Beatles videos!), and the longer it takes to perform a hard disk backup or restore.

Do not delete a program unless you are absolutely certain you have no use for it.

If your computer came with antivirus software other than Norton AntiVirus and you want to switch to Norton, you must remove the preinstalled antivirus program as well.

There is another important reason you might choose to remove a preinstalled program from your new computer. Some preinstalled programs can be heavily watered down OEM versions of the real, complete program, which you might want to install yourself. When I purchased my last computer, it had an OEM version of Easy CD Creator that was missing some important features. I removed the OEM version so that I could install the full version I had purchased.

Step 3: Uninstall Programs

Once you have decided which programs to uninstall, remove them following the instructions in Appendix B.

Step 4: Install Your Applications and Application Patches

Now you are ready to install each of your software applications, including the tools recommended in Chapter 2. However, hold off on installing your software firewall and antivirus software until later.

Perform the following steps to install each application:

1. Create a restore point if necessary. If the application is not System Restore compliant—that is, if it does not trigger the automatic creation of a system restore point—use the System Restore feature to create a manual restore point. Give the restore point a clear name—for example, `Prior to installation of <insert application name>`—that you will recognize if you need to use the restore point later. When in doubt, create a manual restore point.

2. Install the application following the instructions in Appendix B.

3. Immediately after installing an application, reboot your system to make sure that it boots up normally, without any error messages. Open the application and work with it a bit to confirm that it is functioning normally. Create a test document; then, delete the document when you are through and empty your recycle bin.

Don't Install Multiple Applications at Once!

Be sure to reboot and test the application immediately after you install it. If you install several applications before rebooting, and if there is a problem, you will be uncertain as to which application caused the problem. Your only recourse at this point would be to work backward, uninstalling applications one by one until the problem disappears.

Some applications provide the option of registering online as you install the application. As you are not yet connected to the Internet, you should decline this option and register your products later if you choose to do so.

4. Take any necessary corrective actions. If you observe any anomalies during the reboot process or while using the application, you have two choices:

  • **You can try to resolve the problem**—If you are getting some type of error message or abnormal condition, try using your old computer to search the software vendor's Web site knowledge base for the solution to the problem, or try calling the software vendor's technical support number.

  • **You can uninstall the application**—You might decide to uninstall the application for now so you can proceed with the transition process without further delay. You can always reinstall the application later. If you decide to uninstall the application, remove it following the instructions in Appendix B and *then* restore your system to the restore point you created just prior to installing the application. You should definitely uninstall the application first and then restore your system. Restoring your system, in and of itself, does not uninstall the application. Moreover, the uninstall program can get "confused" if you restore the system first and then run the uninstall program because some things the program is trying to uninstall will have already been removed. Once you have removed all traces of the troublesome program, put it aside for investigation later and go on to the next application.

5. Install any application patches. Once the application has been installed, you might need to install patches you downloaded earlier to bring the application up-to-date. If the application patches are incremental and there are multiple patches, you will need to install the patches in sequence. Install the patches as follows:

  • First, create a system restore point prior to installing each patch.

  • Then, reboot and retest the application after you install *each* patch—do not wait until you have installed all the patches.

6. Configure the application options, settings, and file associations. If you have gotten this far, you have successfully installed the application and any applicable patches. Now it is time to set the application's options, settings, and file associations. Refer to the screen shots you printed out earlier for the application options, settings, and file associations.

7. Repeat the previous steps until each application has been installed.

Express Assist, one of the tools recommended in Chapter 2, is not System Restore compliant as of this writing.

In theory, immediately uninstalling a badly behaved application should return your system to the exact state it was in prior to the installation. However, a poorly written uninstall program can leave behind some remnants of the program in your Windows Registry or other system files. Restoring the system to the restore point *after* you uninstall the application provides extra insurance that you have completely purged the application from your system.

Step 5: Set Options, Settings, and File Associations on Preinstalled Applications

Your computer vendor may have preinstalled some applications that are newer versions of applications you are currently using, such as Microsoft Office applications. You will need to open the preinstalled applications and specify the options, settings, and file associations as they were set on your old computer.

Step 6: Resolve Open Issues and Reinstall Applications

If you encountered any problems that required you to uninstall an application and restore your system, now is a good time to resolve these issues (if you can) and reinstall these applications.

If you are unable to resolve a problem with a particular application, you can delay installing it until you have time to perform more research, or you can begin searching for a different application that will provide the same functionality. In either case, do not let these problems delay you from completing this process. You can always come back and install these applications at a later date when you have resolved the problems or when the vendor has released a patch to resolve the problems.

Step 7: Create a Restore Point and Take a Complete System Backup

This is an optional but recommended step. You've expended quite a bit of time and effort to get to this point. I recommend that you use the System Restore feature to create a manual restore point and then use Norton Ghost to take a complete system backup. This way, should anything drastic happen during the balance of the transition process, you won't have to restore using the virgin backup you created earlier. You can restore your system to this point and avoid having to repeat all the effort you expended to install your applications. Mark the backup "Interim Backup—Creating New Computing Environment." Be sure to put the name of the computer (if you have more than one computer) and the date on each CD, and be sure to number the CDs in sequence. Note that this backup will require several more CDs than the virgin backup you took earlier because you have installed several applications on your computer.

Step 8: Install Your Peripheral Hardware

The next step is to install your printer(s), scanner, and any other peripheral hardware. You should install one piece of equipment at a time. You also need the latest software and device drivers, which you should have downloaded earlier.

I strongly recommend that you use the System Restore feature to manually create a restore point just prior to installing each peripheral. If the installation process causes problems, you can uninstall the device and restore your system to this restore point.

Install the device following the instructions in the user guide or the installation instructions you printed out earlier from the vendor's Web site. Note that some vendors direct you to install their software first, before connecting their equipment, and that others require the software to be installed *after* you have connected their equipment and turned on your computer. Follow the vendor's directions carefully.

Beware of Unsigned Drivers

Windows XP automatically warns you if you attempt to install an unsigned driver. An unsigned driver is a driver that has not met Microsoft's Windows Hardware Quality Lab testing criteria. The term *unsigned driver* means the driver does not have a digital signature certifying it as meeting these standards.

If you get a warning about an unsigned driver, do not proceed with the installation without first investigating whether a signed driver is available. You will need to contact the vendor who provided the driver—for example, the printer manufacturer—to find out why the driver is unsigned.

Step 9: Reactivate Your Preinstalled Antivirus Software or Install and Configure Norton AntiVirus

If antivirus software was preinstalled on your computer, you were instructed to disable it earlier in this process. You should reenable your auto-protect feature now and also make certain that the software is configured to automatically start whenever you boot up your computer.

If you do not have antivirus software on your computer, you should install one now. Again, I highly recommend Norton AntiVirus. Remember that if you're using Windows XP, you can't install an old version of Norton AntiVirus on your new computer—releases prior to Norton AntiVirus 2002 are not compatible with Windows XP.

Norton AntiVirus is System Restore compliant so you do not need to create a manual restore point before installing it on your system.

Many of Norton AntiVirus's default settings are acceptable. However, you should change a few of these settings. Detailed instructions for configuring Norton AntiVirus are found in Chapter 5.

You will not be able to register and update your antivirus software until you are connected to the Internet.

Step 10: Install and Configure Your Software Firewall

Install and configure your software firewall. In Chapter 2, I recommended using ZoneAlarm. Instructions for configuring ZoneAlarm are found in Chapter 5.

Windows XP is configured by default to automatically notify you when critical updates to your operating system, Web browser, and email application are available. Once you have connected your new computer to the Internet, you might receive a notification stating `critical updates are available`. This notification can come at any time. When you receive such a notification, you should follow the instructions to apply the critical updates. Windows XP's System Restore feature automatically creates a restore point prior to applying the critical updates.

Step 11: Connect to the Internet and Configure Your Home Network

Now you are ready to connect to the Internet. If you have a home network, you must also add your computer to the network. You need all the network settings you printed out earlier to accomplish this task.

Windows XP provides two wizards to assist you with the tasks of connecting to the Internet and to your home network. The New Connection Wizard helps you configure your Internet connection, whereas the Network Setup Wizard assists you in adding your new computer to your home network. You can find these wizards by selecting Start, My Computer, Network Tasks.

As you are running these wizards, you will be prompted to enter information from the printouts you made earlier.

Your Internet service provider (ISP) might provide you with specific instructions and perhaps even a CD for configuring your Internet connection. If you encounter any difficulties in setting up your Internet connection, contact your ISP for assistance.

If you encounter any difficulties adding your computer to your home network, I refer you to Que Publishing's *Special Edition Using Microsoft Windows XP Home Edition* (ISBN 0-7897-2628-9) for additional assistance.

Step 12: Register and Update Your Antivirus Software

Once you are connected to the Internet, Norton AntiVirus will automatically prompt you to register your software. You should register the software and run the Live Update feature *immediately* to get the latest software updates and virus signatures. You might have to run LiveUpdate several times, as the updates are incremental in nature in many cases. Symantec may instruct you to reboot your computer in some cases. Reboot your computer and run LiveUpdate again, and keep running LiveUpdate until you receive a message telling you that your Symantec products are up-to-date.

If the antivirus software came preinstalled by your hardware vendor, it may have only come with a 90-day subscription to virus updates. Be sure to renew your subscription at the end of the 90-day period; Norton automatically provides you with reminders when you are within a month of the expiration date. Don't let your subscription expire, or you are an accident waiting to happen.

If you purchased and installed Norton AntiVirus, a year's subscription to virus signature updates is included.

Should You Register Your Other Software?

Now that you have established your Internet connection, you might want to register any other software products you installed. Some vendors require you to register your products to install updates or get support. However, most do not. I avoid registering software where possible because I don't like my name or email address on any more lists than is necessary, and these fields are usually required information when you register software.

Step 13: Tune Your System (Optional)

You can do several things to "tune up" your system and make it run faster. If you are interested in pursuing this, I recommend that you download and install a shareware product called Tweak-XP. Tweak-XP provides a number of ways to tweak both Windows XP and your hardware to improve your system's performance.

You can download this product from the following location:

```
http://www.totalidea.de/frameset-tweakxp.htm
```

Tweak-XP is System Restore compliant.

Step 14: Perform a Fully Configured System Backup

At this point, you have completed every task except for data migration. Before you transfer your data from your old computer to your new computer, use Norton Ghost to take a complete system backup. Label each disk "Fully configured system backup."

I recommend taking two complete, fully configured system backups to provide additional protection against bad backup media.

Keep all the backups you have created thus far—the virgin backups, the interim backup, and the fully configured system backups—offsite in a safe deposit box. *Keep these backups as long as you have your PC.* You might never need to use these backups—if you ever have to perform a disaster recovery, you will probably restore from a later, more current backup. But it is very nice to have these backups as an extra safeguard should you ever need them.

Should You Include Your Data in Your Final, Fully Configured System Backup?

You might have noticed that I have instructed you to take your fully configured system backup before you have loaded any data onto your new computer. This is because your data becomes obsolete within a matter of days after you put your new computer into service. Including your data as part of the fully configured system backup adds no value. If you ever need to use this backup to restore your system to its initial, fully configured state, you won't want to restore this data anyway—you will be restoring data from a more recent backup.

Step 15: Back Up Your Data from Your Old Computer

Back up all your data from your old computer following the instructions in Chapter 6. Note that I did not include this as a pretransition step because you do not want to back up your data until you are almost ready to put your new computer into service. This way, you can continue using your old computer until the transition process is almost complete.

If you have a home network and your old computer is a part of it, you do not need to back up and restore your data. Instead, you can move your data directly across the network from your old computer to your new computer. On my home network, I've set up one shared folder on each computer. I move data from one computer to the shared folder on the other computer, and from there I move it to its final location. This approach gives me connectivity without sacrificing privacy—users can only view the data that is in the shared folder on each computer. If you want to provide more extensive sharing privileges, you can move your data directly to its final location on your new computer.

You should make sure you have successfully migrated all your data to your new PC before you delete it from your old machine.

You can use either the drag-and-drop approach to copy all your data files to CDs or NTI Backup NOW! Deluxe. If you use the backup software, you will also need to use the software to restore the data to your new computer. (You should have already installed the backup software when you installed your applications.)

Some data can't be directly migrated from your old computer to its final destination on your new machine. For example, say you are using Express Assist on your old computer to back up your email messages, accounts, address book, and browser bookmarks. Express Assist stores all this data in a single compressed (Zip) file. You will need to use Express Assist on your new computer to restore the data from the compressed file.

Step 16: Restore the Data to Your New Computer

Restore all your data on your new computer by following the directions in Chapter 8. Granted, you are not recovering from a computer disaster here, but the steps for restoring your data are the same regardless of the reason for doing so.

After you have restored your data, verify that the data has been restored properly by accessing it from within your applications. For example, open your email program and verify that all your messages, email accounts, and address book have been successfully restored. Similarly, if you use Quicken, open Quicken and verify that you can open your Quicken files. Do a thorough job here because you are about to delete your data off your old computer, so you should be absolutely certain that you have not forgotten to migrate any data.

Preparing Your Old Computer for Disposal or Redeployment

You're almost finished! You've put your new computer into service, and now the only task remaining is to prepare your old computer for disposal or redeployment.

What do you plan to do with your old computer? Sell it? Give it to a relative? Donate it to a school? Keep it and redeploy it to your child?

If you are getting rid of your old computer, you should certainly remove all traces of your data from the machine first, lest anyone have access to your confidential information.

With some exceptions (I point these out in the instructions), the same approach applies even if you intend to keep your computer. A different family member will be using your old computer, for a different purpose, and you will probably still want to remove most if not all traces of your data from the computer before putting it back into service elsewhere in your house.

So, I am going to proceed under the assumption that whether you are disposing of your computer or simply redeploying it, you will perform the same preparation process.

You can use your judgment here—perhaps you will want to keep your browser bookmarks and some of the contacts in your email address book if you are keeping your old computer, and perhaps you will not be quite as fanatical about erasing your data beyond recovery.

Before you sell, donate, or redeploy your old computer, you need to do four things:

1. Remove your network settings.
2. Remove applications for which you no longer have a valid license.
3. Delete your data.
4. Scrub your hard disk to erase all traces of your data beyond recovery.

Step 1: Disconnect Your Old Computer from the Internet

If you have a broadband Internet connection, physically disconnect your old computer from the Internet at this time. This prevents you from accidentally receiving any email on your own computer. This would be highly undesirable because you have already migrated your email to your new computer. If you begin receiving more email on your old computer, you might have to transfer your email data again. So stop the vicious cycle cold and disconnect your computer from the Internet. (If you are going to keep your old computer, you might reconnect it to the Internet using a different email account after the preparation process is complete.)

Another reason to disconnect your computer from the Internet is to stop your Web browser from automatically capturing more information about your Web surfing habits. You are going to be scrubbing all that information from your hard disk, so it would be counterproductive to surf the Web while you are in fact trying to erase all evidence of your Web surfing habits.

Step 2: Remove Your Network Settings

Earlier, you were instructed to copy your network settings from your old computer to your new machine. Now you should delete your network settings from your old machine.

Removing Your Static IP Address

An *IP address* is the means by which your computer is uniquely identified on the Internet. Some broadband Internet service providers assign a permanent IP address to each computer, known as a *static IP address*. The more common practice is dynamic IP addressing, in which your computer is assigned a different IP address (from a bank of available IP addresses) each time it connects to the Internet.

If you have a dynamically assigned IP address, there is nothing to worry about and nothing to delete from your computer. But if you have a static IP address, you must delete it—*even if you are keeping your old computer*—because two computers can't access the Internet at the same time with the same IP address. It's easy to see the confusion that would result if this were allowed. An IP address is analogous to a phone number.

If your computer serves as the host for a Web site, it must have a static IP address. Imagine the difficulty someone would have reaching you if you changed your phone number every day. If all you do is surf the Web and use email, you do not need a static IP address. Some ISPs charge extra for a static IP address.

Imagine the problem you would have receiving phone calls if two people had the same area code and phone number. How would the phone company know where to route the call?

If two computers try to connect to the Internet using the same IP address, the one that tries first will be successful. The second computer will be blocked and will receive an error message advising that it has used an invalid IP address. The second computer will be unable to connect until the first computer disconnects.

To find out if you have a static IP address, perform the following steps:

1. Right-click the Network Neighborhood icon on your desktop and select Properties.

2. Click the Configuration tab.

3. In the Network Components window, find an entry that refers to your TCP/IP settings for your network interface card (NIC), select that entry, and click Properties.

4. Click the IP Address tab. If the Obtain an IP Address Automatically box is checked, you have nothing to worry about. If the Specify an IP Address box is checked, you will see an IP address below it. You need to delete it, *even if you are keeping your computer* (see Figure 4.8).

FIGURE 4.8
Check to see if your computer has a static IP address. This computer has a dynamically assigned IP address.

My Most Unusual Computer Disaster

The most unusual computer disaster I ever experienced involved a stolen IP address. I share this horror story with you to emphasize the importance of guarding your IP address.

My former ISP assigned static IP addresses to its customers. One day, I started having difficulty connecting to the Internet. Whenever I tried to log on, I received an error message indicating that I was using an invalid IP address.

An investigation revealed that my ISP had given out a range of IP addresses to a corporate customer, and my IP address was within that range.

My Internet service provider knocked the other person off the Internet so that I could reconnect and told him not to use my IP address. But the next day the same problem occurred again. The fight over my IP address went on for several days, and I became increasingly frustrated.

The ISP eventually solved the problem by taking the drastic step of binding my network interface card to my assigned IP address. Every network interface card in the world has a unique identifier called a *media access control (MAC)* address. Through a process know as binding, the only network card allowed to use my IP address was the card installed in my computer. In other words, the other user was permanently blocked from using my IP address.

Unfortunately, there was a major down side to this solution: A few months later I had to replace my network interface card, so I had to contact my ISP to have my IP address re-bound to my new network card.

So, if you have a static IP address, don't leave it on your computer when you sell it, and *never* reveal it to anybody. Should somebody else get hold of your IP address, you can experience the same problem I did.

Changing Your Logon Method

If you have a home network and are selling your old computer to somebody who does *not* have a home network, be nice and change the Primary Network Logon on the Network Configuration tab from Client for Microsoft Networks to Windows Logon (see Figure 4.9). This will stop the new owner from getting an annoying and meaningless network logon message whenever she boots up her computer.

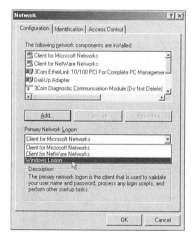

FIGURE 4.9

Changing your primary network logon to Windows Logon.

Removing Your Workgroup ID

You should perform this step only if you are getting rid of your old computer. If you have a home network, the computers on your network share a common workgroup name. This provides your computers with connectivity. To find and delete your workgroup name, right-click Network Neighborhood, click Properties, and click the Identification tab.

Step 3: Uninstall Applications

Your software licensing agreement may not permit you to have the same software application installed on two different computers (unless, of course, you have purchased a new version for your new computer). If this is the case, you should uninstall any applications for which you no longer hold a valid license.

Step 4: Delete Your Data

You've made it to the last, and in many ways most important, part of the transition process. Surprisingly, it's the aspect that most people forget, ignore, or just don't do very well, and it can come back to haunt them.

Before you sell or give your old computer away, you must remove any traces of your existence from the computer. You might think this is a simple, one-step process—and you would be wrong. As I noted in Chapter 2, simply deleting your files does not prevent somebody from recovering them.

But fear not: By the time you are finished following these instructions, nobody will be able to recover a single byte of data from your computer.

Deleting Files

The next step is to delete all your files from your computer.

Assuming you have installed CyberScrub, the disk scrubbing utility recommended in Chapter 2, you can erase these files beyond recovery as you delete them. The simplest way to do this is to right-click the Recycle Bin and select Erase Beyond Recovery.

Alternatively, you can wait until later in this section to do this, when the emphasis changes from deleting files to erasing your data beyond recovery.

Find and delete all your data files. Even if you have made a conscious effort to store all your data in one place—for example, the My Documents folder—you probably have some applications that store data in other locations. For example, my Auction Submit application stores my eBay auction data base in the `C:\Program Files\Auction Submit` folder. I have no control over where this data is stored when I use the application. So, I have to remember where it is when I want to back up the data, or in this case, when I want to delete the data. I recommend that you go through all your applications one by one to make certain you know where all the data associated with each application is stored. If the application does not give you a choice when you save data, the application is automatically determining the storage location.

Some applications also automatically store backups of your data on your hard disk. *You must find and delete the backups as well.* Usually, the backup files are stored in a different folder. For example, my Quicken files are in my `C:\QUICKENW` folder and my Quicken backup files are in my `C:\QUICKENW\BACKUP` folder. Sometimes the backups are stored in the same folder as your data, using the same filename but a different file extension, such as `.BAK`.

If you know what types of files you want to delete, you can also use Windows' search function to search for certain file types, such as .doc, .xls, .ppt, .mp3, and so on.

Deleting Email

For the sake of this discussion, I am assuming you use Outlook Express as your email application. The approach would be similar for other email programs, although you might not have to compact your mail folders (as instructed in the following) for some other email applications.

You will already have restored your email messages, accounts, and address book to your new computer, so now it is time to delete this information from your old computer.

Open Outlook Express and perform the following steps:

1. Delete all your email folders; this moves them to the Deleted Items folder.

2. Empty your Deleted Items folder. You can do this by right-clicking the folder and selecting Empty Deleted Items Folder.

3. Compact all your mail folders. Select File, Folder, Compact All Folders. This removes mail messages that have been deleted. This may come as a surprise to you, but deleting your email messages really doesn't delete them. Even emptying the Deleted Items folder doesn't delete them—it only marks them to be deleted when you compact your mail folders. Compacting your folders is what actually deletes the messages off your hard disk. (More Microsoft magic!)

4. Delete all the entries from your address book. (If you are keeping your old computer, you might want to leave some of the addresses in your address book.)

5. Delete your email accounts. Select Tools, Accounts. Then, select each account, and click Remove.

6. If you have any message rules or blocked senders, delete these as well. Select Tools, Message Rules to find and delete this information.

7. Close Outlook Express.

Deleting this information does not erase it beyond recovery. This will be taken care of when you scrub your hard disk later in this process.

Later, you will use CyberScrub to erase your deleted email messages beyond recovery. If you have not compacted your folders, CyberScrub will not erase your "deleted" email messages. As far as CyberScrub or any other application is concerned, the space occupied on your hard disk by your email messages is not free space until you have compacted your email folders.

Deleting Bookmarks

Open your Web browser and delete the bookmarks. You will also need to delete other browser-related information, such as your Web browser history file, but you will accomplish that objective in the next step. You might want to keep some of your bookmarks if you are keeping your old computer.

Step 5: Scrubbing Your Hard Disk

The last step in preparing your old computer for disposal or redeployment is to erase all your confidential data beyond recovery. This step is especially important if you are getting rid of your old computer.

As you will recall from Chapter 2, deleting files on your hard disk hides but does not actually physically erase the data. Somebody can recover that data with a data recovery utility unless a disk scrubber is used to physically erase the data from the hard disk.

I want to be absolutely clear about what you will be doing here. You will *not* be erasing the applications or operating system. That would render the computer useless to anyone who might want to purchase it. Disk scrubbers are selective erasers for hard disks. They erase the data you want erased without affecting the information you want to keep.

How Disk Scrubbers Work

Disk scrubbers erase two areas of the hard disk: *free space and slack space*. This section explains the meaning of these two terms, which you will encounter frequently in CyberScrub's user interface.

You will recall from Chapter 1 that formatting your hard disk organizes the physical sectors into logical groupings called *clusters*. This is because individual sectors are too small a unit of disk space for the Windows file system to effectively manage.

When you delete a file, the clusters that were occupied by that file become available for use. The data has been hidden, but not erased. These clusters become *free space*, meaning that Windows is "free" to overwrite the data in these clusters.

A particular cluster can contain only one file, but a file can span many clusters. The last cluster a file occupies can contain unused space at the end of the cluster, referred to as *slack space*.

It would be wrong to equate slack space with empty space—space containing no data. When Windows stores a file in a cluster, the file might not require as much space as the file that previously occupied that cluster. This can leave remnants of older files in the cluster's slack space—remnants that can be recovered with the right tool.

To be absolutely certain that you are erasing all the data you previously deleted beyond the possibility of recovery, you must scrub both the free space and slack space on your hard disk. Only a few disk scrubbers have the ability to scan your hard disk and wipe free space, and even fewer have the ability to also wipe slack space. CyberScrub wipes both free and slack space, and it wipes slack space without harming the files stored in these partially used clusters.

How Easy Is It for Someone to Recover Your Data?

It is quite easy for somebody to recover your data if it has not been erased beyond recovery. Numerous utilities are available to help you recover deleted files, and these utilities are useful if you happen to err and delete something important—something you forgot to back up. But file recovery tools are weapons in the hands of people trying to steal your valuable data.

Of course, if you are not too concerned that someone might try to recover your deleted data, you can skip this section. My paranoia meter is set on high because I keep a lot of important information on my computer.

There are two steps to scrubbing your hard disk of confidential data. CyberScrub recommends that these two steps be performed in the following order:

- **Wipe your hard disk of all traces of sensitive information that was stored on your computer *without your knowledge***—Don't be fooled into thinking that the only information on your hard disk is information you intentionally created. Your hard disk also contains information about you that is *automatically* generated by your Web browser and operating system, and this information can be every bit as valuable to people as the information you knowingly created.

- **Wipe your hard disk clean of all traces of previously deleted files**—As you already know from Chapter 2, deleting files from your computer doesn't really delete the files at all—it only gives Windows permission to write over those files in the future. Until the files are actually overwritten by CyberScrub, the deleted files can be recovered with data recovery tools.

Erasing Information That Is Stored Without Your Knowledge

Windows stores sensitive information about you on your hard disk without your knowledge. CyberScrub's Privacy Guard feature removes this sensitive information. The Privacy Guard feature erases sensitive areas related to your Web browser and the core operating system.

Web Browser Sensitive Areas

Your computer automatically stores information about your Web browsing habits. It does this to improve your Web surfing speed and to enhance your Web surfing productivity. If you do not want the next owner or user of your computer to be aware of your Web surfing habits, you should erase this information beyond recovery. CyberScrub's Privacy Guard feature protects your Internet privacy by erasing the following browser information:

- **Temporary Internet files**—These are files that are downloaded to your hard disk when you visit Web sites in order to speed up your Web surfing.

- **Web browser history**—Your Web browser creates a history file of Web sites you have visited in the past. This history makes it easier for you to find and revisit Web sites.

- **Web site addresses you have manually typed in your browser's address bar**—Whenever you manually type a Web site address in your browser's address bar, your Web browser stores the address in a list that can be displayed as a drop-down list from your address bar. (Note: This is not the same thing as your Web browser history file.)

- **AutoComplete history**—The AutoComplete feature saves you time when you are typing in a Web address or entering information on Web pages, such as when you fill out a registration form. This feature displays a list of previously matching entries when you begin to enter information in the field. For example, if you begin to type your street address, the AutoComplete feature displays a list of previously typed street addresses from which you can choose.

You can manually delete much of this information through your Web browser's user interface. However, deleting the information in this manner does not erase it beyond recovery.

This feature saves a lot of typing time, but the information stored in your AutoComplete history may be confidential.

- **Cookies**—Cookies are small files Web sites store on your computer for the purpose of personalizing your Web surfing experience. For example, I belong to the AARP (American Association of Retired People). By filling out certain information on the AARP Web site, my AARP Web surfing experience is personalized to display information about my specific areas of interest. The information about my interests is stored on my computer as a cookie. Because cookies contain personal information, you should erase them beyond recovery before disposing of your computer.

Windows Operating System Sensitive Areas

The Windows operating system might also store sensitive information on your hard disk without your knowledge. The two most critical areas are

- **The Windows swap file**—The swap file is a special file created and used by Windows to store information that exceeds the storage space available in your computer's random access memory (RAM). The information is swapped back and forth between your hard disk and RAM as it is needed. Anything, including your credit card numbers, can end up in the swap file. The contents of the swap file are deleted when you shut down your system, but they are not erased beyond recovery.

- **Temporary files**—Certain applications create temporary files on your computer. These files are supposed to be automatically deleted when you close the application, but this does not always happen. For example, if your computer crashes (does not shut down normally), some temporary files may remain on your computer. These temporary files usually begin with the tilde (~) character and have a file extension of .tmp.

Instructions for Using CyberScrub's Privacy Guard

Perform the following steps to erase all of the aforementioned information beyond recovery:

1. Make sure that all other applications are closed.

2. Open CyberScrub and click Privacy.

3. Check both of the following boxes:
   - Protect Your Computer Privacy
   - Protect Your Internet Privacy

4. Check the box to indicate which Web browser(s) you use (see Figure 4.10).

5. Click the Options button next to Protect Your Computer Privacy and make certain that all the boxes in the Windows Sensitive Areas window are checked. Click OK to return to the Privacy Guard window.

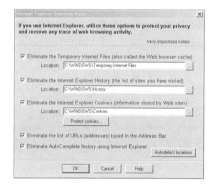

FIGURE 4.10

The Privacy Guard main window.

6. Click the Options button next to your selected Web browser(s) and make certain that all the boxes in the <Insert Browser Name> Sensitive Areas window are checked (see Figure 4.11). Also, make sure that CyberScrub knows the locations for this data. Click OK to return to the Privacy Guard window.

FIGURE 4.11

The Browser Sensitive Areas window.

There is an Autodetect Locations button in the lower-right corner of the Browser Sensitive Areas windows. If the Locations above this button are blank, clicking this button finds a path to these areas of data and fills in the location information.

If you are using the Netscape Web browser, the Autodetect feature works correctly only if Netscape Navigator was installed in the default installation directory. Otherwise, you will have to manually enter the locations of your temporary Internet files, browser history, and cookies in the Location fields.

7. From the Privacy Guard window, click Next to bring up a list called User Defined Sensitive Areas. You can use this window to manually add any other sensitive areas of your hard disk that you wish to target. You probably will not need to do this, however.

8. Click Next, and then click Start.

When the Privacy Guard feature finishes running, you will be prompted to restart your computer. This step is required to delete certain files that are locked when Windows is running, such as the Windows swap file. Privacy Guard "grabs" these files when you reboot (prior to starting Windows) and erases the information in them beyond recovery.

Instructions for Wiping Your Free Space and Slack Space

To scrub your hard disk's free space and slack space, follow these directions:

1. Close all applications before running CyberScrub—open applications can create temporary files that contain critical data. CyberScrub can't destroy the contents of temporary files if the applications are running.

2. Open CyberScrub and select Erase, Erase Options.

3. On the Actions tab, make sure that every box except Use Recycle Bin is checked (see Figure 4.12).

FIGURE 4.12

The Actions tab of the Erase Options window.

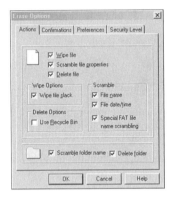

4. On the Security Level tab, check the No Buffering/Caching option. This will make CyberScrub run faster when you wipe your disk.

5. Click OK to return to the CyberScrub main window.

6. Select Erase, Erase for Good. This will display the Erase for Good window.

7. Check the following boxes:

   • Destroy All Files in the Recycle Bin Beyond Recovery

   • Eliminate the Deleted Information on the Following Drives

8. Check the appropriate drive letter(s). Remember to select every partition if your hard disk has multiple partitions.

9. Check the following settings:

   • Wipe the Free (Unused) Disk Space

   • Wipe the Slack of Existing Files (see Figure 4.13)

FIGURE 4.13

The Erase for Good window, with the proper options checked.

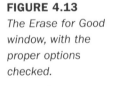

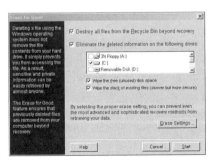

10. Click Erase Settings.

11. Select the Stop Software Recovery Tools wipe method. (See the following note regarding different wipe methods.)

12. Click OK, and then click Start to start the disk scrubbing process.

It can take several hours to scrub your hard disk, depending on which wipe method you selected and how much space needs to be erased. Do not use your system while the disk is being scrubbed.

Step 6: Celebrate

Congratulations. If you have faithfully executed this process, you have significantly reduced your chances of experiencing computer disasters, and you have provided yourself with the ability to restore your computer to its out-of-the-box state, or to its fully configured state. You get as many "do overs" as you need. Go to the head of the class!

The Stop Software Recovery Tools wipe method should be adequate for most users. This method performs 2-pass wiping. The first pass fills the wiped space with random numbers, and the second pass fills the wiped space with 0s.

You can select one of three more secure wipe methods that will prevent the recovery of your data using special hardware tools.

The DoD (Department of Defense) method performs a 7-pass wipe operation. Two other methods go beyond DoD standards: one performs 13-passes, while the other performs 35.

Be advised: The higher the security level, the longer it takes for CyberScrub to scrub your data!

Yes, it's very nice, but wouldn't a firewall have been simpler?

CHAPTER **5**

Protecting Your Computer from Cyber-Terrorists

Revelations

In this chapter you will learn

☐ How your computer can get infected or hacked, even if you are using antivirus and firewall software in the most effective manner possible

☐ Why Norton AntiVirus' Automatic LiveUpdate feature doesn't keep your virus definitions completely up-to-date and what you can do to solve the problem

☐ Why it may make more sense in some cases to restore from a recent hard disk backup than to remove a virus from your computer

☐ How restoring your system from a hard disk backup or using the Windows' System Restore feature can leave your computer more vulnerable to viruses—and what you can do to fix the problem

☐ Why virus hoaxes are even more dangerous than computer viruses

☐ How your data can be hacked even if your computer has not been breached

☐ How to prevent your computer from being hacked from outside your house

Overview

This chapter provides detailed instructions on how to protect your computer from *cyber-terrorists*—my term for virus developers and hackers. It explains how to configure and use (in that order) two of the tools recommended in Chapter 2, "The Threats and the Tools"—Norton AntiVirus (NAV) and ZoneAlarm. It also reveals why these tools are just a first line of defense, and not a panacea for viruses and hackers. You will learn how you can still get infected even if you are using these tools properly, and you will find important information on how to minimize your risk.

This chapter also discusses a new threat on the horizon—spyware—that might prove to be a future weapon for cyber-terrorists.

Because the term *Norton AntiVirus* is used so often in this chapter, I have chosen to use the abbreviation NAV from this point forward.

If you are already an experienced user of NAV, you might be thinking of skipping or skimming the portion of this chapter that discusses this product. I urge you *not* to do so! I share some very important information with you about NAV that is *not* common knowledge—information you need to know to maximize your protection against viruses.

I know many people have the misconception that either they are not vulnerable to viruses or that all they need do to eliminate their vulnerability is install antivirus software. I wish it were that simple, but it's not. To adequately protect yourself against viruses, you must do all of the following:

- Install NAV.
- Configure NAV to afford maximum protection against viruses.
- Use NAV properly. While some functions are automated, there are still some things you must do manually on an ongoing basis to achieve maximum protection against viruses.
- Work around restrictions in Windows that prevent NAV from fixing certain problems.
- Work around vulnerabilities that can be engendered by a disaster recovery.
- Implement procedures to protect your computer against new viruses and to protect your computer when you need to temporarily disable your antivirus software.
- Make changes to other programs you have installed on your computer to maximize protection against viruses.
- Know how to avoid being a victim of a virus hoax.
- Know how to safely remove viruses from your computer in the event that all your precautions have failed to stop an infection.

This chapter shows you how to do all these things and more. And I promise that you will emerge with a new-found awareness of how vulnerable you are and a new-found confidence in your ability to address these vulnerabilities.

Viruses: The Number One Computer Killer

I don't believe there are any official statistics that rank the causes of computer disasters, but I think it is reasonable to assume that viruses are the leading cause of such disasters. Computer viruses can be so destructive that even finding and removing a virus from your computer might not solve your problem if the virus has already delivered a deadly payload. For example, if a virus wipes out critical files on your computer, you might have no choice but to go into disaster recovery mode.

Sadly, I have observed that the same people who tend *not* to protect themselves adequately against viruses also tend not to have any disaster recovery capability, as illustrated by the following story:

> I recently received a call from a friend who works in a small business office. One of her company's computers had become infected with a virus because they were using an old version of NAV that required them to manually run Norton's LiveUpdate to update their virus definitions. They had forgotten to do so for a couple of days, so their virus definitions were out-of-date. A new, virulent virus was running rampant on the Web (the Klez worm) and they were unprotected, so they got infected.
>
> Not surprisingly, they had no backup of their hard disk. They didn't even have a data backup. The virus caused so much damage that they had to reformat their hard disk and manually reload their operating system, drivers, and applications—a task that required several days of effort.
>
> And here's the kicker: *They never completely recovered from the problem!* To this day, they are still getting error messages on their computer when they perform certain tasks—the result of a less-than-completely successful reinstallation. And they never were able to recover their lost data.

So, it is this combination of deadly sins—lack of adequate protection against viruses and lack of a disaster recovery plan—that creates the most common problem of all: the colossal nonrecoverable computer disaster.

How Vulnerable Are You?

Although your computer can get infected in a number of ways (see Chapter 2), the most common source of virus infections today is email. Generally speaking, the more you use the Internet, the more exposed you are to viruses. I operate two Web sites, and my columns have been syndicated on several other Web sites. Hence, my name is very much "out there" in cyberspace. On average, my NAV detects a few virus attacks per day in incoming email messages. During major virus outbreaks, it has detected dozens of virus attacks in a single day. Just recently, I received a dozen infected email messages *at the same time!* And as I write these words, my NAV has already detected three virus attacks today. And it's only 11:30 a.m. on a Sunday morning, a light day for email!

My exposure is certainly much higher than average, but regardless of your relative exposure, the risk of *not* using antivirus software is simply not worth taking. The cost of even one virus infection is so great that all computer users should take maximum measures to protect themselves from computer viruses!

Antivirus Software: Your First Line of Defense

Antivirus software is your first line of defense against virus-related computer disasters. NAV is the most popular antivirus software program on the market and the product that is preinstalled by many PC manufacturers. I think most home users will appreciate NAV's easy-to-understand user interface and the fact that the latest version of the product requires less manual effort to install and configure than previous versions. I also like the fact that NAV has layers of redundancy built into its antivirus protection. If one layer fails to detect a virus, the chances are excellent that another layer will stop the virus from infecting your computer. I also get a lot of value from the support and security response sections of Symantec's Web site.

NAV is not a perfect product, but then, every antivirus software product has its strengths and weaknesses. The important thing is to be aware of the product's shortcomings and understand how to work around them. This chapter provides that information.

Although I make some references and comparisons to earlier versions of NAV, most of this discussion focuses on the latest version of the program, which as of this writing is Norton AntiVirus 2002.

If you have not yet upgraded your software to NAV 2002, here are three compelling reasons you should do so immediately:

- **It automatically updates your virus definitions**—If you are still using NAV 2000, or heaven forbid an even older version of the product, you are at serious risk of becoming infected because these earlier versions do not have the ability to automatically update your virus definitions. With these older versions, it is incumbent upon *you* to take action to update your virus definitions. If you fail to do so, you are at great risk of getting infected. Fortunately, the newer versions of NAV, from 2001 on, provide the ability to automatically update your virus definitions when you are connected to the Internet. The weakest link in the chain—*yourself*—is more removed (but not completely removed) from the disaster prevention process.

- **It automatically scans your incoming email**—In previous releases of NAV, you had to manually configure the software to scan your incoming email. With the latest version, email scanning is automatically enabled. (If you are still using an older version of NAV, I show you how to configure it to scan your email later in this chapter, in the section "How to Activate Email Scanning in Earlier Versions of Norton AntiVirus.")

- **It automatically scans your outgoing email**—In addition to scanning your incoming email, NAV 2002 incorporates a new feature that scans your outgoing email for viruses. Should your computer become infected, this feature can stop you from inadvertently spreading the virus to others.

Additionally, you will need NAV 2002 if you have Windows XP on your machine because previous versions of the product are not compatible with Windows XP. (In point of fact, patches are available to upgrade NAV 2001 for Windows XP compatibility, but I recommend against this approach.)

You should uninstall your older version of NAV before installing NAV 2002.

Why You Should Scan Your Outgoing Email

Although having antivirus software significantly reduces the chances of a virus infection, there are still ways your computer can get infected. For one thing, your machine might have already been infected *before* you installed NAV. You can also become infected with a new virus that spreads rapidly, before Symantec is able to update its virus definitions to protect you. Once your virus definitions *have* been updated to recognize the virus, the virus won't be able to leave your computer.

In addition to sparing you much embarrassment, scanning your outgoing email provides another benefit: awareness of infection. If outbound email scanning detects a virus, this might be the first indication you receive that your computer is infected. You can then take the appropriate steps to remove the virus from your computer.

Configuring Norton AntiVirus 2002

NAV provides numerous configuration options that determine the level of protection NAV provides and the actions NAV takes when a virus is detected. This section assumes that you've been able to install NAV properly and instead focuses on explaining these configuration options. In some cases, I recommend specific changes to the default settings for these options, either to afford a higher level of virus protection or to cause a different action to be taken when a virus is detected.

System Options

NAV groups its configuration options into three main categories: system, Internet, and other. The system options control the features that work within the boundaries of your system—that is, features that do not access the Internet directly. This section discusses how to set the system options.

Auto-Protect Options

Open up your NAV user interface, either by double-clicking the icon on your taskbar or by selecting Start, All Programs, Norton AntiVirus 2002. Click the Options button to open the Options window. The first window is the Auto-Protect options box (see Figure 5.1).

FIGURE 5.1
*NAV 2002 auto-protect
options.*

Given that antivirus
software is constantly
scanning files, it is reasonable to wonder
whether antivirus soft-
ware impacts system
performance. The
answer is yes, and the
reality is that it is a
price we must pay for
living in an unsafe world.

This screen is divided into three sections. The first section, How to Stay Protected,
allows you to define your auto-protection options. All three boxes in this section
should be checked.

When Auto-Protect is enabled, NAV protects your computer against viruses. Auto-
Protect automatically scans any file received from any source, including files you
download from the Internet. It also scans any file anytime it is accessed for any reason, whether you are trying to run a program file, open a file, or move or copy a file.

The only time you should ever disable Auto-Protect is when you are installing a new
program because NAV can interfere with the installation process.

The second box tells Windows to automatically start Auto-Protect whenever you boot
up your computer. You should uncheck this box only if you are going to be rebooting
your computer several times while you install new applications—for example, when
you are putting a new computer into service (see Chapter 4, "A Disaster Prevention
Plan for Your New Computer: Part 2, Before You Try").

Beware Your Internet Connection

If you need to disable Auto-Protect to install a new application, you should
disconnect from the Internet first. If you have an always-on broadband connection, you can do this two ways. The first way is to physically disconnect
your computer from the Internet. For example, if you have a wired connection,
you can unplug your cable from your network card.

The second way is to use ZoneAlarm's Internet lock feature to block all access
to the Internet. (ZoneAlarm is discussed later in this chapter.) However, if you
are going to be rebooting your computer while NAV is disabled, the best
approach is to physically disconnect your computer from the Internet, as
ZoneAlarm is automatically reset to *allow* Internet activity each time you reboot.

Always remember to reenable Auto-Protect immediately after installing a program and before you reconnect to the Internet!

The third box causes the NAV icon to be displayed on your computer's taskbar. You can double-click this icon, rather than go through the Start menu, to open NAV. You can also disable Auto-Protect by right-clicking the icon and selecting Disable Auto-Protect. You can reenable Auto-Protect the same way.

The second section of the Auto-Protect screen allows you to tell NAV how to respond when a virus is found. The installation default is Automatically Repair the Infected File. I recommend changing your setting to the second choice, Try to Repair and Then Quarantine if Unsuccessful because this moves the file to a separate area of your hard disk from which it can be safely deleted.

The third section of the screen allows you to customize Auto-Protect so that only files with specified file extensions are scanned. Leave this on the comprehensive setting. Putting limits on Auto-Protect leaves you at great risk. In fact, I would prefer that this particular option be removed from NAV.

If you click the small arrow next to Auto-Protect, you will see links to two other windows, Bloodhound and Advanced Settings.

Auto-Protect Options: Bloodhound

The Bloodhound setting enables NAV to monitor suspicious activity that might represent a new and unknown virus. Leave this at its default setting. If you increase the setting to the highest level of protection (there are three levels), you may receive false positives, that is, warnings about activities that are not virus threats.

Auto-Protect Options: Advanced

This screen is divided into two sections.

In the first section, What Activities to Monitor for Virus-Like Behaviors, I recommend changing the default values for Low Level Format of Hard Disks and Writes to Hard Disks Boot Record from Ask Me What to Do to Stop the Action (see Figure 5.2).

If you have installed NAV 2002 on a Windows XP system, the advanced options will appear different to you. The first section, What Activities to Monitor for Virus-Like Behaviors, will not be present, and the second section will have only two options. Symantec states that the NAV Bloodhound feature provides this functionality in Windows XP systems. The explanation does not make sense to me, but that is the explanation provided.

FIGURE 5.2
NAV Advanced Auto-Protect options.

Low-level formatting was discussed in Chapter 1, "The Root of All Computer Disasters." You should never have to low-level format your disk, and if NAV detects that such an attempt is being made, this is a sure indication of a virus infection.

The only time you should be writing to the hard disk boot record is if you are format-ting your hard disk with the FORMAT command. As I indicated in Chapter 1, the *PC Fear Factor* approach to disaster recovery eliminates the need for you to ever have to format your hard disk. If NAV detects an attempt to write to your hard disk's boot record, it is a likely indication of a virus.

Leave the Writes to Floppy Disks Boot Record setting at Allow Action because this enables you to format floppy disks.

In the second section of the Advanced Options screen, you should keep the default settings. These settings check your floppy disks for viruses when you are booting up or shutting down your computer, which prevents you from getting viruses from infected media.

You might be tempted to set the script blocking option to Stop All Suspicious Activities and Do Not Prompt Me. I strongly advise you *not* to do this. The problem with this setting is that if NAV blocks a legitimate script from running, you will never know it—you might suspect that there is a bug in your applica-tion when in fact NAV is preventing the applica-tion from running!

Script Blocking Options

A *script* is a small computer program that can be embedded in email attachments and Web pages. Scripts are often written in the Visual Basic programming language. Visual Basic scripts carry the file extension .vbs.

Visual Basic scripts are easy to write and can be run automatically when embedded in Web pages, without your knowledge or permission, which makes them a favorite tool for virus writers. Many worms and Trojan horses are Visual Basic scripts attached to email messages. The infamous Anna Kournikova worm is a Visual Basic script.

NAV 2001 and 2002 have the capability to automatically block unknown, suspicious scripts from running on your machine (see Figure 5.3).

FIGURE 5.3
NAV 2002 Script Blocking options.

If you have the script blocking option enabled (the recommended setting) and your computer attempts to execute a suspicious script, NAV will alert you and ask you what to do. The recommended action is Stop This Script, and unless you are certain that the script is legitimate, you should err on the side of caution and accept this recommendation (see Figure 5.4).

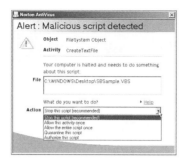

FIGURE 5.4
*NAV 2002 detects a
possible malicious
Visual Basic script and
prompts you for a
response.*

Because many scripts are legitimate, NAV includes a list of exclusions—known legitimate scripts in legitimate computer programs. In addition to updating virus definitions, Norton frequently updates the list of excluded scripts so that your computer will be able to run popular applications without mistaken intervention from NAV.

If you would like to test the script blocking feature to see how NAV responds, Symantec provides a sample pseudo-malicious Visual Basic script on its Web site. You can download the file and double-click it to see NAV's script blocking feature in action. The location for the test script, along with instructions for performing the test, is

http://service4.symantec.com/SUPPORT/nav.nsf/396b6ccde72d4a4d882569fc006071d4/
➡049f1b2057b8d88085256a3900652a0e?OpenDocument

Don't worry—you can't harm your computer even if you chose the wrong option and allow this test script to run.

For a complete and up-to-date list of links mentioned in this book, go to http:// www.alanluber.com/ pcfearfactor/links .htm. This will eliminate the need for you to manually key these links into your Web browser.

Manual Scan Options

The term *manual scan* refers to a virus scan that *you* initiate from the NAV program. The term *manual* is a bit misleading. The scan doesn't require manual effort—you just initiate it manually. You may instruct NAV to scan your entire computer or specific folders and files on your computer. You can also schedule a manual scan to be performed automatically using the Windows Task Scheduler (a seeming contradiction of terms that secretly delights me).

The Manual Scan options tell NAV how to behave when you initiate a virus scan. The Manual Scan options screen is divided into three sections. Leave all three items checked in the first section (What Items to Scan in Addition to Files) to afford maximum virus detection capability (see Figure 5.5).

The default How to Respond When a Virus Is Found setting is Automatically Repair the Infected File. I recommend changing this setting to the third choice, Try to Repair Then Quarantine if Unsuccessful because this automatically moves the file to a separate area of your hard disk from which it can be safely deleted.

The third section of the screen allows you to customize the manual scan so that only files with specified file extensions are scanned. Leave this on the comprehensive setting and scan within compressed files as well. I can't think of a reason to limit the scan to certain types of files or to exclude compressed files.

If you have installed NAV 2002 on a Windows XP system, this window will appear different to you. In the first section, the memory scan option will not be present. I have been unable to find out from Symantec the reason for this difference. There are two possibilities: Either Windows XP renders this option obsolete, or Windows XP prevents Symantec from providing this functionality anymore.

FIGURE 5.5
*NAV 2002 Manual
Scan options.*

For background informa-
tion on the System
Restore feature included
with Windows Millennium
and Windows XP, refer to
Chapter 4 or Appendix
A, "The System Restore
Feature."

If you are using Windows
Millennium and NAV
2000, the C:_RESTORE
folder is *not* automati-
cally excluded from the
virus scan.

If your computer was
infected with a virus at
the time a restore point
was created, the virus
can get into the system
restore folder.

Leave the Manual Scan and Bloodhound settings at the default levels, just as you
did for Auto-Protect.

Exclusions

The Exclusions option is a way to exclude certain file types from the manual scan. I
recommend that you do *not* exclude any files from scanning and that you remove
any default exclusions that are set by NAV.

While we are on the subject of exclusions, this seems like the most appropriate
place to discuss the behavior of antivirus software and Microsoft's System Restore
feature.

(If you are currently using Windows 9x or 2000, which don't have System Restore,
you can skip ahead to the "Internet Options" section.)

If you are using Windows Millennium or Windows XP, you might have noticed that NAV
by default excludes the folder that contains all the files associated with your system
restore points. In Windows Millennium, this is the C:_RESTORE folder (see Figure
5.6). In Windows XP, this is the C:\system volume information folder. For the
sake of brevity, I will refer to both of these locations as the system restore folder.

FIGURE 5.6
*NAV 2002 is automati-
cally excluding the
system restore folder
from virus scans on
this Windows
Millennium system.*

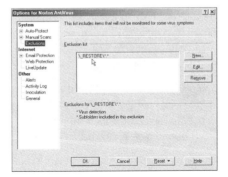

NAV excludes the system restore folder from virus scans because antivirus software programs are unable to repair, quarantine, or delete infected files in this folder. This is because Windows prevents other applications from modifying this folder to protect the integrity of these files.

NAV can scan the system restore folder and detect a virus infection—it just can't do anything to fix the problem.

Nevertheless, I recommend that you remove the _RESTORE or \system volume information folder from the exclusion list and scan it for viruses. Although NAV can't repair, quarantine, or delete the infected files, there are three ways to work around this conundrum and eliminate any virus found in the system restore folder. These three methods are explained later in this chapter in the section "Removing Viruses from Your Computer."

Internet Options

The NAV Internet options control features that involve the use of the Internet, such as the option to automatically update virus definitions. This section explains how to configure these options.

Email Options

NAV scans your incoming email for viruses as you download it from your Internet service provider. The newest version of NAV also scans your outgoing email for viruses.

NAV works with most email applications, including Microsoft Outlook, Microsoft Outlook Express, Eudora, Netscape Messenger, and Pegasus Mail. NAV does *not* work with AOL mail or other Web-based mail applications because these messages reside on a remote server and are not downloaded to your computer unless you choose to have them forwarded. AOL, Hotmail, and Yahoo! Mail provide their own virus scanning capabilities.

AOL, Hotmail, and Yahoo! Mail scan email attachments for viruses before you download them. If you download the attachment to your computer, NAV also scans the attachment for viruses, giving you a redundant layer of virus protection.

Email Scanning: Your Perimeter Defense

According to Symantec, even if you have email scanning disabled, NAV's Auto-Protect feature still protects against viruses should you attempt to open an infected email attachment. For obvious reasons, I have never tested this.

So in a sense, inbound email scanning is redundant with the Auto-Protect feature. However, you should leave email scanning enabled because it is always better to turn the enemy away at the perimeter than to allow him inside the compound.

Having said that, there have been cases where viruses have made it through the outer defense perimeter. Some virus writers have found ways to disguise viruses to go undetected by email virus scanning. In such cases, the Auto-Protect feature usually catches viruses that make it through this outer defense perimeter.

The Email Scanning options screen shown in Figure 5.7 is divided into three sections. The first section tells NAV what to scan. Leave both boxes checked to scan both incoming and outgoing email for viruses.

FIGURE 5.7

The NAV Email Scanning options screen.

I hope that the next version of NAV gives you the option of deleting the file *and* the email message. This would save you the hassle of manually deleting the message from your inbox.

If you try to send email while Norton is still scanning a previous outbound transmission for viruses, you might receive an error message. This typically happens when you have previously sent an email message that has a large attachment that takes a long time to scan. You might have to wait until NAV has finished scanning your previous transmission before you can send additional messages. If you leave the outbound scanning progress indicator turned on, you will know when the scanning operation is complete.

The default setting for the How to Respond When a Virus Is Found section is Automatically Repair the Infected File. This setting is fine, but the description is a little misleading because it doesn't fully describe what the software does when a virus is detected. If the virus can't be repaired, the user is offered the choice of quarantining the file in a special area or deleting the file. I recommend deleting the file—you will only end up deleting it later from the quarantine area.

I strongly recommend *against* using either of the following two email scanning options:

- Repair Then Silently Quarantine if Unsuccessful
- Repair Then Silently Delete if Unsuccessful

I advise against these options because Norton acts silently to quarantine or delete the virus without notifying you, *but it leaves the email message that bore the virus in your inbox.* Because you haven't a clue as to what the message is, you might open it by mistake. Although this is unlikely to do you harm, it exposes you to unnecessary risk in my opinion. By choosing the email scanning option that forces NAV to involve you in the decision-making process, you become aware that there is an email in your inbox that bore a virus, and you know to check your inbox and delete the email.

The third section of this screen tells NAV what to do when scanning email messages. For example, when you send email, NAV 2002 can display a progress indicator as your outgoing messages are being scanned for viruses. These settings are enabled by default and should be left enabled.

LiveUpdate Options

The LiveUpdate options control whether NAV automatically updates your virus definitions file when you are connected to the Internet. Automatic LiveUpdate is enabled by default, and you should *never* disable this feature, as doing so would require you to remember to manually run the LiveUpdate feature to update your virus definitions. Select the Apply Updates Without Interrupting Me option. If you happen to be in front of the computer when updates are applied, you will see a little box (about 2'' square) pop up in the lower-right corner of your screen for about 10 seconds, telling you that your virus definitions have been automatically updated.

As it's a little complicated, allow me to explain how LiveUpdate works. When you install NAV, it automatically sets up a task on the Windows Task Scheduler.

The Windows Task Scheduler is a feature of Windows that enables you to schedule tasks to be run automatically at scheduled intervals. The Task Scheduler starts automatically each time you boot up your computer. It shows in the lower-right corner of your taskbar and has an icon that looks like a calendar and a clock. If you double-click the Task Scheduler, the scheduled tasks are displayed (see Figure 5.8). The task labeled Symantec NetDetect checks for live virus definition updates. If you double-click the task and select the Schedule tab, you will see how often it is set to run. In this example, it checks for live updates every 5 minutes.

Never pause the Task Scheduler or change your system's configuration to stop it from loading when you boot up your computer. Doing so prevents LiveUpdate from updating your virus definitions, putting you at great risk of a virus infection.

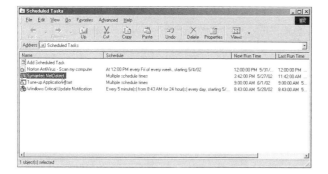

FIGURE 5.8
The Task Scheduler schedules NAV to check for live updates every 5 minutes whenever you are connected to the Internet.

Other Options

Within NAV, the Other Options category is a kind of a catch-all for all other program options not covered under System Options or Internet Options. The following sections address the options found here.

Activity Log Options

NAV keeps a log file of activities it performs. The activity log options determine what information gets written to the log file. Leave all these options at their installed default values.

Inoculation Options

The inoculation options in NAV refer to your computer's *master boot record*—a small program that is executed when you boot up your computer. The master boot record resides on the first sector of your hard disk and tells your computer how to access your hard disk so that it can boot up your computer.

You will probably never need to use the log file, but it is a good idea to keep a historical record of everything NAV does, especially since the log file takes up only 50KB of space on your computer. When the file reaches its size limit, NAV automatically deletes the earliest log file entries to make room for new entries.

A master boot record virus (also called a *boot sector virus*) replaces the master boot record with malicious code. When the computer is booted up, the virus is placed in memory where it can take over control of your computer.

The term *inoculation*, as used to describe these options, is somewhat misleading. NAV is not really inoculating your master boot record against viruses. It records information about the master boot record, and when you perform a virus scan, it compares the master boot record to the information it has recorded. If there is a difference, Norton knows that something has changed the master boot record and gives you the option of restoring your record.

I recommend that you leave NAV at the default settings.

If something changes your master boot record, NAV will notify you and give you two options:

- Update the Saved Copy of My Master Boot Record
- Restore My Master Boot Record

Very few legitimate activities cause your master boot record to change. If you were to upgrade your operating system or repartition your hard disk, your boot record might legitimately change. But most home users—most readers of this book—would not attempt to do such things. My master boot record *never* changes.

There is one other category of options, called Advanced Tools, that really has nothing to do with antivirus protection. My understanding from Symantec is that you only see this option if you have NAV Professional Edition installed. These options have to do with the ability to recover files you have deleted from your recycle bin. This is a useful functionality but not germane to a discussion about virus protection.

Thus, if something has changed your master boot record, it is most likely a virus. Unless you have strong reason to believe that your master boot record has changed for some legitimate reason, the correct option to select is Restore My Master Boot Record. If you know for a fact that the perceived "problem" with your master boot record is not a virus, you can choose to update Norton's "recording" of your master boot record. This is, of course, an *extremely* dangerous option to choose should you be wrong.

Miscellaneous Options

Leave these miscellaneous options at their default values.

One of these options, Enable Office Plug-In, is of particular importance as it adds a layer of protection on top of email scanning and the Auto-Protect feature. Briefly, this plug-in prevents virus writers from fooling Microsoft Office into opening infected documents.

When NAV 2002 is installed, two file types (file extensions .nch and .dbx) are excluded from scanning by default. If you followed my earlier advice and removed these extensions from the default exclusion list, you have nothing to worry about. However, if you left these files on the exclusion list, a virus writer could send you an infected office document, disguised with a file extension of .nch or .dbx. Double-clicking these disguised files automatically executes the infected document. The Office Plug-In feature is designed to detect infected documents that have bypassed email scanning and Auto-Protect.

How to Use Norton AntiVirus

For the most part, NAV functions automatically and unobtrusively in the background.

The Windows Task Scheduler launches a weekly scan of your computer and works with the Automatic LiveUpdate feature to update your virus definitions.

The Auto-Protect and email scanning features work together to automatically scan

- Incoming and outgoing email
- Files you download from the Internet
- Any file you access for any reason
- Media you insert into your computer

When a virus is detected, NAV takes the appropriate action based on the configuration options you have set. In most cases, a window is displayed and you are prompted to make a decision regarding the disposition of the infected file (see Figure 5.9).

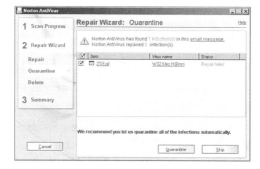

FIGURE 5.9
NAV has detected a virus in an email attachment.

However, there are a number of tasks you must perform manually to maximize your protection against viruses. Specifically, you must

- Work around two significant limitations of the Automatic LiveUpdate feature.
- Configure the Windows Task Scheduler to perform a weekly full system scan at a time when your computer will be on.
- Delete infected files from the quarantine area of your hard disk.
- Manually configure email scanning if you are using an older version of NAV.
- Remove viruses from your system should your computer become infected in spite of your best efforts.

Working Around Norton AntiVirus Automatic LiveUpdate Limitations

Based on conversations I have had with many NAV users, I am convinced that most users have two very important misconceptions regarding the Automatic LiveUpdate feature. Actually, these are not so much misconceptions as logical but false assumptions—assumptions that leave you vulnerable to infection. This section explains these false assumptions and recommends specific actions you can take to maximize your protection against computer viruses.

Automatic LiveUpdate Is Often Out-of-Date

The first false assumption is that NAV's Automatic LiveUpdate feature keeps your virus definitions *completely* up-to-date. This seems like a reasonable assumption to make. I mean, why would Symantec provide an Automatic LiveUpdate function if it didn't keep your virus definitions completely up-to-date?

While a logical assumption, it's still a fallacious one. The Automatic LiveUpdate feature automatically updates your virus definitions but does *not* keep your virus definitions completely up-to-date. There *is* a difference.

Symantec develops new virus definitions daily but generally updates its software with the latest virus definitions only once a week, usually on Wednesday. So, if Symantec develops protection for a new virus on Thursday, you might not receive the update via Automatic LiveUpdate until the following Wednesday.

There is an exception. If there is a major virus outbreak between weekly updates, Symantec releases interim updates, so you might notice your virus definitions being updated more than once a week by the Automatic LiveUpdate feature. But, for the most part, Symantec accumulates new virus definitions between weekly updates and aggregates them for delivery to you in the next weekly update.

It is important to note that you will not get these daily updates *even if you manually run the LiveUpdate feature between weekly updates*. If you manually run LiveUpdate, Symantec tells you that the "products that are currently installed on your computer are up to date," when in fact that may not be true—there may be virus definitions that are being held back for the next weekly update.

Fortunately, there is a way for you to get the daily updates without having to wait for your weekly automatic update. If you want the daily virus definition updates, you must use Symantec's Intelligent Updater, which allows you to manually download and install the absolute latest virus definition updates.

To use the Intelligent Updater, go to `http://securityresponse.symantec.com/avcenter/defs.download.html`.

When you navigate to this link, you will see information about Intelligent Updater and LiveUpdate (see Figure 5.10).

If the total viruses detected by Intelligent Updater are greater than the total viruses detected by LiveUpdate, there have been virus definition updates since the last Automatic LiveUpdate.

Note the date on the Intelligent Updater file. If you have not already downloaded this file, you should download and install it if you want the most up-to-date virus definitions.

Now you probably realize that I chose my words very carefully earlier in this chapter when I advised you to purchase the latest version of NAV because "it automatically updates your virus definitions."

I don't really understand why Symantec calls this the "Intelligent Updater." The user has to manually download a file and then execute the file to install it. Where is the intelligence in Intelligent Updater?

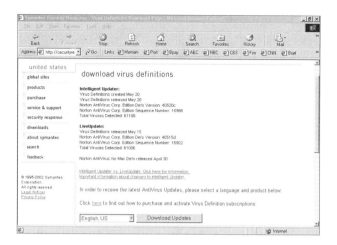

FIGURE 5.10

Symantec's Intelligent Updater allows you to download and install the latest virus definition updates. Note the 5-day difference between the LiveUpdate virus definitions and the Intelligent Updater virus definitions. Note also that the Intelligent Updater protects against an additional 22 viruses.

By now you're probably wondering, "Why doesn't Symantec include the latest virus definitions in Automatic LiveUpdate?" I really don't know. Symantec's explanation for this approach is that the virus definitions that are held back for the next weekly update are "low-risk" viruses. That doesn't really explain *why* it uses this approach— it just explains that you are at minimum risk if you choose *not* to use Intelligent Updater.

Let's examine the minimum risk assertion with regard to one such virus, W32.Benjamin.Worm, a worm that eats up your free disk space. The Benjamin worm is disguised as a popular music, movie, or software file on KaZaA, the heir apparent to Napster. Users of this popular file sharing service are fooled into downloading the worm. This worm was detected on May 18, 2002, and protection was available through Symantec's Intelligent Updater on May 20, 2002. However, the Automatic LiveUpdate feature did not provide protection against this virus until two days later, on May 22, 2002.

Was this a low-risk virus? The answer is yes for people who don't use KaZaA. But KaZaA users were at significant risk for two additional days if they did not manually update their virus definitions using Symantec's Intelligent Updater.

So, I think Symantec's statement that these viruses are "low risk" is, in some cases, a conditional claim. If a virus is indigenous to a specific application that you use, I would argue that you might be at high risk by waiting several days to receive the virus definition update. I also think the premise of "low risk" is fundamentally flawed, given the speed at which viruses can spread across the Internet.

The choice is yours. You can wait for the weekly Automatic LiveUpdate, or you can check the Intelligent Updater every day. It only takes a couple of minutes to use Intelligent Updater, so I choose to keep my virus definitions completely up-to-date. I recommend that you do so also. I think it's only a matter of time before I hear from someone who got infected because he did *not* use the Intelligent Updater.

Automatic LiveUpdate Does Not Apply Program Updates

The second false assumption regarding the Automatic LiveUpdate feature is that it updates your NAV program as well as your virus definitions. Those of you who have used older versions of NAV will recall that the manual LiveUpdate process occasionally downloads program updates as well as virus definition updates. These program updates fix bugs or provide additional features. It would be logical to assume that the Automatic LiveUpdate function also downloads both program and virus definition updates. Logical, but incorrect.

The Automatic LiveUpdate feature does *not* download and install program updates—it only gets the virus definition updates. You still need to manually run LiveUpdate from the NAV program screen to get the latest updates to the core program, and I recommend that you manually run LiveUpdate once or twice a week for this purpose.

Never Skip an Update!

It is very important that you get these program updates because they sometimes fix problems that allow viruses to go *undetected*. For example, in March, 2002, Edvice Security Services (`http://www.edvicesecurity.com/`), an information security testing company, discovered four ways for virus developers to bypass NAV 2002's email scanning feature. Symantec's response to this issue was that there was sufficient redundancy built into NAV to detect the infected files, but Symantec nevertheless responded with program updates that addressed these issues.

Wondering if your computer is infected? See "How Do I Know If I Have a Virus?" in Chapter 2.

I know that it might seem silly to go to these lengths to minimize your risk. I hope that the next version of NAV does *everything* through Automatic LiveUpdate so you do not have to manually run LiveUpdate and Intelligent Updater to maximize your protection.

Performing a Manual Scan of Your Hard Disk

I recommend that you perform a weekly virus scan of your computer to make sure nothing has slipped through email scanning and Auto-Protect. You should also perform a manual scan whenever you have reason to suspect that your computer may have become infected.

Run a manual scan of your computer immediately after installing NAV on any machine to verify that the computer is virus free.

To initiate a manual scan, open the application and click Scan for Viruses. Double-click Scan My Computer to start the scan.

I strongly recommend that you schedule an automatic weekly scan of your hard disk using the Windows Task Scheduler. When you install NAV, it automatically sets up a weekly scan on the Windows Task Scheduler, to be performed at 8 p.m. every Friday. Of course, this scan is performed only if your computer is on at that time. You might wish to change the schedule to a time when your computer is more likely to be running, and a time when you are not likely to be using it. For example, I schedule my weekly scan to run during my lunch hour. Perform the following steps to change the weekly virus scan schedule:

1. Double-click the Task Scheduler to open the window.

2. Double-click the Norton AntiVirus—Scan My Computer task to open the scheduling window for this task.

3. Click the Schedule tab and set the appropriate time and day for your weekly scan (see Figure 5.11).

FIGURE 5.11

Changing the schedule for your weekly computer virus scan.

Deleting Items from Quarantine

NAV can detect viruses three ways: by email scanning, by the auto-protect feature, or by a manual scan of your computer. If a virus is detected by auto-protect or a manual scan, Norton automatically places the infected file in a special area of your hard disk known as the quarantine area. I strongly recommend that you delete these files from the quarantine area as soon as possible. To delete a quarantined file(s), perform the following steps:

1. Open NAV.

2. Click Reports.

3. Click the View Report button next to Quarantined Items.

4. Select the files you want to remove and click the Delete Item button (see Figure 5.12). (If there are several files, you will need to hold down the Ctrl key while clicking to select multiple files.)

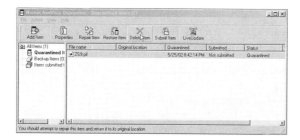

FIGURE 5.12

Deleting infected, quarantined files.

How to Activate Email Scanning in Earlier Versions of Norton AntiVirus

Email scanning is automatically activated when you install NAV 2002. If you are using an earlier version of NAV, you have to manually configure the software to activate email scanning. To activate email scanning in NAV 2000 or 2001, perform the following steps:

1. Open NAV.
2. Click Options.
3. Click Email Protection.
4. Check the boxes corresponding to each email account on the computer.

Removing Viruses from Your Computer

In spite of your best efforts, your computer can still get infected with a virus. For example, a new virus might spread rapidly and infect your computer before your virus definitions have been updated to provide protection.

Removing a virus from your computer is tricky business. Let me begin by noting that it is not always possible or even worthwhile to remove a virus from your computer. If the virus has done substantial damage to your system—for example, if it has deleted hundreds of key files from your system—the best solution is to restore your hard disk from your most recent backup (see Chapter 8, "Disaster Recovery").

If your computer becomes infected with a virus, I recommend that you gain access to the Internet through another, uninfected machine to identify the virus and get instructions or tools to remove the virus from the infected machine. I advise against using your infected machine for these tasks because the removal tool itself can become infected with the virus.

If you have a home network, physically remove the infected machine from the network to isolate the virus from other machines on the network. Run a full scan of your other computers to make sure they have not also been infected.

Once you have isolated your computer and gained access to the Internet from an uninfected computer, the next step is to identify the virus. If you can't determine this from the name of an email attachment that contains the virus, go to Symantec's security response Web page at http://securityresponse.symantec.com/.

This page discusses the latest virus threats and provides descriptions that can help you identify the virus that has infected your computer.

Once you have identified the virus, you need to read about the virus on Symantec's security response page to understand what it might have done to your computer. If the damage appears to be repairable, you need to find out how to remove it from your computer. Symantec's security response Web page provides detailed instructions for removing a specific virus from your system. Symantec's Web page also has automated virus removal tools for some of the more widespread viruses.

Symantec even provides excellent, detailed video and audio instructions for down-loading and running some of these automated removal tools.

If you download a removal tool, you will need to transfer it to the infected machine by copying it to the appropriate form of portable media (floppy disk, CD, or Zip disk).

In some cases, you are instructed to boot your system in safe mode before you follow the instructions to remove a virus.

Losing System Restore Data

If you are using Windows Millennium or XP, you might be instructed in some cases to disable the System Restore function before you remove a virus. Unfortunately, this wipes out all the previously created restore points.

Once the virus has been successfully removed, you must remember to reenable the System Restore function; otherwise, your system will no longer create restore points, leaving you more vulnerable to computer disasters in the future.

You might have to perform a substantial amount of work to remove a virus, even if an automated tool is available. For example, because some viruses corrupt your antivirus software, you may have to uninstall and reinstall NAV after you remove the virus from your system.

After you have removed the virus from your machine (and reinstalled NAV if neces-sary), perform a full virus scan of your computer. If any infected files are detected, instruct NAV to try to repair the files. If the files can't be repaired, quarantine and then delete them from your computer.

It may prove very difficult to remove some viruses. In some cases, there are no automated removal tools and the virus removal instructions are very complex. For example, the removal instructions might require you to delete or modify entries in the Windows Registry. Even if you follow the virus removal directions correctly, some viruses behave in unpredictable ways (because viruses, like all software, contain bugs) and your attempts to remove them and repair the damage they caused might be unsuccessful. If you have been unable to remove the virus, or your computer is still functioning abnormally after the virus has been removed, you may have to restore your hard disk from your most recent backup.

Beware Infected Backups

If you performed a hard disk backup *after* your computer became infected, do *not* use that backup to restore your computer. Use an earlier, virus-free backup. Chapter 7, "Backing Up Your Hard Disk," advises you to keep your three most recent back-ups in case you can't use your most current backup for a reason such as this.

Before you implement any of the following three methods, scan your computer to ensure that it is otherwise virus free. Else, the next system restore point that is created can reinfect this folder, and your efforts will have been for naught.

If you decide to restore your hard disk, I advise *against* taking a *data* backup from the infected machine. Instead, restore your data from your most recent uninfected data backup. If you take a backup from the infected machine, you might end up re-infecting the machine after you restore your hard disk!

Removing Viruses from the System Restore Folder

This section is important only for users of Windows Millennium or Windows XP.

Earlier in this chapter I advised you to remove the system restore folder from the scanning exclusion list in the manual scan options. In Windows Millennium, the system restore folder is called _RESTORE and is found in the system directory. In Windows XP, the system restore folder is the \system volume information folder.

Although Windows does not allow antivirus software to repair, quarantine, or delete any infected files from the system restore feature, there are three ways to eliminate viruses in this folder.

Method 1: Purging All Restore Points

One way to remove a virus from the system restore folder is to purge the folder. This is the easiest but most drastic solution because you will be unable to restore your system to a previous point in time. Unfortunately, this approach may be unavoidable in some cases. If the virus has infected a recent restore point, there is no way to selectively delete the recent restore point to remove the virus.

If you are using Windows Millennium, perform the following steps to purge the system restore folder:

1. Right-click My Computer on the Windows desktop, and then click Properties.
2. Click the Performance tab.
3. Click File System.
4. Click the Troubleshooting tab.
5. Check Disable System Restore, click OK, and then click Close (see Figure 5.13).

FIGURE 5.13
Disabling System Restore to flush your restore points on a Windows Millennium system.

6. Reboot your system. This will purge the _RESTORE folder.
7. As a safeguard, scan your computer for viruses.

If you are using Windows XP, perform the following steps:

1. Click Start, and then click My Computer.

2. Click View System Information.

3. Click the System Restore tab.

4. Check Turn Off System Restore (see Figure 5.14).

FIGURE 5.14

Disabling System Restore to flush your restore points on a Windows XP system.

5. Click Apply, and then click OK.

6. As a safeguard, scan your computer for viruses.

Once you have successfully removed the virus from your machine, you should reenable the System Restore feature so that your system can resume taking restore points. If you forget to do this, you will be much more vulnerable to computer disasters.

Keep System Restore Disabled

Do *not* reenable the System Restore feature until you have removed the virus from your machine; otherwise, your computer may take another restore point, which could reinfect the system restore folder.

Method 2: Waiting and Doing Nothing

Another approach is to wait and do nothing. Here is why this approach will eventually solve the problem.

Whenever a system restore point is created, Windows backs up critical system files and stores them on your hard disk. A certain amount of space is reserved on your hard disk for this system restore data. Over time, as the space limit is approached, Windows automatically purges the oldest restore points to make room for new restore points. This purge process eventually removes the infected files, but it can take some time.

I don't favor this approach because there is a risk that you will restore your system to a point that unleashes the infected files on your computer. (Unfortunately, there is no way to determine *which* restore points are infected.)

Method 3: The Partial Purge Method

The third approach is to perform a partial purge of the system restore folder. It's kind of a compromise between methods 1 and 2. It is the most complicated of all three methods, but it is the preferred approach.

The idea here is to take advantage of the fact that Windows purges old restore points when it needs space to store new restore points and to hasten the purge process (without purging all the restore points) by reducing the amount of Windows System Restore disk space.

Whenever your system restore data exceeds 90% of the allowed disk space, Windows automatically purges enough files to reduce the utilization back to 50%. Thus, if your system restore disk space limit is 500MB, when 451MB has been consumed, Windows purges old restore points until about 250MB of space is available.

You might be able to hasten the purge process by reducing the Windows System Restore disk space. For example, if you currently have 300MB of data in your system restore folder and you reduce the allowed space to 200MB, Windows will immediately purge restore points, beginning with the oldest point, until only about 100MB of data is left in the folder. In this example, you have succeeded in eliminating 200MB of data, and it is possible that you have eliminated the infected files as well.

The minimum amount of space you can reserve for the system restore folder is 200MB. Obviously, if you currently have less than 180MB of data in the system restore folder (90% of 200MB), adjusting the allowed space down to the minimum 200MB will not have an immediate purging effect, but it still hastens the process.

The first thing you need to do is find the system restore folder so you can determine how much data is currently in the folder. If you have a Windows Millennium system, you can do this using the Windows Explorer to find `C:\_RESTORE` or by performing a file search for the `_RESTORE` folder. After you have found the file, right-click it and select Properties (see Figure 5.18). If the file size on the window that appears is less than 180MB, reducing the maximum size to 200MB will not have an immediate purging effect.

If the file size is larger than 180MB, make a note of the file size.

Windows XP

Just for fun, Microsoft decided to make it a bit more difficult for you to find the system restore folder in Windows XP. The folder is hidden by default in Windows XP, so it will not show up on Windows Explorer or when you perform a file search. To unhide the file, perform the following steps:

1. Select Start, Control Panel.
2. Double-click Folder Options.

3. Click the View tab.

4. Uncheck Hide Protected Operating System Files. A warning message will be displayed (see Figure 5.15). Click Yes.

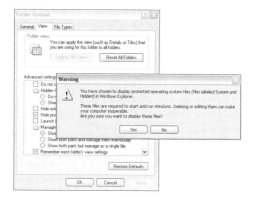

FIGURE 5.15
Unhiding the system restore folder in Windows XP.

5. Click Apply.

After you have done this, you can find the system restore folder by using the Windows Explorer to find C:\system volume information or by performing a file search for the system volume information folder. (I suggest that once you have completed your partial purge you repeat the previous steps and recheck the Hide Protected Operating System Files option.)

To implement the partial purge method, follow the set of instructions that pertains to your operating system.

Windows Millennium

If you are using Windows Millennium, perform the following steps:

1. Right-click My Computer and click Properties.

2. Select the Performance tab.

3. Click File System.

4. Adjust the System Restore Disk Space Use slider control to an amount that is just less than 90% of the current _RESTORE file size, and then click Apply (see Figure 5.16).

5. View the _RESTORE folder properties to confirm that its size has been reduced.

6. Scan the _RESTORE folder for viruses. If a virus is still detected in the _RESTORE folder, repeat steps 4 and 5, gradually lowering the System Restore Disk Space Use to 200MB.

When resizing the system restore folder, do not go all the way down to the minimum size of 200MB immediately. This eliminates more restore points than may be necessary to delete the infected files. You can always try the partial purge approach several times, gradually lowering the size of the system restore folder.

FIGURE 5.16

Reducing the amount of system restore disk space in Windows Millennium.

7. If the virus is still present even after you have reduced the system restore space to the minimum of 200MB, you will need to implement one of the other two previously described methods to eliminate the virus.

8. After the virus has been removed from your computer, return the System Restore Disk Space Use slider to its original position.

If you are using Windows XP, perform the following steps to implement the partial purge method:

1. Select Start, My Computer.

2. Click View System Information.

3. Click the System Restore tab.

4. Click the Settings button.

5. Adjust the Disk Space Usage slider control to an amount that is just less than 90% of the current \system volume information file size, and then click Apply (see Figure 5.17).

FIGURE 5.17

Reducing the amount of system restore disk space in Windows XP.

6. View the \system volume information folder properties to confirm that its size has been reduced.

7. Scan the \system volume information folder for viruses. If a virus is still detected in the \system volume information folder, repeat steps 4 and 5, gradually lowering the Disk Space Usage to 200MB.

8. If the virus is still present even after you have reduced the system restore space to the minimum of 200MB, you will need to implement one of the other two previously described methods to eliminate the virus.

9. After the infected files have been cleared from the system restore folder using this method, return the Disk Space Usage slider to its original position.

Why Virus-Protected Computers Are Still Vulnerable to Viruses

If you think installing antivirus software, configuring it properly, and keeping it up-to-date are all you have to do to protect yourself from computer viruses, you are mistaken. *Badly mistaken.*

Unfortunately for all of us, virus developers are hard at work developing and spreading new viruses every day. Symantec and other antivirus software vendors are working hard to keep pace, constantly updating their software to inoculate your computer against the latest viruses.

But antivirus software vendors are always at a distinct disadvantage to the virus developers because the very nature of their job is *reactive*. A new virus must be in circulation before it can be detected and analyzed, which gives virus developers a head start.

In fact, a new virus can be in circulation for several hours before somebody notices it and reports it to an antivirus software company. Once a new virus has been reported, it might take from several hours to a full day for the antivirus software vendor to analyze it and develop a way of inoculating its customers. Thus, from the time a new virulent virus starts to spread until the time your virus signatures are updated to protect you from the virus, a day or more may have passed. I call this the *time-lag bomb* (see Figure 5.18).

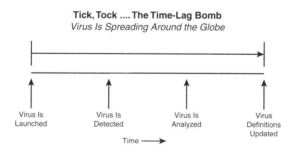

FIGURE 5.18

The time-lag bomb: one of the reasons your computer is vulnerable to viruses.

A few hours or a day might not seem like a very long time to you, but if a virus—particularly a Trojan horse—is packaged attractively, this is more than enough time for the virus to spread all over the world and infect millions of computers.

Such was the case with the Anna Kournikova virus, in which the payload was disguised in what appeared to be a sensational picture of the attractive tennis star. Who could resist such temptation? The answer, apparently, was nobody. It spread like wildfire in February, 2001, bringing corporate networks as well as the Internet to its knees before the antivirus software vendors could respond.

So, even if your antivirus software is configured properly and is as up-to-date as possible, you are always at risk of getting infected because of the time-lag bomb.

And if that is not enough to concern you, consider the following. Until now, most virus developers have been egotistical pranksters—people not intent on causing devastating damage. In fact, many viruses cause no harm whatsoever, other than flooding the Internet with traffic.

That's likely to change. When professional terrorists decide to take aim at the Internet instead of skyscrapers, we can expect a more coordinated, malicious, destructive attack—one in which dozens of new, attractively packaged Trojan horses are simultaneously launched from multiple points of origin around the world. In the face of a massive, coordinated, multipronged attack on the Internet, the time lag between detection and inoculation will be greatly extended, and you will be at even greater risk of a computer disaster.

Tips for Avoiding Virus Infections

Even if you configure and use your antivirus software properly, you are still at risk of getting any new, rapidly spreading virus in a connected world. Here are some tips on how to protect your computer from the time-lag bomb.

Stay Current with the Latest Virus News

Check the Web sites in Table 5.1 first thing every day for the latest breaking news about computer viruses.

Table 5.1   Sources of Breaking News About Computer Viruses

Company	Web Site
CNN	http://www.cnn.com/
Symantec	http://securityresponse.symantec.com/
Trend Micro	http://www.antivirus.com/vinfo/
McAfee	http://www.mcafee.com/anti-virus/default.asp?

By staying up-to-date with the latest virus news, you might be able to recognize a virus and avoid infection even if the virus is so new that protection is not yet available.

Exercise Caution When Opening Email Attachments

There's a piece of oft-dispensed advice regarding computer viruses that makes me cringe whenever I hear it, and it goes something like this:

"Don't open email attachments from people you don't know."

The problem I have with this advice is that it falsely implies that it is safe to open email attachments from people you *do* know. Let's think about this for a moment. One of the ways viruses are designed to spread is by automatically mailing themselves to everyone in your address book.

So, that attachment you just received in the email message from your friend or cousin is just as likely—*perhaps even more likely*—to contain a virus than the piece of spam you just received from an unknown source.

By all means, don't open attachments from people you don't know. But you need to supplement that advice with the following four policies:

- **Don't open email attachments you aren't expecting**—I open attachments from people I correspond with on a regular basis—people who have valid business reasons for sending me attachments. Anything else goes in the trash, unopened.

- **Don't open email attachments from people who don't follow the same security procedures as you**—Many of the people who send me email are friends and relatives who take no precautions against computer viruses. (Hopefully, that will change after they read this book.) I am *much* more suspicious of email attachments I get from them than I am of email attachments I get from colleagues who work in the computer industry—people who I know are as paranoid and fanatical about virus protection as I am.

- **Contact the sender when in doubt**—It only takes a minute to contact the sender and ask questions such as, "Did you send this to me intentionally?" and "Are you certain this attachment is not infected with a virus?"

- **Err on the side of caution, and consider the risks versus the reward**—How important is it to open that funny file somebody sent you? Is it really worth the risk of getting a computer virus? Will your life really be impacted negatively if you just delete the message?

  I have a friend who is fond of saying, "Never miss an opportunity *not* to say something." Extrapolating that philosophy, I advise you to never miss an opportunity *not* to open a questionable attachment.

- **Never open email attachments that has a suspicious file extension**—Microsoft has defined a set of unsafe file extensions for email attachments, which is listed in Table 5.2. The boldfaced items are the ones you will encounter most frequently.

Watch for Double File Extensions

Some virus writers try to disguise their dirty work by using a filename with a double extension, such as `anna.jpg.vbs`. They hope that you will mistake the attachment for a harmless picture. You should never open any file that has a double extension.

Table 5.2   Microsoft's List of Unsafe File Extensions for Email Attachments

Extension	File Type	Extension	File Type
.ade	Microsoft Access project extension	.mde	Microsoft Access MDE database
.adp	Microsoft Access project	.msc	Microsoft common console document
.bas	Microsoft Visual Basic class module	.msi	Microsoft Windows Installer package
.bat	Batch file	.msp	Microsoft Windows Installer patch
.chm	Compiled HTML Help file	.mst	Microsoft Visual Test source files
.cmd	Microsoft Windows NT command script	.pcd	Photo CD image, Microsoft Visual compiled script
.com	Microsoft MS-DOS program		
.cpl	Control Panel extension	**.pif**	**Shortcut to MS-DOS program**
.crt	Security certificate	.reg	Registration entries
.exe	**Program**	**.scr**	**Screensaver**
.hlp	Help file	.sct	Windows Script component
.hta	HTML program	.shb	Shell Scrap object
.inf	Setup information	.shs	Shell Scrap object
.ins	Internet naming service	.url	Internet shortcut
.isp	Internet communication settings	**.vb**	**VBScript file**
.js	**JScript file**	**.vbe**	**VBScript encoded script file**
.jse	JScript encoded script file	**.vbs**	**Windows Script component**
.lnk	Shortcut	.wsf	Windows Script file
.mdb	Microsoft Access program	.wsh	Windows Script host settings file

Beware of Links Inserted into Email Messages

Some virus writers, aware that you are wary of email attachments, include a Web site link instead. When you click the link, you are directed to a Web site that infects your computer. These links typically try to entice you by entreating you to visit a funny or sexy Web site.

Turn Off Your Email Preview Pane

There is a popular misconception that you must open an infected email attachment to get a computer virus. A new generation of sophisticated viruses can deliver their payloads when you view the message in the preview pane of your email application. To avoid this exposure, turn off your preview pane. In Outlook Express, select View, Layout and uncheck the Show Preview Pane box (see Figure 5.19). It's a little inconvenient not to see the message preview, but the convenience of using this feature is not worth the risk, in my opinion.

FIGURE 5.19

Turn off your preview pane to avoid getting a computer virus merely by previewing a message.

Watch for Bad English

As I mentioned in Chapter 2, many email messages that accompany Trojan horses use incredibly bad English. This is a sure tip-off that the attachment is a virus.

However, don't be fooled into opening an attachment just because the story that accompanies it is well-written. Be suspicious of everything.

Don't Suffer Fools Gladly

Let's face it—some people never learn. If the same person is responsible for sending you more than one computer virus, add him to your blocked senders list. In Outlook Express, select Tools, Message Rules, Blocked Senders List and add his name to the list.

Consider Using a Web-Based Email Service

With a Web-based email service, such as Hotmail or Yahoo!, your email messages remain on the server. The only time anything gets downloaded to your computer is if you choose to download an attachment. Thus, Web-based email service providers keep your email messages off your hard disk, reducing the chances of infection. These Web-based email service providers also scan any attachments for viruses.

Don't Be the Victim of an Email Virus Hoax

Every so often, some well-intentioned but misinformed person sends me an urgent email message about a new virus, with instructions on how to remove it. These messages typically tell me to remove certain files from my computer, under the guise that these files should not and would not be on my computer unless it was infected with the virus. For example, the following email message was recently forwarded to me from a business associate. (Note the bad English, a sure indication that something is rotten in the state of Denmark.)

From: <Name withheld to protect the guilty>
Sent: Thursday, May 09, 2002 10:13 AM
Subject: Virus jdbgmgr.exe
Sorry about this but I found out my mail list was infected by an email sent from someone else.
It is not time consuming to get rid but it will be time well spent in the long run.
This virus goes through email lists and since I have you do too. Just follow the simple instructions below. This virus was not detected by Norton or McAfee antivirus systems. The virus stays dormant for 14 days before damaging the system. It is sent automatically by the Messenger and by the address book whether or not you have sent emails to your contacts.
We have checked , found it and deleted from our systems without damage.....so far. The sooner you complete this exercise the better. Here are the instruc-
tions.......
1. Select Start , FIND (or SEARCH) option in the FILES/FOLDER option. Write the name
2. DO NOT OPEN THIS FILE
3. Be sure you are searching your hard drive.
4. Once found, you will notice the little bear icon next to the name **jdbgmgr.exe**
5. Right-click the BEAR icon to delete it. It will then go to the recycle bin.
6. Go to your recycle bin, find the file and right-click again to delete it or empty the entire bin.

IF YOU FIND THE VIRUS YOU MUST CONTACT ALL PEOPLE IN YOUR ADDRESS BOOKS SO THEY CAN ERADICATE IT IN THEIR SYSTEMS.

Such email messages are almost always hoaxes, and they almost always direct you to remove legitimate (and sometimes critical) files from your Windows operating system, which can render your computer inoperable. In this example, if you delete the jdbgmgr.exe file, a legitimate Windows file, you will be unable to run Java applets on your computer. This can impact your ability to surf the Web. Virus hoaxes, in my opinion, are more insidious than viruses for three reasons:

- **They convince you to harm yourself**—The differences between a virus, Trojan horse, and virus hoax can be summed up thusly: With a virus, somebody shoots you in the head. With a Trojan horse, somebody gives you a loaded gun disguised as an ear thermometer. With a virus hoax, somebody convinces you that the growth on top of your neck is dangerous, and they give you a gun, bullets, and detailed directions for loading and using the gun to remove the growth. (A friend of mine wryly observed that if you fall for a virus hoax, the growth on the top of your neck *is* indeed dangerous and ought to be eliminated.)

- **Anybody can write a virus hoax**—I'm a fairly decent writer (or at least, it appears so after the efforts of my copy editor). I am absolutely certain that I could write an extremely convincing virus hoax in an hour—one that would direct people to delete critical operating system files off their computers.

And I bet the net result would be that hundreds if not thousands of people would trash their computers. So without writing a single line of code, I could do as much damage as the most virulent virus on the Web.

- **Virus hoaxes come in the guise of communications from reputable, knowledgeable authorities**—For example, one clever hoax writer made it appear as if the virus warning was coming from Symantec!

The interesting thing about virus hoaxes is that even so-called computer experts fall for these hoaxes and do much harm by distributing them. I have had to chastise several colleagues who should have known better for perpetuating such hoaxes.

Whenever you receive a message from *anybody* warning you about a virus, don't do anything until you investigate it on Symantec's Virus Hoax page at `http://securityresponse.symantec.com/avcenter/hoax.html` or at the Virus Myths Web site at `http://www.vmyths.com/`.

Once you have confirmed that the warning you have received is indeed a hoax, do a "reply all" to the message and let everybody know that it is a hoax. In your reply, include the link that proves it to be a hoax. Hopefully, your reply will be received and read before anybody falls for the hoax. You should also send a separate letter to the originator of the message, rebuking him for sending out information without verifying it first.

Implement the Crosby, Stills, and Nash and *Buffy the Vampire Slayer* Policies

Crosby, Stills, and Nash hit the nail on the head when they sang, "Teach your children well." Chances are you have multiple people in your family accessing the Internet and receiving email, either through one machine or several machines. You must drill virus protection practices into every member of your family. It doesn't do you much good to stand at the front door with Buffy, a cross, and garlic to keep the virus vampires at bay if other family members are at the back door with Bob Barker saying, "Come on down!"

Communicate

As soon as you become aware of a new virus do the following:

- **Confirm that it is not a hoax**—You don't want to be one of the well-intentioned but misinformed people who cause problems instead of solving them by spreading a virus hoax.

- **Send an email to everyone in your address book about the virus**—Remember that not everyone is a diligent as you. By communicating well, you can help prevent the spread of viruses.

If somebody you know sends you an infected file, call and let him know his computer is infected.

Don't Share Floppy Disks

Floppy disks are the number two source of viruses (behind email). Do not stick somebody else's floppy disk in your computer. Always use new floppy disks or floppy disks that have been completely under your control. If the floppy disk has been used before, it's a good idea to scan it for viruses before using it again.

Protect Yourself Against Macro Viruses

As an extra layer of protection, always enable the highest level of macro security in Microsoft Office applications. *Macros* are instructions that are used to automate tasks. Unfortunately, macros are a favorite weapon of virus developers.

To enable Macro protection in Word 97 and Excel 97, select Tools, Options, General and check the Macro Virus Protection box. In Word 2000 and Excel 2000, select Tools, Macro, Security, Security Level, and select High.

Be Careful About Downloading Freeware and Shareware Programs

Some freeware and shareware programs available on the Web are actually Trojan horses. Before downloading and installing such a program, thoroughly check out its reputation to make sure it is a legitimate, proven program. Look for user reviews on various sites, such as http://www.epinions.com/.

Other Situations That Can Leave You Vulnerable to Computer Viruses

Two other situations can leave your computer *extremely* vulnerable to virus infections.

As previously discussed, Windows Millennium and Windows XP have a System Restore feature that allows you to create restore points and restore your system to a previous point in time should your system become unstable.

Unfortunately, if you use the System Restore feature to restore your system to an earlier point in time, Windows can also restore your virus definitions and virus program to that previous point in time. Whenever you restore your system to an earlier point in time, you must manually run LiveUpdate to bring your virus definitions and program back up-to-date. In fact, you might have to run LiveUpdate several times because program patches are incremental. You should keep running LiveUpdate until you receive a message telling you that your program is up-to-date. You should also run Intelligent Updater after you finish running LiveUpdate to get the most recent virus definitions.

You might also find that after using the System Restore function NAV no longer "thinks" you have a valid virus update subscription. Should this occur, you have two choices: call Symantec and try to get the problem resolved, or pay another $9.95 for a year's subscription. The latter may be more expeditious, especially since you don't want to leave your computer unprotected any longer than you have to.

Even worse, if you restore your system to a point prior to when NAV was installed, you will have to reinstall the application and run LiveUpdate repeatedly to bring it up-to-date. Once again, you might have to contact Symantec to work out issues related to your virus subscription or pay for another year's subscription.

Should you ever have to restore your hard disk from a system backup, you will be faced with the exact same problems, and you will have to bring your virus program, definitions, and subscription up-to-date.

The older your restore point or system backup, the more likely you are to have these kinds of problems.

Protecting Your Computer Against Hackers

Antivirus software helps protect you from cyber-terrorists who seek to damage or destroy your data. Firewalls help protect you from cyber-terrorists who want to steal your data or gain control over your computer.

A firewall is a first line of defense against hackers. Because skilled hackers can find ways around a firewall, there are other procedures you should follow to make your system as hack-proof as possible.

Zone Labs' software firewall, the product I will be discussing, comes in three flavors: ZoneAlarm, ZoneAlarm Plus, and ZoneAlarm Pro. ZoneAlarm is a free download for home users. ZoneAlarm Plus costs $39.95 and ZoneAlarm Pro costs $49.95. (Zone Labs occasionally runs special promotions when the software is available at a discount.)

All three ZoneAlarm products offer excellent firewall protection. However, ZoneAlarm Plus and ZoneAlarm Pro provide a few additional firewall-related features not found in the basic, free ZoneAlarm product. For example, both ZoneAlarm Plus and ZoneAlarm Pro provide the option of specifying a blocked zone—a list of computers and networks you explicitly distrust. The computers and networks in the blocked zone are never allowed access to your computer. This provides a layer of protection above and beyond that of a typical firewall.

ZoneAlarm Pro provides an additional anti-hacking feature not found in ZoneAlarm or ZoneAlarm Plus. This feature, *program component control,* makes it more difficult for hackers to hijack programs on your computer and use them for their own nefarious purposes. This feature is discussed in more detail later in this chapter in the section "ZoneAlarm's Program Change Control."

Both ZoneAlarm Plus and ZoneAlarm Pro offer additional features not directly related to firewall protection—features that broach the turf of antivirus software and other software products.

For the most part, I will discuss the free product, ZoneAlarm. I believe that this product will be adequate for most home users. However, I invite you to visit Zone Labs' Web site to compare the three versions of ZoneAlarm and choose the one that best suits your needs:

```
http://www.zonelabs.com/store/content/company/products/znalm/
comparison.jsp
```

Configuring ZoneAlarm

ZoneAlarm provides numerous configuration options that determine the level of protection against hackers. This section assumes you have installed the latest version of ZoneAlarm, which as of this writing is version 3.1.291, and focuses on explaining how to configure ZoneAlarm to afford maximum protection against hackers while allowing legitimate communications to occur.

Setting Program Preferences

Open ZoneAlarm by double-clicking the ZoneAlarm icon in your system tray. ZoneAlarm displays an Overview window that includes three tabs. The first two tabs, Status and Product Info, are informational and do not warrant further discussion. Click the third tab, Preferences, to see the program preferences. The defaults you see here are correct. Do not change them or you might expose yourself to hackers. For example, you would never want to uncheck the Load ZoneAlarm at Startup box, or your computer would not be protected against hackers until you manually started ZoneAlarm.

Setting the Firewall Options

On the left side of the screen, click Firewall to view a window that allows you to configure your basic firewall settings. This window has two tabs: Main and Zones.

On the Main tab, you will see that ZoneAlarm allows you to set a protection level for two different zones—the Internet zone and the trusted zone (see Figure 5.20). As previously mentioned, ZoneAlarm Pro provides an additional zone; the blocked zone.

Internet Zone Security controls communication between your computer and the Internet. Trusted Zone Security (referred to as local zone security in previous versions of ZoneAlarm) controls communication between your computer and other computers that you elect to trust and want to share resources with—for example, computers on your home network. Leave these settings at the recommended defaults—high security for the Internet zone and medium security for the trusted zone. You do not want to set security on the trusted zone to high or other computers on your home network will not be able to see your computer or share its resources.

(If you have no computers in your trusted zone, it makes no difference how you have the security level set.)

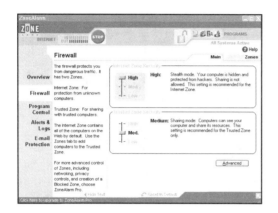

FIGURE 5.20
Leave the zone secu-
rity settings at their
default settings.

Click the Advanced button from the Main tab to bring up the Advanced Security Settings window. Leave all five boxes on this window at their default settings.

The names on the first two boxes—Block Trusted Zone Servers and Block Internet Zone—are not particularly clear. Basically, if these boxes are checked, they prevent your computer from ever acting as a server, either in your trusted zone or on the Internet. You should leave these boxes unchecked (the default setting) because certain software applications on your computer may require server rights to function properly. The term *server rights* means that you have granted an application the right to function as a server. If an application has been granted server rights, it can "listen" for and respond to requests for information from the Internet.

KaZaA, the popular file sharing application, is an example of an application that requires server rights. KaZaA needs server rights so that it can respond to requests from other KaZaA users to download files from your computer. Your risk is controlled because only files from one special folder, the KaZaA shared folder, can be accessed by other KaZaA users. Of course, if you choose to keep nothing in your shared folder, other users will not find anything to download from your computer.

If an application requires server rights to function properly, ZoneAlarm displays a program alert window when the application attempts to function in that capacity (see Figure 5.21). If you click Yes and then select Remember This Answer the Next Time I Use This Program, the application will be granted permanent server rights. (You can always change your mind later by clicking Program Control and selecting the Programs tab to change the server rights setting for that application.)

You need only be concerned about the Zones tab on the Firewall window (refer to Figure 5.20) if you want to allow your computer to share resources with other computers (for example, to perform file and printer sharing on a home network). If you have a home network and your computers are connected through a router, you will probably need to perform the following task to allow your computer to share resources with other computers on the network.

FIGURE 5.21

ZoneAlarm displays a program alert window when an application requests the right to act as a server.

Depending on how your home network is set up (specifically, what networking protocol you are using), you might not need to perform this task. You might want to see if your computers can perform file and printer sharing before you perform this task.

If you have a home network and your computers are connected via a hub instead of a router, and if you are using one of your computers as a gateway to the Internet for all of your computers, you will find it easier to use ZoneAlarm Plus or ZoneAlarm Pro. This will configure your firewall and provide protection against hackers while simultaneously allowing file and printer sharing. The more common networking solution today is the one I previously described, where computers share an Internet connection via a router.

Server Rights = Power

Granting server rights to an application is somewhat risky because you are allowing people on the Internet to get through your firewall. It's possible, for example, that a bug in the application or in Windows could make your system vulnerable to hackers if server rights are granted. If an application requests server rights, I suggest that you try using the application first without granting server rights. Before you grant server rights to an application, try to ascertain why server rights are needed and what information on your computer will be accessed. Grant server rights as a last resort when it is the only way you can use an application. Of course, you should also consider whether the benefits of using an application justify the risk of granting server rights.

1. Click the Zones tab in the Firewall window. You will see an entry for your computer's network adaptor. For example, in Figure 5.22, you see an entry for a 3Com EtherLink PCI adaptor.

2. Under the word Zone you will see that the default setting is Internet. Click this word and change the setting to Trusted (see Figure 5.22).

3. Click the word Apply at the bottom of the window to apply the change. Your computer can now interact with other computers on your home network.

I should point out that ZoneAlarm's documentation is not clear in this regard. In one place, the documentation advises you to place your network adaptor in the trusted zone as I have instructed above. In another place, the documentation advises you to leave your network adaptor in the Internet zone. *Rest assured that my instructions are correct.* I have spoken with the folks at Zone Labs, and they have confirmed that the documentation is misleading, and that you *do* need to place your computer's network card in the trusted zone to allow file and printer sharing.

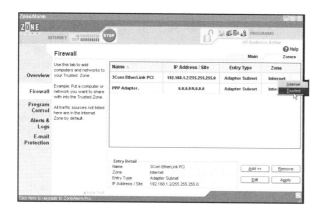

FIGURE 5.22
If you have a home network, place your network adaptor in the trusted zone to allow inbound and outbound communications from and to other computers on your network.

The trusted zone concept is not limited to computers on your home network. For example, you could add grandma's computer to your trusted zone (and grandma can add your computer to her trusted zone) so that you and grandma can share resources. To add a remote computer to your trusted zone, you need to add the computer's Internet Protocol (IP) addresses to your trusted zone. You will recall from Chapter 4 that an *IP address* is the means by which your computer is uniquely identified on the Internet. To add an IP address to your trusted zone, go to the Zones tab, click Add, select IP address, and specify the IP address you wish to add to your trusted zone. This approach only works if the two computers have static IP addresses, that is, if the IP addresses do not change each time the computers log on to the Internet.

Setting the Program Control Options

Click Program Control from the main ZoneAlarm window to display the Program Control window (see Figure 5.23).

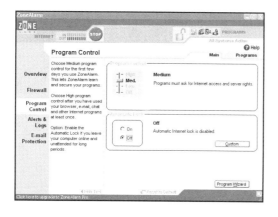

FIGURE 5.23
The Program Control window; Main tab.

On the Main tab, leave the Program Control option at the default setting of Medium. The Medium setting enables ZoneAlarm to monitor outbound communications from your computer (in addition to blocking unauthorized inbound communications).

This feature enables you to stop programs that might be contacting the Internet and sending out information without your knowledge. For example, if a hacker has somehow managed to place a rogue application on your computer that gathers information and sends it back out over the Internet, ZoneAlarm will detect this communication and display a program alert.

If you try to adjust the slider to the High setting you will see a note stating that the High setting is only available in ZoneAlarm Pro. The High setting pertains to the program component control feature that is only available in ZoneAlarm Pro. Program component control is discussed later in this chapter in the section "ZoneAlarm's Program Change Control."

The second option on the Program Control window is the Automatic Lock option. When enabled, this option allows you automatically stop all Internet traffic and provides an extra level of protection against hackers when you are away from your computer. This has the same effect as turning off your machine.

Click the Custom box to view and customize the settings associated with the automatic Internet lock. You can configure ZoneAlarm to automatically engage the lock either after a specified number of minutes of inactivity or when the screensaver activates (see Figure 5.24). If you want to use the automatic lock feature, I recommend that you use a screensaver on your computer and select the Lock When Screen Saver Activates option for the following reasons:

- The lock automatically disengages when you start working at your computer again. With the other automatic locking option, you have to manually disengage the Internet lock.

- The Lock After (x) Minutes of Inactivity method is less reliable as background processes running on your computer can prevent the lock from ever engaging.

FIGURE 5.24

You can configure ZoneAlarm to automatically engage an Internet lock when you are away from your computer as extra protection against hackers.

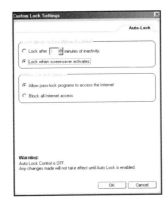

ZoneAlarm also provides the option to enable certain programs to bypass the Internet lock when the lock is engaged. Here is an example of how you might want to use this feature. You might want to download a large video file from KaZaA—one that can take several hours to complete. You can set up KaZaA as a pass-lock program by clicking the Programs tab and checking the Pass-Lock box next to KaZaA (see Figure 5.25).

When you engage the Internet lock in Pass-Lock mode, your download from KaZaA can continue when the Internet lock is engaged, but all other Internet activity is disabled.

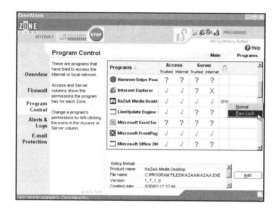

FIGURE 5.25
Selecting the Pass-Lock box allows a program to communicate with the Internet even when ZoneAlarm's Internet lock is engaged.

To allow pass-lock programs to access the Internet when the Internet lock is engaged, check the Allow Pass-Lock Programs to Access the Internet button (refer back to Figure 5.24). If the Block All Internet Access button is selected, pass-lock programs will not be able to access the Internet when the lock is engaged.

Rather than wait for the Internet lock to automatically engage, you can manually engage and disengage the Internet lock at any time simply by clicking the Lock icon at the top of the ZoneAlarm window.

ZoneAlarm also has a separate high-security lock feature that you can engage to stop all Internet activity immediately, *including pass-lock programs.* You can activate this feature two ways: You can right-click the ZoneAlarm icon on the system tray and select Stop All Internet Activity, or you can click the big red Stop button at the top of the ZoneAlarm screen.

If the Internet lock is engaged and an application attempts to connect to the Internet, ZoneAlarm displays a message telling you that access has been denied because the lock is engaged (see Figure 5.26). Pass-lock programs will still be allowed to access the Internet unless the high security lock is engaged.

FIGURE 5.26
ZoneAlarm displays an alert when an application attempts to connect to the Internet when the high security lock is engaged.

On the Programs tab, you see a list of all the applications (programs) on your computer that are being monitored by ZoneAlarm. The columns labeled Access and Server will be described in detail in a later section; "How to Use Zone Alarm."

Setting the Alerts and Logs Options

Click Alerts & Logs to view the alerts and logs options. Leave the Alert Events Shown option set to On. This causes ZoneAlarm to display a Firewall Alert window whenever an intruder is detected (see Figure 5.27). When the Firewall Alert window is displayed, you can then click the More Info button to learn more about the suspicious activity—details about what type of intrusion ZoneAlarm detected, whether you should be concerned, and what action if any you should take.

FIGURE 5.27
ZoneAlarm has detected an intruder and displays a Firewall Alert window. You should click the More Info button to learn more about the attempted intrusion.

The Advanced button enables you to configure when, where, and how ZoneAlarm saves a log of alert messages. There is no need for most users to adjust these settings.

Setting E-Mail Protection

Click E-mail Protection to set ZoneAlarm's email protection settings. ZoneAlarm's MailSafe option provides functionality similar to script blocking in Norton AntiVirus. ZoneAlarm recommends turning this option off if you are using antivirus software because it can cause a conflict with other mail-checking software. The default setting is Off, so you do not have to make any changes here, assuming you are using antivirus software.

How to Use ZoneAlarm

ZoneAlarm works unobtrusively in the background, monitoring unauthorized attempts to communicate with your computer, stopping such inbound communication, and displaying firewall alerts.

But ZoneAlarm monitors outbound communications as well. This feature enables you to stop programs that might be contacting the Internet and sending out information without your knowledge. For example, if a hacker has somehow managed to place an application on your computer that gathers information and sends it back out over the Internet, ZoneAlarm will detect this communication and display a program alert.

ZoneAlarm errs on the side of caution with respect to outbound communications. When you first begin using ZoneAlarm, you see a program alert window whenever a program on your computer attempts to access the Internet (see Figure 5.28).

FIGURE 5.28
ZoneAlarm displays a program alert window when a program on your computer attempts to connect to the Internet.

When the program alert is displayed, you can do any of the following:

- **Deny access by clicking No**—You will be prompted for a response again the next time this application tries to access the Internet.

- **Deny access permanently by clicking No and selecting the Remember This Answer the Next Time I Use This Program box.**

- **Allow access by clicking Yes**—You will be prompted for a response the next time this application tries to access the Internet.

- **Allow access permanently by clicking Yes and checking the Remember This Answer the Next Time I Use This Program box**—By doing so, you are in effect declaring this application to be a trusted program. You will not receive future program alerts for this application.

ZoneAlarm and AntiVirus Software

ZoneAlarm's documentation states that in order to receive automatic updates from your antivirus software vendor you must add the domain that contains the updates to your trusted zone. This is not true, at least with respect to Norton AntiVirus. I suspect that it is also not true with respect to other popular antivirus software applications.

You will continue to receive automatic updates with Norton AntiVirus without having to configure ZoneAlarm in any special way. This is due to the fact that the automatic update process is initiated from inside your firewall via the Windows task scheduler. The first time the process is launched, you will receive a program alert telling you that the Norton AntiVirus agent is attempting to access the Internet. At this point, you can allow permanent Internet access to this program.

ZoneAlarm's Program Change Control

You may be wondering: If one confers trusted program status to an application, doesn't that defeat the purpose of monitoring outbound communications? Couldn't a hacker use this feature to her advantage by hijacking a trusted program?

For example, suppose you have made Internet Explorer a trusted program. This means you have granted Internet Explorer the right to access the Internet without manual intervention (approval) from you. In rare cases, a hacker can hijack your program's Internet access rights. This means that the hacker can gather information on your computer and use the trusted application to send the information back to herself.

Fortunately, ZoneAlarm provides protection against program hijacking. In order to hijack a trusted program, a hacker would have to make changes to the program itself. All programs carry a digital fingerprint known as a digital signature or MD5 signature. If a program has been changed, its digital signature automatically changes. When the digital signature changes, ZoneAlarm displays a Changed Program alert. You then have the option of allowing or denying access to the Internet (see Figure 5.29).

FIGURE 5.29
ZoneAlarm detects that a program's digital signature has changed and displays a Changed Program alert when the application tries to access the Internet. In this case, the change was legitimate—I had recently installed a new version of the program, which had caused its digital signature to change.

There may be legitimate reasons for a program's digital signature to change. Installing a new version of a program causes the signature to change. The first time the updated program attempts to contact the Internet you will receive a Changed Program alert.

ZoneAlarm Pro takes anti-hijack protection one a level deeper with a feature called program component control. This feature authenticates the components associated with a program's main executable file. If you are using ZoneAlarm Pro, and if a hacker has hijacked a program component, you will see a Program Component alert (similar to a Changed Program alert), which lets you know that a program is using a component that is new or has changed. To activate the program component alert feature, change the setting on the Program Control Main tab from its default setting of Medium to High (refer back to Figure 5.30). Note that you will only be able to change the setting if you have purchased ZoneAlarm Pro.

The ZoneAlarm Programs Window

If you click Program Control and select the Programs tab, you see a list of all the applications (programs) on your computer that are being monitored by ZoneAlarm.

The settings for each application determine whether the application is allowed to access the Internet, whether it has server rights, and whether it is allowed to bypass the Internet lock. *ZoneAlarm automatically maintains these settings based on your responses to program alert windows (refer to Figures 5.35 and 5.36).*

However, you can change these options any time you want by going directly to the Programs window.

An application will not show in this window until it has attempted to connect to the Internet. Thus, when you first install ZoneAlarm, this window is empty. As applications attempt to connect to the Internet and are either allowed or denied access, they are automatically added to the Programs window.

The Access column determines whether the application has permission to access other computers in the trusted zone and the Internet zone. There are three possible settings: Allow, Block, and Ask (see Figure 5.30).

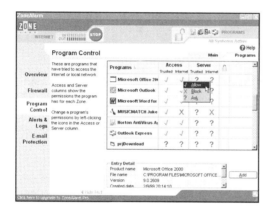

FIGURE 5.30

ZoneAlarm maintains a record of Access and Server permissions for each program that attempts to access other computers in the trusted zone or Internet zone.

For example, if you have a question mark under the Allow Connect column for Internet Explorer, ZoneAlarm displays a program alert window when Internet Explorer attempts to access the Internet. Depending on how you respond to the program alert, ZoneAlarm can change the setting for that program, as indicated in Table 5.3.

Table 5.3   How ZoneAlarm Automatically Updates Program Settings When an Application Tries to Access the Internet

User's Response to Program Alert	Remember This Answer Box	ZoneAlarm Does This to the Program Settings
Yes	Checked	Access is allowed. ZoneAlarm changes the program setting to a check mark. You are making this a trusted application.
Yes	Unchecked	Access is allowed. ZoneAlarm leaves the program setting as a question mark. You will be prompted the next time this application attempts to contact the Internet.
No	Checked	Access is not allowed. ZoneAlarm changes the program setting to an "X". You never want this application to access the Internet.

Table 5.3   Continued

User's Response to Program Alert	Remember This Answer Box	ZoneAlarm Does This to the Program Settings
No	Unchecked	Access is not allowed. ZoneAlarm leaves the program setting as a question mark. You will be prompted the next time this application attempts to contact the Internet.

The Server column indicates whether Server rights have been granted to an application. The values are set based on how you respond to a program alert (refer to Figure 5.21), and they can be manually changed in the Programs window.

Other Hacker Prevention Measures

"And we can treasure our freedoms behind our locked doors."

—John Mellencamp

John Mellencamp's lyrics pretty much sum up the situation we face everyday as we try to balance our desire for easy access to information with our need for security from hackers.

Whenever we browse the Web, we invite strangers into our computers. We expect these strangers to behave properly, but just in case they don't, we rely on Microsoft to provide security to prevent them from wandering around our computers and helping themselves to our data.

At the same time, we want Microsoft to provide us with convenience and ease of use. Unfortunately, security and convenience/ease of use are conflicting objectives.

We face the same issue elsewhere everyday in our lives:

- Do we lock our valuable jewelry securely in a safe deposit box, where we are unable to enjoy using it, or do we wear our jewelry and take some reasonable precautions against theft?

- Do we implement airport security procedures that are so tight that we have to get to the airport 6 hours before our flight, or do we settle for less-than-perfect security?

- Do we use a different random password for every document we generate and every e-commerce activity we perform and spend days trying to commit these all to the locked doors of our memory, or do we use a few different passwords that we can easily remember?

The only sure way to have 100% security from hackers is to turn off our computers. There *is* no other solution. (I chose my words carefully here, by the way. If you have your computers on and are not connected to the Internet, you can still be hacked if you have a wireless network.)

Short of turning off our computers, we could set our browser security settings and firewall security settings so high we would constantly be prompted to make decisions about whether information should be allowed to flow one way or the other.

Perfect security, if it exists at all, is paradoxically an anathema because it controls us and strips us of our ability to experience all that life has to offer.

In the end, we try to set our security levels high enough to afford adequate protection without spoiling the overall experience. And because there is no perfect solution, we leave ourselves somewhat exposed to hackers.

So we look for that middle ground, and everybody's middle ground is different. Because I am quite active and visible on the Internet, I am willing to sacrifice more convenience and ease of use than most people to achieve a higher level of security. There is no right answer here. If your security measures are inadequate, you will only be able to make that determination in hindsight.

With all this in mind, I offer the following recommendations to reduce your vulnerability to computer hackers—recommendations that will make you safer without making your life miserable.

Apply Critical Updates from Microsoft

Microsoft periodically provides critical security-related updates to its operating system, Web browser, and email applications. These updates plug security holes that, left unplugged, allow hackers to find back doors into your computer, even if you have a firewall installed.

For example, Windows XP includes a new feature—Universal Plug and Play—that is intended to make home networking easier and more convenient. As is often the case with features designed to provide ease of use and convenience, this Universal Plug and Play has caused very serious security problems.

Universal Plug and Play is designed to extend the plug-and-play capability of a single machine across your home network. With previous versions of Windows, plug-and-play could (in theory) automatically detect new devices attached to or installed in your computer and load the device drivers so that you could immediately use the device without having to perform any additional setup tasks.

Universal Plug and Play performs a similar function for your home network by enabling devices on the network to automatically detect each other and work together. For example, with Universal Plug and Play, if you install a printer on your home network, all the computers on the network automatically detect the printer and are able to use it immediately—no manual setup is required to configure the printer as a shared device. Home networking has never been easier. *And neither has hacking.*

Shortly after Windows XP was released, two critical vulnerabilities were discovered in the Universal Plug and Play feature. Hackers could exploit these vulnerabilities to either take complete control of your machine or launch a denial-of-service attack against your machine to slow it down or stop it from functioning all together. Basically, by opening the kimono and allowing this automatic interaction among devices on the network, hackers could exploit these vulnerabilities to interact with your computers as well.

Although a firewall reduced the risk of being hacked in this manner, it didn't eliminate the risk entirely.

Microsoft responded with a patch to Windows XP that fixed these vulnerabilities, which brings us back to the main topic of this discussion: keeping your operating system, browser, and email application up-to-date with the latest security patches.

Fortunately, Microsoft makes this easy to do by providing a Windows Update Web page that enables you to obtain and apply the latest antihacking security updates to your system.

Interestingly, one of the updates you can install (I believe it was a recommended update, rather than a critical update, if memory serves me correctly) sets up a task on your Task Scheduler to automatically check for new, critical updates (see Figure 5.31). Microsoft calls this the Automatic Critical Update Notification feature. This feature is installed by default on Windows XP and Windows Millennium systems, but not on Windows 98 systems.

FIGURE 5.31

This Windows 98 computer has a task on the Task Scheduler to automatically check the Microsoft Web site every 5 minutes for critical updates.

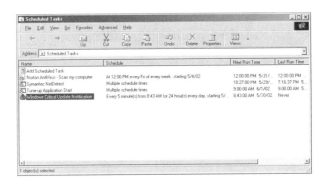

To manually check for both critical and recommended updates, perform the following steps:

1. Go to the Windows update Web page at `http://windowsupdate.microsoft.com/`.

2. Click Product Updates. Microsoft then searches your computer to determine which operating system, Web browser, and email application you have installed. This can take about 30 seconds with a broadband connection, or a few minutes with a dial-up connection. Microsoft needs to do this to determine which specific updates are applicable to your computer. Basically, you are trusting Microsoft not to access other critical information on your computer. At some point, you have to trust somebody.

3. Microsoft displays a list of all critical updates and service packs applicable to your computer (see Figure 5.32). You should immediately download and install these critical updates and service packs. If there are no critical updates, you receive a message that says No updates of this type are available at this time.

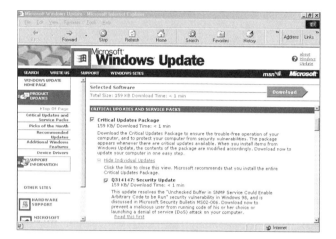

FIGURE 5.32
Microsoft has deter-mined that critical updates need to be installed on this com-puter.

4. Download and install the critical updates and service packs. If this is your first time performing this task, you may have to repeat this process several times, as the patches are often incremental. This means you have to down-load and install one patch before you can download and install another. The instructions are always very clear in this regard. Also, in some cases you will be instructed to reboot your computer to complete the installation process.

If you have the automatic critical update notification process set up on your Windows Task Scheduler, you won't have to remember to manually check for critical updates—you will see a pop-up window on your screen telling you that critical updates are available. If you indicate that you want to apply the updates, you are automatically taken to step 3 in the previous procedure.

You should note that the Microsoft Web page also displays a second category of updates—a list of recommended updates. You can read about these updates individu-ally and decide which ones to install. The general subject of keeping your computer up-to-date is discussed in more detail in Chapter 9, "Keeping Your Computer in Top Shape."

From the "No Good Deed Goes Unpunished" Department

You really must install Microsoft's critical updates. If you don't, you are asking for trouble. Unfortunately, if you do, you may also be asking for trouble. It's a sad fact of life that software patches intended to fix problems often cause problems, and Microsoft is not exempt from that maxim.

A critical update I installed while writing this book created a number of problems with my Internet Explorer, the most serious of which being that it trashed my AutoComplete function.

After installing this update, when I entered an email address on a Web form, AutoComplete displayed an email address I had not used in two years, instead of displaying the two email addresses I currently use. Many other AutoComplete entries just disappeared.

I conferred with a colleague, who suggested that I use the Internet Explorer repair function to see if that fixed the problem. I was fortunate—it did. (I show you how to find and use the Internet Explorer repair function in Chapter 8.)

But it is a never-ending source of frustration for me—and constant validation of my contention that computers are unstable equilibriums—that for every problem software vendors fix, they often create another.

Clean Old Data Off Your Computer

If it ain't there, they can't steal it.

One way to prevent hackers from stealing your data is to erase deleted files beyond recovery using CyberScrub.

The easiest way to delete files beyond recovery is to take advantage of CyberScrub's right-click integration with Windows. Simply highlight the file(s) or folder(s) you want to delete and erase, right-click, and select the Erase Beyond Recovery option. CyberScrub gives you a couple of opportunities to confirm your intentions, so don't have a heart attack if you accidentally select the wrong files. You can use the same approach to erase the contents of your recycle bin—right-click the recycle bin and select Erase Beyond Recovery.

I also recommend that you keep a minimum amount of email messages in your Sent folder and that you regularly review and delete messages from other folders as well. Once you have deleted these messages, you should compact your email folders as instructed in Chapter 4 in the section "Preparing Your Old Computer for Disposal or Redeployment." The compacting process marks the space occupied by the messages as free space, which enables CyberScrub to erase these messages beyond recovery.

For good measure, you should use CyberScrub periodically to erase the free space and slack space on your hard disk as instructed in Chapter 4. This erases your deleted email messages beyond recovery, as well as any other files you might have deleted but forgotten to erase beyond recovery. If you have a significant amount of confidential information in your deleted emails, you may want to do this fairly often as it is the *only* process that erases deleted emails beyond recovery.

Toss Your Cookies

As you may recall from Chapter 4, cookies are small files Web sites store on your computer for the purpose of personalizing your Web surfing experience.

Your cookies might contain information that is of value to a hacker, such as passwords to Web sites. These passwords are encrypted, but a skilled hacker can decrypt them.

Chapter 4 explains how to use CyberScrub to erase all of your cookies when you are preparing your computer for disposition or redeployment.

For a machine that is to remain in service, you might wish to modify this approach.

In Chapter 4, we didn't care about deleting all your cookies because you were going to dispose of or redeploy your old computer. On an ongoing basis, however, you might want to keep some cookies on your computer, particularly if they make your Web surfing experience more enjoyable. For example, if you have customized your Web surfing experience on a particular Web site, the customized settings are stored in a cookie. In most cases, the name of the cookie indicates whether it is worth saving. If this is the case, the easiest approach is to navigate to the `C:\WINDOWS\Cookies` folder, highlight the cookies you want to erase, right-click, and select the Erase Beyond Recovery option. I suggest that you keep a shortcut to this folder on your desktop to make it easy for you to toss your cookies everyday, so to speak.

Should I Disable Cookies?

Your Web browser is set by default to enable (accept) cookies. You have the ability to change this option to either prompt you whenever a Web site wants to place a cookie on your computer or to disallow cookies altogether. I have found that either of these two options makes my Web surfing experience miserable. Some Web sites won't work at all if you disallow cookies, and turning on the prompt option requires constant intervention on your part to allow or disallow cookies. So I have concluded that it is better to leave cookies enabled and purge them at the end of each day.

Don't Install a Wireless Home Network

Wireless Ethernet networks are all the rage now because they enable home networks to be installed without running cables through your walls. (They are also very popular on college campuses for the same reason.) But wireless networks have proven to be a hacker's paradise. Although they utilize a security protocol called WEP (Wired Equivalent Privacy), this protocol has proven to be easy for skilled hackers to crack, leading to a phenomenon known as drive-by hacking, lanjacking, or wardriving.

In drive-by hacking, the hacker pulls up outside your house with a laptop, a wireless networking card, an aerial, software to detect nearby wireless networks (a favorite product of hackers is a Windows-compatible utility called NetStumbler), and packet sniffing software (the network equivalent of wire tapping).

Firewalls can't prevent this type of hacking, as the data being stolen is not behind a firewall—it is traveling over the airwaves.

Traditional wired Ethernet networks are much more secure and much faster than wireless networks. And wireless networking can be a false economy, especially in a home network. The equipment cost for a wireless network is currently about double that for a wired network, offsetting the cost of running cables through the walls.

Use Multiple Passwords

You should protect all sensitive Microsoft Word, Excel, and Quicken documents on your computers with passwords. I suggest that you use a different password for each type of document. That way, if one password gets hacked, your other passwords might still be secure.

For your e-commerce activities, use at least three different passwords: one for your online banking, another for your online brokerage, and a third password for other e-commerce activities.

Choose passwords that are meaningful to you but obscure to anyone else. That way, you can easily remember them, but they can't be easily guessed. Avoid all the obvious choices—birthdays, street addresses, maiden names, pet names, and so on and change your passwords periodically.

Remember to change the password to your email account periodically as well. Be aware that you might have to change this password in two places—on your Internet service provider's server as well as on your computer.

Observe Safe Surfing Rules

Avoid surfing "questionable" Web sites that are more likely to contain malicious hacking-related content.

Be cautious about accepting browser plug-ins from Web sites. *Browser plug-ins* are miniapplications that extend the capabilities of your Web browser. For example, plug-ins can enable you to play streaming audio or video files. Most plug-ins add value to your Web surfing experience, but the problem is that you have absolutely no control over what functionality is added to your computer, and a malicious plug-in can provide hackers with a back door into your computer.

Configure Instant Messenger Tools to Minimize Risk

Internet messenger tools such as AOL Instant Messenger (AIM) provide yet another doorway into your computer. AIM provides the ability to transfer files between users, a feature that can be used to hack into your computer. To prevent this, you should set your AIM preferences to require you to approve any attempt to transfer a file to your computer. Follow these steps:

1. Open AIM. Select My AIM, Edit Options, Edit Preferences.
2. Click File Transfer and select Display Approve Dialog.

I also suggest that you click File Sharing and select Don't Allow to prevent other users from accessing files from a shared file location.

There is no need to manually configure AIM to work with your antivirus software—this happens automatically.

Protect Your Identity

When filling out a Web form, provide the minimum required information. Protect your true email identity. Create an email account on Hotmail or Yahoo! if you need to provide an email account in a Web form. That way, if you get flooded with spam or somebody embeds a virus or hacking tool in an email attachment, the email never makes it to your hard disk.

Message boards, AIM, and other Web-based applications often provide you the opportunity to post a personal profile that others can see. Many of these profiles allow you to share your name, address, email address, phone number, and other personal information with the world at large. My strong advice is that you never, under any circumstances, create a personal profile on the Web. Anytime this information is available to others, somebody will find a way to use it to target you for spam, computer viruses, a hack attack, or even a personal attack. For the same reason, you should never share any personal information while in any kind of chat room.

Never use your actual name or anything close to it as a screen name, and never respond to emails from strangers requesting personal information for any reason.

As an adult, you might realize many of these things instinctively, but I assure you that your children do not, and I implore you to teach your children well in this regard.

Limit Physical Access to Your Computer

We have a rule around our house—our computers are strictly off limits to visiting relatives and friends. Relatives and friends are not aware of your antivirus and anti-hacking policies, and probably don't care in the least if their actions precipitate a computer disaster for you. Your computer is likely to become much more unstable if you allow visitors and houseguests to have access.

Spyware and Adware: The Newest Hacking Threats

> "Every move you make, every step you take, I'll be watching you."
>
> —Sting

Spyware is an application that resides on your computer, gathers information *without your knowledge or permission*, and sends it back to the spyware developer via the Internet.

Adware does pretty much the same thing as spyware, but the difference is that adware developers disclose that their software is being installed on your computer, usually in tandem with a legitimate application you have chosen to install.

So, without the disclosure, an application that gathers information about you is spyware; with disclosure, that same application is adware.

But I think the distinction runs deeper than one of simple disclosure versus nondisclosure.

I think that it is reasonable to assume that spyware programs are more nefarious than adware programs. Adware developers disclose who they are and what they are doing and ask your permission to gather the data (in small print, mind you, but they do ask). The point is, adware developers don't hide from your view, and I think that makes them less likely to do something illegal with the data they gather.

Spyware vendors operate stealthily, and although there may be some legitimate uses for spyware (such as parents monitoring their children's Internet activity), I think we can safely assume that if a spyware program is on your computer it is up to no darn good.

How Does Adware Get on Your Computer?

Adware is frequently tightly bundled with useful software applications. For example, the file sharing service KaZaA includes two adware products, Brilliant Digital and Cydoor. If you decline to install Cydoor or use a special tool to uninstall it later, KaZaA will not function. It's not that Cydoor provides functionality to KaZaA, but that KaZaA has intentionally been written in such a way that it functions only if the adware is installed, thus the phrase *tightly bundled*. So, you need to decide whether the functionality provided by KaZaA is important enough to you to allow adware on your computer.

A spyware program might monitor your every keystroke and steal all your passwords, credit card numbers, bank account numbers, and brokerage account numbers. It can record your instant messages and steal your email. In short, spyware is the electronic equivalent of somebody looking over your shoulder, watching and recording every move you make.

Spyware can be installed on your computer a number of ways without your knowledge—it can be included in a freeware application you download from the Web, or it can be downloaded from a Web site you visit.

Spyware and adware programs are well hidden on your computer—you can't stop them from running by removing them from your list of startup items, and they don't show up on your add/remove programs list.

Firewalls like ZoneAlarm that monitor outbound as well as inbound communications can detect spyware when it tries to transmit data to the Internet, but they can't detect the specific spyware programs that may be installed on your computer.

Getting Rid of Spyware

Spycop, discussed in Chapter 2, scans your computer for known spyware programs and is updated frequently to recognize new spyware programs. Like antivirus software, you need to keep your software updated to have maximum protection.

Spycop is very easy to use—you basically install it, open it, and click the Scan Now button. Spycop uses a brute-force approach to examine every file on your hard disk, and it takes a while. To speed up the process, Spycop provides an option to only scan files that were created on your computer since the previous scan.

Although Spycop can detect the specific spyware programs on your system, it can't remove them. You must search the Internet to find a third-party program to eliminate any spyware programs found by the scan.

Getting Rid of Adware

Another product, Ad-aware, complements Spycop and finds adware on your computer. Ad-aware is a free tool that can be downloaded from `http://www.lavasoft.nu`.

Unlike Spycop, Ad-aware enables you to delete adware products installed on your computer. But you need to be aware of whether deleting such products will stop an application such as KaZaA from functioning. I downloaded and ran Ad-aware. It found the two adware applications that are installed by KaZaA: Brilliant Digital and Cydoor. I deleted Brilliant Digital because I knew from my research that I could do so without disabling KaZaA. But I left Cydoor on my computer because deleting it would have disabled KaZaA, eliminating my ability to download audio and video files.

Ad-aware lets you take a backup of the files you are deleting. If removing the files disables an application, you can easily restore the deleted files at the click of a button.

Spyware and adware are relatively recent phenomenons. As of this writing, it is too early to determine whether a product like Spycop will become as essential as, say, antivirus software.

You *Aren't* the Weakest Link

Let's say, for the sake of argument, that you've installed antivirus software, firewalls, and antihacking tools to detect spyware and adware. You've learned how to use these tools effectively and are diligent about keeping your software up-to-date. You've even implemented all my other recommendations for minimizing your exposure to cyber-terrorists.

Good for you. But before you get too comfortable, I hasten to point out that the chain is only as strong as its weakest link. And in this case, the weakest link might be another computer—specifically, a computer hundreds or thousands of miles away at an e-commerce company with whom you have willingly shared personal and financial data.

As I sit here putting the final touches on this chapter, the following email message has fluttered into my inbox from a personal computer e-tailer with whom I have done business:

From: <Name of company>
To: <my email address>
Wednesday, May 29, 2002 12:59 PM
Dear Customer,
We have discovered that a hacker has accessed our computer systems, potentially including our customer databases. While there is no indication that any customer information has been compromised, as a precautionary measure, we have taken immediate steps to protect you by contacting the U.S. Secret Service and the FBI. Since speaking with law enforcement we have discovered who the hackers are and their motives. Just recently another internet company was a victim of "Zilterio".
Lead by a man who calls himself "Mr. Zilterio," they wanted $50,000 transferred to a bank account that was traced through Russia to Yemen.
The threat? Zilterio claimed that they had, or might be able to access confidential customer information, to include credit card numbers.
Here are some of the details that we have learned.
We quickly learned, from talking to law enforcement authorities and other victims, that the same criminal and his associates had extorted as much as $4 billion from other companies using similar tactics.
We found that they may, in fact, have exploited an obscure and previously unknown hole in a common commercial software program we use, one that's supposed to be very secure.
We quickly plugged that hole and have now taken extraordinary additional steps to put customer data where it can't be accessed except locally by authorized staff.
We notified the major credit card companies of the threat and they have placed a special watch on your credit card numbers -- this will NOT affect your ability to use the card, but some of you might get occasional calls from your credit card issuer just to make sure that certain charges were, in fact, made by you.
Respectfully,
<Name of company>

Five hours later, I received another email informing me that credit card information had in fact been compromised:

From: <Name of company>
Wednesday, May 29, 2002 6:16 PM
Dear Customer,
After conferring with the FBI, Secret Service and several valued customers, it has become clear that your personal and credit card information might have been compromised. In fact, some customers even received their credit card numbers from this self-confessed cyber-terrorist over a non-secure internet

connection. Because of this most unfortunate development, we highly recommend that all previous customers contact their credit card company, inform them that your card might be compromised and seek their recommendation for a course of action.

In addition, we are pleased to report we have discovered and repaired the hole which this criminal used to violate each of us. Unfortunately, Microsoft made the public aware of the hole just last week. In addition to repairing the hole, we are now changing the way our customer information is stored. Customer data will no longer be accessible by anyone, even our internal staff, over any type of Internet connection.

Again, thank you for your patience and understanding. We hope to service your computer needs in the near future.
Regards,
<Name of company>

According to my research, this company was hacked by the same hacker who hacked into the webcertificate.com Web site in August 2001, and tried to blackmail its parent company, Ecount.

The previous emails are similar to several others I have received in the past from other e-commerce companies. They serve as sober reminders that we can be victims of cyber-terrorists even if our own computer hasn't been breached.

I don't have much to offer in the way of solace. It is clear that security is lax at many e-commerce Web sites. Hopefully, things will improve in time, but for now, it seems that hackers are having a field day.

CHAPTER 6

Backing Up Your Data

Revelations

In this chapter you will learn

- ☐ The advantages and disadvantages of three data backup strategies and how to select the strategy that is right for you

- ☐ The two fundamental technical flaws inherent in every backup strategy and what you can to do mitigate their impact

- ☐ The difference between protecting your data and protecting your data backup

- ☐ How to find and back up data your applications may be hiding from you

- ☐ Some tricks for storing your daily backups offsite without ever leaving your house

- ☐ A technique called progressive revisioning that can protect your data from yourself

Overview

Then again, maybe it won't happen. According to my mother, the probability of a disaster is inversely proportional to the time one spends preparing for said disaster. I first heard this theory of hers when, as a small child during the Cold War, I watched as she prepared a makeshift bomb shelter in our basement. I asked her why she was doing this, and she responded with total equanimity, "Because if I do, World War III will never happen." In retrospect, it's hard to argue with her logic. *So far.*

This chapter and Chapter 7 assume that you are backing up your data to CD media and that you are using the tools recommended in Chapter 2, "The Threats and the Tools," for these tasks: Easy CD Creator or Backup NOW! for data backups and Norton Ghost for disk imaging. Refer to Chapter 2 for an explanation as to why CD media is the logical choice today for data and hard disk backups. This chapter does not explore backing up using slower, less reliable media such as tape.

If I may be permitted to amend an old aphorism, there are *three* inevitable things in life: death, taxes, and computer disasters.

In spite of your best efforts to prevent computer disasters, you will probably experience at least one major disaster during the life of your computer. Even if you diligently follow all the disaster prevention advice contained in *PC Fear Factor*, there are things that you just can't control. It's the fundamental nature of an unstable equilibrium. My computer is two years old, and I have already experienced two major disasters—and I am probably more diligent than 99.9% of personal computer users in taking all possible disaster prevention measures.

I can't predict what will happen to you or when it will happen—only that if you use computers long enough, it *will* happen.

This Chapter and Chapter 7, "Backing Up Your Hard Disk," prepare you for this inevitable eventuality.

If you diligently follow these backup instructions, you will be able to easily recover from even the worst possible computer disaster—a disaster that either physically or logically trashes your hard disk.

This chapter explains the four things you need to be fully protected against data loss:

- A data backup strategy (three basic backup strategies will be presented)
- A data backup protection strategy (how to protect your backups from fire, theft, flood, and family members)
- A data storage strategy (how to store your data on your hard disk to facilitate data backups)
- A data backup preparation plan (the steps you should perform just prior to backing up your data)

This chapter provides an in-depth understanding of three data backup strategies. It explains the basics of each approach, the circumstances that might lead you to choose a particular approach, and the advantages and disadvantages of each approach relative to the others. This enables you to select the backup strategy that is most appropriate for your particular situation. Suggestions for tweaking these three strategies to design your own personal strategy are provided as well.

You will learn about two fundamental flaws inherent in any backup strategy and what you can do to minimize their impact.

Detailed, step-by-step instructions for executing each backup strategy are included, along with instructions for restoring individual files from a data backup. (Chapter 8, "Disaster Recovery," provides instructions for restoring all your data from a backup.)

Finally, you will learn a technique for protecting yourself against self-inflicted computer disasters.

Backup Terminology

This section defines nine terms that are used extensively throughout the chapter. You must know what these terms mean to understand, select, and execute a backup strategy.

File Backup Software

File backup software is software that has special features to aid in backing up and restoring data. The file backup software product I recommend is NTI's Backup NOW! Deluxe.

If you have very little data to back up, you do not need file backup software. You can back up your data by using DirectCD, a component of Roxio's Easy CD Creator software, to drag and drop all your data files to a CD-R or CD-RW. You might even be able to take a complete backup of all your data on a daily basis.

If, on the other hand, you have enough data to fill several CDs, you should give serious consideration to using file backup software, as it makes your task much easier and less error prone.

Even if you plan on using the drag-and-drop approach for backing up your data, I strongly recommend that you read this entire chapter, as much of the material presented is applicable (and valuable!) regardless of your backup strategy.

The Projected Rise and Fall and Rise in the Demand for File Backup Software

Just three years ago I could back up all my data to a single 100MB Zip disk. I had no need for file backup software—the drag-and-drop approach was quite adequate for my needs.

My data explosion was precipitated by three events: broadband, my interest in digital photography, and the availability of higher-capacity hard disks.

At first, I was able to store all my data on one CD-RW. The drag-and-drop approach was still adequate for my needs.

Soon, I found that I needed three CD-RWs to back up all my data: one for my MP3 files, one for my digital photographs, and one for all my other data. It was still easy to use the drag-and-drop approach because I could simply drag the appropriate file folders to the appropriate CD-RWs.

Eventually, I reached the point where I had so much data that the drag-and-drop backup strategy was no longer viable. At this point, I needed a formal file backup software solution to address my backup needs.

The demand for file backup software is currently increasing rapidly as more and more users' data storage requirements grow beyond the practical limits of the drag-and-drop backup approach.

As we make the transition over the next few years from CD-based backups to DVD-based backups, the demand for file backup software will diminish because the drag-and-drop approach will allow users to copy 4.7GB of data onto one DVD.

But the demand for file backup software will gradually increase again as our data storage requirements grow beyond the practical limits of even DVD drag-and-drop backups.

Baseline Backup

A *baseline* backup is a complete backup of all your data. It is also referred to as a *full* backup, *complete* backup, or *normal* backup. I prefer the term *baseline* because it correctly implies that this backup is a starting point—that there is a supplemental process you should perform to keep your baseline backup up-to-date. This supplemental process backs up files that have been modified or created since the baseline backup was performed. The next three definitions define and explain this supplemental process.

Differential Backup

A *differential* backup is one of two methods provided by file backup software (the other being an incremental backup) to keep your baseline backup up-to-date.

By definition, a differential backup backs up all files that have been modified or created since the last baseline backup, as illustrated by the following simplified example:

> On day 1, you take a baseline backup of all your files: `file01`, `file02`, `file03`, and `file04`.
>
> On day 2, you modify `file01` and create a new file, `file05`. A differential backup backs up `file01` and `file05`.
>
> On day 3, you modify `file02` and create a new file, `file06`. A differential backup backs up `file01`, `file02`, `file05`, and `file06`. Note that `file01` and `file05` are backed up again because the differential backup process is cumulative—it backs up *every* file that has been modified or created since the baseline backup was taken on day 1.

Because a differential backup is cumulative of all changes (including new files), the data restore process is a relatively simple two-step process:

1. You restore your baseline backup.
2. You restore only your latest differential backup. This restores all files that have been modified or created since the baseline backup. (The earlier differential backups are not needed.)

Incremental Backup

Incremental backups are the second method provided by file backup software to supplement a baseline backup.

By definition, an *incremental* backup backs up only those files that have modified or created since the last backup, as illustrated by the following simplified example:

> On day 1, you take a baseline backup of all your files: `file01`, `file02`, `file03`, and `file04`.

On day 2, you modify `file01` and create a new file, `file05`. An incremental backup backs up `file01` and `file05`.

On day 3, you modify `file02` and create a new file, `file06`. An incremental backup backs up `file02` and `file06`.

On day 4, you modify `file01` again and create `file07`. An incremental backup backs up `file01` and `file07`.

Essentially, a differential backup is cumulative, whereas an incremental backup is additive.

Because each incremental backup backs up only those files that have been modified or created since the previous backup, the data restore process is much more complicated.

Note that in the previous example, `file05` can only be found on the incremental backup taken on day 2, and `file06` can only be found on the incremental backup taken on day 3.

Note also that `file01` is included on the incremental backups taken on day 2 and day 4 because it was modified on both of these days. The most up-to-date version of `file01` is on the day 4 incremental backup.

To restore your data from incremental backups, you must restore your baseline backup and then restore every one of your incremental backups in sequence, from oldest to latest. By restoring the incremental backups in this sequence, if a file exists on several incremental backups, the latest version will automatically overwrite the earlier version.

Differential Versus Incremental Backups

Differential backups require more CD media and take more time to perform than incremental backups because each differential backup backs up every file that has changed or been created since the baseline backup was performed. However, restoring from differential backups is a simple two-step process.

Incremental backups require a minimum amount of CD media and can be performed very quickly, but restoring your data is a complex, multistep process. For example, if you have a baseline backup and 10 incremental backups, you must perform 11 steps to restore all your data. And if you are trying to find just one file to restore—well, happy hunting.

Archive Bit

The archive bit is a feature in Windows that facilitates differential and incremental backups. You should understand what an archive bit does because it will help you understand how file backup software works. It will also help you understand one of the limitations of incremental backups, which is explained later in the section "How Many Backup Sets Do I Need?"

If you right-click any file in a My Computer or a Windows Explorer window and select Properties, you see a list of file attributes (see Figure 6.1).

FIGURE 6.1

The archive bit facili-tates differential and incremental backups. If the archive bit is checked, a differential or incremental backup will back up the file. Baseline backups ignore the archive bit and back up everything.

The archive bit is one of these file attributes. It is used to determine whether file backup software will back up a specific file. If the archive bit is set (checked), the file will be backed up when you perform a differential or an incremental backup. In essence, the archive bit is saying, "Back me up, Scotty." When the archive bit is cleared, differential and incremental backups ignore the file.

Which brings us to the logical question: What conditions cause the archive bit to be set or cleared?

Let's start with the baseline backup. Baseline backups don't care whether the archive bit is set. Whenever you perform a baseline backup, all the selected files are backed up and the archive bit on every file is automatically cleared as part of the baseline backup process.

When a file is modified or created subsequent to the baseline backup, Windows sets (checks) the archive bit and the file is backed up again when a differential or an incremental backup is performed.

The fundamental difference between differential and incremental backups is reflected in what they do to the archive bit.

Differential backups do not clear the archive bit—they leave the archive bit set. This is why differential backups are cumulative—once the archive bit is set, it doesn't get cleared until the next baseline backup is performed. For example, if file01 is modified subsequent to the baseline backup, the archive bit on file01 is set and file01 is backed up every time you perform a differential backup, even though it might have only changed one time.

Incremental backups clear the archive bit after the file is backed up successfully. This is why incremental backups only back up files that were modified or created since the previous backup. If file01 is modified (setting the archive bit), the incremental backup backs up file01 and clears the archive bit. Unless file01 is modified again, which would reset (recheck) the archive bit, the next incremental backup will *not* back up file01.

Don't Mix Backup Methods

Because of the fundamental difference between how differential and incremental backups manage the archive bit, you should never mix these two methods. The only time you can choose one or the other method is immediately following a baseline backup. You must then stick with that method until the next baseline backup, or you can create a self-inflicted computer disaster.

Backup Set

A *backup set* is the complete set of media (either CD-R or CD-RW if you are backing up to CDs) associated with a backup. It includes all the discs from the baseline backup and all the discs from the differential or incremental backups that have been performed to supplement the baseline. When we talk about restoring data, we're talking about restoring a specific backup set (usually, the most current set).

You do not have to use a separate CD for each differential or incremental backup. As long as there is free space on the disc, you can append these backups to prior backups. If you take baseline backups weekly, it is possible that all the differential or incremental backups taken between baseline backups will fit on a single CD.

How Many Backup Sets Do I Need?

You should always keep at least three backup sets on hand: your current backup set and the two previous backup sets. If you have to restore all your data and are unable to restore from your current backup due to corrupted media, you will still have older backups to fall back on. Of course, you will lose some data if you have to restore from an older backup.

If you are truly paranoid—an admirable quality in a system administrator—you can keep *two* complete current backup sets on hand. For example, you can take two baseline backups and keep two sets of differential backups. This is called a *dual backup strategy*. This way, if a restore fails due to corrupted media, you have another current backup set you can use.

The dual backup strategy is viable with either drag-and-drop backups or differential backups. It will *not* work with the incremental backup strategy. You can't create two separate, current sets of incremental backups because incremental backups clear the archive bit on the files that were backed up. If you were to attempt to take a second incremental backup immediately after taking an incremental backup, nothing would get backed up! This is the limitation associated with incremental backups that I referred to in the earlier discussion of archive bits.

Backup Set Rotation

The term *backup set rotation* refers to the fact that CD-RWs are reusable. Once you have accumulated the desired number of backup sets, you can begin reusing the media from the oldest backup set. In this manner, you are always rotating your backup sets, replacing your oldest set with your newest set.

If you are using CD-R media, you can't rotate your backup sets because the media is not reusable. You simply destroy old backup sets that are no longer of value.

Should I Use CD-R or CD-RW Media for My Backups?

There is no right answer to this question. If your most important objective is to minimize the time to perform backups, use CD-R discs because software can write to CD-Rs much faster than it can write to CD-RWs.

If your most important objective is to minimize costs, use CD-RW media. CD-RW discs cost more than CD-Rs, but you save money in the long run because the discs are reusable.

My personal preference is CD-R media. I find that the benefit of quicker backup speeds is worth the extra cost.

Backup Job

A *backup job* is simply a set of backup instructions that can be created, saved, and executed on a repetitive basis when you are using file backup software. The backup job specifies all the parameters related to the backup, including

- The files to be backed up
- The type of backup to be performed (baseline, differential, or incremental)
- Whether data should be compressed as it is being backed up to save space on the backup media
- Whether the backup is password-protected

Backup jobs eliminate the need for you to remember where your data is stored each time you want to take a backup. If your data is scattered about in several places on your hard disk, you can identify those places one time when you define your backup job. For example, most of my data is in the `My Documents` folder, but I have some applications that automatically create and store data in other folders. So long as I specify all these locations when I define the backup job, I can easily back up all my data without having to constantly remember where my data is stored.

To avoid confusion in this chapter, where a backup file and data are being discussed in the same paragraph, I will use the term *data file* to refer to data that is being backed up to distinguish it from the backup file—the file containing all the backed-up data files.

Backup File

Whenever you use file backup software to create a backup—whether it is a baseline backup, a differential backup, or an incremental backup—that backup is stored as a single backup file on your CD media. This is true even if the backup spans multiple discs.

Each backup file has a unique name that includes the date and time the file was created. You can define the name to make it meaningful to you. For example, if you are using Backup NOW!, a backup file named `baseline backup job_020604_152156.NBF` indicates that the backup was performed on June 4, 2002, at 3:21:56 p.m.

This completes the definitions of the nine backup-related terms that are used throughout this chapter. You now have the background required to understand the fundamental technical flaws with any backup strategy.

The Fundamental Technical Flaws in Any Backup Strategy

Before we proceed with a discussion of backup strategies, you should be aware that all backup strategies have two fundamental technical flaws:

- They may restore too much data.
- They may restore data to the wrong location on your hard disk.

Allow me to explain why this is so, and what you can do to minimize the impact of these inherent flaws.

As you use your computer, you constantly create, modify, and delete files. You also reorganize your data, moving files from one folder to another. For example, I frequently reorganize my collection of digital photographs.

Over a long period of time, you might delete hundreds, even thousands, of files you don't need anymore. You also might move dozens or even hundreds of files to different locations (folders) on your computer.

Should you have to restore your data from a backup, you will inadvertently and unavoidably restore any files you have deleted off your hard disk since the baseline backup was taken. For example, if your baseline backup contains `file01` and `file02`, and if you deleted these two files *after* the baseline backup was taken, restoring your data from the baseline backup restores `file01` and `file02` to your computer, *even though you don't want them anymore*. The restore process isn't intelligent—it doesn't know and doesn't care that you don't want these files anymore.

Unfortunately, you will have no choice but to go back through all your restored data files and re-delete the files you no longer want. (Alternatively, you could deselect these files from the restore process so they are not restored, but the process is fundamentally the same—you still have to go through all your files and identify the ones you no longer want.)

But that's not the only problem: Under certain circumstances, different versions of the same file can be restored to different locations on your hard disk, as illustrated in the following scenario:

> `file01` is located in `folderA` when a baseline backup is taken. `file01` is then moved to `folderB` and modified, which sets the archive bit. If you take a differential or incremental backup, `file01` will be backed up because it has been modified since the baseline backup. If you have to restore your data, the latest version of `file01` will be restored to `folderB` and the earlier baseline version of `file01` will be restored to `folderA`.

> The earlier version of the file in `folderA` should be deleted after the data has been restored.

Obviously, if a file is moved and modified several times between baseline backups, several different versions of the file could be restored to several locations.

This creates a confusing and potentially dangerous situation, should you start working with the wrong (older) version of the file after your data has been restored.

You can mitigate the impact of these two flaws by taking baseline backups often. Regardless of which backup strategy you employ, I strongly recommend that you take a new baseline backup weekly. This way, if you have to restore your data, the worst-case scenario is that you will have to fix problems created during a seven-day period. You can mitigate the impact even more by leaving any deleted files in your recycle bin until you take your next baseline backup and keeping a log of which files you have moved between baseline backups. This enables you to identify which files you need to re-delete if you have to restore your data from a backup.

The Importance of a Data Backup Protection Strategy

It's not enough to have a strategy for backing up your data—you must have a strategy for protecting your backups as well.

I was recently chatting with a neighbor about *PC Fear Factor*. As we were talking, he told me about his backup strategy. I was most interested in what he had to say on the subject because he is a computer expert.

He started telling me about his RAID configuration. No, not Raid, the insecticide. RAID stands for redundant array of inexpensive disks. Basically, if you have a RAID configuration on your computer, all your data is written to two different hard disks. This means that even if one of the hard disks fails, you will not have lost any data— hence the term *redundant*.

I looked at him and said, "You don't have a valid backup strategy."

He replied, "What do you mean? I just told you about my RAID configuration."

To which I replied, "The most elaborate RAID configuration in the world still doesn't protect you against fire, flood, or theft."

He immediately saw my point and nodded in agreement.

A RAID configuration is not a valid backup strategy, and copying your data across a home network to a computer in another room is also not a valid backup strategy because neither strategy protects your backup from these exogenous factors.

Strategies for Protecting Your Baseline Backup

Simply stated, you *don't* have a valid backup strategy unless the strategy allows you to store your current backup offsite.

At an absolute minimum, your current baseline backup should always be stored off-site in a safe deposit box. If you are not willing to go to this effort, you are really just kidding yourself. You are only protecting yourself against data loss caused by computer viruses, a hard disk crash, human error, and so on. You are not protecting yourself against fire, flood, and theft. Nor are you protecting yourself from the kid who goes into your closet and "borrows" your CD-RWs.

Until recently, getting into your safe deposit box was a pain. You had to get a bank employee to assist you, and two keys—yours and theirs—had to be inserted to open the box. Most banks today provide single-key access to safe deposit boxes. Getting in and out is a breeze, so if you don't have a safe deposit box, get one and store your backups offsite. You'll thank me later.

Be they angels or devils, kids are still kids. A family member once borrowed the CD wallet where I store all my software CDs. Not only did she borrow the wallet, she removed and destroyed all the stickers that contained the software registration keys—the printed stickers that were marked "URGENT. DO NOT REMOVE." in 36-point print. My blood boils anew at the sheer memory of this episode. On the plus side, I now have one less person to feed and clothe.

Not-So-Safe Deposit Boxes

If you have single-key entry to your safe deposit box, make absolutely certain that the key does not have the box number stamped on it and that the little envelope in which the key is stored does not indicate the name of the bank. This way, should your key be lost or stolen, the person can't walk into the bank and empty your safe deposit box—the key is too small a needle in too large a haystack. I further suggest that you commit your safe deposit box number to memory and not have any documents in your house that identify the bank or box number.

Make certain that your bank follows good security procedures regarding single-key access. I walked into my bank last year and found the safe deposit box card index sitting in the vault. If somebody had my key and my name, all he would have to do is look up the box number on the index file. I chastised the branch manager for such poor security. It has not been a problem since.

Strategies for Protecting Your Daily Backups

Unless you live next door to the bank, you aren't likely to take your daily differential or incremental backups to your safe deposit box. But fear not—here are some off-site storage alternatives that might work for you:

- Make a copy of the disk and entrust it to a neighbor.

- Email your daily backup file to a trusted friend or relative, or configure ZoneAlarm's local (trusted) zone to allow you and a friend or relative to directly share files between computers. Perhaps you can work out an exchange agreement—you can store your daily backups on a friend's computer, and he can store his daily backups on your computer.

- Email copies of your daily backups to yourself at a third-party, server-based email account. This way, you are storing your backups on a Hotmail server or Yahoo! server.

Backup NOW! Deluxe, the file backup software recommended in *PC Fear Factor*, provides the ability to password-protect your backup files. It's always a good idea to password-protect your backup files, but it is *extremely important* that you do so if you are going to email them to anybody or store them on a third-party server.

The Importance of a Data Storage Strategy

To facilitate data backups, I strongly recommend that you keep all your data in one central folder location. This should be a root (top-level) folder. If you store your data in multiple unrelated folders, you will have a more difficult time remembering where all your data is, and you might forget to back up important data.

I strongly recommend that you use Windows' top-level root folder C:\My Documents folder as your data repository for the following reasons:

For the balance of this chapter, I will assume that you will be storing the bulk of your data in the C:/My Documents folder. If you choose to store your data in some other location, you can mentally substitute that folder name in the discussion.

- **The My Documents folder is strictly *verboten* for the System Restore feature found in Windows Millennium and Windows XP**—In theory, the System Restore feature will never harm your data, even if it is stored in other folders. In practice, you provide yourself with an additional layer of security by keeping your data in the My Documents folder, which is explicitly off-limits to System Restore.

- **Most of your applications try to store and find data in the My Documents folder by default anyway**—So, accepting the default folder saves you time when you save or open documents.

Of course, you can organize your data within the My Documents folder however you like—create as many folders and as many levels of folders as you like, so long as they all fall under the root My Documents folder.

Are Your Applications Playing Hide-and-Seek with Your Data?

In some situations, storing data in the My Documents folder will be impossible. Certain applications play hide-and-seek with your data. They automatically determine where data is stored and never give you the option of choosing a storage location. The real challenge you face in backing up your data is finding out which applications do this and where the data is stored.

For example, I use the United States Postal Office Shipping Assistant Software to generate priority mail labels. This software allows me to create an address book, which it stores locally on my computer, but I can't control where the address book is stored—it is automatically stored in the following folder:

```
C:\Program Files\USPSShippingAssistant\DefaultAddressBook
```

And, of course, your email, Windows address book, and browser bookmarks are not stored in the My Documents folder.

You might need to conduct some research to find out where this "hide-and-seek data" is stored. A good place to start looking is in the program file directory for the application. If you know the file extension of the data file, you can do a search for all files having a particular extension. If you can't find the data, you may have to contact the software vendor for assistance.

I recommend that you document all this information so you don't lose track of any of your data.

Selecting a Backup Strategy

At this point, you should now understand backup terminology, the inherent technical flaws in any backup strategy, the importance of protecting your backup as well as your data, and the importance of a data storage strategy.

Congratulations! You are now ready to consider alternative backup strategies and select the strategy that is most appropriate for your needs.

There is no single correct answer to the question, "What is the best backup strategy?"

Any one of several strategies, carefully planned and diligently executed, will work just fine. With that in mind, in this section I offer three backup strategies for your consideration. The following information is provided for each of the three strategies:

- A brief description of the strategy
- Situational considerations, that is, situations where the strategy might be the most logical choice
- Advantages and disadvantages relative to other strategies

Once you have reviewed the three basic strategies, I suggest that you select the most appropriate strategy for your situation. Later sections of this chapter provide detailed step-by-step instructions for executing each of these three strategies.

You can also design your own backup strategy by tweaking any of these strategies. I offer some ideas on how to do this at the end of this section.

The Importance of Intra-Day Backups

All three of these backup strategies are based on a timetable of weekly baseline backups supplemented by daily backups. I would be remiss in not pointing out the benefits of intra-day backups of critical data. For example, I consider this chapter that I am typing to be critical data. If I lose a full day's worth of work, it will set me back a great deal. So I save my work to my hard disk every few minutes, and I back up my work to another computer on my home network or to a CD-RW every half hour. I have been rewarded for my diligence in taking intra-day backups of critical data on many occasions. These intra-day backups, however, do not replace my end-of-day differential backups.

The Drag-and-Drop Strategy

With the drag-and-drop strategy, you use DirectCD, a component of Roxio's Easy CD Creator, to copy all your data files to a CD-R or CD-RW to create a baseline backup.

If you have too much data to fit on one CD, you must manually parse the data into CD-size chunks and drag the appropriate folders to each CD. For example, you might put all your MP3s on one CD, your digital photographs on another CD, and all other data on a third CD.

On a daily basis, you should drag and drop all files you have modified or created since your baseline backup to a separate CD-RW. This provides the drag-and-drop equivalent of a differential backup.

The drag-and-drop strategy is a logical one if all your data can fit on one CD, or if your data can easily be parsed into CD-size chunks.

Advantages

- This approach is an extension of what you already know how to do—copy files from one location to another.

- You don't need to purchase file backup software.

- This approach is compatible with a dual backup strategy should you elect to keep two current backups of your data.

Disadvantages

- You can encounter software compatibility issues if you use this method to migrate data from a Windows 98 or Windows Millennium computer to a Windows XP computer. The latest version of Easy CD Creator must be installed on *both* computers or the Windows XP computer will not be able to read the backup disk you created on the Windows 98 or Windows Millennium computer.

- This strategy is cumbersome if you have a great deal of data because you have to manually parse the data into CD-size chunks.

- Restoring individual files from daily backups is more difficult than with file backup software because daily drag-and-drop file backups don't keep track of the file's location on the hard disk. For example, suppose you create `file02` in the `C:\My Documents\Alan's Pictures` folder on your hard disk. The file wasn't included in your baseline backup, so you copy it to a CD-RW to have a backup. Should you have to restore all your data, you must remember that `file02` belongs in the `C:\My Documents\Alan's Pictures` folder. File backup software would automatically restore `file02` to the `C:\My Documents\Alan's Pictures` folder—you would not have to remember the restore location.

- The backup can't be password-protected.

The Differential Strategy

With the differential strategy, you use file backup software to take a weekly baseline backup and supplement it with daily differential backups.

The differential strategy is a good approach if you need many CDs to back up all your data and if the convenience of a simple two-step restore process is more important than saving time and media costs when you perform your daily backup.

Advantages

- This approach provides an easy two-step restore process.
- This approach is conceptually easier to understand than the incremental backup strategy.
- This approach is compatible with a dual backup strategy should you elect to keep two current backups of your data.
- Files from daily backups are automatically restored to the correct folders (unlike the drag-and-drop restore process).

Disadvantages

- Daily backups require more media space and take more time than incremental backups.

The Incremental Strategy

With the incremental strategy, you use file backup software to take a weekly baseline backup and supplement it with daily incremental backups.

The incremental strategy is a good approach if you need many CDs to back up all your data and if the convenience of a fast backup process is more important than saving time when you restore your data.

Advantages

- This approach requires a minimum amount of media and time to perform daily backups.
- Files from daily backups are automatically restored to the correct folders (unlike the drag-and-drop restore process).

Disadvantages

- This approach is not compatible with a dual backup strategy because incremental backups clear the archive bit on backed up files.
- The incremental backup strategy has the most complicated restore strategy of all three basic backup strategies. To perform a complete restore of your data, you have to restore your baseline backup and then every incremental backup in sequence from oldest to newest.

- It is particularly difficult to find and restore a single data file. You have to search through every backup file in your backup set in reverse sequence from newest to oldest, starting with the latest incremental backup and working your way back to the baseline backup, until you find the data file you are seeking. (Because you are going from newest to oldest, the first version of the data file you find will be the latest version—the version you should restore.)

Designing Your Own Backup Strategy

You can design your own backup strategy by tweaking any of the strategies that have been presented. Here are some ways to tweak your backup strategy:

- **Change the time interval between baseline backups**—If you want to take a baseline backup more often than once a week, I applaud your dedication. Of course, if you take a baseline every day, there is no need for differential or incremental backups. You can also increase the time interval between baseline backups, provided you are mindful that this gives you greater exposure to the fundamental technical flaws inherent in any backup strategy discussed earlier in this chapter.

- **Change the time interval between differential or incremental backups**—Take these supplementary backups every two or three days, if you are willing to risk losing up to two or three days' worth of data.

- **Use a dual backup strategy**—Although CD media is far more reliable than tape, you might still occasionally experience a problem with corrupt media. If you don't want to incur the risk of restoring from an older backup, take and maintain two current backup sets. The incremental backup strategy is not compatible with the dual backup strategy.

CD Care and Handling

When handling CDs, keep the following information in mind:

- Do not write on the disc with an ink/ballpoint pen; use a felt-tip pen.
- Handle CDs by the edges because fingerprints cause read errors due to refracting the laser.
- Avoid direct sunlight and high heat because it is harmful to the dye of CD media.
- Avoid scratches; do not lay the CD face down on a surface.
- Store your CDs in jewel cases or a CD wallet. Slim jewel cases do not take up much room in a safe deposit box.
- If your media is worth backing up then it is worth backing up on quality, name-brand media. Cheap media often denotes poor quality.

- **Keep additional backup sets on hand**—I always recommend that you keep three complete backup sets. You can choose to keep four or five backup sets on hand for extra safety. Under no circumstances should you keep fewer than three backup sets on hand.

- **Back up over a home network**—If you have a home network, I encourage you to do a drag-and-drop data backup to another computer on your home network. If you do this often, you might be able to use this backup to restore your data instead of using your CD media. However, I caution you again that backing up your data over your home network is not in and of itself a valid backup strategy because it does not allow for offsite storage. Home network backups should only be used to complement CD media backups.

Recommendations

All things considered, I recommend the drag-and-drop strategy if all your data can fit on one CD or if it can be easily and logically parsed into a few CDs.

Otherwise, I recommend using Backup NOW!, and I prefer the differential backup approach to the incremental approach. You can restore your data much more easily with differential backups than with incremental backups, and you can use a dual backup strategy if you choose.

Preparing for a Data Backup

Regardless of which backup strategy you choose, you need to perform some tasks in preparation for a data backup. These tasks should be performed *just prior* to taking a backup to ensure that you are backing up the latest information.

Some of the following preparation steps apply only to baseline backups, whereas others apply to both baseline and daily differential/incremental backups. Some steps are applicable only to certain backup strategies. All this is clearly indicated in the description of each step.

Step 1: Clean Up Your Data

This step is applicable only to baseline backups.

Go through your data and delete any files you no longer need. The more data you get rid of prior to taking your baseline, the less time and fewer discs you need to perform the backup. This includes deleting old email messages.

Step 2: Back Up Your Email, Address Book, and Browser Bookmarks

This step is applicable to both baseline and daily differential/incremental backups because you should back up this information every day. (Exception: While I advise against it, if you are willing to risk losing up to a week's worth of email, you do not need to perform this step between baseline backups.)

There is one other approach worth mentioning in passing. If you have a super-fast CD writer and less than 5GB of information in total (data, applications, and operating system) on your hard disk, you might want to use Norton Ghost to take a complete backup of your hard disk every day. As mentioned in Chapter 2, Norton Ghost has a Ghost Explorer that allows you to restore data files without restoring your entire hard disk. This approach has the singular advantage of providing an up-to-date hard disk backup and data backup every day. Refer to Chapter 7 for more details.

The following sentence is *not* a misprint:

Before you can back up your email-related information and browser bookmarks, you need to back up your email-related information and browser bookmarks.

You may be thinking, "What ever does he mean by that?"

What I mean is this: Express Assist, the application that backs up your email-related information and browser bookmarks stores all this backed-up data in a single backup file. The information can subsequently be restored from this file. Once you have created this backup file, you still need to include it in your data backup, just like any other file. That way, in the event of a hard disk crash (or if you are simply migrating this information to another computer), you can restore all this information.

So, what you have here is a two-step backup process. First, you use Express Assist to back up all this information into a single file, and then you use your backup strategy to transfer this file to CD media for safekeeping.

Express Assist backs up Outlook Express–related email information, including your

As of this writing, AJS Systems, the developer of Express Assist, is working on a new omnibus version of the program called EaZy Backup that can also back up Netscape bookmarks and all email-related information from these other email applications: Microsoft Outlook, Incredimail, and Eudora.

- Email folders and messages, including any message attachments
- Email account information
- Address Book
- Email preferences (the information under Tools/Options in Outlook Express), message rules, blocked senders, and all other email-related information

In addition, Express Assist backs up your Internet Explorer Favorites (your bookmarks).

Perform the following steps to take a backup with Express Assist:

1. Open Outlook Express.
2. Compact all your mail folders. Select File, Folder, Compact All Folders. This removes mail messages that have been deleted. (Simply deleting your email messages really doesn't really delete them—it just marks them to be deleted when you compact your mail folders.) Compacting your folders gets rid of the deleted messages, which means that less time and space is required to back up your email.
3. Exit Outlook Express—you can't back up your data if Outlook Express is open.
4. Open Express Assist.
5. Click Make Backup.
6. Click Select All (see Figure 6.2). This causes Outlook Express to back up everything it possibly can. Click Next Step.
7. Click Browse and select the My Documents folder as your backup location. Click Next Step.
8. The next window is informational and tells you the name of the backup file that will be created. Simply click Next Step.

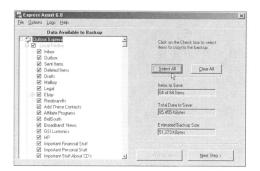

FIGURE 6.2
Click Select All to back up your email messages and folders, address book, preferences, message rules, and Internet Explorer bookmarks.

9. Click Make Backup and wait for the backup process to complete; this can take a few minutes.

10. Assuming this is not the first time you've performed this backup, you'll also find your old backup file in the My Documents folder. Because the date and time is automatically built into the filename, it's easy to tell them apart. For example, the backup I just created has the name `Express5Backup.Main Identity.2002-06-07-10-32.eaz`. Delete the previous Express Assist backup file—you don't need it anymore.

Step 3: Create a Local Backup of Your Web Site

You can skip this step if you do not have a Web site.

This step is applicable to both baseline and daily differential/incremental backups because you will probably want to back up this information every day. (Exception: If your Web site is inactive or doesn't change much from day to day, you may need to perform this step only prior to baseline backups.)

If you have a Web site, you should not assume that your Web hosting service is backing up the site. You should "publish" a copy of your Web site to your hard disk and store it in the My Documents folder so that it gets backed up along with all your other data. The following instructions assume you are using Microsoft FrontPage.

To create a local copy of your Web site, do the following:

1. Create a folder named `Local Copy` within the My Documents folder.

2. Open your Web site in Microsoft FrontPage.

3. Select File, Publish Web and browse to the `Local Copy` folder.

4. Click Options and select the Publish All Pages, Overwriting Any Already on the Destination option (see Figure 6.3).

5. Click Publish.

Once you have published (copied) your Web site to your Local Copy folder, I suggest that you delete it just prior to the next time you copy it to the Local Copy folder. If you do not delete your old local copy, pages you have deleted from your actual Web site remain on your local copy, cluttering up your hard disk with data you do not want. (This also means that these old pages would get copied back to your actual Web site in the event that you ever have to restore your Web site from your backup.)

FIGURE 6.3

Publishing your Web site to your hard disk gives you a backup in case your Web hosting service is not backing up your Web site.

Step 4: Update Your Data

This step is applicable to both baseline and daily differential/incremental backups.

You might have some applications that import data from the Internet. For example, I use Auction Submit to submit auctions to eBay. This application allows me to import and keep track of my current auctions. Before I back up my data, I import the latest information from eBay.

Step 5: Copy Data from Other Locations to the My Documents **Folder**

This step is applicable *only* if you are using the drag-and-drop approach to backing up your data.

This step is applicable to both baseline and daily backups.

You will recall that some applications play hide-and-seek with your data, automatically store your data in folders of their choosing.

I find that the easiest way to perform a drag-and-drop backup is to copy all the hide-and-seek data into the My Documents folder before I take a backup. That way, I only have to worry about backing up everything in the My Documents folder when I perform my drag-and-drop backup.

This step is not necessary if you are using file backup software because you can create backup jobs that remember the locations of your data.

Copy, Don't Move, Your Hide-and-Seek Data

Make sure you copy—not move—the data from its hide-and-seek location to the My Documents folder. If you move the data by mistake, the application that uses the data won't be able to find it. If you move the data by accident, don't panic—simply copy it back to its original location. If you don't remember the original file location and haven't documented it, contact the software vendor for assistance.

Step 6: Defragment Your Hard Disk

This step is applicable only to baseline backups.

Whenever you save a file to your hard disk, Windows stores that file wherever it can find room. Windows is perfectly content to break the file into multiple pieces and store those pieces in different places on your hard disk. Windows keeps track of where all these pieces are and automatically reassembles the pieces for you when you open or access a file for any reason, such as when you take a data backup.

Over time, your hard disk becomes more and more fragmented, meaning that more and more files have been broken into multiple pieces and stored in many different places on your hard disk. If your hard disk is very fragmented, data backups take longer because it takes time for Windows to reassemble these pieces when you back up the files.

Microsoft Windows provides a utility called Disk Defragmenter (Defrag, for short) that reorganizes all these files on your computer so each file is stored in one contiguous set of clusters on your hard disk. Running Defrag prior to performing a baseline backup reduces the amount of time required to back up your data and improves the overall performance of your computer. You might not want to run the Defrag utility *every time* to take a data backup, but if you use your computer a great deal, I recommend that you run this utility at least monthly.

Prior to running defrag, it's a good idea to purge your computer of all debris: temporary files, files in your recycle bin, and so on. For instructions on how to do this, refer to "Take Out the Trash," in Chapter 7. This enables Windows to do a better job of defragmenting your hard disk.

Perform the following steps to defragment your hard disk:

1. The Defrag utility wants exclusive access to your hard disk, so give it that access. I have found that it does not run well if you boot up Windows normally because other processes that continually access your hard disk are running in the background. Each time this happens, the Defrag utility starts over again, and it will never be able to run to completion.

   Before you run Defrag, turn off your screensaver if you have one installed. The screensaver accesses your hard disk and prevents Defrag from running to completion.

   Boot up your computer in safe mode to prevent other background processes from loading, thereby ensuring that Defrag will have exclusive access to your hard disk. To boot up your computer in safe mode, restart your computer and repeatedly press the F8 function key until the startup menu is displayed. Then, select the Safe Mode Boot option.

2. Select Start, All Programs, Accessories, System Tools, Disk Defragmenter.

3. If you are running Windows 98 or Millennium, the first time you run Defrag, you will need to configure the settings. Click Settings and select these two options: Rearrange Program Files So My Programs Start Faster and Check the Drive for Errors. Select the Every Time I Defragment My Hard Drive option as well so you will not have to configure these settings again.

Changes to Disk Defragmenter in Windows XP

The Windows XP disk defragmenter program, which evolved from Windows 2000, is not the same program as the Windows 98 or Millennium operating system. In the Windows XP version of disk defragmenter, the user no longer has the option to select Rearrange Program Files So My Programs Start Faster. Apparently, Microsoft can't provide this functionality in Windows 2000 or XP. According to Microsoft, the reason is that the beginning of the hard disk is reserved for a system file called the master file table (MFT). Microsoft states, "Because Windows reserves the MFT for exclusive use, Disk Defragmenter doesn't move files to the beginning of volumes."

Also, the Windows XP version of disk defragmenter has a tool called Analyzer. This gives you a graphical representation of how fragmented your disk is and a recommendation as to whether the disk needs to be defragmented. Microsoft has tried something like this before in previous versions of Windows, and I have not found it to be a very accurate tool. My recommendation is to just go ahead and defragment your hard disk.

4. In Windows 98 or Millennium, in the Select Drive window, select your drive and click OK to start. In Windows XP, select your drive and click Defragment (see Figure 6.4).

FIGURE 6.4

The Windows XP Disk Defragmenter user interface.

5. The Defrag utility may take several hours to run. It goes through your entire hard disk, sector by sector, and reorganizes all your files so that each file is stored as one set of contiguous clusters. In Windows 98 and Millennium, Defrag moves programs you use most frequently to the beginning (outer edge) of your hard disk so they will open more quickly.

6. When you are finished defragging your hard disk, reboot your computer. After the computer reboots, you might need to rearrange the icons on your desktop.

The Drag-and-Drop Approach: Step-by-Step Instructions

This section provides detailed instructions for performing a drag-and-drop baseline backup and a drag-and-drop differential backup and for restoring individual files from your backup.

First, here is some background information on DirectCD, the tool I use and recommend for performing your drag-and-drop backup. You will understand why this background information is important when you get to step 6 of the detailed instructions for taking a drag-and-drop data backup.

DirectCD allows you to copy or save files to a CD-R or CD-RW just as you would a floppy disk, Zip disk, or any other portable or fixed media.

DirectCD employs an industry-standard file system called UDF (universal disk format) that facilitates data interchange. This means that other computers can access the CD-R or CD-RW you create, even if the other computers use different operating systems than your computer.

Baseline Backup Instructions

Take a weekly baseline drag-and-drop backup using the following instructions:

1. Prepare your data for the baseline backup following the directions provided earlier in this chapter.

2. If you are using CD-RWs that have been written to previously, delete all the files before you begin your baseline backup.

   If you are using CD-R media, you should always use new media to perform drag-and-drop backups. Deleting files from CD-R media does *not* free up usable space. It merely makes the files invisible on the disc. Deleting files from CD-RW media, on the other hand, does make the space available to be used.

3. Format the media. If you are using brand-new media—either CD-R or CD-RW— you need to format the media using Roxio's DirectCD before you can copy files to the media. Do the following:

   3.1. To format the disc, select Start, Programs, Adaptec DirectCD, DirectCD Wizard. This places a small icon in your system tray (the lower-right side of your task bar).

   3.2. Right-click the icon and click Format. This displays a Format Disc window.

   3.3. Click Next.

   3.4. You can enter a name for your disc if you like or leave it blank—it matters not. I always leave it untitled.

You may find that after starting DirectCD and inserting unformatted media into your CD writer, DirectCD automatically launches a wizard that walks you through the previous steps to format your CD.

3.5. Leave the Enable Compression on This Disc box unchecked. If you enable data compression, all data stored on the CD is compressed. You should leave this blank because your backups will proceed much faster if you do not compress your data. You might need to use a few extra discs, but the savings in time is worth the added expense.

3.6. Click Finish, and then click OK.

4. If you have not already done so, open the DirectCD Wizard now. Select Start, Programs, Adaptec DirectCD, DirectCD Wizard. You need to have the DirectCD Wizard open so you can properly eject the CDs in step 6.

5. Take the backup. Take a baseline backup by dragging and dropping all the data files in the My Documents folder to the CD media. Label each disc with the words "baseline backup", the date, and the disc number if you have to use multiple discs.

6. Eject the disc. When you have completed your drag-and-drop backup, *do not* press the button on your CD writer to eject your CD media, and *do not* shut down your computer before properly ejecting the media. If you do either of these two things, the disc can become unstable or unreadable. This is because there is a small amount of UDF data that must be written to the disc before you eject it. To eject the disc without risk of rendering it unreadable, follow these steps:

6.1. Right-click the DirectCD icon on the Windows taskbar.

6.2. Select Eject from the drop-down list. DirectCD will finish writing the UDF data to the disc and eject it.

7. Label the disc(s). Each disc should have the following information: baseline backup, the date, and the disc number (for example, disc 1 of 3).

8. Test the backup by dragging and dropping a file from each disc to an alternative location on your hard disk. You can set up a folder called Test Restore on your desktop for this purpose and drag files into this folder.

9. Take the baseline backup set to your preferred secure location. As I mentioned earlier, I prefer a safe deposit box.

Daily Backup Instructions

Between weekly baseline backups, you should take a daily drag-and-drop backup of any files that have been modified or created.

I recommend that you use a CD-RW, not a CD-R, to perform your daily drag-and-drop backups and that you use the same CD-RW all week long, provided that all the data you need to back up can fit on one disc. However, you should remember to eject the CD-RW from your computer before shutting down, using the previous instructions.

It is important that you use a CD-RW because, if you modify a file several times during the week, each time you drag and drop it onto a CD-RW, you overwrite the previous copy with the latest copy. This drag-and-drop daily backup approach is the functional equivalent to a differential backup because restoring your data is a simple two-step process. (If you want the functional equivalent of an incremental backup, use a different CD every day, in which case it won't matter if you use a CD-R or CD-RW.)

For the *first* daily backup, you need to prepare the CD-RW media, just as you did for the baseline backup, either by deleting all the files on it if it has been used previously or by formatting the disc if it is new. You must *not* prepare the media again for subsequent daily backups taken during the week, or you will wipe out the data on the media.

Perform your daily backup per the following instructions:

1. Prepare your data for the daily backup following the directions provided earlier in this chapter. Specifically, back up your email and browser bookmarks, back up your Web site, update your data, and copy your hide-and-seek data from other locations on your hard disk to the My Documents folder. Use your judgment here. Obviously, if you have not used an application, there is no need to back up that application's hide-and-seek data.

2. Label the media to relate it to a specific baseline backup set.

3. Drag and drop any files that have been created or modified since the last daily backup to the CD-RW, overwriting any previous versions on the CD-RW. If you need to, make a note of where each file is stored on the hard disk. This enables you to restore the data to the proper location should it become necessary to do so.

4. Use one of the alternatives presented earlier in this chapter for moving your daily backups offsite. Be especially careful because you do not have the ability to password-protect a drag-and-drop backup the way you can do with file-based backup software.

5. When you eject the media from your CD writer, be sure to do this properly: Open the DirectCD Wizard, right-click the DirectCD icon, and click Eject.

Restoring Your Data

You might need to restore an individual file if you accidentally delete it or make an undesirable change to the file. To restore it, follow these steps:

1. Check first to see if the file you wish to restore is on the CD-RW that contains your differential backup. If it is, restore the file from there. Otherwise, restore the file from your baseline backup.

2. Drag and drop the file back to its proper location (subfolder) within the My Documents folder.

3. If the file you are restoring is hide-and-seek data, copy it from the My Documents folder back to its hide-and-seek location on your hard disk (refer to Figure 6.4). (If you prefer, you can restore the file directly to its ultimate destination.)

If for some reason, your computer is having difficulty reading the media when you try to restore a file, all might not be lost. DirectCD comes with a program called ScanDisc (not the same program as Windows' ScanDisk) that can often fix errors on DirectCD-formatted media. To run ScanDisc, selt Start, (All) Programs, Adaptec DirctCD, ScanDisc.

You need to restore all your data if you have suffered a hard disk crash or extensive damage from a computer virus, or if you are migrating your data to a new computer (see Chapter 4, "A Disaster Prevention Plan for Your New Computer: Part 2, Before You Try"). Detailed instructions for restoring all your data are found in Chapter 8.

An Introduction to Backup NOW! Deluxe

This first window will go away in version 3.0 of Backup NOW!, currently under development. Instead, you will launch the File Backup/Restore program from a separate icon.

This section provides instructions on how to use certain features of Backup NOW! Deluxe. This information will help you back up and restore your data using the detailed instructions provided later in this chapter.

My quest for a file backup software package that I could recommend with confidence in *PC Fear Factor* was surprisingly long and arduous. There are many file backup software applications on the market that either don't work, lack important features such as the ability to perform differential backups, or have a user interface that would perplex Albert Einstein. In fact, Backup NOW! Deluxe is the *only* file backup software package I have found that works, has robust functionality, and is easy to use.

Launching Backup NOW! Deluxe

When you open Backup NOW! Deluxe, the first window you see asks if you want to use the product's File Backup/Restore function or Drive Image Backup/Restore function. Click OK to accept the default selection, File Backup/Restore (see Figure 6.5).

FIGURE 6.5
The Backup NOW! Deluxe opening window. Select the default File Backup/Restore function.

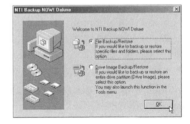

Creating Backup Jobs with Backup NOW!

You should create two backup jobs: one to perform a baseline backup and one to perform a differential or incremental backup, depending on which approach you use. Each time you perform a backup, you will execute the appropriate job.

You need to know the locations of all your hide-and-seek data to create these jobs.

This section shows you how to create these backup jobs. The section "Taking a Baseline Backup: Step-by-Step Instructions," later in this chapter, provides step-by-step instructions for using these jobs you have created to perform backups.

Creating a Baseline Backup Job

Follow these instructions to create a baseline backup job after you have opened the software application:

1. Select Job, New from the menu bar.

2. Select (check) all the folders you want to include in your backup. In addition to the My Documents folder, be sure to include the locations of all your hide-and-seek data. For example, notice that in Figure 6.6 I have selected the My Documents folder and a file named storage.mdb in the C:\Program Files\ Auction Submit subdirectory. This file is a Microsoft Access database where my Auction Submit application stores information about my eBay auctions.

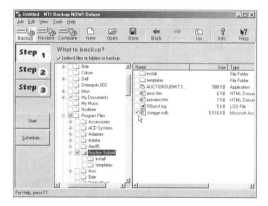

FIGURE 6.6
Select the folders to include in your backup job. Make sure to select all your hide-and-seek data as well as the My Documents *folder.*

3. Click the step 2 button. Select your CD writer as your backup device. Note that you do not name the backup job at this point.

4. Click the step 3 button. Select the All Selected Files option (the default). By doing so, you are in effect telling Backup NOW! Deluxe to perform a baseline backup—in other words, to back up all the selected folders and files and clear the archive bit (see Figure 6.7).

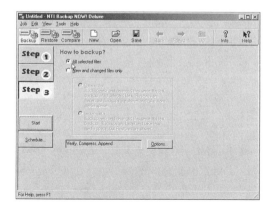

FIGURE 6.7
Select the All Selected Files radio button for a baseline backup.

There are certain features of Backup NOW! Deluxe that are not explained in *PC Fear Factor* because I feel they are not relevant for most of you. For example, Backup NOW! has a scheduler that enables you to schedule backup jobs. This is not a useful tool for CD-based backup strategies because the backup jobs can't be run unattended—you have to be there to switch CDs when one CD is full. (The scheduler is useful in corporate environments when you are backing up over a network.) Backup NOW! also has a Compare feature that is not explained in this chapter, as it is not essential for backing up or restoring your data.

If you have a Windows 98 system, you need to create a third backup job for the specific purpose of backing up the Windows Registry every day. You do not need to do this if you have Windows Millennium or Windows XP because the System Restore function automatically handles that task.

5. Click Options and select No Data Compression. This requires more media, but your backup also proceeds much faster. Leave the Compare Backup Files and Their Original at the default (checked) value.

6. Click the Password tab on Backup Options screen, check the Enable Password Protection box, and specify a password. In the event that your backup is lost or stolen, this prevents somebody else who has Backup NOW! from restoring your backup to her computer.

7. Select Job, Save and enter a filename of **baseline backup job**; then, save the file.

Creating a Differential or Incremental Backup Job

It is absolutely critical that you select the exact same folders and files for your differential or incremental backup job as you did for your baseline backup job. If you fail to do this, your baseline and differential/incremental backups will not function as a synchronized set.

Here is a trick that enables you to do this easily and accurately. The easiest way to create a differential or incremental backup job is to open your baseline backup job, make a few changes, and then resave it under a different job name. Follow these steps:

1. Select the Job, Open function and open your baseline backup job. Notice that your files are already selected.

2. Click step 3.

3. Select New and Changed Files Only, and then select Differential or Incremental, depending on your strategy.

4. Select Job, Save As. Be careful to select Save As, not Save; otherwise, you will end up changing your baseline backup job, which you do not want to do. Selecting Save As gives you the opportunity to save the job under a different name.

5. Enter a filename of **differential backup job** or **incremental backup job**, depending on your strategy, and save the file.

You now have created two backup jobs. One performs a baseline backup, and the other performs a differential or incremental backup.

You can open these jobs and modify them anytime you like. For example, you might need to select some additional folders to include in your data backup. Just be careful that your baseline and differential/incremental backups always select the same exact folders and files.

Creating a Windows Registry Backup Job (Windows 98 Users Only)

Whenever you perform a data backup with Backup NOW!, you have the option of backing up the Windows Registry. As you will see in Chapter 8, having a number of backups of your Windows Registry (the more the better) can help you recover from some types of computer disasters.

There are many ways to back up the Windows Registry, but I find Backup NOW! to be an easy-to-use tool for this purpose.

However, there are two small problems to overcome if you use Backup NOW! to back up (and, if necessary, restore) your Registry:

- Backup NOW! can't *just* back up the Registry—it can back up the Registry only when it backs up other data.
- Backup NOW! can't *just* restore the Registry—it can restore the Registry only when it restores other data.

You could back up the Registry each time you take a baseline differential or incremental backup, but you will be forced to restore at least one file from your data backup to restore the Registry.

I prefer the following solution because it allows you to compile a large collection of Registry backups and keep them all together on one disc.

Create a small file on your desktop. For example, create a Microsoft Word or Notepad document and name it Dummy file.

Create a Registry backup job in Backup NOW! as follows:

1. Select Job, New from the menu bar.
2. Select the Dummy file as the only file to be included in your backup.
3. Click step 2 and select your CD writer as the backup device.
4. Click step 3 and select the All Selected Files option.
5. Click Options to display the Backup Options window.
6. Select No Data Compression.
7. Click the Advanced tab and select the Backup Windows Registry box.
8. Click the Password tab on the Backup Options screen, check the Enable Password Protection box, and specify a password.
9. Select Job, Save and enter a filename of **registry backup job**; then, save the file.

I suggest that you keep all your Registry backups on a separate CD-R and that you run the Registry backup job daily. Because you are only backing up one data file in addition to the Registry, you can store many Registry backups—about 50—on one CD-R. When this disc is filled, I suggest that you start a second disc and keep two full discs of Registry backups on hand.

You will learn how to restore the Registry in Chapter 8.

Using the My Catalog Feature

Backup NOW! has a feature called My Catalog that captures information about each backup file in a folder on your hard disk. The catalog provides a list of every data file that was backed up when the backup file was created. Note that the catalog is just a list of data files in the backup file—not the actual data files.

Until you have actually used Backup NOW! and created some catalog files, the My Catalog *folder is empty.*

This feature is very useful if you need to find and restore a specific file to your hard disk. Instead of having to load the CD media into your CD writer to search for a file, you can search through the online catalog. This capability is particularly useful if you are using the incremental backup strategy because the same data file can exist in several backup files. Without the My Catalog feature, you would have to load each incremental backup in reverse sequence (newest to oldest) to search for the file. With the My Catalog feature, you can search through the online catalog files, find the most recent incremental backup that contains the file, and *then* load the media to restore the file.

This section explains how to use the My Catalog feature to find a specific data file within a backup file. The section "Using Backup NOW! to Restore Individual Files," later in this chapter, explains how you can select one or more files from the catalog file and restore them to your hard disk.

To view the detailed contents of a specific catalog file in My Catalog, open Backup NOW! and perform the following steps:

1. Click Restore.

2. In the From drop-down list, select My Catalog (see Figure 6.8). This displays a Catalog File window, which provides a list of all the files in the My Catalog folder.

FIGURE 6.8

Viewing a list of all the catalog files.

3. Select the catalog file you want to look at and click Load. This loads the contents of the catalog file in the window. (You can select and load multiple catalog files at one time if you wish.)

4. You will have to expand the catalog file directory by clicking the plus (+) signs in the left window (see Figure 6.9). Keep clicking until there are no more plus signs. You can then click any folder to see a list of all the data files that were backed up. (Unfortunately, Backup NOW! can't do this expansion for you automatically.)

Suppose the file you are looking for is not in the catalog file you loaded. You will probably want to load and check a second catalog file. If you want to view another catalog file, you have to first click the From box and select Backup File from the drop-down list; then click the From box again and select My Catalog. If you do not recycle or reset the software in this manner, Backup NOW! will not display the Catalog File window again.

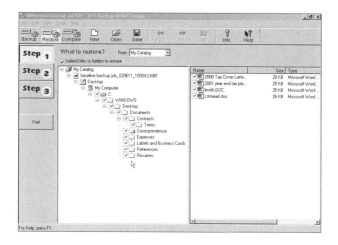

FIGURE 6.9

Expand the catalog "tree" by clicking the + signs in the left window.

Backup NOW! provides an alternative feature, the Find Files feature, to help you find data files within file catalogs. I do not find this feature to be very useful because it does not provide enough information about the files that it finds. For example, if you load several catalog files to search for a file (a logical use for this feature), it does not identify the catalog in which the file was found. Furthermore, if your backup set spans multiple discs, the find files feature does not identify the disc number within the backup set that contains the file. I suggest that you do not use this feature until NewTech Infosystems enhances it to provide more information about the data files it finds.

Cleaning Up and Backing Up Backup NOW! Data

Backup NOW! creates data just like any other application, and it stores that data in folders on your hard disk.

You should clean up this data from time to time and back up some of this data, just as you would any other data.

Assuming you use the default installation options, Backup NOW! stores the catalog files in the following location:

```
C:\Program Files\New Tech Infosystems\NTI Backup NOW!\Catalog
```

I suggest that you back up this folder as part of your data backup.

You can also delete files in the catalog folder that you no longer need—that is, catalog files from backups you no longer have.

The backup jobs you created are stored in the following location:

```
C:\Program Files\NewTech Infosystems\NTI Backup NOW!
```

If you used the names I suggested, the files are named as follows:

- `baseline backup job.BJF`
- `differential backup job.BJF`
- `incremental backup job.BJF`
- `registry backup job.BJF` (Windows 98 users)

You should back up these files as well. Also, feel free to delete any backup jobs (files ending in `.BJF`) that you have created and no longer use.

Finally, Backup NOW! generates reports each time you run a backup or restore job. These reports are stored in the following locations:

- `C:\Program Files\New Tech Infosystems\NTI Backup NOW!\Report Files\Backup`
- `C:\Program Files\New Tech Infosystems\NTI Backup NOW!\Report Files\Restore`

You should periodically delete these reports as they consume space on your hard disk. There is no need to back up this data.

Using Backup NOW! to Back Up Your Data

Now that you have created your backup jobs, you are ready to learn how to execute these jobs to take baseline and differential or incremental backups. This section provides step-by-step instructions on how to perform these tasks.

Taking a Baseline Backup: Step-by-Step Instructions

Taking a baseline backup of your drive consists of sets of steps:

- Preparing the media
- Taking the backup

The next two sections break down the steps necessary for the execution of both processes.

Preparing Your CD Media

Before taking the backup, the first step in performing a baseline backup is to prepare the backup media. In the case of a CD backup, you need to use either unformatted, new CD-R media or unformatted CD-RW media.

If you have already formatted a CD-RW using DirectCD, you have to perform a physical erase of the media before you can use it with Backup NOW! Deluxe. Note that deleting files from the CD-RW is *not* the same thing as physically erasing the media.

Backup NOW! provides a CD eraser for this purpose. Perform the following steps to erase your disc:

1. Insert your CD-RW in the CD writer and open Backup NOW!
2. Select Tools, Erase CD-RW Disc.
3. Select Full Erase and click Start. New Tech Infosystems, the developers of Backup NOW!, recommend a full erase, which takes more time than a quick erase but is more thorough.

Taking the Backup

Once you have prepared enough discs to store your data, perform the following steps to take a baseline backup:

1. Select Job, Open.

2. Select `baseline backup job.BJF` and click Open. (You will recall this is the baseline backup job you created earlier.)

3. Click the Start button. A Ready to Backup window will be displayed and the software will begin a 30-second countdown, during which you can cancel the job if you want.

4. Click Start Backup Now anytime during the countdown. You will see a Backup in Progress window. Do not use your computer for anything else until the backup is completed.

5. If the backup spans multiple CDs, Backup NOW! automatically ejects the CD when it is full and displays a message instructing you to insert another blank CD. Insert the next CD-R or CD-RW, and click OK to continue. Number the discs in sequence (1, 2, 3, and so on) as you eject them from your CD writer, but do not write a filename on the CDs yet. (You won't know the backup filename until the backup is complete.)

6. When the backup is complete, you will receive a message indicating that the backup was completed successfully. Click the View Report button. Backup NOW! automatically ejects the last disc and displays the report. Look at the report to verify that no errors occurred during the backup process, and to see the backup filename that was assigned by Backup NOW! (see Figure 6.10).

Make sure the backup jobs you previously created are up-to-date and that they identify all the data files you need to back up.

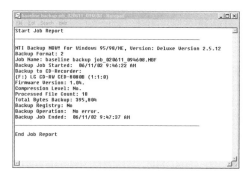

FIGURE 6.10
Check the backup report to verify that no errors occurred during the backup process. Notice that Backup NOW! has appended the date and time to the backup job name to create a backup filename.

Notice that Backup NOW! has assigned a filename of `baseline backup job` + date + time.

7. Add the filename to each disc in the backup set.

8. Take the baseline backup set to your secure location, like a safe deposit box.

Differential and Incremental Backups

The steps for performing differential and incremental backups with Backup NOW! are exactly the same as the steps for performing the baseline backup except that you should select your differential or incremental backup job instead of the baseline backup job.

When you label the media, you should cross-reference the backups to the specific baseline backup set. You might be able to fit several differential or incremental backups on one disc. Be sure to include the filename of each differential backup on the disc label.

After you take your differential or incremental backup, consider one of the previously presented strategies for storing a copy of your backup offsite.

Registry Backups

The steps for performing a Registry backup with Backup NOW! are exactly the same as the steps for performing the baseline backup except that you should select your Registry backup job instead of the baseline backup job. You should be able to store about 50 Registry backups on a single disc. Label the disc "Registry backups," and put the date range on the label—for example, "Registry Backups, 6/1/02 through 7/20/02."

Consider one of the previously presented strategies for storing a copy of your backup offsite. Alternatively, start with a fresh disc each week and keep the older Registry backup discs in your safe deposit box.

Using Backup NOW! to Restore Individual Files

This section explains how to use Backup NOW! to restore individual files. You can restore files to their original locations on your hard disk or to an alternative location of your choice.

Earlier in this chapter, I explained how to use the My Catalog feature to search for a specific data file (or files) within a catalog file. Once you have used this feature to locate a file, you can load the corresponding CD media, open the backup file, and restore the data file to your hard disk.

The skill is in knowing where to look for the file(s) you want to restore. If you are using the differential backup strategy, you should always search first in the latest differential backup catalog file. If the data file is not there, you should find it in the baseline backup file.

If you are using the incremental backup strategy, you should search through every backup file in your backup set in reverse sequence from newest to oldest, starting with the latest incremental backup and working your way back to the baseline backup, until you find the file you are seeking. Because you are going from newest to oldest, the first version of the file you find will be the latest version—the version you should restore.

To restore one or more data files, perform the following steps:

1. Load the catalog file and drill down and select the data file(s) you want to restore by checking the boxes next to the filenames (see Figure 6.11). Note that there is a column labeled Disc in the far right side of the window. This column identifies the disc in your backup set that contains the data file. This is an especially useful piece of information if your backup set spans multiple CDs. Make a note of the disc number that contains the data file you want to restore.

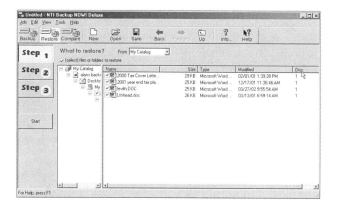

FIGURE 6.11
The file to be restored has been selected on the right side of the catalog window. Note that the disc number from the backup set is also identified in the far right column.

2. Click step 2. Note that Original Location is selected by default. Unless you want to restore the data file to an alternative location, do not change this setting.

3. Click step 3. Change the How to Restore? option from Never Replace a File with Its Backup Copy to Always Replace a File with Its Backup Copy (see Figure 6.12).

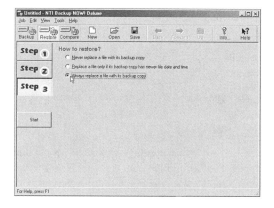

FIGURE 6.12
Be sure to select the Always Replace a File with Its Backup Copy; otherwise, the file may not be restored.

4. Insert the CD media that contains the data file you wish to restore and click Start. You need to match the name of the catalog file to the name of the backup file, and you need to select the correct disc number from within that backup set.

(Don't worry if you select the wrong disc from your backup set—Backup NOW! will prompt you to enter the correct disc should you attempt to restore the file from the wrong one.)

5. In the Open window, navigate to your CD media, select the proper backup file, and click Open.

6. If you have password-protected the file, you will be prompted to enter a password. Enter the password and click OK. Backup NOW! will begin restoring the selected data file(s). Note that if you are restoring multiple data files from within the catalog, you may be prompted to enter more than one disc.

7. When the restore is complete, the following message is displayed: `Restore was completed successfully`.

Testing Your Backup

It's a good idea to test each backup you perform by restoring some randomly chosen individual files.

Instead of restoring the files back to their original locations, create a new folder on your desktop and name it **Test Restore**. Restore the selected files to this alternative location. This way you can be absolutely certain the files are being restored because there is nothing in the folder when you begin the restore operation.

Use the instructions provided in the previous section to restore several files from each backup you take, including daily backups, to this alternative location. Be sure to specify the Restore to Alternate Location option. (Delete the files from the alternative location when you have finished testing so that the folder will be empty and ready for your next test.)

If your backup set spans multiple discs, restore at least one file from each disc to verify that each disc works.

If Backup NOW! is unable to read the media, your media has probably become corrupted in some way.

If the differential backup media is corrupt, you can just perform another differential backup on a different disc.

However, this approach will not work if your incremental backup media is corrupt. You will recall that the archive bit is cleared when incremental backups are taken, so it is not possible to take another incremental backup. If your incremental backup media is corrupt, you should immediately take another baseline backup.

Destroying Old Backups

If you use CD-RW media for backups and rotate through three sets of backups, you don't have to worry about destroying old backups. However, if you use CD-R media, you do have to be careful. Don't throw your old backups in the trash, and don't try to break a CD with your bare hands—you will likely get hurt.

Here are three suggestions for destroying your old CD-R backups:

- Cut your CDs in half with a good, heavy-duty scissors.
- Hold the CD-R with a pair of pliers and run an electric pad sander over it for a few minutes.
- Put the discs in a bag, take them outside, and smash them to bits with a hammer. Wear safety goggles, please.

Some people suggest that you nuke your old discs in the microwave. I do not recommend this: It's a good way to start a fire or create poisonous fumes. Don't barbecue your discs either because they will leave a poisonous residue on your grill.

Progressive Revisioning: Protecting Your Data from Irreversible Human Error

Sometimes, the most important thing you can do is to protect your data from yourself.

Consider the following scenario:

You have been hard at work restoring a scanned photograph for several hours. You have made hundreds of modifications to remove blemishes, fix scratches, and adjust the sharpness and exposure. You have been diligent about saving your work every few minutes to avoid losing any changes should you experience a power failure. And then, just after saving your work for the hundredth time today, you realize you have made a terrible photo-editing mistake that can't be undone. Perhaps you accidentally saved a color image as a grayscale image. Perhaps you made some errors editing the photo. Whatever the cause, the picture is ruined!

Do you have to rescan the photo and start over?

Not if you use a trick that I call *progressive revisioning*. Whenever I am restoring a digital image, I don't just save my work every few minutes—I save it under a *different* filename every few minutes. Each filename has a progressively higher revision number—for example, revision 1.1, revision 1.2, revision 1.3, and so on.

By creating a new file every few minutes, I can go back to my most recently saved known good revision of the file and start from there if I make a mistake I can't fix. Instead of losing a day's worth of work because I made an irreversible error, I am never in danger of losing more than 10 minutes' worth of work.

As you can see, this practice is very useful when you are working with digital images. But it is also useful in any type of complex application where you might make an irreversible mistake!

For example, whenever I use Microsoft Project to create or maintain a project schedule, I frequently save my file under a different revision number. Microsoft Project is such a complex application that it is very easy to make a mistake that causes your project plan go haywire. It can be extremely difficult (if not impossible) to find the mistake that caused the problem. By saving multiple copies of the file under different revision numbers, I am never at risk of losing more than a few minutes' worth of work, even if I do something that destroys my project plan.

Backing Up Across a Home Network

If you have a home network, you can do all your backups from one computer as long as you provide shared access to the appropriate folders on other computers. That is, you can back up data on computer B to a CD writer on computer A. This is true whether you use DirectCD or Backup NOW! This eliminates the need for you to purchase these products for each computer you own (although you might want to purchase multiple copies of Easy CD Creator for other reasons, such as to burn music CDs on each computer).

CHAPTER 7

I don't think that's what the boss had in mind when he said to make a copy of your hard disk.

Backing Up Your Hard Disk

Revelations

In this chapter you will learn

☐ The one task even computer experts fear

☐ When it is *not* a good idea to back up your hard disk

☐ Why you might want to delete some of the data off your hard disk before you take a hard disk backup

☐ Why it is extremely important to keep a running log of changes you make to your computer

☐ How you still might be able to use Norton Ghost even if it is not compatible with your CD writer

Overview

A hard disk backup is the ultimate safety net for the inevitable, unavoidable PC disaster. Rebuilding a new hard disk from scratch—reloading the operating system, device drivers, and applications and getting everything to work properly—is a challenging task that even computer experts fear. It is something to be avoided at all costs.

This chapter explains a strategy and process for backing up your hard disk. It also provides a strategy for keeping records that will enable you to easily bring your hard disk up-to-date should you have to restore from a backup that is weeks or months old.

Norton Ghost is the most widely used, reliable disk imaging software solution on the market today. Although Norton Ghost is easy to use, its user interface is not intuitive and the product documentation is geared for the technical user. This chapter addresses these limitations by providing simple, step-by-step instructions for using Norton Ghost to back up your hard disk.

The detailed instructions include a two-step alternative for backing up your hard disk if Norton Ghost is not compatible with your CD writer.

Norton Ghost, the hard disk backup tool recommended in *PC Fear Factor*, is a disk imaging or cloning tool. For the purposes of this discussion, the terms *imaging*, *cloning*, and *hard disk backup* are interchangeable.

When I use the phrase "rebuild the hard disk from scratch" I am referring not to a physical process but to the logical process of creating all the logical structures on the disk and loading the operating system, device drivers, and applications.

Are You a Disaster Waiting to Happen?

A friend of mine is scrupulous about backing up his data. Oh, he probably misses some of the hide-and-seek data (see Chapter 6, "Backing Up Your Data"), but at least he makes a serious attempt to protect his data. I applaud his efforts—as far as they go—but they don't go far enough.

Recently, he experienced the worst of all computer disasters—a hard disk crash. Fortunately, his computer was under warranty and he was able to get his hard disk replaced. He didn't even have to install the disk—his computer vendor did it for him. That's when he learned, much to his surprise, that his new hard disk was as empty as a politician's promise. In fact, the hard disk was not even partitioned or formatted (see Chapter 2, "The Threats and the Tools," for an explanation of these terms).

My friend assumed (if he gave it any conscious thought at all) that the hardware vendor would send him a new hard disk that had everything he needed but his data—the operating system, device drivers, and applications. In other words, he expected that the mere act of having a new hard disk installed would restore his computer to its virgin out-of-the-box state. He believed that all he would have to do is reinstall some other applications and restore his data, and he would be back in business.

He understands now that this was a very bad assumption, and he paid a dear price for his mistake. First, he tried unsuccessfully for a week, with whatever help he could get, to rebuild his hard disk from scratch—a difficult task even for computer experts.

In the end, he was forced to conclude that this task was far beyond his capabilities. He was faced with two options:

- Pay an expert several hundred dollars to rebuild his hard disk (and hope that the job was done right!)
- Buy a new computer

He purchased a new computer—he couldn't see the logic of spending several hundred dollars to repair a computer that was two years old and on the verge of being obsolete anyway.

My friend is not unusual. In fact, he did a better job than most people do in taking precautions to prevent computer disasters. Based on my observations, most people don't back up *anything*, and those that do only back up (most of) their data.

This means that most people would be in the same position (or worse) as my friend if they experienced a hard disk failure.

Just how difficult is it to rebuild a hard disk from scratch? Allow me to digress for a moment.

> My neighbor, a British chap, is an automobile expert who rebuilds MGBs. He buys old cars and literally guts them, rebuilding them from the ground up. I think that you have to have the same kind of expertise relative to computers that my neighbor has relative to MGBs to rebuild a hard disk from scratch. The task of rebuilding a hard disk—partitioning it; formatting it; reinstalling an operating system, device drivers, and applications; *and getting everything to work again in harmony*—is incredibly complex and beyond the capabilities of mere mortals. It's probably the only task more difficult than upgrading to a new Windows operating system.
>
> Even if you have a friend who has the skills to help you, she probably won't—the task is just too time-consuming. It would be like me buying an old MGB and asking my neighbor to restore it because I'm a nice guy in need of help. I help my neighbor—who is as ignorant about computers as I am about cars—with minor computer problems, and he helps me with minor car problems, but we both understand implicitly where the line is drawn—at an hour's worth of support per incident, be it car or computer. I don't ask him to do a valve job (whatever the heck that is), and he doesn't ask me to rebuild his hard disk. It's an arrangement that has served both of us well.

If you back up your data, I applaud you. But if you don't back up your hard disk, you, like my friend, are still a disaster waiting to happen.

Happily, I am about to pull you back from the brink of disaster by showing you how to back up your entire hard disk.

A Hard Disk Backup Strategy

Home users should back up their entire hard disks *at least* once every three months, and more often if they make substantial changes to their computing environments. For example, if you add several new applications to your hard disk, you might want to immediately take a new backup rather than wait until your next scheduled backup. Otherwise, you will have to reinstall all these applications in the event of a hard disk crash.

If you are rich enough to buy a new computer whenever your hard disk crashes, just back up your data and skip this chapter! And please adopt me. I promise to be a good son.

Ever wonder why vendors don't provide ready-to-use hard disks? For example, why does Dell, who has a record of every PC they've built, give you an empty hard disk when it installs an in-warranty replacement? Why don't they preload the hard disk with everything that was on the computer it shipped to you?

It's a good question— and a missed marketing opportunity for companies like Dell.

You should also make a hard disk backup prior to making any high-risk change to your computer. The definition of "high risk" is somewhat subjective, but it should include the following kinds of activities:

- **Installing a new hardware device in your computer**—New hardware devices require new device drivers, and new device drivers always have the potential for creating problems.

- **Installing an application of unknown pedigree**—By this I mean an application that has not been proven in the market to be a reliable, trouble-free product. For example, I would not be concerned about installing Microsoft PowerPoint, but I wouldn't download and install unproven shareware utilities before taking a hard disk backup.

- **Installing an updated device driver on a Windows 98 or Windows Millennium system**—Windows XP includes a device driver rollback feature that can "untrash" your computer in most cases if a new device driver trashes it. (Instructions for using this feature are in Chapter 9, "Keeping Your Computer in Top Shape.")

The more often you back up your hard disk, the less work you will have to perform to bring your hard disk back up-to-date should you need to restore from a backup.

Like data backups, your most recent hard disk backup should be stored in your safe deposit box or some other secured, offsite location.

The first time you back up your hard disk, I strongly recommend that you take two backups as extra protection against corrupt media.

Whenever you purchase a new computer, you should take several hard disk backups as part of the process of putting your new computer into service. The number and timing of these backups are described in Chapter 4, "A Disaster Prevention Plan for Your New Computer: Part 2, Before You Try." You should keep all these backups until you get rid of your computer.

In addition, you should always keep your three most recent hard disk backups. The objective is always to restore from your most current backup, but the other two backups provide fallback positions should you experience a problem with corrupt media.

When NOT to Back Up or Restore Your Hard Disk

It is equally important to know when *not* to back up or restore your hard disk. If your hard disk has suddenly developed problems—for example, if you are unable to open certain files or are having difficulty writing to your hard disk—you should not attempt a backup, as your operating system, applications, and data may have become corrupted.

Nor should you assume that it is safe to restore your hard disk from a recent backup because your hard disk might have suffered physical damage. At this point, you should perform a thorough surface scan of your hard disk to determine if there are any bad sectors. If you are using Windows XP, see Chapter 4 for instructions for using TUFKAS (the utility formerly known as ScanDisk) to check your hard disk for errors.

If you are using Windows 98 or Millennium, use ScanDisk to perform a thorough surface check of your hard disk. To run ScanDisk, perform the following steps:

1. Select Start, Programs, Accessories, System Tools, ScanDisk. This opens the user interface to ScanDisk (see Figure 7.1).

FIGURE 7.1
Configuring ScanDisk to perform a thorough surface scan.

2. Click Thorough. Do not check Automatically Fix Errors. If there is a bad sector, ScanDisk will notify you as soon as it is found. Click Options.

3. Check System and Data Areas and Do Not Repair Bad Sectors in Hidden and System Files. You want to know if you have a bad sector anywhere. Click OK.

4. Click Start.

5. If ScanDisk finds a bad sector, you can cancel the program. There is no need to continue—as soon as your hard disk begins to develop bad sectors, you should replace it immediately. Hard disks never get better once they start to go bad; they only get worse. After a hard disk starts to develop bad sectors, the end is near.

If ScanDisk runs to completion without any errors, your hard disk problem is likely not physical, and restoring from your most recent hard disk backup will probably solve the problem. Instructions for restoring your hard disk are found in Chapter 8, "Disaster Recovery."

Preparing for a Hard Disk Backup

You should perform several tasks in preparation for a hard disk backup. Some of these tasks reduce the amount of data (and therefore the amount of media and time) that you will need to back up, and some of these steps reduce the amount of effort required should you ever have to restore from your hard disk backup.

Update Your Computer

If you are going to go to the trouble of backing up your hard disk, it only makes sense to bring your computer as up-to-date as possible before taking your disk image.

Utilities are typically small, special-purpose applications. For example, IrfanView is a popular graphics viewer utility. The developers of such utilities typically do not issue patches; they release complete new versions that replace the older version. Prior to my most recent hard disk backup, I uninstalled version 3.61 of IrfanView and installed version 3.70 so that my backup would include the latest version.

This means updating your applications with the latest software patches, updating your device drivers, and in some cases installing the newest versions of utilities.

The following example illustrates the importance of updating your computer prior to taking a hard disk backup.

> Suppose that you check all your applications and drivers and determine that you need to apply 20 updates to your computer to have the latest software releases, patches, drivers, and so on. Suppose that you wait until the day *after* you perform your hard disk backup to apply these updates. It takes you a full day to apply all the changes. A week later, your hard disk crashes. You install a new hard disk and restore from your most recent hard disk backup. And that's when you realize you have to reapply all the changes you just made last week because you made them *after* you took your backup.

Of course, you need to strike a balance here. I have no concerns, for example, about installing a new version of IrfanView. I know from experience that it will work and that it won't trash my computer. If you have reason to suspect that a particular change, however necessary, might have adverse implications, you are better off taking your hard disk backup first. In the event that the change *does* trash your computer, you will then be able to restore your computer to a point just prior to the change.

The extent to which such considerations are important depends on which operating system you have. Windows 98 users need to be more cautious with respect to updating their computers than Windows Millennium or Windows XP users. The System Restore feature in Windows Millennium and XP significantly reduces the risk of applying updates to your computer. The System Restore function, which was explained briefly in Chapter 4 and is described in detail in Appendix A, "The System Restore Feature," is essentially an "untrash" function. If you make a change that trashes your computer, the System Restore function can, in most cases, restore your computer to its prior untrashed state. There are third-party products, such as Roxio's Go Back, that provide similar functionality for Windows 98 systems.

Additionally, Windows XP has a Driver Rollback feature that reduces the risks associated with updating device drivers on your computer.

Before you proceed with updating your computer, you should read Chapter 9. This chapter provides you with how-to instructions on the topic of keeping your computer up-to-date. More importantly, it discusses the pros and cons of keeping your computer up-to-date and discusses why the risks of performing some updates may not be worth the reward.

Take Out the Trash

> "Take out the papers and the trash."

> —"Yakety Yak," composed by Jerry Leiber and Mike Stoller, 1958

The more information on your hard disk, the longer it will take to back up and the more CDs you will require. At any given point in time, often unbeknownst to you, there is a lot of debris on your computer—data you don't need and certainly don't want to back up.

Just prior to backing up your hard disk, you should perform the following steps to clean the debris off your system:

1. Delete unwanted email messages and compact your mail folders. Be sure to empty your Deleted Items folder before compacting your mail folders. To compact your folders from within Outlook Express, select File, Folder, Compact All Folders.

   The mere act of deleting your email messages and emptying your Deleted Items folder does not physically delete your messages from and free up space on your hard disk. You must compact your mail folders to really delete the email messages. Otherwise, even though you don't see them in your Deleted Items folder, you will still be backing up your deleted email messages.

2. Delete your temporary Internet files (Web browser cache) and Web site history. Chapter 4 provides detailed instructions on how to do this using CyberScrub. Alternatively, Internet Explorer users can delete their browser caches from within IE by doing the following:

   2.1. Select Tools, Internet Options.

   2.2. Under the Temporary Internet Files section of the General tab, click Delete Files.

   2.3. In the pop-up window, check the box labeled Delete All Offline Content and click OK (see Figure 7.2).

   2.4. Within the same window, click the Clear History button to delete a history of links to Web pages you have recently visited.

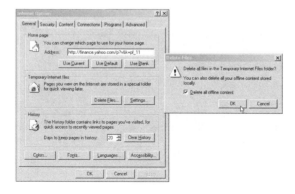

FIGURE 7.2
Use either CyberScrub or your Web browser (pictured here) to delete your temporary Internet files prior to backing up your hard disk.

3. Delete all temporary files on your computer. A number of applications create temporary files, and some applications, such as America Online Instant Messenger, do a poor job of removing them. Perform a file search to find all files named *.tmp and delete all these files (see Figure 7.3). If your computer won't allow you to delete some of these files, it is because they are in use at the moment.

Try shutting down open applications; then you should be able to delete the files. If you are still unable to delete a few of these files, you can try rebooting your computer because this might automatically eliminate them. In any event, don't worry if you are unable to delete some of these files—there is no harm in leaving them on your computer.

FIGURE 7.3

Find and delete all the temporary files on your computer prior to backing up your hard disk.

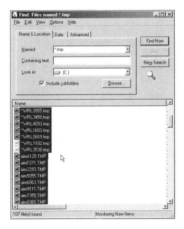

4. Empty your recycle bin. If you fail to do this, your hard disk backup will include everything in your recycle bin. To empty the recycle bin, just right-click the desktop icon and select Empty Recycle Bin from the menu that appears. You must perform this step last.

5. Run a full virus scan of your computer to make sure the hard disk is not infected with a virus.

Things NOT to Delete

Your restore points. I've come across some backup experts on the Web who advise people to disable the System Restore feature found in Windows Millennium and Windows XP prior to taking a hard disk backup. As you will recall from Chapter 4, disabling the System Restore feature automatically flushes *all* your restore points from your computer, potentially eliminating several gigabytes worth of information that would otherwise be included in a hard disk backup. *Don't do it!*

Flushing all your restore points just to save some time and CDs in the hard disk backup process is perhaps the single most imprudent, penny-wise-and-pound-foolish thing you can ever do to your computer. By doing so, you can leave yourself no other option but to restore from your hard disk backup in the event of a computer disaster.

If your system restore folder has really gotten huge, you might consider doing a partial flush of your oldest restore points using the technique described in Chapter 5, "Protecting Your Computer from Cyber-Terrorists."

If you decide to ignore my advice and disable the System Restore feature to flush your restore points, you should immediately reenable it following your backup so that your computer will continue to create restore points in the future.

Files in the applog folder. (Windows 98 and Millennium users only.) You also might receive what I consider to be bad advice to take out the trash in the `C:\Windows\Applog` folder. Deleting the contents of this folder won't hurt anything, but it could impact the performance of your computer. These files keep track of how often you use each program. When you defrag your hard disk (see Chapter 6), the defrag utility places the programs you use most often at the beginning of the hard disk so they open faster.

Delete Noncritical Data (OPTIONAL!)

Only experienced users should consider this step.

If you take your hard disk backup *immediately* following a data backup, you can (optionally) delete your noncritical data off your hard disk prior to taking a hard disk backup and then restore your data to your hard disk after you take your hard disk backup.

By noncritical data, I am referring to things such as MP3 files and video files (other than home video!) that consume a significant amount of space on your hard disk. (My MP3 and video files account for 70% of all of my data.)

Here is why you might want to consider this.

The primary purpose of taking a hard disk backup is to back up your operating system, device drivers, and applications. If you are only taking a hard disk backup every two or three months, there is no real value in backing up your data—you will have to restore your data from your most recent data backup anyway in the event of a hard disk crash.

If you delete your noncritical data prior to taking a hard disk backup, your backup will proceed much more quickly and require fewer disks.

If you have a home network, you can back up your data two ways prior to deleting it and taking a hard disk backup: You can take a data backup on CDs, and you can copy all your data across the network to another computer. This gives you two ways of restoring the data to your computer after performing a hard disk backup. You can either copy it back across the network (the easier method since you don't have to keep inserting discs in your computer) or restore from the CD backup. More importantly, if one method fails for some reason, you have the other method to fall back on.

There is absolutely no harm in leaving all the data on your hard disk. I delete my MP3s and videos because by doing so, I can back up my hard disk on seven CDs instead of sixteen CDs. *If you are at all squeamish at the thought of deleting even noncritical data and then restoring it, don't do it.*

If you *do* decide to delete your data, remember to empty your recycle bin before backing up your hard disk. Otherwise, your data will still be backed up from the recycle bin, and you will have failed to accomplish your objective in deleting the data.

If you use Express Assist, you can also delete its most recent backup file from your hard disk. In my case, deleting this file saves me from backing up another 30MB of data on my hard disk backup. Make sure you have a current backup of this file on CDs before you delete it from your hard disk. The nice thing about this suggestion is that you don't even have to restore this file from your CD backup—you can just run Express Assist and take another backup immediately following your hard disk backup. Chapter 6 contains detailed instructions for backing up your email information using Express Assist.

(Actually, your recycle bin has a size limit, and once the capacity is exceeded—which is likely if you are deleting a lot of data—deleted files bypass the recycle bin and get deleted immediately.)

Do Not Delete Important Data

I do not recommend extending this suggestion to delete *all* your data. Even if you have multiple backups of your critical data, I see no reason to incur even the slightest amount of risk by deleting your digital photographs, financial records, and other important data from your hard disk just to make your backup go faster.

Please don't confuse the expression "easy to use" with "intuitive." There is nothing at all that is intuitive about Norton Ghost, which is why I describe it in Chapter 2 as an application that is difficult to understand but easy to use.

Therefore, you must be of a mindset to follow the instructions in *PC Fear Factor* without bemoaning the fact that such detailed instructions would be unnecessary if the application were truly intuitive.

For the record, I did test some hard disk backup solutions that were more intuitive than Norton Ghost, but I did not find them to be as reliable.

Norton Ghost: The Author's Perspective

I think Norton Ghost is by far the most critical application discussed and recommended in *PC Fear Factor*. You can do all the right things to protect yourself against computer disasters, but unless you have a tool that enables you to recover from the inevitable, unavoidable disaster, you are still walking a high wire without a net.

Norton Ghost is quite easy to use, but most home users would probably be intimidated by the product documentation, which reads somewhat like a manual for defusing a nuclear weapon. In defense of Symantec, it does explicitly state that Norton Ghost is geared toward the professional user. *But it doesn't have to be that way.*

Normally, I would not dissuade users from reading product documentation, even though I have been told by two software vendors that *PC Fear Factor* does a better, more accurate, more comprehensive job of describing their products than their own documentation.

In the case of Norton Ghost, however, I specifically encourage you *not* to read the documentation except as a last resort—in other words, if Norton Ghost gives up the ghost. Even then, you are more likely to find answers on the Symantec Web site than in the product documentation. (My enthusiastic contact at Symantec asked me to assure you that "the online support team rocks!")

You're probably wondering, "Why does Alan recommend Norton Ghost if the documentation is so confusing?"

The answer is simple: because it works and because it really is easy to use if you follow the instructions in *PC Fear Factor*.

The problem with choosing a hard disk backup tool is that you will never really be 100% certain that the product works until you have to restore your hard disk. Of course, you could restore your hard disk from a backup just to verify that the restore process works, but that's a high-risk proposition I don't advocate.

I know Norton Ghost works. I have backed up to various makes and models of CD writers, including one that is not on the official supported list, without a problem. I have actually had to restore disk images I created with Norton Ghost, and the restore process went off without a hitch.

Norton Ghost: Creating Boot Discs

Norton Ghost is a DOS (Disk Operating System) application that functions completely outside of Microsoft Windows. To take a backup with Norton Ghost—in other words, clone an image of your hard disk—you boot up your computer from a special floppy boot disc and take your backup without ever entering Windows. The restore process works in a similar fashion.

Why Does Norton Ghost Work Outside Windows?

Every so often, I come across a disk imaging tool that claims to work from within Windows. I am very wary of any tool that claims to be able to back up something it is using—in this case, the operating system. To me, this seems as illogical as trying to build a new house with the bricks from the old house without tearing down the old house until the new house is built! One package that claims to work within Windows really doesn't if you read the small print. It allows you to enter your backup job parameters within Windows (an admittedly user-friendly feature), but it then automatically reboots your system in DOS to perform the backup.

As far as restoring your hard disk, I hope that it is self-evident that it is beneficial to you that Norton Ghost works outside Windows. If it didn't, and if you were restoring to a new hard disk, you would have to partition and format the disk and then reinstall Windows before you could restore your hard disk. *This is the very thing we wish to avoid!*

This section explains how to use Norton Ghost to create the special boot discs needed to launch the backup (disk imaging) process and restore process.

To use Norton Ghost, you must create two special floppy "boot" discs: one that allows you to boot up your computer and create an image of your hard disk and one that allows you to boot up your computer and restore your hard disk from that image. You can't use the same boot disc for both functions. (This is just one of several things that are not very clear in the Ghost documentation.)

In theory, you need to make only one set of boot disks. However, floppy disks are so unreliable that I strongly urge you to create a new set each time you take a backup. This way, if one set fails, you have other sets to fall back on. As a caution against computer viruses, always use new floppy disks that you know are not infected with viruses.

Do Not Run Norton Ghost from a DOS Window Within Microsoft Windows!

Some readers are probably proficient enough with computers to know how to open a DOS window and run a DOS application from *within* Microsoft Windows. Do *not* attempt to run Norton Ghost in this manner, as the resulting backup will not be viable. You must always run Norton Ghost from a pure DOS environment, using the special boot discs you will learn how to create in this section.

Creating the Backup Boot Disc

Although the backup and restore functions are performed from outside of Windows, the actual boot discs are created from within Windows using the Norton Ghost Boot Wizard tool.

To create your backup boot disc, do the following:

1. Insert a floppy disc into your computer.

2. Select Start, Programs, Norton Ghost 2002, Norton Ghost Boot Wizard. The Norton Ghost Boot Wizard window is displayed (see Figure 7.4).

FIGURE 7.4
The Norton Ghost Boot Wizard.

3. Select the first option, Boot Disk with CD-R/CD-RW, LPT and USB Support, and click Next. This creates a boot disk that will be used to perform backups. (I know, I know—it's not obvious. That's why you're reading *PC Fear Factor*.)

4. Select the Include Adaptec SCSI Drivers option on the next screen and click Next (see Figure 7.5). For some undocumented reason, you need to select this option even if your CD writer does not use these drivers. (Do not select either of the peer-to-peer options. These are used when you are connecting two computers together via a parallel port cable or USB cable to back up one hard disk to another hard disk.)

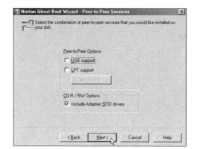

FIGURE 7.5
Select the Include Adaptec SCSI Drivers option.

5. On this screen you have two options for how to create the boot disc: PC-DOS or MS-DOS. Select the PC-DOS DOS version and click Next (see Figure 7.6). PC-DOS is IBM's version of the Disk Operating System (DOS), which is used to boot your computer from the floppy disc. PC-DOS works for most computers. If it does not work for you—if your computer can't boot up from a PC-DOS floppy disc—you will need to create a boot disc that uses Microsoft's version of DOS, MS-DOS.

This Needs a Sidebar Head!!!

I have recommended that you select PC-DOS simply because creating MS-DOS boot discs with Norton Ghost is not easy.

If you try to create an MS-DOS boot disc with Norton Ghost, you will probably receive an error message.

I considered including an explanation of this error message and instructions for working around the error message in *PC Fear Factor*.

I ultimately decided not to include such information because very few people (less than 1% according to my sources at Symantec) will be unable to use the PC-DOS boot disc, and I didn't want to include a rather complicated solution to a problem that very few people will experience.

In the unlikely event that you are among the 1% who are unable to use PC-DOS discs, the Symantec knowledge base contains information on how to work around the problem creating MS-DOS discs. The URL for the Web page containing this information is incredibly long—too long to print here—but you will find the link at http://www.alanluber.com/pcfearfactor/links.htm. The link name is How to Replace the DOS Files and is shown under the list of links for Chapter 7.

---

6. If you accepted the default install directory when you installed Ghost, the next window will display the location of the Ghost executable program—the program that backs up your hard disk (see Figure 7.7). This program must be loaded onto the floppy disc. If you did not accept the default install location, you need to browse your hard disk and locate the file GhostPE.exe within the Norton Ghost 2002 directory. Click Next.

FIGURE 7.6

Select the PC-DOS version (the default) and click Next.

FIGURE 7.7

Select the location of the Ghost executable file.

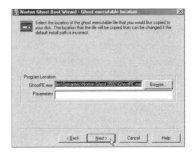

7. The destination drive (the floppy disk drive) window will be displayed (see Figure 7.8). Accept all the defaults, click Next, and then click Next again.

FIGURE 7.8

Accept the destination drive defaults and click Next; then click Next again.

8. Click Start to format the floppy disk (see Figure 7.9). Unfortunately, when the format process is completed, this window does not close. You must close the Format—3 1/2 Floppy window for the process to continue. If you don't close this window, you and your computer will engage in a staring contest. Your computer will win.

9. Norton Ghost now creates the backup bootable floppy disk. Wait until the process is complete (see Figure 7.10).

10. Once the process is complete, eject the disk from the floppy disk drive and label it "Norton Ghost Backup Boot Disk."

11. Click Start Again to create the restore boot disk. Proceed to the next section of these instructions.

FIGURE 7.9
*Click Start to format
the floppy disk.*

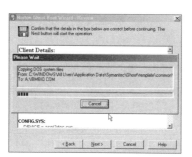

FIGURE 7.10
*Norton Ghost is now
creating the backup
boot disk.*

Creating the Restore Boot Disc

After you click the Start Again button mentioned in the previous section, Ghost
returns you to the initial wizard screen (shown earlier in Figure 7.4). To create your
restore boot disk, follow these steps:

1. Select the third option, CD-ROM Boot Disk, and click Next. This creates a boot
   disk you can use to restore your backup from your CD writer or CD-ROM to
   your hard disk.

2. Select the PC-DOS DOS version (rather than MS-DOS) and click Next.

3. If you did not accept the default install location when you installed Norton
   Ghost, you need to browse your hard disk and locate the file GhostPE.exe.
   Then click Next.

4. The destination drive (the floppy disk drive) window will be displayed. Accept
   all the defaults, click Next, and then click Next again.

5. Click Start to format the floppy disk. Close the format window when the
   process is complete.

6. Norton Ghost will now create the restore bootable floppy disk. Wait until the
   process is complete.

7. Eject the disk from the floppy disk drive and label it "Norton Ghost Restore
   Boot Disk."

Norton Ghost: Backing Up Your Hard Disk Directly to CDs

The following instructions explain how to create a hard disk backup that is *not* password-protected. If you wish to password-protect your backup, read the sidebar at the end of this section *before* you begin your backup, as the steps are slightly different.

To back up your hard disk to CDs, you must either use new CD-R discs or unformatted CD-RW discs to take your backup. Norton Ghost will not write to formatted CD-RWs.

If you are taking a backup on previously used or formatted CD-RWs, you must perform a physical erase first. I recommend using Backup NOW!'s full erase feature to erase your CD-RW, rather than DirectCD's CD-RW Eraser tool. My version of DirectCD seems to only perform a quick erase, whereas Backup NOW! allows you to perform a more reliable "deep erase." A quick erase erases the CD's table of contents but leaves the data on the disc, whereas a full erase erases everything on the disc and leaves it in a more reliable state.

Instructions for erasing CD-RWs with Backup NOW! are provided in Chapter 6.

Norton Ghost will tell you approximately how many CDs you will need when you begin your backup (it always seems to overestimate by one or two discs).

Norton Ghost supports automatic media spanning. That is, the hard disk image is automatically split into CD-size chunks of data called *file segments* as it is written to CDs. You do not have to select any settings in Norton Ghost to enable this feature when you are cloning directly to CDs.

To back up (clone) your hard disk directly to CDs, do the following:

1. Shut down your computer.

2. Insert the Norton Ghost backup boot disc you created into the floppy disk drive.

3. Turn on your computer. Your computer will boot up into DOS instead of Windows. You may see several ugly error messages as your computer is booting up, telling you that diagnostics tests have failed. *Don't be concerned.* Ignore these messages and allow the computer to continue booting up. You will eventually see the Norton Ghost splash screen on your monitor (see Figure 7.11).

FIGURE 7.11

Norton Ghost launches automatically when you boot up your computer from the Norton Ghost backup boot disk.

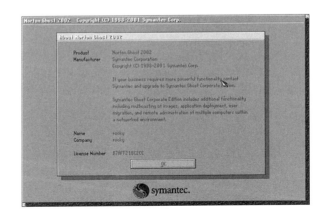

4. Write down the serial number displayed on the Norton Ghost splash screen. You will need this serial number when you restore your backup. Click OK.

5. Select Local, Disk, To Image (see Figure 7.12). This tells Ghost you want to clone your local hard disk to an image. If your disk has more than one partition, all partitions will be backed up.

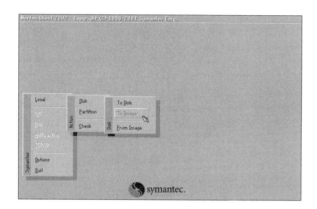

FIGURE 7.12
Instructing Norton Ghost to create an image from your local disk.

6. Select the drive to be backed up and click OK (see Figure 7.13). (If you have more than one hard disk in your computer, you must choose which one to back up.)

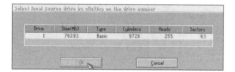

FIGURE 7.13
Selecting the disk to be backed up (cloned).

7. Norton Ghost prompts you to select the place where you want to copy your disk image. Click the box labeled Look in from the top of the dialog box and select your CD writer (see Figure 7.14).

FIGURE 7.14
Selecting your CD writer as the location for the cloned image of your hard disk.

8. Norton Ghost then asks if you wish to compress the backup file (see Figure 7.15). I suggest that you answer No to this question. The backup will require more CDs, but it will proceed much faster than if you use compression.

FIGURE 7.15

The backup will proceed much faster if you select no compression.

9. Norton Ghost then asks if you want to copy a bootable floppy to the CD (see Figure 7.16). If you respond Yes to this question, Norton Ghost makes the first CD in your backup set bootable. This means you would not need the restore floppy boot disk you created earlier if you ever have to restore your hard disk—you can boot into Norton Ghost directly from the first CD in your backup set.

However, it is important to note that a bootable CD will only function on your computer if the computer's BIOS is configured to check for your CD drive(s) during your computer's boot sequence. (Refer to Chapter 3, "A Disaster Prevention Plan for Your New Computer: Part 1, Before You Buy," for an explanation of BIOS.)

If you responded No to the "copy a bootable floppy to the CD" question, proceed directly to step 11. If you responded Yes, proceed to step 10.

What Is a Boot Sequence?

The term *boot sequence* refers to the order in which your computer checks devices to look for the information it needs to boot up your computer. The BIOS on most computers checks the floppy disk drive first for a bootable floppy and then defaults to the hard disk as its boot device if nothing is found in the floppy disk drive. This is what enables you to boot up Norton Ghost from your floppy disk drive—your computer sees the floppy disk drive before it ever sees your hard disk.

Many newer computers have their BIOSes preconfigured to include the CD drive(s) in the boot sequence. This enables your computer to recognize a bootable CD.

If your computer does not check your CD drive(s) when booting up, it is possible to change your BIOS settings to include your CD drive(s) in the boot sequence. I have elected not to show you how to change your computer's BIOS settings in *PC Fear Factor* because it is not essential that you make your CD bootable to use Norton Ghost.

Making the CD bootable is entirely optional. And in any event, it does no harm to make the CD bootable even if your CD drive is not included in your computer's boot sequence.

FIGURE 7.16
Norton Ghost is asking if you wish to make the first CD in your backup set bootable.

10. When you respond Yes in step 9, Norton Ghost asks you if your bootable floppy is in drive A:. *Do not respond Yes just yet.* First, you must eject your backup boot disk and insert your restore boot disk into the floppy disk drive. Then, click Yes, and Norton Ghost copies your bootable restore floppy to your CD media. You must copy your restore floppy disk to the CD because it contains the drivers that will enable you to read the backup set from your CD drive(s).

After you have made your CD bootable, replace your restore floppy disk with your backup floppy disk before proceeding with the backup.

11. Next, Norton Ghost displays a Ready to Proceed message and tells you approximately how many CDs are required for the image (see Figure 7.17).

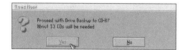

FIGURE 7.17
Norton Ghost tells you how many CDs will be required for the image. The estimate is usually one or two CDs too high.

12. Once the backup begins, you will see a progress indicator across the top half of the screen (see Figure 7.18). When a CD is full, Norton Ghost automatically ejects the disc and prompts you to enter another. There is no time limit here—if you happen to be out of the room when the disc is ejected, Norton Ghost waits patiently for you.

Label each disc as you remove it. Include the words "Norton Ghost Hard Disk Backup," the name of the computer (if you have more than one), the date, and the disk number. Write down the Norton Ghost serial number on the first two discs. Norton Ghost asks for the serial number when you do a restore.

13. When the backup is complete, Norton Ghost ejects your last disc and displays the message Dump Completed Successfully.

Congratulations! You have taken a complete backup of your hard disk.

Do not start the backup unless you have enough CDs to finish. If you stop the backup part way through, you can't pick up again where you left off, and you will have wasted your time (and your media if you are using CD-R discs).

FIGURE 7.18

Norton Ghost tracks the progress of your backup.

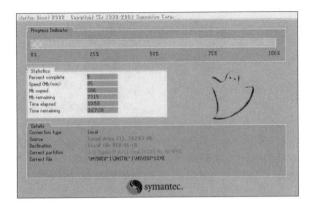

Creating a Password-Protected Disk Image

If you wish to create a password-protected backup, you need to follow slightly different instructions when you create your hard disk image.

You can run Norton Ghost with command-line switches that change the behavior of the program. One of these command-line switches enables you to create a disk image that is password-protected.

When the Norton Ghost splash screen is first displayed, click OK and select Quit. Answer Yes to `Are you sure you want to quit?` This puts you back to a DOS prompt:

`A:\GHOST>`

Restart Ghost by typing the following after the DOS prompt and pressing the Enter key:

`ghostpe.exe -pwd`

Note that `-pwd` is a command-line switch that tells Norton Ghost to prompt you for a password during the backup process.

Be patient—it may take a minute or two for the Ghost splash screen to be displayed again.

Continue with step 4 of the previous instructions to create your image. When you complete step 7, Norton Ghost prompts you for a password. After you enter your password, Ghost prompts you to confirm your password.

Working Around Norton Ghost CD Writer Compatibility Issues

As of this writing, Norton Ghost officially supports about 90 CD writers, and most of these are older models. The next release of the program will probably support additional models of CD writers. However, because manufacturers are developing new models all the time, it is still unlikely that the newest, fastest CD writers will appear on Symantec's revised list of supported CD writers.

If your CD writer is not compatible with Norton Ghost, you can perform a two-step backup process to work around this issue, provided that your hard disk has two partitions. (Refer to Chapter 1, "The Root of All Computer Disasters," for an explanation of hard disk partitions.) This approach works best when you have a blank hard disk partition that is used exclusively for Ghost images.

In step 1, you create an image of the partition that contains all the information you want to back up (your operating system, applications, and data) and save it onto a blank hard disk partition.

In step 2, you copy the resulting image to CDs using software that is compatible with your CD writer. I recommend that you use Roxio's Easy CD Creator, rather than DirectCD, to perform this process as it makes an exact image of this file on your CDs, just as if the image had been written directly to your CDs in the first place.

You can even use a command-line switch to direct Norton Ghost to automatically break the image file into CD-size file segments on your hard disk partition.

Ideally, your blank partition should be as big as the partition that contains your operating system, applications, and data. But even if the blank partition is somewhat smaller, you may still be able to store a disk image of the other, larger partition by using Norton Ghost's compression feature to compress the disk image. If you are using Ghost's highest rate of compression, you will require only about 60% of the space you would normally need to store a disk image.

Important Hard Disk Partition Requirements

You *must* have (at least) two partitions on your hard disk to use this approach. You can't back up the C: partition to the C: partition—this would clearly be circular logic.

This approach will *not* work if you have a Windows XP system and if your second partition uses the Windows New Technology File System (NTFS). As previously noted in Chapter 2, Norton Ghost can't create a backup image on an NTFS hard disk partition because Ghost is a DOS-based application and DOS is fundamentally incompatible with NTFS. (Norton Ghost can restore an image to an NTFS partition, so in that sense it is compatible with Windows XP.)

If you do not have two partitions on your hard disk and wish to use this approach, there are software tools you can use to split your hard disk into multiple partitions. The most popular hard disk partitioning tool is PowerQuest's Partition Magic. You can learn more about this product at http://www.powerquest.com/partitionmagic/.

Finally, I should note that if you only have one partition on your hard disk but you have a home network, it *is* possible with Norton Ghost to back up your hard disk to a hard disk on another computer. It's possible, but not easy. I consider this to be much too complex a solution for most home users, and for that reason I have elected not to elaborate on the specifics of this approach in *PC Fear Factor*.

Users who are able to back up their hard disks directly to CDs can skip this section, which provides a workaround for users whose CD writers are not compatible with Norton Ghost.

As I noted in Chapter 2, I have had success using Norton Ghost on a CD writer that was not on the official supported list. I suspect that Norton Ghost will work on a much larger number of CD writers than appear on the official list.

For a complete and up-to-date list of links listed in *PC Fear Factor*, go to http://www.alanluber.com/pcfearfactor/links.htm. This will eliminate the need for you to manually key these links into your Web browser.

However, if you want to learn more about this approach, I direct you to the following link:

```
http://service2.symantec.com/SUPPORT/ghost.nsf/docid/2000111914205025
```

Other Hard Disk Backup Solutions

Because a hard disk backup tool is so critical, I was hoping to have an alternative tool I could recommend in the event that Norton Ghost is *not* compatible with your CD writer and you are unable to use the two-step backup process described previously.

With that objective in mind, I did test some other disk imaging products. I was even prepared to throw caution to the wind for you, dear reader, and test the restore process with these applications. (I knew I could always restore from my Norton Ghost backup if I had to do so.)

However, I never got that far. Each application I tested failed in some manner exclusive of the restore function.

The fact that I cannot recommend these other products does not necessarily mean these products won't work for you.

The Two-Step Backup Process

This section provides instructions for the two-step backup process described previously. If your CD writer is compatible with Norton Ghost, you can skip this section.

Step 1: Creating the Partition Image

The image file needs to be split into CD-size file segments so it can be copied to CDs. Norton Ghost provides two ways to do this. One approach uses a tool called the Norton Ghost Explorer to split the file into CD-size segments after the backup file is created. I don't recommend this approach because I find the other approach much easier.

The easiest way to split your image file into CD-size file segments is to use a command-line switch to instruct Norton Ghost to automatically split the image file into CD-size file segments as it is being created. This is the approach used in the following instructions.

To create an image of one hard disk partition and save it on another partition, do the following:

1. Shut down your computer.
2. Insert the Norton Ghost backup boot disc you created into the floppy drive.
3. Turn on your computer. Your computer will boot up into DOS instead of Windows. The Norton Ghost splash screen displays automatically.
4. Click OK and select Quit to exit back to the DOS prompt.

5. After the A:\GHOST> prompt, type **Ghostpe.exe -split=680 -auto** and press Enter. If you are using older, 650MB CDs instead of 700MB CDs, use the number 620 instead of 680. In theory, you could make the file segment the exact size as your CD capacity, but I recommend leaving a small buffer. You can experiment with this if you like.

6. When the Norton splash screen is displayed, click OK. Then select Local, Partition, To Image to indicate that you want to make an image of a partition. *Be very careful to select Partition instead of Disk, as you are cloning a partition and not the entire hard disk.*

7. Norton Ghost displays a window labeled Select Local Source Drive by Clicking on the Drive Number. Select the source drive and click OK. The source drive is the hard disk containing the partition you wish to clone. If you have only one hard disk on your computer, as most people do, you will see only one drive to select.

8. Norton Ghost displays a window labeled Select Source Partition from Basic Drive. Select the partition you wish to clone and click OK. This will be the partition that contains your operating system, applications, and data.

9. Norton Ghost displays a window labeled File Name to Copy Image to. Select the destination partition for the cloned image. This will be the partition you use to store your images. Make sure that the destination partition is large enough to hold your cloned image. You will only need about 60% as much space on the destination partition as the source partition if you use high compression, and 70% as much space if you use fast compression.

10. Enter a filename for the image in the Filename box. Because Norton Ghost is a DOS application, you must limit the name to eight characters.

11. Norton Ghost asks you if you want to compress the backup file. If your destination partition is large enough to accommodate an uncompressed image, click No. Otherwise, click either Fast or High, depending on how much you need to compress the image to make it fit on the destination partition.

12. Norton Ghost asks if you are ready to proceed with your partition dump. Click Yes to create the partition image. When the process is complete, you receive a message that the dump has been completed successfully.

Step 2: Copying the Image to CDs

Once the partition has been cloned, you can copy each file segment from the destination partition to CDs and store your backup offsite. Use Roxio's Easy CD Creator to perform this task, and follow these steps:

1. Open Easy CD Creator and click the option to create a data CD project. You'll then see a window like the one shown in Figure 7.19.

2. Insert an unformatted CD-R or CD-RW in your CD writer.

FIGURE 7.19

The Easy CD Creator 5 user interface for creating a data CD.

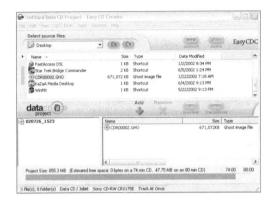

3. In the top half of the window, where it says Select Source Files, browse to the hard disk partition containing your image file segments.

4. Select the file segment you want to copy and drag it into the lower-right window underneath the arrow labeled Add.

5. Click File/Record CD.

6. When the recording process is complete, eject and label the CD. Be sure to include the file segment number, date of the backup, and name of the computer on the label.

7. Repeat this process until each file segment has been copied to a CD.

Testing Your Hard Disk Backup

Norton Ghost provides a tool to check the integrity of your image, but I find that it takes as much time to run the image integrity check as it does to create the image.

And even then, short of restoring your image to the hard disk, there is no way to be absolutely certain that the restore process will work.

However, there is a way to perform some limited testing using the Norton Ghost Explorer. This tool enables you to view your backup set and either restore individual files to their original locations or copy files to a new location. By using this tool to randomly select and copy some files to your computer's desktop, you can feel confident that your backup set will work should you need to perform a full restore.

Here is how to test your backup by copying some of the files in your backup set to your desktop:

1. Open the Norton Ghost Explorer by selecting Start, Programs, Norton Ghost 2002, Norton Ghost Explorer.

2. Insert the first CD from your hard disk backup set in your computer.

3. Select File, Open; navigate to the disc drive containing the CD; and select the disc (see Figure 7.20). Note that the title bar of this window says Open. You will see the first file segment in the backup set, CDR00001.

FIGURE 7.20
Select the first file segment in the backup set and click Open.

4. Select CDR0001 and click the Open button.

5. Notice that the window named Open has been replaced by another window titled Please Select the File for the Last Segment in This Image File.

   This second window prompts you to remove the first CD in your backup set and insert the last CD in the backup set. Insert the last CD, right-click inside the window and click Refresh (see Figure 7.21). Alternatively, you can press the F5 key to refresh the display.

Watch Your Windows!

It is very easy to miss the fact that this second window has replaced the Open window because they look exactly alike (except for the titles), are the same exact size, and are placed in the same exact location on your screen. It all happens in the blink of an eye, making it even more difficult to detect the fact that a new window has been displayed. Many Ghost users fail to notice this second window.

If you receive an error message stating, `Corruption in image file`, or `media not present`, you probably have not followed the previous instructions properly. If you just try to open the first file segment without inserting the CD containing the last file segment, you will see this error. A significant number of Ghost users experience this problem because they miss the fact that the Ghost Explorer has displayed a second window prompting them to enter the last CD in the backup set.

FIGURE 7.21
After inserting the last CD in your backup set, right-click inside the second window and select Refresh, or press the F5 key to display the last file segment in the backup set.

6. Notice that the last file segment is listed (in this case, it is CDR00009). Select the segment and click Open. The directory for the entire backup set is now displayed. Select View, Explode All to explode the directory tree on the left side of the explorer (see Figure 7.22).

FIGURE 7.22

The directory for the entire backup set is displayed in the Norton Ghost Explorer.

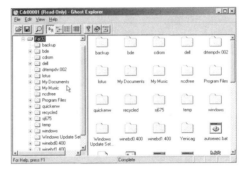

7. Select a folder at random from the left side of the window, right-click it, and click Copy. (Try not to pick an extremely large folder.) Alternatively, you can double-click a folder and select a specific file on the right side of the explorer. When you click Copy, you are prompted to enter the disc in your backup set that contains the selected folder (see Figure 7.23).

FIGURE 7.23

The Norton Ghost Explorer prompts you to insert the CD from your backup set that contains the folder or file you want to copy to your hard disk.

8. Insert the disc as directed and click Retry.

9. Right-click anywhere on your desktop and click Paste. The folder and its files should appear on the desktop.

10. Repeat steps 7–9 several times. If possible, exercise every disc in your backup set. Unfortunately, this is a trial-and-error process—the Norton Ghost Explorer does not indicate which files are on a particular CD. When you are done testing, delete the files you copied to the desktop.

11. After testing your hard disk backup to your satisfaction, take it to your safe deposit box or another secure offsite location.

The Importance of Tracking Changes to Your Computing Environment

It is extremely important that you keep a permanent system log of all changes you make to your computer. This enables you to easily determine which changes you need to reapply to bring your hard disk back up-to-date after you have restored it from a backup.

Your log should be a permanent, running system log—not just a log of changes you have made since your most current hard disk backup. In the event that you are forced to restore from an earlier hard disk backup, you will have a record of every change you have made to your computer since that backup.

The log should include the following information for each entry:

- The date of the change

- A description of the change—for example, "Installed Easy CD Creator 5"

- Any special instructions for performing the change. This will help you if you have to reapply the change after a hard disk recovery.

You should track the following types of changes in your system log:

- New application installed

- Application uninstalled

- Change to an application setting (option or preference)

- Patch or application update installed

- Addition of new internal or peripheral hardware to your computing environment

- Installation of new or updated drivers

- New BIOS or firmware installed (see Chapter 9 or the Glossary for a definition of firmware)

Obviously, you should include an entry in the log each time you perform a hard disk backup. This enables you to track your starting points for reapplying changes.

An Alternative Backup Strategy

If you take a complete backup of your hard disk weekly, you can use your hard disk backup as a data backup and do without a file backup software tool.

The advantages of this strategy include

- You will have a more current complete backup of your hard disk.

- You won't need to purchase file backup software.

However, there are also significant disadvantages, including

- Your weekly backups will take longer and use more CDs because you are backing up the entire hard disk and not just the data.

- Because Norton Ghost is not a file backup tool, it does not support differential or incremental backups. This means you will need to use DirectCD to supplement your weekly hard disk backups with daily drag-and-drop backups of files you have modified or created.

- You can select only one folder at a time to restore. This is not a major problem if you store most of your data in the My Documents folder, as I recommend in Chapter 6.

As I mentioned in Chapter 6, there is no single correct backup strategy, and that statement extends to whether you should use one or two tools to do the job.

Clear! Don't die on me now!

CHAPTER 8

Disaster Recovery

Revelations

In this chapter you will learn

- [ ] Why what most people would consider the worst kind of computer disaster is actually the "best" kind of disaster

- [ ] Why restoring your hard disk after a computer disaster can be the wrong thing to do

- [ ] How a counterintelligence technique called *walking back the cat* can help you recover from computer disasters

- [ ] A class of applications that is infamous for creating the appearance of computer disasters

- [ ] What you need to do immediately after you restore your hard disk to prevent another disaster

Overview

In spite of your best efforts to prevent computer disasters, sooner or later, you will experience some type of disaster. It might be an obvious one—you might hear your hard disk in its death throes one day as you are working at your computer. Or, a fire or flood might leave your PC in ruin. More likely, it will be a disaster of some mysterious unknown origin.

This chapter tells you how to recover from such disasters, quickly and easily, without fear or worry, provided you have followed the procedures provided in Chapter 6, "Backing Up Your Data," and Chapter 7, "Backing Up Your Hard Disk."

You will learn how to troubleshoot computer disasters and find solutions that are less radical than restoring your hard disk, and you will learn how to restore your entire system to a previous stable state when troubleshooting fails to solve the problem.

The "Best" Kind of Computer Disaster

What's the worst kind of computer disaster imaginable?

I think that for most people the response to this question would be, "A hard disk crash."

It certainly sounds catastrophic. After all, what can be worse than losing everything on your disk?

Well, I'll let you in on a little secret. If you have followed the advice in Chapters 6 and 7—if you diligently back up your data and hard disk—a hard disk failure is the *best* kind of computer disaster you could possibly have. (This is especially true if your computer is under warranty, in which case you won't have to pay for a replacement.)

You're probably thinking, "What does he mean by that? Has he lost his mind? Can I get my money back on this book?"

Well, no folks, I've not lost my mind. Other than the fact that I am obsessed to the point of paranoia with keeping my computers in their delicate state of unstable equilibrium, I am quite sane, thank you very much.

The reason a hard disk crash is the best kind of disaster is that you know how to fix the problem! You install a new hard disk, restore from your latest hard disk backup, bring your hard disk up-to-date with any changes you made since your last backup, restore your data from your latest data backup, and you're back in business! The last time I did this, the entire process took but a few hours.

If you've been somewhat less diligent—if your most recent hard disk backup is a year old—the process can take a few days instead of a few hours. But it's still a well-defined process that has the assurance of success.

The Worst Kinds of Computer Disasters

"It's the worst that can happen to me."

—"The Worst That Can Happen," by Jim Webb, 1969

The worst kinds of computer disasters are the disasters of mysterious unknown origin because they are so difficult to diagnose and fix. Sadly, the vast majority of computer disasters fall into this category.

There are so many causes of disasters of mysterious unknown origin that it would be fruitless to try to mention them all. These disasters are almost always software related. Either you made a change or combination of changes that caused the disaster or some files on your computer have become corrupted with no "help" from you whatsoever.

One day, your computer is functioning normally, and the next day when you boot it up a mysterious, continuous sound emanates from your speakers. (And as soon as I finish writing this book, I am going to try to find out what is causing this problem.) One day, all is normal, and the next day an application that has functioned perfectly for years suddenly develops a mind of its own and decides to crash your computer every time you use it. One day, your computer shuts down normally, and the next day it automatically reboots whenever you try to shut it down.

But these disasters of mysterious unknown origin don't faze you because you've read and followed the advice in Chapters 6 and 7. You have current backups of your data and your entire hard disk. At the first hint of a disaster of unknown origin, you are ready to spring into action with your hard disk backup. But in the words of Richard Nixon, "That would be wrong."

Think about it. What do you do immediately after you restore your hard disk? You bring it up-to-date with all the changes you made since you took the backup. In other words, you replicate your current environment. And if you replicate your current environment, there's a fair chance that you will replicate the disaster of mysterious unknown origin. For some reason, the only decent line of lyrics Paul McCartney has written in the last 30 years comes to mind: "I go back so far, I'm in front of me." In other words, your efforts to solve your problem by restoring your hard disk might land you in the same place.

Don't get me wrong—in some cases, restoring your hard disk *will* solve the problem. For example, if your computer has become infected with a virus, restoring from a preinfected backup will eliminate the virus. But wouldn't you like to know for certain before you go to the trouble of restoring your hard disk? And wouldn't you prefer a simpler solution if one could be found?

The hard disk restore is the biggest, baddest gun you can use against computer disasters, but it can misfire. And just as you don't use a gun to kill a fly, you shouldn't use a hard disk restore to solve every type of computer disaster. There are often simpler, less risky solutions available.

You're traveling through another dimension.... Sometimes, I feel like the character Bartlett Finchley in Rod Serling's famous *Twilight Zone* episode, "A Thing About Machines." Finchley hates all the machines in his house, but guess what—they hate him even more, and they conspire to eliminate Finchley, who at the end of the episode is face down in a swimming pool. Is this what my computers have in store for me? I wonder. That would certainly explain why they all seem to develop problems at the same time.

Troubleshooting Computer Disasters

When you visit a doctor's office with, for example, a sore throat, the doctor's primary goal is not to make the symptom go away but to figure out what is causing it in the first place. After all, a throat lozenge might make swallowing less painful for a short while, but if you have strep throat, it's not going to cure the condition. The same kind of thinking must go into solving a mysterious computer disaster.

When good computers go bad, you need to try to diagnose the problem first to determine the appropriate course of action. I'm not asking you to spend days troubleshooting a computer disaster. What I am suggesting is that, if you spend a reasonable amount of time diagnosing the problem, you might find an easier, more certain fix.

How Much Time Should You Spend Diagnosing a Disaster?

If you are not a computer expert, there is no sense in spending days trying to fix a problem that an expert might be able to fix in minutes or hours. In my opinion, there is absolutely nothing wrong with using your backup as a substitute for expertise. The fact that an expert might have been able to find an alternative solution is irrelevant.

If you can't solve the problem after a few hours—my definition of a reasonable amount of time—and if you are reasonably certain that the problem is not mechanical, restore your hard disk.

So, whenever your computer's delicate state of unstable equilibrium is disrupted, don't run to the safe deposit box and get your backups. Instead, try the following first.

Eliminate the Obvious

The first thing to do when you experience a computer disaster of mysterious origin is to eliminate the obvious: a computer virus. Make sure you have the very latest virus definitions installed (run Symantec's Intelligent Updater and install the latest definitions as directed in Chapter 5, "Protecting Your Computer from Cyber-Terrorists"), and scan your computer for a virus. If a virus is found, try to remove it from your computer using the instructions and tools on Symantec's Web site.

If you are unable to remove the virus successfully, or if the virus has done irreparable damage to your computer, you will have to restore your hard disk to eliminate the problem.

If you have a Windows Millennium or Windows XP system, restoring your computer to a restore point prior to the date of infection will probably *not* solve a virus-related problem. That is, it will not eradicate the virus from your system.

Look for Clues

Troubleshooting a PC is all about detective work. If your PC has a problem or stops working for some reason, use what you know about the problem to help fix it. Ask yourself the following questions and take the appropriate actions.

Did the Problem Start Immediately After a New Application Was Installed?

If the answer is "yes," uninstall the application following the instructions in Appendix B, "How to Install and Remove Programs from Your Computer." If you have a Window Millennium or XP system, after uninstalling the application, follow the instructions in Appendix A, "The System Restore Feature," to restore your system to a point just prior to the install. You should definitely uninstall the application first and then restore your system. Restoring your system, in and of itself, does not uninstall the application. Moreover, the uninstall program can get "confused" if you restore the system first and then run the uninstall program because some things the program is trying to uninstall will have already been removed.

If uninstalling the application solves the problem, you should check the software vendor's customer support knowledge base for information about known problems and conflicts. There is a good chance that you will be able to determine what is causing the problem, and then you can reinstall the application. The vendor might already be aware of the problem and have a patch available that you can download and install to solve the problem. Sometimes the solution is as simple as turning off some optional feature within the application that either has a bug or creates a conflict with another application or your operating system. (Such is the case with my version of Easy CD Creator—the animated helper (CD Guide) in the jewel case creator crashes my system, so I just turn the feature off.)

In any event, do not reinstall the application unless you really need it and know (or believe you know) how to solve the problem.

Did the Problem Start After You Updated a Driver?

If you have a Windows XP system, try using the Driver Rollback function described in Chapter 9, "Keeping Your Computer in Top Shape," to fix the problem.

If you have a Windows 98 system, try to find and reinstall the old driver.

Does the Problem Occur Only When Your Pop-up Blocker Is Running?

> "It's a sad, sad situation, and it's getting more and more absurd"
>
> —"Sorry Seems to Be the Hardest Word," Elton John and Bernie Taupin, 1976

Pop-up ads are the scourge of the Internet. They make your Web surfing experience miserable and consume your bandwidth, slowing down your connection. *Pop-up blockers* are utilities that detect and block pop-up ads from appearing on your screen. I honestly don't understand how anybody can live without such a tool. Every so often, I forget to start my pop-up blocker and am immediately deluged with pop-up ads. The latest, most obnoxious pop-up ads move around the screen—you have to chase them with your mouse to catch them and shut them down.

Pop-up blockers have become very popular. There are dozens of choices out there, and many of them are free downloads. If you don't have a pop-up blocker, get one.

If the problem appears to have been triggered by the installation of an application patch, rather than the application itself, you might still have to uninstall the application. Most applications do not provide a means of uninstalling only specific patches. If you installed the application some time ago, I do *not* recommend using the System Restore feature after you uninstall the application, as you will inadvertently undo many other changes you have made to your computing environment since you installed the application.

Message to Internet advertisers: Your pop-up ads are so annoying, pervasive, and obnoxious that I will go to any lengths *not* to use your products. May somebody replace your Tinea Cruris cream and your Preparation H with Bengay.

If you do have one, be prepared to deal with a whole other set of problems. I have tried numerous pop-up blockers, and they *all* cause problems—problems that can easily be mistaken for computer disasters. But I put up with the problems because, compared to the ads themselves, these problems are by far the lesser of two evils.

One of the reasons pop-up blockers cause problems is that they are sometimes unable to distinguish between legitimate windows and pop-up ads. Another reason they cause problems is that, as a class of applications, they just seem to be ill-behaved programs.

Pop-up blockers can cause such consistent and pervasive problems that you could easily and incorrectly conclude you are the victim of a computer disaster, as illustrated by the following example:

> My home page is my Yahoo! stock portfolio. At the bottom of this page is a Download Spreadsheet link that allows me to download my portfolio into an Excel spreadsheet. One day, I realized that I was no longer able to use this feature. Every time I clicked the link, my computer hung. Pretty soon, I noticed that the problem wasn't limited to this specific activity. Whenever I tried to download a music clip from Amazon, the same thing happened. In fact, I was suddenly unable to download *any* file from the Internet.
>
> I tried everything to fix the problem—nothing worked. No help was forthcoming and I was at my wit's end.
>
> In the meantime, I had what I thought was an unrelated problem. My pop-up blocker was causing all sorts of conflicts on my computer. I knew it was at fault because a window would suddenly flash up on my screen telling me that my pop-up blocker was unable to function and would be automatically shut down.
>
> Fed up, I uninstalled the pop-up blocker, and that is when I discovered that it had been the direct cause of my other problem. As soon as I uninstalled the program, I was once again able to download files from the Internet.
>
> (I now use another pop-up blocker. It has its own ugly set of problems, but fortunately this one is not among them.)

Short of living without a pop-up blocker—an unacceptable solution for many users—how do you solve the problems they cause?

Most pop-up blockers allow you to temporarily disable the program by holding down the Ctrl key while you are trying to perform some activity. Unfortunately, this approach does not always work. Sometimes you have to close the program completely to work around the problem. For example, I have noticed that sometimes when I receive hyperlinks in email messages, I can click through to them successfully only if I shut down my pop-up blocker completely.

If you are experiencing problems of the following nature, try bypassing your pop-up program or closing it completely if the Ctrl-key bypass doesn't solve the problem:

- **You are unable to download files from the Internet.**

- **You click a link and nothing happens**—For the longest time, I thought that Paul McCartney's Web site was broken. None of the links worked. I would click them, and my computer would sit there and stare at me. Then, by accident, I discovered one day that pop-up blockers are often overzealous—they stop some legitimate activities as well as pop-up windows. (I admit there is one other possible explanation. Perhaps my pop-up blocker was actually filtering out objectionable content. Any software product that prevents you from hearing McCartney singing, "One, two three, four, five, let's go for a drive. Six, seven, eight, nine, ten, let's go there and back again," might have been intentionally designed to filter out vomitus content.)

- **Your virtual private network (VPN) doesn't work**—A *virtual private network* is a means of using the infrastructure of the Internet in a secured fashion to access your employer's network. With a VPN, you can sit at your desk at home and access your company's network to check email, get to your company's internal Internet pages, and so on. VPNs use *tunneling*, a protocol for providing a specific secure path (tunnel) through the Internet from your home to your company's network. Unfortunately, pop-up blockers often interfere with virtual private networking. If you are unable to connect with your company's network, your pop-up blocker is probably to blame.

Pop-up blockers cause all these problems and more, and still I put up with them because the only thing worse than having a pop-up blocker is not having one.

Is the Problem Confined to Internet Explorer?

If you are having problems with Internet Explorer, you should attempt to fix the problem using the Internet Explorer repair function, rather than by restoring your hard disk.

The Internet Explorer function is well hidden within Windows. (Would Microsoft have it any other way?) Here is how to find it:

1. Navigate to the Windows Control Panel and double-click Add/Remove Programs (this is a single-click option in Windows XP).

2. Select Microsoft Internet Explorer and click Add/Remove. (Don't be concerned—we are not actually going to do something as silly as removing Internet Explorer.)

3. Select Repair Internet Explorer and click OK (see Figure 8.1).

FIGURE 8.1

Following the mysterious, illogical path to the Internet Explorer repair utility.

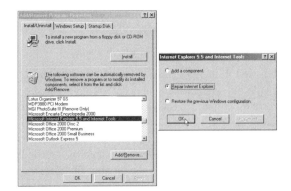

Did the Problem Start When You Booted Up Your System Today?

If everything was working just fine last night when you shut down your computer and everything was decidedly *not* fine when you booted up your computer today, there is a good chance that your Windows Registry has become corrupted.

If you have a Windows Millennium or XP system, restore your system to the most recent settings using the System Restore feature (see Appendix A). This will restore your Registry to a point where the problem should no longer occur.

If you have a Windows 98 system and have been backing up your Registry daily using Backup NOW!, restore your Registry from your most recent backup.

If you have a Windows 98 system and you have *not* been backing up your Registry with Backup NOW!, you can still restore your Registry (although not as easily), as Windows 98 automatically keeps backup copies of your Registry for the past five days.

To restore your Windows 98 Registry "the hard way," perform the following steps:

1. Restart your system in MS-DOS mode. Select Start, Shutdown, Restart in MS-DOS Mode; then click OK.

2. After your system reboots in MS-DOS mode, type **scanreg /restore** and press Enter.

3. Your system will present a list of backups, each one having a date. Select the most recent backup and press Enter. This starts the Microsoft Registry checker, which attempts to replace your Registry with the backup you have selected.

4. When the restore is complete, reboot your computer.

Does the Problem Occur When You Are Running a Certain Program, or When You Have Some Combination of Programs Running at the Same Time?

If you can consistently replicate the conditions that cause your computer to crash, you can begin searching the Internet for solutions. In this respect, it is important to get as specific as possible. For example, if your computer always crashes when application A and application B are running at the same time, try to narrow in on the specific action that is causing the crash.

The more you can hone in on the details of your disaster, the more easily you will be able to find a solution by searching the Internet. Chances are, unless you are using some really unusual applications, others have encountered the same problem and have found a solution. Start with the software vendors' Web sites, and if they fail to yield a solution, try several free computer help forums available on the Internet. On many occasions, complete strangers who, having read my detailed description of the problem, were able to suggest a solution.

Has Somebody Else Been Using Your Computer?

If someone else has been using the computer, read them their Miranda rights and then interrogate them without food or water for as long as it takes to find out what they did. If you have to, force them to listen to Cher singing "Do You Believe in Love?" 24/7 until they crack. This might seem cruel and unusual, but the ends jus-tify the means here, my friends.

Suspect anyone. It's not just the neophytes who cause problems. In fact, sometimes I think the computer experts are more dangerous. I once made the mistake of allow-ing a relative—a computer science major—to use my computer to check his email. The unspeakable horror that ensued is still so fresh in my mind after all these years that I can't bring myself to discuss the details.

Once the suspect has confessed, you might at least be able to figure out how to recover from the disaster.

Walk Back the Cat

> "Meow, Meow, Meow, Meow"
>
> —The Meow Mix commercial

If none of the previously mentioned simple troubleshooting steps solve the problem, try *walking back the cat*. My inspiration for this technique, which I explain momentar-ily, was Robert Littell, the best darn writer of spy novels ever. (His latest book, *The Company*, is an incredible tour de force. Buy it and read it—you'll thank me.)

The counterintelligence agents in Littell's books frequently employ a technique called *walking back the cat* to retrace an operation that has gone bad and determine the source of the deception—in other words, the double agent.

In Chapter 7, I recommended that you keep a log of all changes you make to your computer, the primary purpose of that log being to enable you to bring your hard disk back up-to-date after a restore.

But this log serves another important purpose: It enables you to walk back the cat on your computer and find out if a "double agent" caused your computer disaster.

Using your system log as your guide, undo the recent changes you have made to your system, one by one, in reverse order. (Keep track of the "undos" in your system log.) After each undo, reboot your system to determine if the problem has been resolved.

Unfortunately, there is no way to easily determine if the tenth most recent change was the sole double agent in your computer, or if it had a coconspirator. For example, the disaster might have been caused by the tenth most recent change in combination with another change.

If the problem appears to be mechanical, rather than software related—for example, if you are having difficulty accessing your hard disk—run ScanDisk (TUFKAS if you have Windows XP) to check for bad sectors on your hard disk. See Chapter 7 for details. You do not want to restore your hard disk if it has a mechanical problem.

This process enables you to determine if a specific change you made caused your disaster. For example, suppose you walk back the cat, and after undoing your tenth most recent change, your problem is solved and your system becomes stable. This tells you that your tenth most recent change was the double agent. When you walk the cat forward again, do *not* reapply this change.

Once you have determined the cause of the disaster, you can conduct research on the Internet to determine whether there is a fix.

Obviously, the key to being able to walk back the cat is to have a detailed, accurate system log.

If all these attempts to troubleshoot the disaster fail to yield a solution, the chances are good that something has become corrupt on your system and that a hard disk restore will solve the problem.

Restoring Your System

There are exactly three disaster-related circumstances under which you should restore your hard disk:

- You have installed a new hard disk to replace an old one that failed.
- The data on your hard disk has been irreversibly damaged by a computer virus.
- You have experienced a computer disaster of mysterious unknown origin, and all reasonable attempts to troubleshoot and fix the disaster have failed.

This section takes you through the 10-step process of restoring your computer system:

1. Restore your hard disk backup.
2. Update your virus definitions.
3. Reapply Microsoft critical updates.
4. Use your system log as your roadmap, bring your system up-to-date.
5. Verify that the preceding steps have resolved your problem.
6. Restore your data.
7. Clean up the restored data.
8. Restore your email and browser bookmarks.
9. Take a fresh data backup.
10. Take a fresh hard disk backup.

Step 1: Restore Your Backup Image

This section provides instructions for two scenarios for restoring your backup image:

- Scenario A: From Image to Disk Restore
- Scenario B: From Image to Partition Restore

The "from image to disk" restore is the simpler of the two restore scenarios. It is applicable when you have backed up your entire hard disk directly to CDs. Quite simply, the hard disk is backed up in its entirety and restored in its entirety.

When the image is restored, the entire hard disk is completely overwritten. If your backup image contains one partition, the restored hard disk will contain one partition. If the backup image has two partitions, the restored hard disk will have two partitions, and so on.

With the "from image to partition" restore, you restore a backup image to a specific partition on the hard disk. The restore process overwrites the partition—not the entire hard disk.

The "from image to partition" restore is applicable when the backup image was created using the two-step process described in Chapter 7. With the two-step process, you first back up one partition on your hard disk to an image file on another partition and then copy the image to CDs. (You might recall that this workaround can be used when Norton Ghost can't write directly to your CD writer.)

In such cases, you would usually be restoring the backup image to the partition that was the source for the image.

For example, if you backed up partition C: to an image file on partition D: and then copied the image file to CDs, you would restore the image to partition C:.

Before you begin, retrieve your most recent hard disk backup and data backup from your secure location.

Image to Disk Restore: Detailed Instructions

Follow these instructions to restore your image to a hard disk:

1. Insert your Norton Ghost restore boot disk in your computer and boot up your computer.

2. The Norton splash screen will be displayed. If you have not already written down the license number that is visible on this screen, do so now. You will need it to restore your image. (I don't know why Symantec requires this, but it does.) Click OK to continue.

3. Select Local, Disk, From Image (see Figure 8.2). This instructs Norton Ghost that you are restoring the local disk from an image.

4. Norton Ghost displays a window titled File Name to Load Image from. Insert the first CD from your backup set in your CD writer, navigate to it, and select the image (see Figure 8.3).

5. Norton Ghost will display a window and ask you for your license number. Enter the license number and click OK to continue.

With scenario B, if your old hard disk has failed and you are restoring the image to a new hard disk, you will have to partition the new hard disk first using the Microsoft FDISK utility. Norton Ghost provides its own disk partitioning utility, but I think FDISK is easier to use.

Alternatively, if your old hard disk has failed, you can perform an image to disk restore (scenario A) on your new hard disk and use Partition Magic to split the hard disk into multiple partitions after the image has been restored. I think most home users will find this to be the easiest approach.

If you password-protected your backup, Norton Ghost will also require you to enter your password when you restore your image.

FIGURE 8.2

Instructing Norton Ghost to restore your local disk from an image.

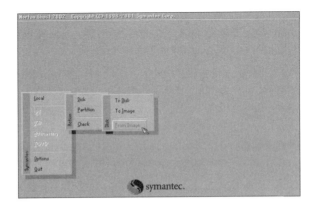

FIGURE 8.3

Selecting the image to restore.

6. Select the local destination drive—that is, the drive to which you will be cloning the image. Most people only have one hard disk on their computer, so only one drive will be displayed (see Figure 8.4). However, if you *do* have two drives, make certain you choose the correct drive. Overwriting the wrong drive would not be a good thing. Click OK.

FIGURE 8.4

Select the destination drive. Most personal computer users will see only one choice here.

7. Click OK again on the destination drive details screen. (This screen is displayed only if your drive has already been partitioned.)

8. Norton Ghost will display a message stating Proceed with disk load? Destination drive will be permanently overwritten. (see Figure 8.5). Make certain that this is what you want to do, and then click Yes.

FIGURE 8.5
*Take a deep breath,
relax, and make sure
this is what you want to
do before you proceed.
There is no turning back.*

9. Norton Ghost will begin the restore process. The application knows that the disc is part of a spanned media set. When the first disc is restored, Norton Ghost ejects it and prompts you to enter the next disc. Enter the next disc and click OK to continue.

10. When the restore is complete, Norton Ghost displays a message indicating that the restore was completed successfully.

What Does Norton Ghost Do on an Image-to-Disk Restore If Your New Hard Disk Is Larger Than Your Old One?

If your new hard disk is larger than your old one and your backup image contains one partition, Norton Ghost automatically expands the size of the partition when it is restored to your new hard disk. For example, if your old hard disk was 40GB and your new hard disk is 80GB, Norton Ghost automatically creates one 80GB partition when you restore your image to the new disk.

If your new hard disk is larger than your old one and your image contains multiple partitions, Norton Ghost automatically maintains the same size ratio between the new disk partitions.

Here's an example: Your old 40GB hard disk had a 10GB partition and a 30GB partition. Your new hard disk is 80GB. When you restore the image to your new disk, Norton Ghost creates a 20GB partition and a 60GB partition, maintaining the ratio between partition sizes.

Image to Partition Restore: Detailed Instructions

Follow these instructions to restore your image to a specific partition on a hard disk:

1. Insert your Norton Ghost restore boot disk in your computer and boot up your computer.

2. The Norton splash screen is displayed. If you have not already written down the license number visible on this screen, do so now. You will need it to restore your image.

3. Select Local, Partition, From Image. This instructs Norton Ghost that you are cloning *to* the local partition from an image. Be sure to select Partition and not Disk.

4. Norton Ghost displays a window titled File Name to Load Image from. Insert the first CD from your backup set in your CD writer, navigate to it, and select the image.

5. Norton Ghost displays a window and asks you for your license number. Enter the license number and click OK to continue.

6. Norton Ghost displays a window titled Select Source Partition from Image File (see Figure 8.6). If you only have one partition in your image file, you will see only one choice. Select the source partition and click OK.

FIGURE 8.6

Select the partition in your image file that you will be restoring. The partition you select will be restored to a hard disk partition. If your image file contains only one partition, you will have only one choice.

7. Norton Ghost displays a window titled Select Local Destination Drive by Clicking on the Drive Number (see Figure 8.7). If you have only one hard disk on your computer, you will see only one choice. Select the drive and click OK.

FIGURE 8.7

Select the local destination drive to which you will be restoring the image.

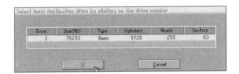

8. Norton Ghost displays a window titled Select Destination Partition from Basic Drive (see Figure 8.8). Be careful to select the correct destination or you can overwrite the wrong partition! Click OK to continue.

FIGURE 8.8

Select the correct destination partition.

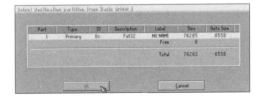

9. Norton Ghost displays a message stating Proceed with partition load? Destination partition will be permanently overwritten. Make certain that this is what you want to do, and then click Yes.

10. Norton Ghost begins the restore process. The application knows that the disc is part of a spanned media set. When the first disc is restored, Norton Ghost ejects it and prompts you to enter the next disc. Enter the next disc and click OK to continue.

11. When the restore is complete, Norton Ghost displays a message indicating that the restore was completed successfully.

Step 2: Update Your Virus Definitions

Do *not* browse the Web. Do *not* check your email. Your virus definitions are out of date—perhaps very badly out of date, depending on how old your hard disk backup was—and your computer is very susceptible to a virus infection at this point.

After you have restored a disk image to your hard disk or hard disk partition, you should immediately run Norton LiveUpdate to update your virus definitions. You might have to run LiveUpdate several times, as the updates are incremental in nature in many cases. Symantec might instruct you to reboot your computer in some cases. Reboot your computer and run LiveUpdate again. Keep running LiveUpdate until you receive a message telling you that your Symantec products are up-to-date.

If for some reason Norton AntiVirus no longer recognizes that your virus definition subscription is paid and precludes you from running LiveUpdate, you will have to contact Norton by phone to get this issue resolved. This should be your number one priority.

Step 3: Reapply Microsoft Critical Updates

You will need to reapply critical security updates Microsoft has issued since your last hard disk backup. You might find that your system notifies you regarding these critical updates as soon as you boot up after restoring your hard disk. However, you still need to manually reapply the updates. Instructions for applying Microsoft critical updates are provided in Chapter 5.

Note that Microsoft critical update patches are also incremental and that you might have to download and install several critical updates in sequence.

Avoid Self-Inflicted Disasters: Don't Skip Steps!

Under no circumstances should you proceed any further with the recovery process until you have performed steps 2 and 3. Otherwise, you risk becoming the victim of another computer disaster while you are still trying to recover from the previous one!

Under no circumstances should you check your email until after you have performed step 8 in the restore process. If you check your email before you have restored your email messages from your backup, the restore process will overwrite any new email messages you received!

Step 4: Bring Your Hard Disk Up-to-Date

Using your system log as a roadmap, bring your hard disk back up-to-date by reapplying all the changes you've made, in sequence, since your last hard disk backup. If you are installing applications or application patches and have a Windows Millennium or XP system, don't forget to take restore points along the way.

Step 5: Verify That the Problem Has Been Resolved

This step is not applicable if you are replacing a failed hard disk. It is applicable only if you are trying to fix a computer disaster of mysterious unknown origin.

You are now at the point where, except for your data, you have completely restored your hard disk. Before you go any further, test to ensure that this process has fixed your computer disaster.

In the unlikely event that you are still having problems, you might have to restore from an older backup—perhaps even your virgin backup—and start over again. But this is an unlikely scenario.

Step 6: Restore Your Data

When you restored your hard disk, you also inadvertently restored old data to your hard disk—the data that was backed up when you took your hard disk image.

Delete this data now. Delete all the folders in the My Documents folder as you are going to replace this old data with your current data backup. You don't want to overwrite your old data because this would leave files on your hard disk that you had deleted since taking your hard disk backup.

You do not have to delete your hide-and-seek data—overwriting this data when you perform your restore should work just fine. For example, the file in my Auction Submit application, storage.mdb, will be overwritten when I restore my data.

Restoring Your Data from a Drag-and-Drop Backup

Refer to Chapter 6 for a description of the drag-and-drop data backup strategy.

To restore all your data from a drag-and-drop backup, do the following:

1. Drag and drop all the data from your baseline backup to the My Documents folder on your hard disk.

2. Drag and drop all updated and new files from your differential backup CD-RW to the appropriate locations in the My Documents folder. You will have to manually determine where each file belongs.

3. Drag and drop your hide-and-seek data from the My Documents folder back to the appropriate locations on your hard disk. If you followed the instructions in Chapter 6, you will have a record of all these locations.

Restoring Your Data from Your Backup NOW! Backup Set

Perform the following steps to restore your baseline backup from the most recent backup set you created using Backup NOW!:

1. If you have not already done so, retrieve your most current backup set from your secured location.

2. Open Backup NOW! and click Restore.

3. Insert the first disc from your baseline backup set into your drive.

4. Navigate to the drive and select the backup set (see Figure 8.9). (Note: You do not need to use the My Catalog feature to assist you because you know exactly what you are going to restore—you have the discs in your hot little hands.)

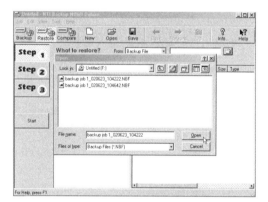

FIGURE 8.9
Select the backup set to restore.

5. Select the check box next to the C: drive (see Figure 8.10).

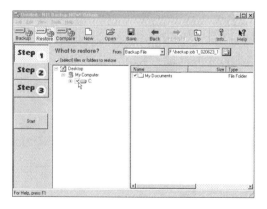

FIGURE 8.10
Select the box next to the C: drive letter to restore all the files.

6. Click the Step 2 button, and you will notice that the files are restored to their original locations by default. This is exactly what you want.

7. Click the Step 3 button. Select Always Replace a File with Its Backup Copy from the list of available options (see Figure 8.11). It is important that you do this because you have not deleted your hide-and-seek data from your hard disk, and you want the backup to replace these files.

FIGURE 8.11

Select Always Replace a File with Its Backup Copy.

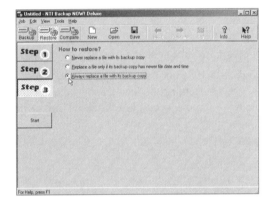

8. Click Start to begin the restore process. If your backup spans multiple discs, Backup NOW! prompts you to insert another disc when it is finished restoring the data from the current one.

9. When the restore is complete, you will receive a message stating that the `Restore was completed successfully`. Click View Report to make sure there were no errors during the restore process.

10. If you are using the differential backup strategy, repeat steps 3–9 using your latest differential backup file. If you are using the incremental backup strategy, repeat steps 3–9 for each incremental backup, going in sequence from earliest incremental backup to latest incremental backup.

Step 7: Clean Up Your Data

Chapter 6 discusses two fundamental flaws inherent in any data backup and restore strategy:

- They might restore too much data.
- They might restore data to the wrong location on your hard disk.

If you have been taking new baseline backup sets every week, you should not have a difficult time cleaning up your data. You will need to go through the restored data and delete any files that were restored that you don't want anymore. You will also need to check to make sure that the same file was not restored to the wrong location or to multiple locations. See Chapter 6 for a detailed explanation of these issues.

Step 8: Restore Your Email and Internet Explorer Bookmarks

One of the files you restored from your differential or incremental backup was your latest Express Assist backup file. You now need to use Express Assist to restore your email and Internet Explorer bookmarks from this backup file. Do the following:

1. Open Express Assist and click Restore or Copy Folders.

2. Browse to the Express Assist backup file if it does not show up automatically, click Do a Full Restore of All Mail Folders from the Backup, and click OK (see Figure 8.12).

FIGURE 8.12

Restoring your email folders.

3. Scroll down in the next window and select all the items that are not already checked: the Windows address book, the IE favorites, your email accounts, your list of blocked senders, your Outlook Express preferences, the remote access information, the message rules, and the electronic signatures (see Figure 8.13).

    This is very important! If you do not select these items, they will not be restored.

    Click Next Step.

FIGURE 8.13

Select your address book, IE favorites, and all the other items to be restored.

4. Click Restore Now.

When the restore is completed, open Outlook Express and confirm that everything has been restored.

I should note that Express Assist is good for much more than doing a total restore. Should you accidentally delete a folder, you can use Express Assist just to restore a selected folder.

Step 9: Back Up Your Data

Take a fresh baseline backup of your data following the instructions in Chapter 6.

Step 10: Back Up Your Hard Disk

Use Norton Ghost to take a complete backup of your hard disk following the instructions in Chapter 7.

CHAPTER 9

Keeping Your Computer in Top Shape

Revelations

In this chapter you will learn

❏ Why your computer will likely experience performance and stability problems with the sheer passage of time and what you can do to fix the problem

❏ When the "If it ain't broke don't fix it" approach to updating your computer makes sense

❏ Why you might be more inclined to keep a Windows Millennium or Windows XP system up-to-date than a Windows 98 system

❏ A great tool that takes much of the risk and effort out of keeping your computer up-to-date

Don't get me wrong. I'm not saying you shouldn't put as many applications on your computer as you need (although I am reminded of the time a tech support specialist blamed *me* for my computer problems because I had changed the computer's out-of-the-box configuration by < gasp > installing applications!). No, what I am leading up to here is that the actual installation process can make changes to your system configuration that have a negative impact on your computer's performance and stability.

Overview

In previous chapters, I've discussed some very specific causes of computer disasters, such as computer viruses, hackers, ill-behaved applications, and hard disk crashes. I've explained how to protect your computer from avoidable disasters and how to prepare for and recover from unavoidable disasters.

In this chapter, I focus on a less obvious cause of computer disasters: time. A friend of mine was recently complaining to me, "When I purchased my computer last year, it worked great. Now it's slower than an arthritic turtle, and I have to reboot the damn thing five times a day. I'll never buy a <brand name deleted> computer again."

It turns out that my friend was wrong in assigning blame to the computer manufacturer. He was experiencing performance and stability problems that afflict most computer owners with the sheer passage of time, regardless of make or model. His computer was out-of-date and cluttered with applications that were slowing it down and ultimately causing it to crash several times a day.

This chapter shows you how to avoid the ravages of time by keeping your computer up-to-date and streamlining its operation.

I present and reconcile two sharply different views on whether you should keep your computer up-to-date with the latest application software and system software. (*System* software is software that makes your computer function—the operating system, drivers, BIOS, firmware, and so on.) The pros and cons of updating your computer are discussed. Specific recommendations are provided to help you determine when the risk of updating your computer is worth the reward and how to manage risk and minimize the chances of destabilizing your computing environment when you apply an update.

What Is Firmware?

Firmware is software that, like your computer's BIOS, is permanently (firmly) stored on a memory chip. Firmware is typically found in devices such as CD writers, DVD-ROMs, and scanners. It interprets instructions sent by device drivers and generates commands that actually control the operation of the delicate electronics within that device.

The manufacturers of devices containing firmware occasionally update their firmware to improve the device's performance or fix problems. These updates can be downloaded either from the device manufacturer's Web site or, in many cases, from your computer manufacturer's Web site.

This chapter also explains why the simple act of installing new applications can impact your system's performance and destabilize your computing environment, and it provides a solution for this problem.

Should You Keep Your Computer Up-to-Date?

I considered naming this section "Damned If You Do, Damned If You Don't" because it perfectly describes the ambivalent feelings I and many people share about keeping one's computer up-to-date.

There are two diametrically opposed opinions on this issue. One position is "If it ain't broke, don't fix it," and the other position is that you should keep your computer as up-to-date as possible with the latest application and system software updates. The truth, as you will see, lies between these two extreme views.

There is support for both of these positions. You are already well aware of the primary argument against updating your computer: Computers are unstable equilibriums, and any update can precipitate a computer disaster. It's a strong argument.

The argument for keeping your computer up-to-date is that it makes it less susceptible to disasters down the line. For example, as your computer gets older, the likelihood of incompatibilities increases if you haven't kept your computer up-to-date. Recently, I purchased a software package that would not write data to my CDs. It turns out that the software package was incompatible with my CD writer's firmware. I had not updated the firmware since I purchased the computer two years ago. Once I updated the CD writer's firmware, the program worked. The point here is that software developers tend to develop products that work with the latest versions of drivers and firmware, and if your computer is out-of-date, you may be out of luck. In a more extreme case, I installed a piece of hardware that completely trashed my computer because the hardware was incompatible with an old video driver.

Another benefit of keeping your computer up-to-date is that the latest software patches frequently add new features, fix bugs, or make your computer less susceptible to hackers.

As you can see, there is no easy answer to the question, "Should you keep your computer up-to-date?"

I don't think you can make a blanket decision in this regard. For one thing, even if you are in the "If it ain't broke don't fix it" camp, you should always apply Microsoft critical updates to your system to protect it from hackers. Similarly, you should upgrade to the newest releases of tools that protect your computer from cyber-terrorists, and you should keep your antivirus software up-to-date with the latest virus definitions.

Beyond these obvious exceptions, the waters get murkier. My recommendation is that you evaluate each available update on a case-by-case basis and make your decision whether to apply the update based on the criteria presented in the following sections.

As I have pointed out in earlier chapters, you can do everything you are supposed to do in this regard and still end up an innocent victim. Microsoft critical updates have created problems on my system, and antivirus software updates have on occasion created very serious problems for customers. There is *nothing* more frustrating than applying an update that is supposed to protect you from disasters, only to have it precipitate a disaster!

You might care about updating the video driver if you plan to install Windows XP on your Windows 98 computer, but in Chapter 10, "Tips for Avoiding PC Disasters," I do everything in my power to convince you that changing operating systems on your computer is the single worst computing decision you can ever make.

Is There a Benefit to Be Gained from Applying the Update?

Generally, updates add features or fix bugs (some do both). I recommend that you read the description that accompanies an update and make sure you will receive some benefit from applying the update before doing so. Some updates add features or fix problems that are either not important to you or not applicable to your computing environment. For example, if you have a Windows 98 system, you could care less if a driver is updated to make your video card compatible with Windows XP.

If there is nothing to be gained, don't apply the update, as it will not help you and can in fact hurt you by destabilizing your system.

If the benefit is questionable, I urge you to err on the side of caution and *not* apply the update.

Is the Update Incremental, or Is It Differential?

I am less inclined to keep my computer up-to-date when updates are differential (cumulative) rather than incremental (additive) in nature.

My Dell Dimension 4100 currently has version A06 of the BIOS program installed. There have been four BIOS updates since then, A07–A10, that I have *not* applied to my system because they either added support for features I do not have (such as support for Pentium III B stepping processors) or fixed problems that are not applicable in my computing environment. For example, BIOS update A09 fixed a communication problem with USB keyboards. Since I do not have a USB keyboard, I would gain no benefit from applying the update.

I know that BIOS updates are differential. If they were incremental—if you had to apply updates A07–A10 before you could apply A11—I might be more inclined to keep my BIOS up-to-date. As it is, if Dell comes out with a version A11 that provides benefits to me, I can install it without having to first install the previous BIOS updates.

What Is the Risk Associated with Applying the Update?

This is admittedly a subjective assessment. However, it is generally true that system software updates are riskier to apply than application software updates. System software updates—and in particular, driver updates—have a well-deserved reputation for creating problems. If there is a place for the "If it ain't broke, don't fix it" philosophy, this is it.

With application software updates, you need to assess the nature of the change itself, the complexity of the application, the stability of the application within your computing environment, and the software vendor's reputation for reliability. I am more hesitant, for example, to apply upgrades to Easy CD Creator—a complex application that has given me trouble in the past—than I am to install a new version of IrfanView, my graphics viewer. In general, if I have difficulty getting an application to work in harmony with everything else in my computing environment, I leave well enough alone once I have achieved a state of equilibrium, so long as the functionality meets my needs.

How Easy Will It Be to Recover If the Update Trashes Your Computer?

The answer to this question depends on which operating system you have. I am generally less inclined to apply updates to my Windows 98 system than I am to my Windows Millennium or XP systems because Windows 98 does not have a System Restore feature. If a change trashes my Windows 98 system, my only recourse in some instances is to restore my hard disk from a backup, following the instructions in Chapter 8, "Disaster Recovery."

New Windows XP Disaster Prevention and Recovery Features for Driver Updates

As previously mentioned, driver updates have a well-deserved reputation for creating problems. With this in mind, Windows XP provides a driver disaster recovery feature, Driver Rollback, and a driver disaster prevention feature, Driver Signing.

The Windows XP Driver Rollback feature can help you recover from computer disasters caused by ill-behaved drivers. This feature automatically keeps a backup copy of your old driver whenever you install an updated driver and can be used to roll back your system to the previous version of the driver if the new version causes problems. If you are updating a driver on a Windows XP system, the Driver Rollback feature should be sufficient to protect you from disaster; it is not necessary to create a system restore point.

If the driver-related disaster prevents you from booting up your computer, you will need to boot up in safe mode to prevent the driver from loading. Instructions for booting up in safe mode can be found in Chapter 4, "A Disaster Prevention Plan for Your New Computer: Part 2, Before You Try."

After booting up, perform the following steps to view the Driver Rollback option for a device:

1. Select Start, My Computer to display the My Computer window.

2. Click View System Information to display the System Properties window.

3. Click the Hardware tab, and then click Device Manager.

4. Click the plus sign next to the device type for the device you are interested in.

5. Select a device, right-click, and select Properties to see the device properties.

6. Select the Driver tab, and you will see the Roll Back Driver button (see Figure 9.1). Clicking this button uninstalls the current driver and reinstalls the previous version of the driver. If the Driver Rollback feature is not applicable to this device (see the following warning), the Roll Back Driver button will be disabled.

FIGURE 9.1
The Driver Rollback feature can be used to uninstall a driver update that causes system problems and to reinstall the old driver.

The addition of the Driver Rollback and Driver Signing features to Windows XP is another indication that Microsoft recognizes the need to include more "undo" functions in each new release of Windows as our computing environments become more complex and more delicately balanced in a state of unstable equilibrium.

When Driver Rollback Will NOT Help You

The Driver Rollback feature can be used only if the problem was caused by updating a driver. This is because the rollback feature uninstalls the updated driver and reinstalls the previous version of the driver. If you installed a new driver, there is no previous version for Driver Rollback to use. This situation would occur if you were installing a new hardware component on your machine. If you are installing a new hardware device inside your computer, I advise you to create a System Restore point first and to also take a hard disk backup. If the install trashes your computer, you can try recovering using the System Restore feature. This usually works, but it is nice to have the redundancy of a hard disk backup available to you.

The Windows XP Driver Signing feature helps prevent driver-related disasters. This feature automatically checks to determine whether a driver you are attempting to install has a digital signature that indicates it has passed testing standards established by Microsoft. Such drivers are called *signed drivers*. Windows XP warns you if you attempt to install an unsigned driver. You can also configure the Driver Signing feature to automatically block the installation of unsigned drivers. You need to access this feature only if you want to disable it (not recommended!) or change the default behavior from warning you about unsigned drivers to blocking the installation of unsigned drivers.

To change the Driver Signing option, select Start, My Computer. In My Computer, select View System Information and select the Hardware tab. Click the Driver Signing button to view the Driver Signing Options window.

Should You Install an Unsigned Driver?

An unsigned driver is not necessarily an ill-behaved driver. It may be a new driver (for a newly developed hardware device) that has not yet passed the testing standards established by Microsoft. In fact, your computer may have come with some preinstalled unsigned drivers.

If you change the default behavior of the Windows XP Driver Signing feature to block the installation of unsigned drivers, you might be unable to install and use some new piece of hardware on your computer.

Usually, if you are installing an unsigned driver, there is no previous version of the driver installed, so the Driver Rollback feature will not help you recover from a driver disaster. However, you can always use the System Restore feature to recover from a driver disaster.

In any event, your only other choice—not being able to use the equipment—is probably unacceptable, so you might have no other viable alternative other than to install the unsigned driver. You may want to contact the vendor to determine when a signed driver will be available.

Where Are You in the Life Cycle of Your Computer?

Just as doctors generally don't perform major surgery on 80-year-old patients, one generally does not perform the equivalent of major surgery on older computers. My rule of thumb is that if I intend to replace my computer within the next year, there is little to be gained from doing anything that might disrupt its unstable equilibrium.

Keeping Your Computer Up-to-Date

You might have purchased your computer from Dell, Hewlett-Packard, or Gateway, but the fact remains that your computer's system software is a multivendor affair. The sound card, video card, network interface card, DVD-ROM, CD writer, monitor, hard disk, and so on are all manufactured by different companies, and they all require software drivers—and, in some cases, firmware—to function.

On top of the multivendor system software environment, you probably have dozens of applications installed.

If you had to manually check every system software component and application software component, updating your computer would be a difficult, error-prone task. You would likely miss some important updates, and you might install the wrong driver, precipitating a self-inflicted computer disaster.

Fortunately, CatchUp, the free utility from CNET that I recommend in Chapter 2, "The Threats and the Tools," makes this process a lot simpler and safer.

Keeping your computer up-to-date with CatchUp is a simple four-step process (after you have installed the application):

1. Allow CatchUp to scan your computer to compile an inventory of installed application and system software.

2. Allow CatchUp to find the updates you want to consider installing.

3. Determine which updates to install.

4. Install each update.

As software vendors are constantly updating their software, I suggest that you run the CatchUp program weekly to check for new updates.

Step 1: Scanning Your Computer/Compiling the Inventory

To run CatchUp after you have installed it, go to the CNET's CatchUp Services Web site at `http://catchup.cnet.com/`, click Launch Software Scan, and select the drive you want to scan (see Figure 9.2).

FIGURE 9.2

Launch the software scan to scan your PC for out-of-date software.

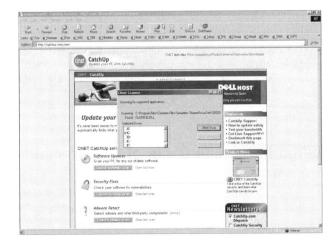

CatchUp analyzes your system and compiles a list of the system software and application software components installed on your computer (see Figure 9.3). The following information is reported for each item on the list:

- The filename
- The installed location on your computer
- The version currently installed on your computer

You then have the opportunity to uncheck any applications for which you do not want update information.

FIGURE 9.3

CatchUp has scanned your computer and is displaying the scan results.

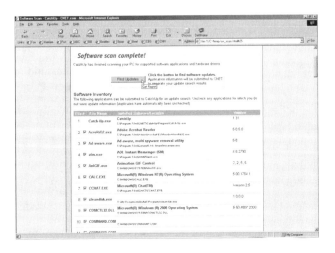

Step 2: Finding the Updates

The next step is to find the updates you want to install. Simply click the Find Updates button (refer to Figure 9.4). CatchUp examines each checked item on the inventory list to determine if an update is available.

Note that CatchUp is going to find the updates but is not going to automatically apply the updates, so clicking the Find Updates button does not alter your computer's configuration in any way.

One of the nice features about CatchUp is that it only recommends updates that are applicable to the release of an application software package you currently have installed. For example, two major releases of Easy CD Creator are currently in use, versions 4.0 and 5.0 (version 6 is scheduled for release in 2003). Each major release has had patches (updates). If you have version 4.0 installed on your computer, CatchUp only recommends updates that are applicable to version 4.0.

CatchUp also alerts you if a major upgrade is available and provides a price comparison link on the right side of the screen if such an upgrade is available.

CatchUp displays a list of available software updates. The following information is reported for each item on the list:

- The software name
- The latest version available
- A Get Update link that you can click if you decide to get more information about the update
- The version currently installed on your computer
- A File Location link that takes you back to the previous page (refer to Figure 9.4) if you need to refer to the inventory of applications installed on your computer

Step 3: Determining Which Updates to Apply

Use the criteria provided earlier in this chapter, in the section "Should You Keep Your Computer Up-to-Date?" to investigate each update to determine whether you want to install it. To do this, click the Get Update link. Note that this does not actually install the update; it takes you to a Web page where you can learn more about the update and download it should you decide to proceed with the update. Usually, this information (as well as the link for downloading the update) is displayed on a CNET Web page. In some cases, you will be taken directly to the software vendor's Web site.

For example, my Software Update Results list tells me that I currently have version 9.41.1 of the Logitech Mouse Driver installed and that I should consider installing version 9.6.1 (see Figure 9.4).

To learn more about this update, I click the Get Update link and see that the new version of the driver provides support for Windows XP. Since this particular computer is Windows 98, I decide not to install the update.

For a complete and up-to-date list of links listed in *PC Fear Factor*, go to http://www.alanluber.com/pcfearfactor/links.htm. This will eliminate the need for you to manually key these links into your Web browser.

You may be understandably nervous about allowing an application to scan your computer for information. According to CNET, CatchUp does not scan your computer for personal information and the application has no communication capabilities of its own—that is, it can't communicate with the Internet except when you initiate a scan. (Of course, if the application did try to initiate contact with the Internet on its own, ZoneAlarm would stop this activity.)

FIGURE 9.4
CatchUp is indicating that a newer version of the Logitech mouse driver is available.

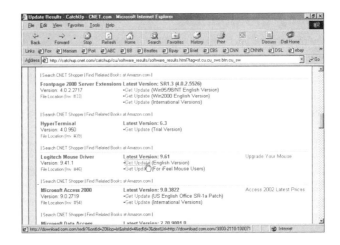

Prior to installing an update to your BIOS or to a device's firmware, download the version you currently have installed onto a floppy disk in case you need to recover from a computer disaster. BIOS and firmware updates are programmed directly into computer chips. This information does not exist on your hard disk, and therefore neither the System Restore feature in Windows Millennium or Windows XP nor a hard disk restore will enable you to recover from a disaster caused by a BIOS or firmware update. Reinstalling the old version from a floppy disk is the only solution that will work.

In some cases, the CNET Web page does not provide enough information about the update to enable you to make a decision, and you will have to visit the software vendor's Web site for additional information about the update.

Step 4: Applying the Updates

To apply an update, you must first download it to your computer. Downloading the update does not actually install it—it just downloads a setup program you can then run to install the update.

For application software updates, see Appendix B, "How to Install and Remove Programs from Your Computer," and follow the installation instructions to install the update. It is important that you follow these instructions because they include steps that enable you to recover if you experience a computer disaster as a result of applying the update. For system software updates, follow the installation instructions included with the update.

Before applying the update, create a system restore point if you are running Windows Millennium or XP. If you have reason to believe that the update is particularly risky, you also might want to perform a hard disk backup before applying the update, particularly if you are running Windows 98.

Be Especially Careful When Installing Driver Updates

Some companies manufacture components specifically to computer OEM specifications. For example, NVIDIA manufactures video cards to Dell's specifications. The drivers for these cards can be found *only* on Dell's Web site, so there is no benefit at all to checking NVIDIA's Web site for updates. In fact, you can do yourself a world of harm by downloading video drivers from NVIDIA's Web site in this case.

Finding and Installing BIOS and Other Firmware Updates

CatchUp is a great tool, but it is limited to popular freeware, shareware, commercial software applications, and device drivers. It will *not* find firmware or BIOS updates. To find these updates, I suggest that you go to your computer manufacturer's Web site.

BIOS and firmware downloads are typically organized by product family (computer model) within a computer vendor's Web site. The trick is to find out which downloads are applicable to your specific computer by comparing the version number on the vendor's Web site to the version number that is installed on your computer.

Your installed BIOS version shows in the upper-left corner of your computer screen for a few seconds every time you boot up your computer. If you have difficulty reading this, you can access the BIOS program by repeatedly tapping the Delete key when you boot up the computer. The BIOS screen will tell you which version you currently have installed. You exit the BIOS program by pressing the F10 function key on your keyboard.

Typically, devices such as DVD-ROMs and CD writers have firmware. You need to compare the firmware revision level on the vendor's Web site to the firmware revision level displayed on the device under Device Manager. The firmware version for your device can be found on the Settings tab for the device properties (see Figure 9.5).

FIGURE 9.5
Viewing the firmware revision number for a device.

Make sure you have and understand the instructions for downloading and installing the BIOS or firmware update. Updates to your BIOS or device firmware need to be downloaded to a bootable floppy disk because they need to be applied from outside Microsoft Windows. (Such updates create the bootable floppy disk for you.)

After You Apply the Update

Immediately after applying an update, reboot your system and verify that it is still functioning properly. If the update was supposed to fix a specific problem, verify that the problem has been fixed. If the update added new features, verify that the features function properly and don't cause other problems.

Do *not* install multiple updates before rebooting your system and verifying that it is still functioning properly. If you install multiple updates and there is a problem, you will be unable to determine which update caused the problem. You will therefore have to uninstall all the updates and start over.

Stop Sluggish Performance and System Crashes

You were zipping right along when you purchased your computer last year, but now your computer is slower than Wes Covington and crashes more often than Evel Knieval. (Wes Covington and Roy Sievers both played for the Philadelphia Phillies in the early '60s. Neither player was fleet of foot. There is an unsubstantiated rumor that they once had a foot race and nobody won.)

Here is what is probably causing your problems.

Most software programs are like small children: They think they are the center of universe. Whenever you install an application, the installation program assumes (incorrectly in most cases) that you automatically want to launch the program whenever you start your computer. The installation process automatically places the application in Windows' list of startup items.

Some programs at least give you an option during the install process, displaying a message asking, Do you want this program to start automatically when you start your computer? But many programs don't even give you that option; they just insert themselves into your computer's list of startup items without ever asking your permission.

If you see a great many icons in the system tray (the lower-right corner of your Windows task bar) when you boot up, your computer is probably launching too many programs.

Loading too many programs or background processes can consume limited system resources and cause a system crash. Additionally, the more programs you have open, the more opportunity there is for these programs to conflict with each other, which can also cause a system crash.

All About System Resources, System Crashes, and Memory Leaks

The term *system resources* refers to an amount of memory Windows uses to store information used by each program. Each open program consumes a certain amount of system resources. This area is not unlimited and can be exhausted when you have too many applications open.

The problem of insufficient system resources is exacerbated by something called *memory leaks*. When a program is started, it consumes a certain amount of system resources. In theory, when the program is closed, all the resources it consumed are freed.

Even if you do *not* see a large number of icons in your system tray, your computer may still be loading a significant number of unnecessary background processes. A *background process* is something that runs undetected without input from the user. Some background processes are essential, such as the process that automatically checks for virus definition updates. But many programs place background processes on your computer that are not necessary and not to your benefit. These processes just make it easier for the software vendor to pester you with reminders and promotions.

In practice, some programs don't do a very good job of letting go. The amount of resources not made available is called a *memory leak*.

To view the amount of available system resources, right-click My Computer, select Properties, and click the Performance tab (see Figure 9.6).

FIGURE 9.6
Viewing available system resources.

The percentage of System Resources consumed is not viewable on Windows XP, which was derived from the Windows NT operating system and is not as susceptible to system crashes. However, all operating systems are susceptible to sluggish performance caused by having too many programs loaded at once.

On a related subject, each new version of Windows promises to deliver the holy grail: a crash-proof system. If you believe such claims, I would like to sell you some shares of Enron.

When your system resources become dangerously low, your computer seizes up like an engine without oil. This is called a *system crash*. A system crash, or computer crash, does *not* refer to a physical hard disk crash. Rather, it refers to a situation where the computer stops functioning and may need to be rebooted. In some cases, you might see the blue screen of death (a bright blue screen with white text obscurely describing an error that has occurred). In other cases, the computer may simply stop responding. System crashes are frequently caused by software conflicts or lack of resources, both of which can be caused by having too many applications open. Frequent system crashes are more than an inconvenience—they can lead to loss of data or corruption of system files because they often result in the abnormal shutdown of Windows.

Escaping from a Windows Crash

Sometimes, you can escape from a system crash by shutting down an application that is not responding. To see a list of applications and processes currently running on your computer, press Ctrl+Alt+Del (see Figure 9.7). On Windows XP computers, the applications and processes show on separate tabs (see Figure 9.8).

If any application or process in the window has the words "Not responding" next to it, click the application to highlight it and then click the End Task button. This shuts down the application. You might have wait a while, or you might have to repeat this step several times before the application shuts down. Sometimes, Windows displays a second window asking if you want to end the program. Click Yes if this window appears.

Of course, the real solution to this problem is *not* to Ctrl+Alt+Del your way out of a system crash, but to prevent these unnecessary programs and processes that are causing your problems from loading in the first place.

FIGURE 9.7

Press the Ctrl+Alt+Del keys simultaneously to view a list of applications and processes that are running on your computer. This figure shows the applications and processes running on a Windows 98 system. Windows Millennium systems have a similar appearance.

FIGURE 9.8

On Windows XP systems, the applications and processes show on different tabs.

The Solution

Microsoft provides a System Configuration Utility that allows you to disable items in your startup list to prevent them from loading automatically when you boot up your computer.

Microsoft originally intended for this utility to be a troubleshooting tool, but its real value is in allowing you to stop all this junk from loading up and consuming system resources.

To run the System Configuration Utility, do the following:

1. Select Start, Run.

2. In the Open text box, type **msconfig** and click OK.

3. Click the Startup tab. This displays a list of items that have been placed in your startup list by applications installed on your computer (see Figure 9.9). Any item that has a check mark next to it starts automatically whenever you boot up your computer. (If you are using the Normal startup mode, *every* item has a check mark. (Refer to the General tab.)

FIGURE 9.9

The Startup tab displays a list of items that have been placed on your computer's startup list.

You may notice many applications on your startup list, such as America Online Instant Messenger, MusicMatch Jukebox, RealPlayer, Adaptec DirectCD, Create CD, KaZaA, and so on. With the possible exception of America Online Instant Messenger, there is absolutely no benefit to starting these applications when you start your system. You can and should uncheck all these boxes.

Although *PC Fear Factor* does not deal specifically with Windows 2000, I thought it worth mentioning that Windows 2000 does not include the System Configuration Utility. This means you have to modify the Windows Registry to stop applications from loading automatically when you boot up your computer. As you can see, Windows 2000 was not intended for the average home user.

System Configuration Utility "Do Nots"

You can improve the performance of your computer and reduce the likelihood of system crashes by disabling the right startup items, but you can also buy yourself a big heap of trouble by disabling the wrong startup items.

Do not disable any startup items having anything to do with ZoneAlarm, Norton, or Symantec. These items load ZoneAlarm and Norton AntiVirus when you start up your computer, as well as certain options such as Symantec's script blocking capability. Disabling these items leaves your system vulnerable to virus infections and hackers.

Do not disable CriticalUpdate or Microsoft will not be able to check for critical updates. This leaves you vulnerable to hackers, as many of these critical updates fix security flaws in Internet Explorer, Outlook, or Outlook Express.

Do not disable the SchedulingAgent (`mstask.exe`). This leaves your system vulnerable to virus attacks and hackers. If the SchedulingAgent is disabled, Norton AntiVirus does not check for virus definition updates or perform a weekly scheduled scan of your computer, and Microsoft does not execute the CriticalUpdate job to check for critical updates.

Do not (with a little less emphasis on not) disable the TaskMonitor (`taskmon.exe`); otherwise, Microsoft's defrag utility will not be able to rearrange your program files so that the programs you use most often open faster. It's not the end of the world if you disable the TaskMonitor, but your Windows 98 or Millennium computer will not perform as well. (This does not apply to Windows XP systems because the defrag utility works differently.)

Do not change any of the settings on any of the other tabs on the system configuration utility unless instructed to by an experienced technical support specialist, and then only to troubleshoot some sort of computer problem. Changing any of these settings could leave your computer in an unstable state.

If you click the General tab and select Normal Startup, all the boxes in your startup group are automatically rechecked. You do *not* want to do this—you *always* want to be running in the Selective Startup mode. As soon as you uncheck any box on your startup list, you are in the Selective Startup mode by default.

Paul Collins, a hardware engineer who hails from England, has put together an excellent, comprehensive, alphabetized list of startup group items. He has included comments that will help you determine whether it is safe to disable a specific item in your startup group. The list can be found at `http://www.pacs-portal.co.uk/startup_pages/startup_full.htm`.

Nice job, Paul!

Because things have a way of getting added to your startup list without your knowledge over time, I suggest that you run the System Configuration Utility once a week and disable any items you don't want loaded when you start your computer.

RealPlayer Is Just Real Obnoxious

RealNetworks' RealPlayer application is particularly obnoxious with respect to its startup behavior. You can disable this application in `msconfig` if you like, but you are wasting your time. RealPlayer will immediately recheck the item as soon as you close `msconfig`.

Fortunately, there is a way to disable RealPlayer from your startup list, although it is not very obvious. To disable RealPlayer, open the application and select View, Preferences. On the General tab, under StartCenter, click Settings.

Uncheck the Enable StartCenter box and click OK. This prevents RealPlayer from loading when you boot up your computer.

If you are experiencing problems like this with other applications, I suggest that you look in the application's user interface under Options or Preferences for a way to stop the application from loading.

How many items will you be able to disable? Your results will vary depending on how many applications you have installed. I have 47 items in my startup group and have disabled all but 20 of them. The difference this makes in performance and stability is incredible.

If you are currently running in Normal startup mode, check your system resources as soon as you boot up. Now, disable the unnecessary startup items, reboot your computer, and check your system resources again. In my case, the available system resources after booting up using the normal startup is under 50%. After disabling the unnecessary startup items and rebooting, my available system resources are 79%. (You can't perform this check under Windows XP.)

Tips for Avoiding PC Disasters

Revelations

In this chapter you will learn

☐ Why you should beware of most freeware

☐ Five high-risk changes to your computing environment to avoid whenever possible

☐ How to avoid self-inflicted computer disasters

☐ Why a system administrator should also be a preacher

☐ Why redundancy is good. Why redundancy is good. Why redundancy is good

☐ How to tell when somebody is leading you down the path to disaster

☐ How a party PC can act as an important buffer against computer disasters

Before You Read

This chapter provides a few general tips for avoiding computer disasters that go above and beyond the material covered elsewhere in *PC Fear Factor*. These tips are mostly procedural do's and don'ts. Each section stands on its own, but they all stand together in their common objective of helping you avoid computer disasters.

Don't Change Your Operating System

"Danger, Will Robinson! Danger!"

—The Robot, *Lost in Space* television series

Do you have a Windows 98 or Millennium system? Are you thinking of installing Windows XP? I have three words of advice for you: *Don't do it!*

Sure, Windows XP is a much better product than Windows 98 or Windows Millennium. It has a cleaner interface, more stable performance, and some great disaster recovery features. Unfortunately, if you attempt to install it on your old machine, you are more likely to *have* a disaster than to get a great new disaster prevention tool.

Whenever Microsoft releases a major new version of Windows, it unleashes a whole new world of incompatibilities. It's a sure bet that many of your installed software applications and many of your computer's internal components aren't compatible with Windows XP. The older your computer, the more incompatibilities you will have. You will spend many days (perhaps weeks) trying to resolve these incompatibilities— searching for new drivers, buying new software, and trying to fix problems of mysterious unknown origin. You may even end up replacing some hardware components. The manufacturer of your three-year-old, obsolete CD writer has absolutely no incentive to provide Windows XP drivers for a product it no longer sells: The manufacturer wants you to buy a new CD writer.

And that's not all. Each new release of Windows requires more memory and more disk space, which means your old computer might not be up to snuff anyway.

In my opinion, you just don't change operating systems on computers! The gain is never worth the pain. Until you buy a new computer, your old operating system should serve you very well.

Apparently, most people already agree with me, so perhaps I am preaching to the choir here. The vast majority of sales for Windows XP are coming not from retail sales, but from the OEM market. In fact, each new release of Microsoft Windows sells fewer retail copies than the previous release, even though there are more PC users than ever before. The reason, according to analysts, is that more users upgrade their operating systems by buying new computers, rather than buying new releases of Windows to install on old PCs.

That's not to say that people rush out and buy a new computer whenever Microsoft releases a new version of Windows. But the data indicates that people wait until they buy a new computer to get a new operating system. I suspect there are two reasons for this:

- **The gain is incremental**—When Windows 95 came out, there were compelling reasons to upgrade from Windows 3.1, not the least of which were multi-tasking and the Windows desktop. With each new release of Windows, the reasons to upgrade are less compelling. People can wait.

- **The pain is monumental**—Consumers are sadder but wiser. They understand how difficult it is to change operating systems on a computer. Many have been burned in the past when they tried to upgrade Windows 3.1 to Windows 95 or Windows 95 to Windows 98. The old adage, "Fool me once, shame on you. Fool me twice, shame on me," seems to apply particularly well here.

Now, I am sure some people out there have successfully installed Windows XP on their Windows 98 computers. But, if you are like everyone *I* know who has attempted to install Windows XP on their old computers, you will admit defeat in the end and reinstall Windows 98. If I may paraphrase Ernest Thayer:

> Oh somewhere in this favored land a man shouts out in glee
>
> He changed his operating system on his old PC
>
> The install went extremely well, no problems, fuss, or pain
>
> But anyone I know who tried has been declared insane.

Don't Install Freeware

Don't download and install freeware utilities and applets (small applications) you find on the Web. Freeware applications are more likely to be ill-behaved than commercial applications, and some freeware applications contain Trojan horses or spyware.

There are obvious exceptions to this rule. My graphics viewer, IrfanView, is freeware. But it is used by thousands, if not tens of thousands, of people, and the developer has an excellent reputation for quality. It is for all practical purposes managed as a commercial software product.

If you can't resist the urge to download freeware, I implore you to follow the instructions in Appendix B, "How to Install and Remove Programs from Your Computer," which includes tips on how to evaluate a software application to determine if it is well-behaved.

Avoid High-Risk Changes Wherever Possible

We know that computers are unstable equilibriums. Common sense dictates that you should try to avoid high-risk changes—changes that are most likely to engender computer disasters. Here is my top five list of risky changes to your computing environment you should try to avoid:

1. Changing operating systems
2. Installing new drivers or device firmware (unless the update fixes a bug or adds a feature that you require)
3. Installing new hardware. (I'm speaking of internal components here, not printers and scanners, or other USB devices)
4. Updating your BIOS (unless the update solves a problem)
5. Installing unproven applications

Don't Be Bold

This piece of advice goes hand-in-hand with the previous tip.

I was sitting next to a parachute instructor on a plane recently. He was telling me about people who, after having made a number of successful jumps, get cocky and bold and end up killing themselves. He called them "100 jump wonders."

I think it's a useful analogy for what I am about to discuss.

Now that you are confident in your ability to recover from even the worst possible computer disaster, you may feel inclined to take more risks with your computer, such as downloading freeware, installing unproven applications or betaware, making multiple changes to your computing environment at once, letting other people use your computer, and so on.

I beseech you: Don't get bold, or you may become the personal computer equivalent of a 100 jump wonder.

First, some types of damage just can't be undone, even with a hard disk restore. If you boldly download freeware, only to learn later that it contains spyware that has compromised your personal data, there is no way to undo the damage.

Secondly, it's never a good idea to take unnecessary risks. I don't speed and run red lights because I have seat belts and air bags, and I wouldn't walk through a snake pit just because I had anti-venom. As always, the name of the game is risk management.

There are unpredictable consequences of computer disasters, so I caution you to exercise good judgment. Disaster recovery should be the exception, not the rule.

Preach What You Practice

Your computing environment is only as stable as its weakest link, and the weakest link is usually human—a family member who does not practice safe computing. While it may be too much to expect everyone in your family to read *PC Fear Factor*, you *must* instruct family members regarding safe computing practices.

Implement Procedures to Minimize Risk

Good procedures can add stability to your computing environment and are especially important if you have more than one computer, or even multiple people using one computer.

Of course, I would prefer it if you would purchase a copy of *PC Fear Factor* for each family member. It also makes a lovely gift.

I recommend that you implement a few simple procedures to minimize the risk of a computer disaster:

- **No family member should install or update a software application on her computer without the prior approval of the system administrator (that's *you*)**—My youngest daughter is so diligent in this respect that she even asks my permission to apply Microsoft CRITICAL UPDATES.

- **Computers are off-limits to all visitors**—It's difficult enough getting family members to apply safe computing practices—anytime you allow a guest to use your computer, you are asking for trouble. Once again, my youngest daughter is most diligent in this regard—so much so that she has declared her computer off-limits to other family members as well. I find her attitude interesting and, quite frankly, refreshing. She is very technology oriented (she developed http:// www.alanluber.com, the companion Web site for *PC Fear Factor*) and seems to have a greater appreciation of the fact that computers are unstable equilibriums than other family members. If we have house guests, she even puts a sign up on her computer politely advising people that her computer is off-limits.

- **Do not open email from people you do not know**—And don't open any attachments you are not expecting, even if they come from people you *do* know. Because some viruses can activate themselves without opening the message, you should turn off your preview pane on your email messages.

- **Users of Norton AntiVirus should run LiveUpdate once a week to get any Norton program updates**—If you use a different virus protection program, be sure to use whatever tools it has available to keep it up-to-date.

- **Keep a system log of any changes you make to your computing environment**—This includes even changes in program preferences. This will be a big help in disaster recovery.

You might want to implement additional procedures if you are willing to delegate the tasks of taking data backups and hard disk backups, but you will have to spend some time training family members to do that using the step-by-step instructions in Chapter 6, "Backing Up Your Data," and Chapter 7, "Backing Up Your Hard Disk."

Incorporate Redundancy into Everything You Do

When it comes to disaster prevention and recovery, redundancy is the key to success. Two firewalls—a software firewall and a hardware firewall—provide more protection from hackers than one firewall. In the world of personal computing, redundancy is goodness, and faith in a single solution to any problem—one backup set, for example—is an invitation to disaster.

Avoid Self-Inflicted Disasters

Each version of Windows has a Disk Cleanup tool that can help you clean out these files. Select Start, All Programs, Accessories, System Tools, Disk Cleanup to run this tool.

Many computer disasters are self-inflicted. A friend of mine recently called me because his computer speakers stopped working. It seems that he decided to clean up his hard disk and deleted a lot of stuff he didn't need. Apparently, one of the things he didn't need was his sound card driver.

Limit your PC cleanup activity to things you *know* are safe to delete: temporary Internet files, Windows temporary files, old documents, and so on.

And as you will see in Appendix B, you don't remove a program from your computer simply by deleting an icon off the desktop or by finding the program folder and deleting the folder. You must use whatever uninstall feature is available for the program (usually through the Windows Add/Remove Programs tools). Failure to do so will result in partially removed programs that could render your system unstable.

Don't Let Somebody Talk You into Doing Something Stupid

At some point, you are going to have some kind of problem, either with your PC or your broadband Internet connection that requires technical support.

For the most part, technical support specialists are pretty savvy, helpful individuals. But every once in a while, you will come across someone who is either lazy or stupid (or both). This person will spend a few minutes troubleshooting a problem with you and then try to convince you to make some major changes to your system. Such changes are almost *always* unnecessary and very harmful! Whenever somebody suggests that you change the configuration of your system, all sorts of warning bells should go off in your head. Whenever a technical support specialist sounds as if he is guessing about the cause of your problem—that he is directing you on a "try this, try that" adventure—it's time to hang up and call back in hopes of getting somebody competent on the line.

Be *especially* careful with Internet service provider help desks. Some ISP help desks operate under the assumption that *you* are somehow at fault when you lose your Internet connection—that you have changed a setting on your computer or done something to cause the problem. These people will immediately want you to change all sorts of setting on your computer. *Don't* do it! The problem is not on your end. Insist that they investigate the problem on their end first.

Let's apply a little common sense here. One second, your computer was connected to the Internet and everything was working just fine. The next second, you've lost your connection. Now I ask you: Have you done anything that might have caused you to lose your connection? Of course not. Invariably, your ISP is the source of the problem. It either has a server down or some type of network infrastructure problem. The help desk just doesn't know it yet. But don't let them put the blame back on you, and don't start making changes to your machine because then you *will* have a problem.

I have never understood this mentality—this arrogant assumption that the customer has done something wrong, when 99.9% of the time the ISP is to blame. Now, I suppose it's possible that your network interface card, router, or cable modem suddenly died or that a connection has come loose, but if your Internet connection is working one second and then suddenly dies, it is extremely unlikely.

If you are going to get a router, be aware of the advantages of having a solution that is supported by your ISP. See the sidebar, "Your Shared Internet Connection and Your ISP" in Chapter 2, "The Threats and the Tools." The information in this sidebar applies whether you have one or multiple PCs connected through the router.

Use Your Old PC As a Playpen

"We are havin' a party"

—Sam Cooke, 1962

Here's a novel idea. The next time you buy a new computer, don't sell or give away the old one. Use it as a playpen—a party PC, so to speak.

A party PC can serve as an important buffer between your newer, more important computers and a computer disaster. Here are some ways to use your party PC:

- If you use certain applications that contain adware, install them only on your trash system. For example, install KaZaA on your party PC, download the files you need, and then move them to your other computers either by copying them to CD or moving them across a home network. Don't expose your other computers to spam-inducing adware.

- Install applications that don't play well with others on your party PC.

- If you have certain legacy applications—applications that only work with older versions of Windows—install them on your party PC.

- If you want to try freeware or new applications, try them on your party PC.

- If you want to try to install a new operating system, do it on your party PC.

Of course, you shouldn't store any valuable data on your party PC or rely on this system for any critical applications. Nor should you treat this system any differently than any other computer you own with regard to virus protection or firewalls.

Before you put your old computer into service as a party PC, take a complete backup of the hard disk. Once you start partying, you should *not* take any more backups. At this point, you may no longer have a stable system. If you experience a complete computer disaster on your party PC, the best thing to do is restore your hard disk to a configuration you know is stable—the hard disk backup you took just before you put the computer into service as your party PC.

APPENDIX **A**

Wouldn't it be easier to use Windows' System Restore feature?

The System Restore Feature

Revelations

In this appendix you will learn

☐ Why some application install and uninstall programs create a vicious cycle I call the *DO Loop of Despair*

☐ When you should manually create restore points in addition to those automatically created by System Restore

☐ How to determine which disaster recover tool to use: System Restore or Driver Rollback

What Is the System Restore Feature?

Windows XP has an excellent disaster recovery feature called System Restore that is quite useful in helping users recover from certain types of computer disasters. (This feature is also found in Windows Millennium but is not present in older versions of Windows.)

System Restore is essentially a limited "do over" tool. It takes snapshots of critical system files on your computer whenever you make a significant change to your computing environment. Each snapshot is called a *restore point*. Each restore point has a unique date and time stamp. If a change to your computing environment renders your computer unstable, you can use the System Restore feature to restore your computer to a previous stable state.

The really remarkable thing about System Restore is that it is able to restore your system to a prior, stable point *without causing any loss of data*. So, if you restore your system to a restore point from two weeks ago, you *won't* lose any documents, data files, email, or browser bookmarks created in the past two weeks.

Activities That Trigger the Automatic Creation of Restore Points

System Restore requires very little manual effort to use because it creates restore points for you automatically. The following activities trigger the automatic creation of restore points:

- **Installation of applications that are System Restore compliant**—An application is System Restore compliant if its install program is written specifically to integrate with the System Restore feature to trigger the creation of a restore point just prior to the installation.

- **Installation of Microsoft Critical Updates**—Microsoft periodically provides critical security updates to the Windows operating system, Web browser, and email applications. It is a good thing that Windows automatically creates a restore point prior to installing these updates, as I have found that these software updates, which are intended to fix problems, sometimes cause problems.

- **Installation of an unsigned driver**—You will recall from Chapter 9, "Keeping Your Computer in Top Shape," that an unsigned driver is a driver that has not passed testing standards established by Microsoft's Windows Hardware Quality Lab (WHQL). Windows XP automatically creates a restore point before an unsigned driver is installed because in some cases you may not be able to use the Driver Rollback features (see the following sidebar).

- **A System Restore operation**—Now this is really clever, but it's a bit difficult to understand. Microsoft was smart enough to recognize that you might accidentally chose the wrong restore point when you restore your system, and that you might want to undo the restore operation. So just prior to executing your command to restore your system, Microsoft creates *another* restore point.

This gives you the ability to undo your undo, that is, restore your system to the point just prior to when you restored your system.

- **Use of your computer**—Once a day, every day you use your machine, even if none of the previously mentioned activities take place, System Restore creates a restore point. (System Restore waits until your machine is idle before taking the restore point.) This is very helpful in fixing computer disasters of sudden, mysterious origin. If you boot up your system in the morning, only to find that it is exhibiting some strange and abnormal behavior, you can restore your system to the restore point created the previous day.

System Restore also automatically creates a restore point prior to performing a backup recovery with the Microsoft backup utility. However, this is somewhat of a moot point because most Windows XP users do not have access to this utility. Microsoft did not see fit to include the backup utility in the OEM version of Windows XP or provide Windows XP users with a means of downloading and installing the utility. So, if you purchased a computer with Windows XP, the only way presently to acquire this utility is to go to the store and buy Windows XP, which is kind of silly.

Should I Use System Restore or Driver Rollback?

Windows XP has two disaster recovery "undo" functions: System Restore and Driver Rollback. In some cases, you have no option but to use the System Restore feature. The Driver Rollback feature can only be used if updating a driver caused the problem. If you installed a new driver, there is no previous version for Driver Rollback to use.

If you *do* have a choice of using either the System Restore feature or Driver Rollback feature to recover from a driver-related disaster, you should try the Driver Rollback feature first because it is a more focused, less intrusive disaster recovery tool than System Restore. System Restore undoes all the changes you have made to the system since installing the driver, whereas Driver Rollback affects only the driver itself.

If, for some reason, the Driver Rollback feature does not solve the problem, you can try the System Restore feature.

How Do I Know if an Application Is System Restore Compliant?

How can you determine if an application will automatically trigger the creation of a restore point when it is installed?

You can safely assume the latest version of all Microsoft applications are System Restore compliant. You can also reasonably assume that software products that are logo certified for Windows XP are System Restore compliant.

Not sure if an application is System Restore compliant? Err on the side of caution and create a restore point prior to installing the application. There is absolutely no harm done if you manually create a restore point and then the installation process triggers the creation of another restore point.

Beyond that, you should attempt to confirm whether a specific application you intend to install is System Restore compliant before you install that application. Unfortunately, my experience has been that application software vendors do not post such information prominently on their Web pages. You are going to need to search the knowledge base on the software vendor's Web site or contact technical support to ask the following specific question:

> "Is your application's install program System Restore RestorePT.API compliant? That is, will the application trigger the automatic creation of a restore point when it is installed on a Windows XP system?"

If you get an affirmative response from a knowledgeable authority, you can reasonably assume that the installation process will trigger the automatic creation of a system restore point.

If the application is *not* System Restore compliant, or if you are unable to definitively make that determination, you should manually create a restore point just prior to installing the application.

Manual Restore Points

You can manually create a restore point at any time. I recommend that you create a restore point

- **Prior to installing or upgrading an application, if you are not absolutely certain that the application is System Restore compliant.**

- **Prior to installing new hardware**—Manually create a restore point prior to installing new hardware in your computer, or installing any peripheral device.

- **Prior to allowing another person to use your computer**—I strongly advise against letting people outside your immediate family use your computer, but if you have no choice, create a manual restore point first in case they do something to precipitate a computer disaster.

- **Anytime you are making any unusual change to your computing environment that might render your computer unstable.**

Should You Create a Manual Restore Point Prior to Uninstalling an Application?

Poorly written uninstall programs can cause computer disasters, either by removing things they shouldn't remove or by leaving files on your computer (or entries in your Windows Registry) that they should remove.

Restoring your computer to a point just prior to an application uninstall might fix a disaster caused by an uninstall program, but it will also reinstall many of the files associated with the application, defeating the purpose of uninstalling the application in the first place!

And if you were uninstalling the application to fix a problem caused by the application (and not just because you didn't need the application any more), restoring your system to fix a problem caused by the *uninstall* program may just cause you to bounce back and forth between two problems. I call this the infinite *DO Loop of Despair*.

The real solution—the only way out of the DO Loop of Despair—is to uninstall the program and then restore your system to a restore point prior to when the program was installed.

How Windows Manages Restore Points

Windows Millennium stores all restore points in the C:_RESTORE folder, and Windows XP stores this information in the C:\system volume information folder.

Obviously, a large amount of disk space is required to store all these system snapshots, even though the files are automatically compressed to save room. If older restore points were not purged periodically, the restore point files would eventually consume your entire hard disk!

While Microsoft does not set a limit on the number of restore points it retains, there is a limit on the percentage of disk space that restore points can consume. The limit is preset to the maximum allowable percentage—12% of your hard disk space—and can be adjusted by the user. (I've no idea how Microsoft arrived at this arbitrary number. Why not 10%?)

Windows automatically purges old restore points as the limit on hard disk space is approached. Whenever your system restore data exceeds 90% of the allowed disk space, Windows automatically purges enough restore points to reduce the utilization back to 50% of the allowed space. Windows purges restore points on a first-in-first-out basis, so that the oldest, least important restore points are purged.

System Restore needs a minimum of 200MB of free space on your hard disk. If less than 200MB of free space is available, System Restore automatically stops creating restore points until more space becomes available.

Limitations of the System Restore Feature

System Restore is most useful if you *immediately* notice a problem after making a change to your system. If you determine that a problem was caused by a change you made a month ago, you might not want to use the System Restore feature. If you do, other changes you have made to your system since that point will also be undone, which can create an even bigger problem than the one you are trying to fix.

The System Restore feature will not help you fix certain types of problems, even if you notice them immediately. System Restore will not help you fix problems created by updating your system's BIOS or any other firmware, as these changes are *not* stored on your hard disk—they are "burned" into chips in your computer and would not be undone by reverting to an earlier restore point. Also, you generally can't undo the damage done by a virus by restoring your system.

Enabling the System Restore Feature

The System Restore feature is enabled by default within Windows, so you won't have to worry about activating this feature when you get your new computer.

Do Not Disable System Restore Except Under Extreme Circumstances

Disabling the System Restore feature doesn't just stop System Restore from creating new restore points—it flushes all existing restore points down the drain!

You should only disable System Restore under the extreme circumstances described in Chapter 5, "Protecting Your Computer from Cyber-Terrorists," if it is necessary to flush all restore points to rid your system restore folder of a computer virus. Even then, you should immediately reactivate System Restore once the virus has been eliminated from your computer so that it begins working for you again.

What Files Are Included in the System Restore Snapshot?

System Restore takes a snapshot of the Registry, critical system files, and any file on your computer having one of over 600 files extensions that are monitored by System Restore.

A complete list of monitored file extensions can be found on Microsoft's Web site at `http://msdn.microsoft.com/library/default.asp?url=/library/en-us/sr/sr/monitored_file_extensions.asp`.

Basically, System Restore monitors everything except files with known document extensions such as .doc, .xls, .ppt, and any files in the My Documents folder, which is strictly off-limits to System Restore.

It is important that you do *not* create any documents that use any of the monitored extensions, as these documents would be automatically included in the System Restore snapshot and restored to their older versions in the event that you have to restore your system. (If you look at the list of monitored file extensions, you will see that it is unlikely that you would use any of these intentionally.)

Using System Restore

System Restore functions unobtrusively in the background, automatically creating new restore points and periodically purging old restore points.

There are only four times when you will need to manually intervene to use the System Restore feature:

- **If you need to temporarily disable the System Restore feature**—You might need to do this to purge all restore points if your system restore folder has become infected with a virus. Instructions for disabling the system restore feature are found in Chapter 5.

- **If you want to change the amount of hard disk space allotted for restore points**— Reducing the amount of hard disk space allotted to restore points can force a partial purge of restore points, as explained in Chapter 5. You might want to do this for either of two reasons: to try to purge a virus from your system restore folder without purging *all* of your system restore points, or to reduce the amount of data that has to be backed up when you take a hard disk backup.

- **To manually create a restore point.**

- **To restore an unstable system to a stable restore point.**

How to Create a Manual Restore Point

To create a restore point, do the following:

1. Select Start, All Programs, Accessories, System Tools, System Restore.

2. Select Create a Restore Point and then click Next (see Figure A.1).

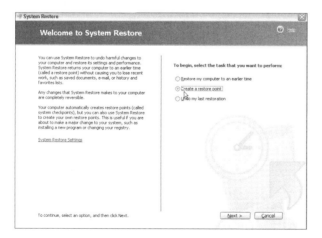

FIGURE A.1

Creating a restore point: initiating the process.

3. Enter a description of the restore point and then click Create (see Figure A.2). A good description is important because it is the only piece of information you have to guide you in selecting a restore point should you later need to restore your system.

FIGURE A.2

Enter a description for the restore point.

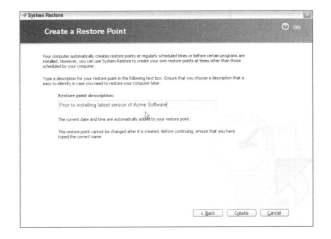

That's all there is to it: Windows will take a snapshot of all the monitored files and create a restore point.

How to Restore Your System to a Restore Point

To restore your system to a restore point, follow these steps:

1. Select Start, All Programs, Accessories, System Tools, System Restore.

2. Select Restore My Computer to an Earlier Time and then click Next (see Figure A.3).

FIGURE A.3

Restoring your computer to an earlier time.

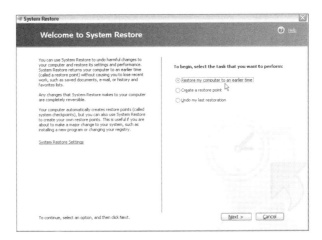

3. Select a restore point. Choose the most recent restore point that you believe will solve the problem you are experiencing. To select a restore point, click a date; you will see a list of restore points available for that date (see Figure A.4).

Notice that the date and time are displayed for each restore point, as well as the description of the restore point. Daily restore points taken by Windows have the description "System Checkpoint." Write down the information about the restore point that you intend to use. *You are not going to restore your system just yet. First, we have some preparation work to do.*

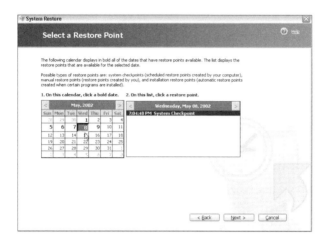

FIGURE A.4

Selecting a restore point. Choose the most recent restore point that you believe will solve the problem.

4. Once you have selected and made note of the date and time of the restore point you intend to use, exit System Restore and uninstall all applications that have been installed since that date and time. You should have a record of all these applications in your system log. Refer to the sidebar following these instructions for an explanation of why you need to uninstall these applications.

5. Repeat steps 1–3. This time, when you select a restore point, click Next.

6. You will see a window asking you to confirm your restore point selection (see Figure A.5). Read the instructions, verify that you have selected the right restore point, and click Next to restore your system. If this does not solve your problem, you may need to repeat the process, choosing an earlier restore point.

Once you have returned your system to a stable state, you will need to reinstall any applications you uninstalled.

If you had installed a hardware component subsequent to the restore point, your system will no longer recognize that hardware component after the restore operation. However, Windows' plug-and-play functionality should prompt the reinstallation of the hardware component when you reboot your computer.

FIGURE A.5

Confirm your restore point selection.

When Restoring My System, Why Should I First Uninstall Applications That Were Installed Subsequent to the Selected Restore Point?

Restoring the system renders applications that were installed subsequent to the restore point inoperable, but it does not do the same thing as a clean application uninstall—remnants of the application can remain on your system.

Furthermore, if you try to uninstall the applications after you restore your system, the uninstall program may abort because it is unable to find things it is looking for.

So, the proper sequence is to uninstall your applications and *then* restore your system to the selected restore point.

APPENDIX **B**

How to Install and Remove Programs from Your Computer

Revelations

In this appendix you will learn

- [ ] How to avoid a computer disaster before you install a new program
- [ ] How to save disk space during the installation process
- [ ] How *not* to uninstall a program
- [ ] How to avoid a computer disaster during the uninstall process

Avoiding Disaster Before You Buy

In Chapter 3, "A Disaster Prevention Plan for Your New Computer: Part 1, Before You Buy," I discussed how to avoid a disaster before you purchase a new computer. It is equally important to know how to avoid a disaster before you purchase and install new software.

Computer disasters are often caused by ill-behaved software applications. Many of these disasters could be avoided if more people would stop and ask themselves the following question *before* installing a software package:

> Should I install this application on my computer?

I find that many people just assume that any software package they can buy at their local computer store that comes in an attractively designed box is a quality product. In truth, there is a lot of attractively packaged junk out there. Before buying any software package, you should check out reviews from other people who have actually used the software. The two best places on the Web for user reviews of software products are Epinions and CNET. Software reviews can be found at `http://www.epinions.com/cmsw-Software-All` and `http://home.cnet.com/software/0-8888.html?tag=st.re.9870989.dir.8888`.

If the reviews are favorable, go to the software vendor's Web site and check out its knowledge base for issues, bugs, and complaints.

Checking out the package in this manner will help you understand whether the package is reliable and whether there are any potential conflicts with anything in your computing environment.

Don't put much stock in software reviews in computer magazines. More often than not, the reviews are nothing more than regurgitated press releases or marketing brochures. My impression is that the people writing these reviews have never actually installed and used the software. The only reviews that count for anything in my book are reviews written by real users.

Regardless of your source of information, an important consideration should be the number of reviews. If a product has only a few reviews, be they good or bad, that is just not a large enough sample to form an educated opinion. If, on the other hand, a product has 100 reviews and a significant percentage—say 20%—are negative, this is a clear indication that there is some type of problem.

You should also consider the quality of the review, as well as the content:

- Did the reviewer do to a thorough job? For example, did the reviewer clearly explain the reasons for a positive or negative rating? Did the reviewer evaluate all the major features of the software?

- Did the reviewer give the product a negative rating because of the lack of a feature that might be unimportant to you?

- Did the reviewer use the product as directed, for the purpose intended? Some negative ratings can be unfairly conferred.

Another Great Source of Technical Support

I have found some incredibly detailed, well-written user reviews of both hardware and software products I have purchased. You can often tell from reading a review if the person is a knowledgeable expert with regard to the product being reviewed or the related discipline. For example, you might be able to determine, based on the content of the review, that a reviewer of a particular photo quality printer is an expert in the field of digital photography.

Quite often, the reviewer includes an email address. This is particularly true of reviews on epinions.com. Many of these reviewers have become willing and gracious sources of support for me when I install a new piece of software or hardware peripheral, or if I have questions about the field of knowledge related to the software or hardware.

Another good source of information about software packages is TechTV (`http://www.techtv.com/techtv/`).

Downloading a Trial Version

Many vendors allow customers to download a trial version of their software at no cost.

Once you are satisfied that other customers are generally happy with the product, I would suggest that you download and install the trial version before you actually purchase the product. By downloading the trial version, you can make certain the product satisfies your requirements before you purchase it. (Follow the same instructions for installing a trial version of a software package as you normally would when installing any application.) In most cases, the trial version is the complete, functional product, but you will be able to use it for only a limited period of time—usually 30 days. In other cases, you can use the product as much as you want, but certain key features are disabled that limit its usefulness.

Unless you have a party PC (see Chapter 10, "Tips for Avoiding PC Disasters"), exercise caution before downloading trial versions of software.

Don't download that trial version until you have checked user reviews and the vendors' knowledge base to verify that you are installing a quality product. The practice of downloading and trying software packages without checking references and reviews first is a dangerous one.

Purchasing the Product

If you have downloaded a trial version of a software product and later decide to purchase it, you can usually complete your purchase over the Web. Typically, the vendor provides you with a license number via email that you must simply input into the program. If the program was set to expire or if key features were previously unavailable, you should now find that these restrictions have been lifted. However, if the software package is available through multiple distribution channels and not just directly from the software vendor, it will usually be much cheaper to buy the software through one of these other channels. The best buys are usually found on eBay. If you can't find the product there, go comparison-shopping on CNET.

Whenever you purchase a software product, be certain that you are buying the latest available version of the product. Even the version you find at your local computer store may be out-of-date. Why spend $60 or $70 on a package that is already out-of-date?

If you purchased the product by downloading it over the Web, be sure to keep the license number provided by the software vendor and the install program you downloaded in case you ever need to reinstall the application. For example, you will need to reinstall the program if you replace your computer. I keep all my software license numbers in a separate folder in my email application.

If your party PC and production PC are running different versions of Windows, the value of loading it first on your party PC is somewhat diminished. If there is a problem, you may be unable to determine whether the problem is related to an incompatibility with the operating system.

Installing the Software Package

Before installing the software package, try to find out if it is System Restore compliant. Refer to Chapter 4, "A Disaster Prevention Plan for Your New Computer: Part 2, Before You Try," for information on how to do this.

If you have a party PC (see Chapter 10), try installing the package on this machine first. If you are running the same version of Windows on both machines, and if the application runs well on your party PC, there is a good possibility it will run on your production machine as well. Since there are other differences between your computing environments, you can never be completely certain that a software application that works on one machine will work on another. For example, earlier in this book I made mention of an application that was incompatible with certain video cards.

If you are running the same version of Windows on both machines and the application does *not* run well on your party PC, you should not install it on your production machine until you are able to determine the cause of the problem.

The following steps describe a typical install process. The process can vary a bit from package to package—the order of the steps may change, and some steps might not apply to some installations—but this example, based on the installation of MGI PhotoSuite, will give you a good idea of what to expect.

Perform the following steps to install the package:

1. Check the vendors' Web site to determine if any patches are available for the application you are about to install. Download the patches so that they will be on your desktop, ready to install, as soon as you have installed and tested the application.

2. If you have a broadband Internet connection, you should either physically disconnect your computer from the Internet or enable your Internet lock on ZoneAlarm. (Remember: If you reboot your system after enabling the Internet lock, the Internet lock is automatically disabled again.) You need to do one of these two things because you will be disabling your antivirus software, and you do not ever want to be connected to the Internet without virus protection.

3. Disable your antivirus software because it can interfere with the installation process.

4. Close all other open applications.

5. If you have Windows Millennium or Windows XP, and if you are uncertain whether the software is System Restore compliant, use System Restore to create a manual restore point (see instructions in Appendix A, "The System Restore Feature").

6. Initiate the setup process. If you have downloaded the package from the Internet, double-click the setup program. If you are installing from a CD, insert the CD into your optical drive, for example, a CD-ROM or DVD-ROM. In most cases, the installation program starts automatically. If the installation does not start automatically, navigate to the drive containing the CD, find the setup program, and double-click it to begin the installation process. The setup process should display a welcome screen, as shown in Figure B.1. Click Next to continue.

FIGURE B.1
The setup welcome screen.

7. This is usually the point at which you're presented with a software license agreement (see Figure B.2). Review the terms of the agreement, and click Yes to accept the terms of the agreement and continue. If you were to click No, the installation program would end.

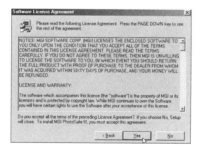

FIGURE B.2
Accepting the terms of the license agreement.

8. Depending on the program, you may be asked to enter user information and a license number or product "key" (see Figure B.3). Enter the information and click Next to continue.

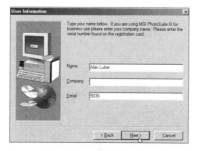

FIGURE B.3
Enter the user information and license number on this screen.

9. Many programs will ask you if you want to perform a typical, full, or custom installation (see Figure B.4). If you are unfamiliar with the product and don't understand the options presented by a custom installation, select the typical option. However, it is usually better to select the custom installation when given the option. This gives you the opportunity to see if the application is installing a lot of optional features that take up disk space—features you may not want or use. By choosing the custom installation, you can prevent such features from being installed. After making your choice, click Next to continue. (Note that if you select the custom installation and change your mind because you do not understand which options to select, you can always go back to the previous step and choose the typical installation.)

You are also given the choice here to change the default installation directory (destination folder)—that is, the location on your hard disk where the program will be installed. I recommend that you accept the default directory. Other applications might interact with this application, and they may expect to find it in the default directory. If they can't find the application in the expected location, you might have to manually intervene and play traffic cop.

FIGURE B.4

Selecting a typical, full, or custom installation.

10. If you selected custom installation, you should see a list of components to select (see Figure B.5). Notice that in this example I can save a whopping 705MB of space on my hard disk by not installing the templates and photo tapestry tiles. Notice that the installation process may also provide the opportunity to associate certain file extensions with the application. For example, if you were to select JPEG, anytime you double-click a JPEG file, it will open within this application. Select the components and options you want and click Next to continue.

FIGURE B.5

Selecting the list of components to be installed.

11. While the process can vary from program to program, this is usually the point at which your program is installed. If the installation process gives you an option to start the program automatically when you boot up your PC, decline the option. This prevents the software package from automatically being added to your startup list.

   During the installation process, you may be given the opportunity to register the software. If the option is available, you should do this later, when you are connected to the Internet.

   This is also usually the point at which you are given the option of specifying where the program will appear on your Start menu—that is, under which Program group. I always accept the default suggestion, as it keeps applications from the same vendor grouped together. This is just a matter of personal preference.

   You may also be asked if you want the application to create a desktop icon—a shortcut on your desktop from which you can launch the application. If you will be using the application frequently, you will probably want to create a desktop icon. You can always change your mind at a later date and either create a shortcut or delete it by dragging it to the recycle bin.

Drag Shortcuts, Not Applications, to the Recycle Bin

When you delete a desktop icon, make sure it is a shortcut to the application and not the application itself. As you will see in the next section, "Uninstalling the Software Package," this is not the proper way to uninstall an application.

It is usually self evident if an icon is a shortcut: There typically is a little curved arrow that appears as part of the icon in the lower-left corner. If you are not certain whether an icon is a shortcut, right-click the icon and select Properties. If the icon is a shortcut, there will be a Shortcut tab under Properties.

12. Once the program has been installed, you will receive a message indicating that the setup is complete (see Figure B.6). This message also might ask if you want to review the Read Me file or perform some other task. I recommend that you review the Read Me file, as it often has late-breaking information about known incompatibility issues and recent news about the program that might be important to you. This information might not have made it into the manual, if one was provided with the software. If the Read Me file has nothing of value to you, you may wish to find and delete it from your hard disk.

13. You might be instructed to reboot your computer after the installation is complete so that the application can update some settings in your Windows Registry. Even if you are not specifically instructed to reboot your computer, you should do so and verify that everything is functioning normally.

FIGURE B.6
Setup is complete. View the Read Me file to see the latest information about the program and learn about known incompatibility issues.

Avoid installing multiple applications at the same time. Use a new application for a few days before installing another application. In the event of a problem, this makes isolating variables and determining the root cause of the problem easier. It also makes fixing problems using the System Restore feature easier.

14. If a software patch is available, install the patch now. Use System Restore to create a restore point prior to installing each patch.

15. After installing the patch, reboot your system and verify that everything is functioning normally. Repeat step 14 and this one if necessary to install additional patches. This would be necessary only if the software vendor issues incremental patches—patches that must be applied in sequence—rather than differential patches, which are cumulative.

16. Reenable your antivirus software and reconnect to the Internet if you have a broadband connection.

17. Run msconfig (see Chapter 9, "Keeping Your Computer in Top Shape") and disable the software package from your startup list if it has been placed there automatically—unless, of course, you really want the package to start up every time you boot up your computer.

18. You might want to register your software at this point. Usually, you will find information about the registration process by looking under the application's Help.

Uninstalling the Software Package

Contrary to what some users believe, you do *not* uninstall software by deleting the shortcut from your desktop or by finding the folder that contains the software program executable and deleting that folder.

All application software packages come with an uninstall program. If the program is written well, it will remove all traces of the application—including Registry entries—from your system.

Perform the following steps to remove the software package:

1. Navigate to your Control Panel and select Add, Remove Programs. Select the program you wish to remove and click Remove. (Some programs may include an uninstall shortcut in their program group within the Start menu.)

2. You will receive a message asking you to confirm that you really want to uninstall the software (see Figure B.7). Click Yes to continue.

FIGURE B.7
Confirm that you want to uninstall the program.

3. During the uninstall process, you may receive a message to the effect that a file is no longer needed and can be deleted (see Figure B.8). The message typically reads as follows:

> The system indicates that the following shared file is no longer used by any programs. If any programs are still using this file and it is removed, those programs may not function. Are you sure you want to remove the shared file?

You should respond No to All to this question, as leaving the file on your system will not harm the computer, whereas removing the file may cause harm.

Although it appears as if Microsoft Windows is removing the program, Windows really has nothing to do with the uninstall process. Windows simply locates and executes the application's uninstall program. In fact, you can also find the application's uninstall program by going directly to the application's program files folder.

Beware of Uninstall Mind Games

In 1964, John Lennon and Paul McCartney wrote, "I don't care what they say, I won't live in a world without love." Well, we may not live in a world without love, but we certainly do live in a world without standards, and nowhere is this more evident than in uninstall programs.

Be very careful when responding to this type of question during the uninstall process. Different uninstall programs ask the same question different ways—there are no standards. For example, one uninstall program may ask if you want to *keep* the file and others like it. You should respond Yes to All.

And I once came across an uninstall program that asked, "Do you *not* want this file?" I admit I had to scratch my head for about 10 minutes before I figured out the right answer.

FIGURE B.8
Do not remove shared files during the uninstall process because doing so can prevent other programs from functioning.

4. When the uninstall is complete, reboot your computer and confirm that it is functioning normally. A poorly written uninstall program can precipitate a computer disaster by deleting files it should not delete or by not removing things it *should* delete.

Years ago, uninstall programs, if they existed at all, were written almost as an after-thought and did a very poor job of removing all traces of the application from your computer. These days, things have improved markedly. I can't recall the last time I experienced computer problems after uninstalling an application.

Occasionally, an uninstall program leaves behind some empty folders, such as the folder in which the program was installed. It is easy to find and delete these, but leaving them on your computer causes no harm.

Glossary

actuator   The component of the hard disk that moves the arms back and forth across the surface of the hard disk. See also *arm*.

adware   Software that resides on your computer, gathers information about your Web surfing habits, and transmits that information back to the adware developer via the Internet. It is similar to spyware, the difference being that adware developers disclose that their software is being installed on your computer, usually in tandem with a legitimate application you have chosen to install. Also, adware is less likely to be designed to steal data off your computer than spyware. See also *spyware*.

antivirus software   Software that detects and blocks viruses from infecting your computer. Antivirus software scans any file that is accessed for any reason and alerts you if a virus is detected.

applog   A special folder where Microsoft Windows 98 and Me captures information about how often you use each application on your computer. This folder is used by the defrag utility to rearrange your program files so that the programs you use most often open faster. Not applicable to Windows XP. See also *defrag*.

archive bit   A file attribute that facilitates differential and incremental backups. Baseline backups clear the archive bit. Whenever a file is created or modified, the archive bit is set (checked). Differential backups do not clear the archive bit, but incremental backups do clear it. See also *differential backup* and *incremental backup*.

arm   The component of the hard disk that moves back and forth across the platters to move the read/write heads to specific locations on the hard disk. All the arms move across the platters as a fixed-assembly unit to occupy the same respective position over each platter. See also *platter* and *cylinder*.

Autocomplete   A feature in certain Microsoft products, such as Internet Explorer, Microsoft Word, and Microsoft Excel, that displays a list of previously matching entries when you begin to enter information in a field. This feature saves data entry time.

automatic media spanning   The ability of backup software to automatically span a backup set across multiple CDs if the amount of data to be backed up can't fit on one CD.

background process   A program that runs undetected without input from the user. Some background processes are essential, such as the process that automatically checks for virus definition updates. But many programs place background processes on your computer that are not necessary and not to your benefit.

backup file   Whenever you use file backup software to create a backup—whether it is a baseline backup, differential backup, or incremental backup—that backup is stored as a single backup file on your CD media. This is true even if the backup spans multiple discs. See also *file backup software*.

backup job   A set of backup instructions that can be created, saved, and executed on a repetitive basis when you are using file backup software. Backup jobs eliminate the need for you to remember where your data is stored each time you want to take a backup. See also *file backup software*.

backup set   A complete set of CD media (either CD-R or CD-RW) associated with a backup. It includes all of the disks from the baseline backup and all of the disks from the differential or incremental backups that have been performed to supplement the baseline. See also *file backup software*.

baseline backup   A complete backup of all your data, which serves as a starting point for daily differential and incremental backups. See also *differential backup*, *file backup software*, and *incremental backup*.

binding   The process of associating a specific network interface card with a specific static IP address so that no other computer can access that IP address. Binding is only possible if your computer has a static IP address. Binding is a solution of last resort because if you want to switch computers or you get a new network interface card, the binding process must be performed again. Your ISP performs binding. See also *IP address*, *ISP*, *media access control (MAC) address*, and *network interface card*.

BIOS   A program that your computer's microprocessor uses to get the computer started when you turn it on. The BIOS is stored on a programmable chip on the computer's motherboard and can be updated with new versions.

blocked senders list   A list of people from whom you do not accept email. People who you know are prone to spread viruses should be added to your blocked senders list.

blocked zone   A list of computers and networks that are explicity forbidden to have access to your computer. A firewall prevents all communications between computers in the blocked zone and your computer. The ability to specify a blocked zone is a feature found in ZoneAlarm Plus and ZoneAlarm Pro.

blue screen of death (BSOD)   An error generated by the Windows operating system that appears on an ominous-looking blue screen. Such errors are usually indicative of some type of software conflict. You may also get a blue screen of death if your system is running very low on system resources. When you receive a blue screen of death, you usually have to reboot your computer to return it to a stable configuration.

boot sector virus   See *master boot record virus*.

boot sequence   The order in which your computer checks devices to look for the information it needs to boot up your computer. The boot sequence is determined by your computer's BIOS. See also *BIOS*.

bug   A piece of software with errors in the program code.

CAT 5   A popular specification for Ethernet cable. Category 5 cable contains four twisted pair of 24-gauge copper wire that can transmit data at high speeds. See also *Ethernet cable*.

cloning   See *disk image*.

cluster   One of the logical structures on the hard disk imparted by the high-level formatting process. A cluster is a group of sectors on a hard disk. Clusters are used to effectively manage data on the hard disk. Individual sectors are so small that it makes sense to organize these physical entities into larger logical structures. The cluster represents the minimum amount of space that can be occupied by a file. If the file size (number of bytes) is smaller than the cluster size, there will be wasted space at the end of the cluster. See also *cluster size*, *formatting*, *sectors*, and *slack space*.

cluster size   The number of physical sectors in a logical cluster. The cluster size on a hard disk partition is a function of three things: which version of Windows you have installed, which file system your version of Windows is using, and the size of your hard disk partition. Large partitions using Windows XP and NTFS have clusters that consist of 128 sectors. See also *cluster*, *New Technology File System (NTFS)*, and *sectors*.

cold reboot   Rebooting your computer by completely powering it down and then restarting it. A cold reboot completely resets everything on your computer and is the best approach to use to clear a computer problem that has resulted in a blue screen of death. See also *blue screen of death*.

command-line switch   Switches that can be entered when starting a program to change the behavior of the program. For example, one command-line switch causes Norton Ghost to prompt the user for a password when creating a backup set.

commodity item   A mass-produced, unspecialized, consistent, reliable product for which price is the only purchase criterion.

computer disaster   A major computer problem resulting in the loss or theft of irreplaceable data or the loss of use of your computer for an extended period of time. Computer disasters typically have a long, painful recovery process if the user is not prepared to deal with such disasters.

computer virus   See *virus*.

cookies   Small files that Web sites store on your computer for the purpose of personalizing your Web surfing experience. Cookies are stored in the `C:\WINDOWS\Cookies` folder on your computer. You should periodically purge your computer of cookies that add no value to your Web surfing experience, as some cookies track your movements on the Web.

customer no-service   An all-too-common business model, in which a company tries to cut costs by keeping customers at arm's length. Customer no-service techniques include voice mail and email-only support.

cyber-terrorist   A person intending to do harm to your computer either by infecting it with a virus or by hacking into your computer to steal valuable data or to use it as a base to launch attacks on other computers. Cyber-terrorists probe the Internet for easy targets—computers not protected by firewalls.

cylinder   All the arms on a hard disk across the surface of the platters in unison as a fixed-assembly unit. Thus, all the arms are always located over the same respective position on each platter, forming an imaginary cylinder. See also *arm* and *platter*.

data migration   The process of transferring data from your old computer to your new computer. A variety of data migration strategies can be employed, including a home network, a direct cable between computers, and copying data from the old computer onto CDs and transferring it to another computer.

defrag (disk defragmenter) A Microsoft Windows utility that reorganizes all the files on your computer so that each file is stored in one contiguous set of clusters on your hard disk. Running defrag improves the performance of your computer by reducing file access times. Running defrag prior to performing a baseline backup reduces the amount of time required to back up your data and improves the overall performance of your computer. See also *applog*.

device driver See *driver*.

Device Manager A feature in Microsoft Windows that allows you to view and change the properties associated with devices installed in or attached to your computer.

differential backup A file backup method that backs up all files that have been modified or created since the last baseline backup. Because a differential backup is cumulative of all changes (including new files), the data restore process is a relatively simple two-step process: You restore your baseline backup and then you restore only your latest differential backup. See also *archive bit*, *baseline backup*, and *file backup software*.

digital signature A digital fingerprint associated with a program. If the program is changed, either by legitimate or illegitimate means, its digital signature automatically changes. A legitimate change occurs when a program is updated to a new release. An illegitimate change is one made by a hacker to hijack an application for his own nefarious use. ZoneAlarm uses the digital signature to determine when a program has been changed, and displays a changed program alert when the application attempts to access the Internet. The digital signature is also referred to as an MD5 signature.

direct seller A computer OEM that sells directly to the end customer, over the phone or over the Internet, instead of through retail distribution channels. Dell Computer and Gateway Computer are the two largest direct sellers of computers. See also *OEM*.

disk defragmenter See *defrag*.

disk image An exact image or clone of your hard disk. Disk imaging is the best technique for backing up your hard disk.

disk operating system See *DOS*.

disk scrubber A software packages that permanently erases files that have been deleted from your computer so that the data can't be recovered by software packages designed to recover deleted files.

DO loop of despair A situation that results when installing an application causes one type of computer disaster and uninstalling the application causes another disaster. The only way out of the DO loop of despair is to uninstall the application and then use the System Restore feature to restore your system to the point just prior to the installation of the program. See also *System Restore*.

DOS An acronym for disk operating system. The original standard operating system for IBM-compatible personal computers. Applications such as Norton Ghost that need to work outside Windows boot your computer into DOS using a special boot floppy disk.

Download Manager A software tool that speeds up the process of downloading files from the Internet and optimizes the use of your bandwidth. A download manager breaks the file into several pieces, downloads the pieces concurrently from multiple locations, and then reassembles the pieces.

drag-and-drop An approach to backing up your data by copying (dragging and dropping) data files from your hard disk to a CD-R or CD-RW.

drive-by hacker A hacker who attempts to hack into wireless networks. The drive-by hacker drives around with a laptop, a wireless networking card, an antenna, software to detect nearby wireless networks (a favorite product of hackers is a Windows-compatible utility called NetStumbler), and packet sniffing software (the network equivalent of wire tapping). Also known as lanjacking or wardriving. See also *hacker*.

driver   A small computer program that enables your computer's operating system to communicate with some type of internal or external device. The manufacturer of the device develops drivers. See also *driver rollback*, *signed driver*, and *unsigned driver*.

Driver Rollback   A feature in Windows XP that allows you to roll back a badly behaved driver to a previous version if a previous version exists on your computer.

e-Tailer   A retailer who does business primarily or exclusively over the Web, usually at discount prices. e-Tailers are good sources of computer software, computer supplies, and copies of *PC Fear Factor*!

Ethernet cable   A cable used to connect computers on a local area network. Ethernet cables connect the computer's network interface card to a residential gateway. Ethernet cables facilitate high data transfer rates across networks. Ethernet cable can be produced to a variety of specifications, the most popular spec being CAT 5. See also *CAT 5*, *local area network*, *network interface card*, and *residential gateway*.

Ethernet card   See *network interface card*.

FAT32   A file system used mainly in Windows 98 and Windows Me. It can also be used in Windows XP, but this legacy file system will eventually be replaced by the New Technology File System (NTFS). See also *file system* and *New Technology File System*.

fat outlet   An outlet on a surge protector that has a lot of space on either side so that a transformer plugged into the outlet does not block other outlets. See also *surge protector*.

FDISK   A special system command used to create one or more partitions on a hard disk. See also *partitioning*.

file allocation table (FAT)   One of the logical structures imparted to the hard disk by formatting. The file allocation table is an address table that keeps track of where everything is located on the hard disk and directs the read/write heads to specific locations. See also *formatting*.

file association   The association of a particular file type with a specific application. When you double-click a user-editable file, it opens with the associated application. For example, when you double-click a "doc" file type, the file opens with Microsoft Word. Some file associations are unique. For example, "doc" is uniquely associated with Microsoft Word, "xls" with Microsoft Excel, and "ppt" with Microsoft PowerPoint. Many file associations are not unique, but they still have a default file association. See also *file extension* and *file type*.

file backup software   Software designed specifically to back up data on your computer. It typically supports baseline backups, differential backups, and incremental backups.

file extension   No, this is not what you do to extend your tax deadline. The file extension is a three-character suffix following the period after the filename. For example, if the filename is `alan.jpg`, the file extension is `jpg`. See also *file association* and *file type*.

file segment   A CD-size chunk of data. Norton Ghost automatically splits an image into file segments when a hard disk image is written directly to CDs.

file system   The method used to store and organize files on your hard disk. The two file systems in use today on Microsoft Windows personal computers are FAT32 and NTFS (New Technology File System). Windows XP supports both types of file systems. Older consumer versions of Windows support only the older FAT32 file system. See also *FAT32* and *New Technology File System*.

file type   A classification that enables your computer to recognize and manage a file with the appropriate application. The file type is denoted by the file extension. See also *file association* and *file extension*.

firewall   A piece of hardware or a software application that prevents computer hackers from using the Internet to gain access to your computer.

Firewalls inspect packets of data arriving at your computer to ensure that the data is part of an ongoing "conversation" that was initiated by your computer, rather than an independent, unauthorized attempt on the part of someone to communicate with your computer. See also *packet filtering*.

firmware   Software that, like your computer's BIOS, is permanently (firmly) stored on a memory chip. Firmware is typically found in devices such as CD writers, DVD-ROMs, and scanners. Firmware interprets instructions sent by device drivers and generates commands that actually control the operation of the delicate electronics within that device.

formatting   The process of applying logical structures to the hard disk to facilitate easy access to data. Formatting organizes individual hard disk sectors into groups called clusters and applies a directory structure (file allocation table) to the hard disk. Formatting is accomplished with a special system command, FORMAT. The computer OEM formats your hard disk. Also referred to as high-level formatting. See also *cluster*, *file allocation table*, and *OEM*.

free space   Clusters on a hard disk where Microsoft Windows is allowed to write file information. These clusters can be empty or can contain data from files that have been previously deleted but not yet overwritten with new files. See also *cluster* and *slack space*.

freeware   Small applications and utilities that can be downloaded for free on the Internet. Freeware applications can be badly behaved or can contain adware or spyware. See also *adware*, *shareware*, and *spyware*.

hacker   A person who attempts to gain access to your computer over the Internet to steal information or take control of your computer and use it to launch attacks on other computers. The term *hacker* used to have a benign definition, meaning anyone who was interested in computers. See also *cyber-terrorist*, *drive-by hacker*, and *firewall*.

hard disk crash   The catastrophic failure of your hard disk. It may or may not produce an audible sound from within the computer, but it is guaranteed to produce an audible sound from within your mouth.

hide-and-seek data   User data that applications automatically store in locations not of the user's choosing. Certain applications automatically choose the location (folder or file) where data is stored. It is up to the user to find out where the data is stored in order to back it up. The application hides the data, and the user must seek it out. What fun!

high-level formatting   See *formatting*.

home network   See *local area network*.

imaging   See *disk image*.

incompatibility   A conflict that prevents your computer from functioning properly. Serious incompatibilities can precipitate computer disasters. There are many types of incompatibilities. A software application can be incompatible with a particular version of Microsoft Windows, another software application, a driver, or a hardware component. A hardware component can be incompatible with a particular version of Microsoft Windows, a software application, a driver, or another hardware component. All computers are incompatible with users who fail to follow safe computing practices.

incremental backup   A file backup method that backs up only files that have modified or created since the last backup. Because incremental backups are additive of all changes, whereas differential backups are cumulative of all changes, the data restore process for incremental backups is much more complicated—you must restore your baseline backup and then restore every one of your incremental backups in sequence, from oldest to latest. See also *archive bit*, *differential backup*, and *file backup software*.

inoculation   A technique used by antivirus software to protect your computer from master boot record viruses. It records information about the master boot record, and when you perform a virus scan, it compares the master boot record to the information it has recorded. If there is a difference, the antivirus software knows that something has changed the master boot record and gives you the option of restoring your record. See also *master boot record* and *master boot record virus*.

Internet lock   A feature in a firewall software application that allows you to block all access to the Internet.

Internet zone   All computers and networks that have not been explicitly designated as being in either the blocked zone or trusted zone. A firewall prevents unauthorized communication between computers in the Internet zone and your computer. See also *blocked zone* and *trusted zone*.

intra-day backup   Backups taken several times during the course of the day of critical, active files. If you back up such data only once a day, you risk losing up to a full day's worth of changes to such data in the event of a computer disaster.

IP (Internet protocol) address   The means by which your computer is uniquely identified on the Internet. Some broadband Internet service providers assign a permanent IP address to each computer, known as a *static* IP address. The more common practice is *dynamic* IP addressing, in which your computer is assigned a different IP address (from a bank of available IP addresses) each time it connects to the Internet.

ISP   An Internet service provider. High-speed Internet service providers use either cable modem or DSL technology to deliver high data transfer rates.

knowledge base   An area of a software or hardware vendor's Web site that contains answers to questions and solutions to problems pertaining to the vendor's products.

lanjacking   See *drive-by hacker*.

local area network (LAN)   A group of computers, usually in a small, local area, that are connected together so that they can share information with each other, common peripheral devices such as printers, and a common broadband Internet connection. Within the context of a home, a local area network is also referred to as a home network. See also *residential gateway*.

logic board   A board that contains the electronics that control the components of the hard disk.

logical drive   Another name for disk partition. See also *partitioning*.

Low-level formatting   The process of applying physical structures (tracks and sectors) to the hard disk. The hard disk manufacturer performs this process.

master boot record   A small program that resides in the first sector of your hard disk that is executed when you boot up your computer. This program tells your computer which partition of your hard disk to use for booting up your computer.

master boot record virus   A virus that replaces the master boot record with malicious code. When the computer is booted up, the virus is placed in memory where it can take control of your computer. Also called boot sector virus. See also *master boot record* and *virus*.

MD5 signature   See *digital signature*.

media access control (MAC) address   The unique identifier on a network interface card. The MAC address can be used to bind a specific static IP address to a specific network interface card to prevent people from stealing your IP address. See also *binding*, *IP address*, and *network interface card*.

memory leak   When a program is started, it consumes a certain amount of system resources. In theory, when the program is closed, all the resources it consumed are freed. In practice, some programs don't do a very good job of letting go. The amount of resources *not* made available when a program is closed is called a memory leak.

motherboard   The main circuit board on your computer. All other circuit boards plug into the motherboard. Your computer's BIOS resides on a memory chip on the motherboard. See also *BIOS*.

Msconfig   See *system configuration utility*.

network address translation (NAT)   Software on a residential gateway that routes information from the Internet to a computer on the local area network. NAT acts as a natural firewall between the Internet and your computers. See also *local area network* and *residential gateway*.

network cable   See *Ethernet cable*.

network interface card (NIC)   A card inserted into your computer that allows the computer to be connected via Ethernet cable to a local area network. See also *binding*, *Ethernet cable*, *local area network*, and *media access control address*.

New Technology File System (NTFS)   A file system employed by Windows XP. NTFS has many performance and security advantages over the older FAT32 file system. See also *FAT32* and *file system*.

OEM   An original equipment manufacturer, such as Hewlett-Packard, Dell, or Gateway Computer.

packet filtering   A technology used by firewalls to determine whether data arriving at your computer is part of an ongoing conversation initiated by your computer. Arriving packets of information are filtered (checked) for an acknowledgment bit. If the data is missing an acknowledgment bit, the packet filter knows that someone is attempting unauthorized access to your computer and blocks the communication. See also *firewall*.

partitioning   The process of dividing the hard disk into one or more logical sections called partitions. Each hard disk has at least one partition, which is called the primary partition. Additional partitions, if they exist, are called extended partitions. Multiple partitions make it appear as if you have multiple, independent hard disks on your computer. Partitions are applied to a hard disk through a special system command called FDISK. Partitions can also be applied using a variety of disk management utilities.

party PC   An old PC used to test applications or install applications that contain adware. The purposes of the party PC are to serve as a buffer between your production personal computers and the Internet and to minimize the risk of installing new software on your production computers.

pass-lock program   A program that is allowed to access the Internet even if the firewall's Internet lock is engaged.

patch   An interim release of a software package that provides bug fixes, support for new devices or operating systems, or new features. Patches can be downloaded from the vendor's Web site.

payload   The destructive content of computer virus.

peripheral device   A device that connects externally to your computer, such as a printer, scanner, or camera. Some peripheral devices can be shared by all computers on a local area network. See also *local area network*.

platter   A component of the hard disk that contains all the information on your computer—the operating system, drivers, applications, and data. Many hard disks are comprised of multiple platters, stacked on a spindle. The platters are coated with a magnetic media. See also *read/write head* and *spindle*.

Plug and Play   A Microsoft Windows technology that enables your computer to automatically recognize and configure newly installed internal hardware devices or peripheral devices. Because this feature does not always work, it is sometimes referred to as Plug-and-Pray.

plug-in   A software program used to enhance the functionality of another software program. Plug-ins are commonly used to enhance the functionality of a Web browser. Examples of plug-ins are Acrobat Reader, Flash Player, Windows Media Player, and QuickTime.

pop-up blocker   A class of utilities that detect and block pop-up ads from appearing on your screen. Pop-up blockers are necessary but often badly behaved applications that tend to cause problems that can be mistaken for computer disasters.

The only thing worse than having a badly behaved pop-up blocker is not having one.

preview pane The pane in the lower-right corner of your email application that shows you a preview of an email message prior to opening the actual message. Because some viruses can deliver their payloads when the message is viewed in the preview pane, you should turn off the preview pane option in your email application.

program component A file associated with an application software program. A hacker might attempt to hijack a program by changing a program component to do her bidding. ZoneAlarm Pro displays a program component alert window whenever an application attempts to connect to the Internet after a program component has been changed.

progressive revisioning The practice of saving a document that is being modified extensively under a different revision number every few minutes. In the event that the document becomes corrupted, you can revert to the last known good revision number without losing all the changes you have made to the document.

quarantine A special area of your hard disk where Norton AntiVirus places files that are infected by computer viruses. Quarantined files should be deleted from your computer. See also *virus*.

RAID An acronym for redundant array of inexpensive disks. Certain types of RAID configurations eliminate a single point of failure for data storage. If one of the hard disks in the RAID configuration fails, no data is lost. RAID configurations are not yet common on personal computers but will probably become more common in the coming years.

read/write head The hard disk component that retrieves information from and writes information to the hard disk. It does this by converting electrical energy to magnetic fields to write data to the disk and by reversing the process to read data from the disk.

residential gateway A device that sits between the computers in your house and the Internet, connecting your computers to each other and to the Internet. Such devices serve as gateways to the Internet, allowing multiple computers to share one broadband Internet connection. They also allow your computers to share information with each other and to share peripheral devices. Residential gateways also have built-in firewall protection. See also *local area network* and *router*.

restore point A configuration of your computer as of a certain date and time to which your computer can be restored via the System Restore feature. Restore points are automatically created by Windows every day you use your computer and whenever you make a significant change to your system. You can also manually create restore points on your computer. See also *System Restore*.

rogue application An application that was installed on your computer without your permission or knowledge for the purpose of performing dastardly deeds. The two most common types of rogue applications are spyware and Trojan horses.

router A specific type of residential gateway that allows computers to be connected to each other and to the Internet using an Ethernet network. Routers are designed to support either wired or wireless networks. See also *residential gateway*.

safe mode A special way of booting up Windows without loading applications, background processes, and most drivers that would normally load. The only drivers that are loaded in safe mode are the drivers for your keyboard, mouse, and a generic video driver that enables you to view your monitor only at low resolution. Normally, safe mode is used to troubleshoot Windows problems. In some cases, safe mode is used to run an application such as ScanDisk, TUFKAS, or Disk Defragmenter that runs better when it has exclusive access to your hard disk.

ScanDisk A utility in Windows 98 and Windows Millennium that checks your hard disk for errors in logical and physical structures. See also *TUFKAS*.

script   A small computer program that can be embedded in email attachments and Web pages.

script blocking   A feature in antivirus software that stops potentially harmful scripts from running on your computer. See also *script*.

sectors   One of two physical structures on the hard disk—the other being tracks. The sector is the smallest physical unit on a disk that can be accessed. Your hard disk should be replaced when it begins to develop bad sectors—sectors that can't be accessed by read/write heads. See also *ScanDisk* and *tracks*.

server rights   An application has server rights if you have granted an application the right to function as a server. If an application has been granted server rights, it can "listen" for and respond to requests for information from the Internet. Some applications, such as KaZaA, require server rights to function properly because your computer must function as a server to other KaZaA users. See also *firewall*.

shared file   A file on your computer that is shared by more than one application.

shareware   Small applications and utilities that can be downloaded on the Internet. Similar to freeware, except that you are supposed to pay for the application if you decide to use it. See also *freeware*.

signed driver   A driver that has a digital signature indicating it has passed testing standards established by Microsoft's Windows Hardware Quality Lab. See also *driver*.

slack space   A particular cluster can contain only one file, but a file can span many clusters. The last cluster a file occupies may contain unused space. This is referred to as slack space because it is space that can't be used by any other file so long as the cluster is partially occupied. Slack space can contain remnants of other files that previously occupied the cluster. See also *cluster* and *free space*.

slider   A hard disk component attached to the arm. The slider holds the read/write head. See also *arm* and *read/write head*.

software patch   See *patch*.

specialty item   A complex product that is purchased based on value—the lowest total cost in use. A personal computer is a specialty item that is often mistaken for a commodity item because it is mass produced and is getting less and less expensive with each passing year. What many people fail to realize is that computers are also getting more and more complex and that service and support are more important purchase criteria today than ever before. See also *commodity item* and *value*.

spindle   A component of the hard disk. The hard disk platters are mounted on the spindle. See also *platter*.

spindle motor   The component of the hard disk that rotates the spindle and, therefore, the platters that are mounted on the spindle.

spyware   An application that resides on your computer, gathers information without your knowledge or permission, and sends it back to the spyware developer via the Internet. A spyware program might monitor your every keystroke and steal all your passwords, credit card numbers, bank account numbers, and brokerage account numbers. Spyware can record your instant messages and steal your email, and it can be installed on your computer without your knowledge when you download freeware or when a hacker penetrates your defenses. See also *adware* and *freeware*.

startup list   A list of items (application programs or background processes) that automatically load whenever you boot up into Windows. Some ill-behaved programs automatically add themselves to the startup list during the install process without asking your permission. The more items you have in your startup list, the more system resources are consumed, the slower your system's performance, and the more potential you have for application conflicts and system crashes. Items can be removed from the startup list using the system configuration utility. See also *background process*, *system configuration utility*, *system crash*, and *system resources*.

stealth virus   A virus designed to escape detection by antivirus software. See also *virus*.

surge protector   A piece of equipment that protects your computer and its peripheral devices (scanner, printers, cable modem, router, and so on) from voltage spikes.

system administrator   The person responsible for maintaining a trouble-free computing environment. In a home computing environment, this person installs and removes programs, takes data and hard disk backups, fixes problems, recovers from computer disasters, and implements safe computing practices.

System Configuration Utility   A Microsoft Windows utility originally intended as a troubleshooting utility. This utility can be used to prevent applications from automatically loading and consuming precious system resources when you start Windows. See also *startup list*, *system crash*, and *system resources*.

system crash   A situation where your computer freezes up. A system crash is often accompanied by a blue screen of death. System crashes are frequently caused by software conflicts or lack of resources, both of which can be caused by having too many applications open. See also *blue screen of death*, *system configuration utility*, and *system resources*.

system log   A running record of all changes you have made to your computing environment. Used to bring your hard disk up-to-date after a disaster recovery and to walk back the cat to determine the source of a computer disaster. See also *walking back the cat*.

system resources   An amount of memory Windows uses to store information used by each program. Each open program consumes a certain amount of system resources. This area is *not* unlimited and can be exhausted when you have too many applications open, causing a system crash. See also *memory leak* and *system crash*.

System Restore   A feature in Windows Millennium and Windows XP that allows you to restore your system to a previous, more stable configuration.

System Restore folder   The folder in which restore points are stored in Microsoft Windows. In Windows XP, this is the `C:\system volume information` folder. In Windows Millennium, this is the `C:\_RESTORE folder` See also *restore point*.

Task Scheduler   A component of Microsoft Windows that can be used to automatically schedule tasks to run at certain time intervals. The Task Scheduler is an important weapon against computer disasters. It is used to schedule weekly virus scans of your hard disk, check for virus definition updates, and check for Microsoft critical updates. This component should never be disabled in your startup list. See also *startup list* and *virus definitions*.

technical support specialist   A person who provides phone, email, or interactive Web-based support for a specific software or hardware product.

temporary files   Short-lived files that are automatically created by certain applications running on your computer. Such files are supposed to be automatically deleted when you close the application, but this does not always happen. For example, if your computer crashes (does not shut down normally), some temporary files may remain on your computer. These temporary files usually begin with the tilde (~) character and have a file extension of `.tmp`. They can be safely deleted from your computer. See also *system crash*.

temporary Internet files   Files that are downloaded to your hard disk when you visit Web sites to speed up your Web surfing. If you revisit a Web site, the files already stored on your hard disk do not need to be downloaded again unless their content has changed since your last visit to that Web site. Unfortunately, these so-called temporary Internet files are really permanent in nature in that they remain on your computer forever unless you periodically delete them.

time-lag bomb   The elapsed amount of time from when a new virulent virus starts to spread until the time your virus signatures are updated to protect you from the virus. During this period of time, your computer is very vulnerable to being infected.

tracks   One of two physical structures on the hard disk—the other being sectors. Tracks are concentric rings around the disk. See also *sectors*.

trial version   A fully functional version of a software package you can download for free and try for a limited period of time.

Trojan horse   A virus or worm disguised as something that is harmless, funny, or perhaps even helpful. Most worms are packaged as Trojan horses. The disguise comes in the form of the text of an email message that comes with the worm and the name on the worm file itself. For example, the worm file might be disguised as a screensaver or sexy picture.

trusted application   An application on your computer that you allow to access the Internet without manual approval on your part each time the application tries to connect to the Web. This term is applicable to firewalls that monitor outbound communications. See also *firewall*.

trusted zone   A list of computers that you elect to trust and want to share resources with, even when your firewall is engaged.

TUFKAS   The author's acronym for "the utility formerly known as ScanDisk." This acronym is necessary because Microsoft failed to name the utility in Windows XP. See also *ScanDisk*.

tunneling   A protocol for providing a specific secure path (tunnel) through the Internet from your home to your company's network. See also *virtual private network*.

uninterruptible power supply (UPS)   A power supply that contains a battery source of power to prevent your computer from crashing in the event of a power outage. Depending on how much money you spend, a UPS will provide enough power to keep your computer running either for a few minutes,

so you can save your data, close your applications, and shut down your computer or for several hours, so you can continue working during an extended outage. There are several different types of UPS units, the least expensive one being a standby UPS and the most expensive being an online UPS.

Universal Serial Bus (USB)   An external high-speed data transfer standard that allows multiple external components to be connected to your computer. Used to connect peripheral devices such as printers and scanners to a computer.

unsigned driver   A driver that has not passed testing standards established by Microsoft's Windows Hardware Quality Lab. See also *driver*.

unstable equilibrium   A type of equilibrium in which a slight deviation from the point of equilibrium causes the system to become unstable. A rocking chair is a good example of a stable equilibrium. If the rocking chair is disturbed, it returns to its state of equilibrium. A pencil standing vertically on end is an example of an unstable equilibrium. If the pencil is disturbed, it falls over rather than returning to its point of equilibrium. Metaphorically speaking, personal computers are unstable equilibriums.

update sniffer   An application that has the capability to scan your computer, determine which application software and system software (drivers, operating system, and so on) is out of date, and provide links to the available updates.

utility   A small, special-purpose application, such as a graphics viewer.

value   The lowest total cost in use based on price, quality, features, service, and support.

virtual memory   Information that is stored temporarily on the hard disk when your system runs out of real memory (random access memory).

virtual private network (VPN)   A means of using the infrastructure of the Internet in a secure fashion to access your employer's network. See also *tunneling*.

virus   Specific definition: A malicious program that attaches itself to an application (known as the host) and causes damage whenever that application is run. Generic definition: A program usually designed to do damage to your computer and spread to other computers. The generic definition includes worms and Trojan horses. See also *script blocking*, *Trojan horse*, *virus definitions*, *virus hoax*, *virus signature*, and *worm*.

virus definitions   A list of all known virus signatures. You must keep your computer up-to-date with the latest virus definition list to achieve maximum protection against viruses. See also *virus signature*.

virus hoax   An email message intended to convince you that your computer is infected with a virus if you have certain files on your system. The message instructs you to delete these files from your computer, citing grave danger if you leave these files on your system. The actual grave danger is in deleting these important, perfectly legitimate system files.

virus removal tool   A software program developed by an antivirus software vendor to automate the process of removing a specific virus from an infected computer. Antivirus software vendors develop virus removal tools for viruses that are widespread and difficult to remove manually. You must exercise caution when following the instructions for using the virus removal tool, as the removal process may still require several manual steps to be performed.

virus signature   The unique, recognizable pattern associated with a computer virus. Used by antivirus software developers to detect and block computer viruses arriving at your computer. See also *virus* and *virus definitions*.

vulnerability   A weakness that leaves you exposed or prone to a computer disaster. Such weaknesses include failure to install antivirus software, failure to install a firewall, failure to take data backups and hard disk backups, and failure to use any disaster prevention tool diligently.

walking back the cat   The process of undoing recent changes you have made to your system, one by one, in reverse order to determine which change caused your computer disaster.

wardriving   See *drive-by hacker*.

Web browser history   Your Web browser creates a history file of Web sites you have visited in the past. You can control how many days of history are stored on your computer through your Web browser interface. This history makes it easier for you to find and revisit Web sites. You can see the Web browser history by clicking the History button on your Web browser.

Windows Registry   Two files within the Windows directory on your computer that contain critical information about all the hardware and software installed on your computer. If the Registry becomes corrupted, your computer might not work properly, or at all.

Windows swap file   A special file created and used by Windows to store information that exceeds the storage space available in your computer's RAM (random access memory). The information is swapped back and forth between your hard disk and RAM as it is needed.

Windows task scheduler   See *task scheduler*.

wired equivalent privacy (WEP)   A security protocol for wireless networks that can be easily hacked by drive-by hackers. See also *drive-by hacker*, *hacker*, and *wireless network*.

wireless network   A local area network that shares information over the airwaves.

worm   A malicious program designed to automatically spread itself across the Internet, often by mass-mailing itself to the contacts in your address book.

Index

backups, 42, 282
  compacting mail fold-
    ers, 241
  data backup strategies,
    261-262
  deleting applog folder
    files, 243
  deleting email, 241
  deleting noncritical
    data, 243-244
  deleting restore points,
    242
  deleting temporary
    files, 241
  deleting temporary
    Internet files, 241
  deleting Web site histo-
    ries, 241
  emptying recycle bins,
    242
  Norton Ghost, 118,
    250-254
  strategies, 237-238
  testing, 258-260
  updates, 239
  virus scans, 242
bad sectors, 115-117
clusters, 23
crashes, 22, 25, 264
data recovery, 26
defragmenting (baseline
  backups), 217-218
dust, 25
formatting, 23
logic boards, 22
low-level formatting, 22
manual virus scans,
  156-157

platters, 21
  logical structures,
    22-26
  physical structures,
    22-25
read/write heads, 21
ready-to-use hard disks,
  237
restoring, 272
  backup images, image
    to disk restore,
    273-275
  backup images, image
    to partition restore,
    273-276
  data backups, 282
  Norton LiveUpdate,
    277
  reapplying Microsoft
    critical updates, 277
  restoring data,
    278-280
  restoring email,
    281-282
  updating hard disks,
    278
ScanDisk, 28, 239
scrubbing, 68-71,
  131-132, 135-137, 188
sectors, 22-23, 26
sliders, 21
spindle motors, 21
spindles, 21
system logs, 261
TUFKAS (The Utility
  Formerly Known as
  ScanDisk), 115-118,
  238

updating, 278
virtual memory, 19
viruses, 151
hardware
  CD writers, 41-46
  connecting, 114
  drivers, 123
  DVD writers, 46
  installing, 104, 122
  internal hardware,
    installing, 302
  residential gateways,
    72-74
  surge protectors, 38-40
  tape drives, 41
  unsigned drivers, 123
  UPS (Uninterruptible
    Power Supply), 77-78
  vendors, selecting, 84
  Windows XP compatibility,
    102-103
help desks, 305
**Hewlett-Packard computers,
86-88, 104**
high-level formatting. *See*
  formatting
**histories (Web browsers),
  deleting, 133, 241**
home networks
  backups, 234
  data backups, 126
  Internet, connecting to,
    124
  logon methods, changing,
    129
  settings, capturing,
    107-108

Hey, you've got enough worries.

Don't let IT training be one of them.

Get on the fast track to IT training at InformIT,
your total Information Technology training network.

 | **www.informit.com** |